QUANTUM COMPUTING

QUANTUM COMPUTING

Gregory Falco
Maurice Dawson

Kruger Brentt
Publishers

2025

Kruger Brentt Publishers UK. LTD.
Company Number 9728962

Regd. Office: 68 St Margarets Road, Edgware, Middlesex HA8 9UU

ISBN: 978-1-78715-305-9

For information on all our publications visit our website at http://krugerbrentt.com/

PREFACE

"Quantum Computing" is a comprehensive exploration into the transformative potential of quantum technologies, offering insights into the principles, applications, and future directions of quantum computing. This book serves as an essential resource for researchers, students, and enthusiasts seeking to understand the fundamentals of quantum computation and its implications for science, technology, and society.

Quantum computing represents a paradigm shift in information processing, harnessing the principles of quantum mechanics to perform calculations that are infeasible for classical computers. With the promise of exponentially faster algorithms for certain tasks, quantum computing has the potential to revolutionize fields such as cryptography, materials science, drug discovery, optimization, and machine learning.

As editors of this volume, we have endeavored to compile a diverse array of perspectives, methodologies, and case studies from leading experts and researchers in the field of quantum computing. Through a blend of theoretical foundations, practical insights, and real-world examples, this book covers a wide range of topics, including quantum algorithms, quantum hardware, quantum error correction, quantum cryptography, and quantum machine learning.

Our overarching goal in presenting this book is to provide readers with a comprehensive and accessible introduction to the field of quantum computing, inspiring curiosity, critical thinking, and exploration of this rapidly evolving field. By demystifying complex concepts, highlighting key applications, and discussing the challenges and opportunities of quantum computing, we aim to empower researchers, students, and enthusiasts to engage with this transformative technology and contribute to its advancement.

We extend our sincere gratitude to all the contributors who have generously shared their expertise, experiences, and insights in the field of quantum computing.

It is our hope that this book will serve as a valuable resource and inspiration for readers as they embark on their journey into the fascinating world of quantum computation and its potential to reshape the future of computing and technology.

Gregory Falco
Maurice Dawson

CONTENTS

CHAPTER-1

INTRODUCTION TO QUANTUM COMPUTING

Quantum computing is a unique technology because it isn't built on bits that are binary in nature, meaning that they're either zero or one. Instead, the technology is based on qubits. These are two-state quantum mechanical systems that can be part zero and part one at the same time. Quantum computing uses specialized technology—including computer hardware and algorithms that take advantage of quantum mechanics—to solve complex problems that classical computers or supercomputers can't solve, or can't solve quickly enough.

Quantum mechanics is the term we give to the behavior of reality on the most minute scales, nanoscopic to be precise. At the fundamental level, almost nothing works as you would expect it to – particles go through walls and information appears to teleport, all because the world is inherently probabilistic. Advancing the frontier in many fields will require scientists in those research areas to know quantum mechanics. Developing MRIs, car batteries, and computers; identifying molecular structures and chemical properties; searching for dark matter, and measuring gravitational waves are just a few fields that are rooted in understanding these abstract physical phenomena. The beauty of physics is that it will sometimes break your intuition and then provide a clearer picture of the world. This is what makes quantum physics arguably the most fascinating field of all. The beauty of engineering is in applying these unimaginable behaviors to create novel technologies.

Since the mid-20th century, quantum physics has arguably paved the way for many technologies we interact with daily, the computer being a prime example. The earliest advancements came with the discovery of the physical properties of semiconductors, like silicon, which led to the invention of the transistor in the early 1950s. Transistors are the technology responsible for bits, the unit of information in classic computers. Billions of transistors are at the core of all computer chips, like those in your cell phone, laptop, and other smart devices.

Light emitting diodes (LEDs) like those on your computer screen, similar electroluminescent technology, such as digital cameras, and photovoltaic technologies like solar cells can be accredited to discovery in the field of quantum mechanics.

Quantum Computing is a new kind of computing based on Quantum mechanics that deals with the physical world that is probabilistic and unpredictable in nature. Quantum mechanics being a more general model of physics than classical mechanics give rise to a more general model of computing- quantum computing that has more potential to solve problems that cannot be solved by classical ones. To store and manipulate the information, they use their own quantum bits also called '*Qubits*' unlike other classical computers which are based on classical computing that uses binary bits 0 and 1 individually. The computers using such type of computing are known as '*Quantum Computers*'. In such small computers, circuits with transistors, logic gates, and Integrated Circuits are not possible. Hence, it uses the subatomic particles like atoms, electrons, photons, and ions as their bits along with their information of spins and states. They can be superposed and can give more combinations. Therefore, they can run in parallel using memory efficiently and hence is more powerful. Quantum computing is the only model that could disobey the Church-Turing thesis and thus quantum computers can perform exponentially faster than classical computers.

CLASSICAL VS. QUANTUM COMPUTING

Classical computing relies on binary digits (bits) that are either in the state of 0, or 1, while quantum computing relies on quantum bits or qubits. These can be both in the state of 0 and in the state of 1, simultaneously. This is known as superposition.

Classical computing, which is the foundation of our current digital technology, relies on classical bits to process and store information. Classical bits can exist in one of two states: 0 or 1. Classical computers use logic gates and algorithms to manipulate these bits and perform computations. They process information sequentially and use binary representation.

Advantages of Classical Computing:

- **Robust and Reliable:** Classical computers have been extensively developed and optimized over several decades, resulting in highly reliable systems.
- **Wide Applicability:** Classical computing is suitable for a broad range of applications, including data processing, software development, simulations, and many other tasks.
- **Mature Infrastructure:** Classical computing has a well-established infrastructure, including programming languages, compilers, and frameworks, making it easy to develop software and solve problems.

Limitations of Classical Computing

- **Limited Processing Power:** Classical computers face limitations in solving certain complex problems efficiently. As the size and complexity of the problem increase, classical computers require exponentially more time and resources.
- **Inability to Solve Certain Problems:** Some problems, such as prime factorization and optimization in large-scale systems, are inherently difficult for classical computers to solve within a reasonable time frame.
- **Limited Parallelism:** Classical computers process information sequentially, which restricts their ability to perform certain computations in parallel.

Quantum computing utilizes quantum bits, or qubits, which can exist in multiple states simultaneously, thanks to the principles of quantum mechanics. Qubits allow for superposition and entanglement, enabling quantum computers to perform computations in parallel and potentially solve complex problems more efficiently.

Advantages of Quantum Computing

- **Quantum Parallelism:** Quantum computers can process multiple possible solutions simultaneously, which can lead to exponential speedup for specific problems compared to classical computers.
- **Quantum Entanglement:** Qubits can be entangled, allowing for strong correlations between them. This property enables quantum computers to perform certain computations more efficiently, such as solving linear equations or searching large databases.
- **Potential for Breakthroughs:** Quantum computing has the potential to revolutionize fields like cryptography, optimization, drug discovery, and material science by providing faster and more accurate solutions to complex problems.

Limitations of Quantum Computing:

- **Fragile Quantum States:** Qubits are highly sensitive to environmental noise and disturbances, making quantum computations susceptible to errors and decoherence.
- **Limited Scalability:** Building large-scale quantum computers with a high number of qubits is a significant technical challenge. Currently, quantum computers have a limited number of qubits, making them suitable for only certain types of problems.
- **Noisy Intermediate-Scale Quantum (NISQ) Era:** Current quantum computers fall into the NISQ era, where they have a high error rate and

limited coherence times, restricting the complexity of problems they can effectively solve.

The performance of classical and quantum computing depends on the specific problem being solved. Here are some general assessments:

Classical Computing Performance:

- Well-suited for routine tasks like data processing, software development, and general-purpose computing.
- Efficient for problems that can be solved using classical algorithms and do not require exponential time.
- Suitable for small to medium-scale optimization and simulations.
- Limited performance for problems that require massive parallelism or solving complex mathematical equations.

Quantum Computing Performance:

- Potential for exponential speedup for certain specific problems, such as factoring large numbers (relevant to cryptography) and searching large databases (relevant to data mining).
- Suitable for solving complex mathematical equations, simulation of quantum systems, and optimization problems.
- Limited to problems for which quantum algorithms exist or can be developed.
- Current quantum computers are still in the early stages and face technical limitations, making them less efficient than classical computers for routine tasks and small-scale problems.

In summary, classical computing excels in a wide range of everyday tasks and is reliable, while quantum computing holds the potential for significant speedup in specific problem domains but is still in the early stages of development and faces technical challenges.

The two computing methods can be complementary, with classical computers handling routine tasks and quantum computers focusing on specialized problems that benefit from quantum algorithms.

Differences Between Classical Computing and Quantum Computing

The primary differences between quantum and classical computers are as follows:

- **Quantum Computers are Governed by Quantum Mechanics:** Quantum computers rely on quantum mechanics, a branch of physics that operates at the level of atoms. In contrast, traditional computers operate in accordance with the laws of classical physics.

- **Quantum Computers Store Information in Qubits:** Classical computers rely on bits to perform operations. Bits can have a value of either 0 or 1. Qubits, in contrast, can represent a combination of the classical 0 or 1, which is what makes quantum computers so fast.
- **Quantum Computing Operations Rely on Linear Algebra:**.Bits operate according to Boolean algebra because they can produce either 0 or 1. Quantum computing, in contrast, uses linear algebra and matrices to define operations and qubit states.
- **The Power of Quantum Computers Increases Exponentially With Qubits:** Because qubits can simultaneously store both 0 and 1, the power of quantum computers scales exponentially as we add qubits. In contrast, classical computers scale linearly with the number of transistors.
- **Programs in Quantum Computing are Probabilistic:** In quantum programs, each possible output has an associated probability. Classical programs deterministically produce either 0 or 1.
- **Quantum Computing Operations Must be Reversible:** Quantum circuits must be reversible, essentially meaning that we must be able to recover the input state of an operation from its output. Most classical circuits aren't reversible, although they can be.
- **Quantum Computers Have Data Restrictions:** According to the no-cloning theorem, it's impossible to create a copy of an arbitrary unknown quantum state. This severely limits the ability of quantum computers to copy data, which is an issue that doesn't exist on classical computers.
- **Quantum Computers are Better at Data-Heavy Tasks:** Quantum computers are unlikely to fully replace classical computers any time soon. Quantum computers require a lot of maintenance and are costly, making them unreasonable for tasks that classical computers can do much more efficiently. At least initially, quantum computing will be reserved for very demanding applications, such as AI or drug development.
- **Quantum Computers Can't Operate at Room Temperature:** Quantum computers need to be kept near absolute zero to operate reliably – otherwise, qubits break down and lose information. This is one of the main factors that make quantum computers difficult to operate.
- **Quantum Computers Aren't Easily Scalable:** We can scale classical computing technology basically at will. Thanks to this scalability, virtually

infinitely scalable compute resources are now available to anyone through cloud platforms. Quantum computers aren't yet easily scalable – qubits are extremely sensitive to environmental conditions, which considerably complicates scaling.

QUANTUM BITS (QUBITS) AND SUPERPOSITION

Quantum physics has a reputation for being difficult and confusing, exacerbated by (incorrect) references to quantum mechanics in movies to justify their sci-fi plot elements. To help reduce this intimidation factor and ease the introduction of quantum computing, I made a board game called Qubit Touchdown. It is shown in Fig. 1.1, and it is available print-on-demand from The Game Crafter.

Superposition

Zero or One

A quantum bit, or qubit, is both similar to and different from a classical bit in some important ways. First, like a classical bit, a qubit can take two values, 0 or 1. Using bra-ket notation or Dirac notation from quantum physics, we write 0 and 1 enclosed between a vertical bar and an angle bracket called a ket:

$$|0\rangle, |1\rangle.$$

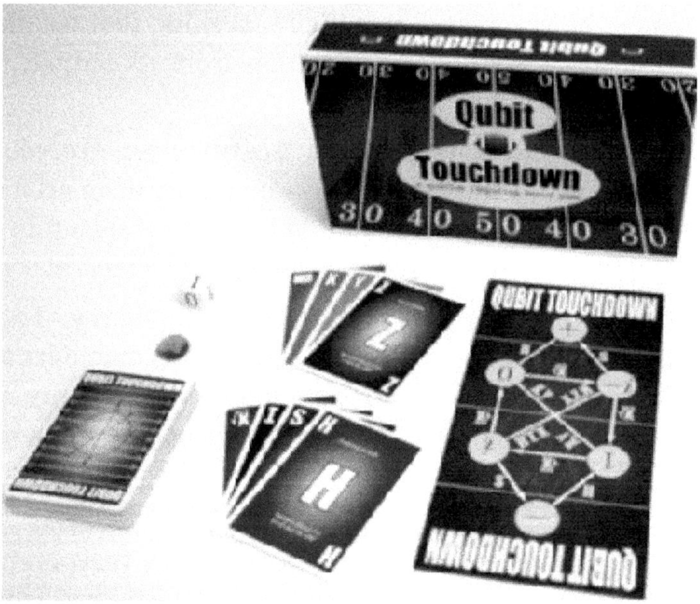

Fig. 1.1: The complete Qubit Touchdown board game.

Although it may seem strange to write a quantum 0 and a quantum 1 like this, it will be very useful later.

We can visualize these distinct states, $|0\rangle$ and $|1\rangle$, as the north and south poles of a sphere of radius 1 called the Bloch sphere:

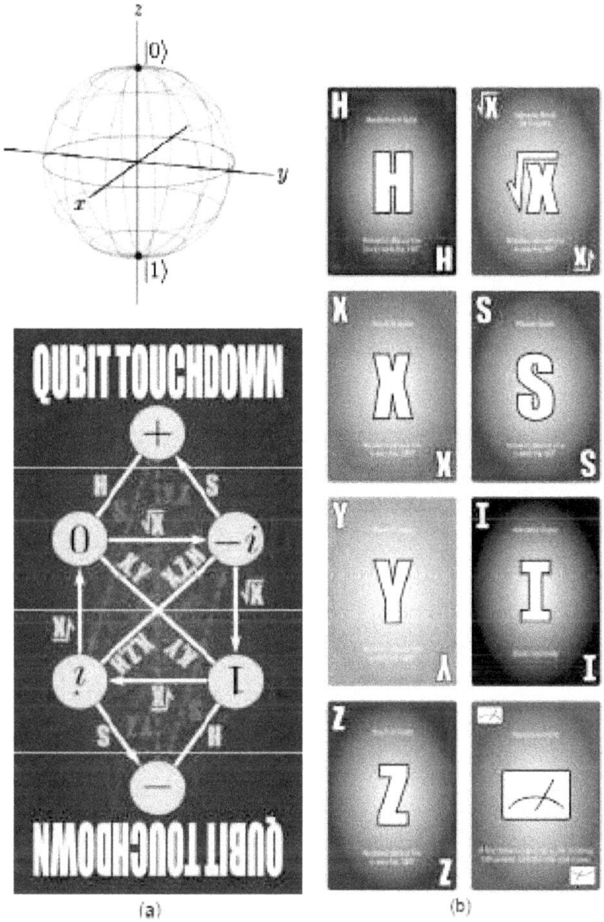

Fig. 1.2: The Qubit Touchdown (a) game board and (b) action cards

Following the standard physics convention, the x-axis comes out of the page, the y-axis points to the side, and z-axis is oriented up. Then, since the Bloch sphere has radius 1, $|0\rangle$ corresponds to the (x, y,z) point (0,0,1), and $|1\rangle$ corresponds to (0,0,-1).

Superposition

If we had a classical bit, $|0\rangle$ and $|1\rangle$ would be the only two states. But, the laws of quantum mechanics allow the state of a qubit to be a combination of $|0\rangle$ and $|1\rangle$, called a superposition of $|0\rangle$ and $|1\rangle$. For example, here is a state that is equal parts $|0\rangle$ and $|1\rangle$:

$$1/\sqrt{2}\,(|0\rangle + |1\rangle).$$

In this state, the coefficient of $|0\rangle$ is $1/\sqrt{2}$, and the coefficient of $|1\rangle$ is also $1/\sqrt{2}$. So, it is equal parts $|0\rangle$ and $|1\rangle$. Given this, it should be on the equator of the Bloch sphere, which is halfway between the north and south poles:

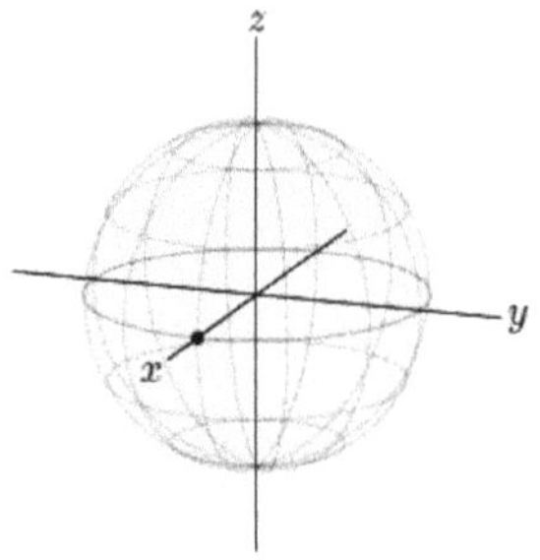

This state is at the (x, y,z) point (1,0,0), where the Bloch sphere intersects the xaxis. Later, we will learn how to calculate these coordinates, but for now, we will focus on building geometric intuition.

There are many other states on the equator of the Bloch sphere, all of which are equal parts $|0\rangle$ and $|1\rangle$. We can reach them by changing the relative phase of $|0\rangle$ and $|1\rangle$. For example, if we instead use a negative sign, we get

$$\frac{1}{\sqrt{2}}(|0\rangle - |1\rangle)$$

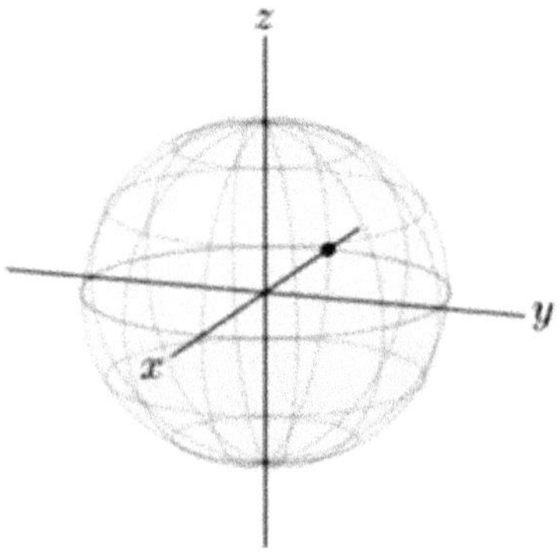

This state is at the point (-1,0,0), on the -x-axis. To reach the y-axis at (0,1,0), we instead use a phase of $i = \sqrt{-1}$:

$$\frac{1}{\sqrt{2}}(|0\rangle + i|1\rangle)$$

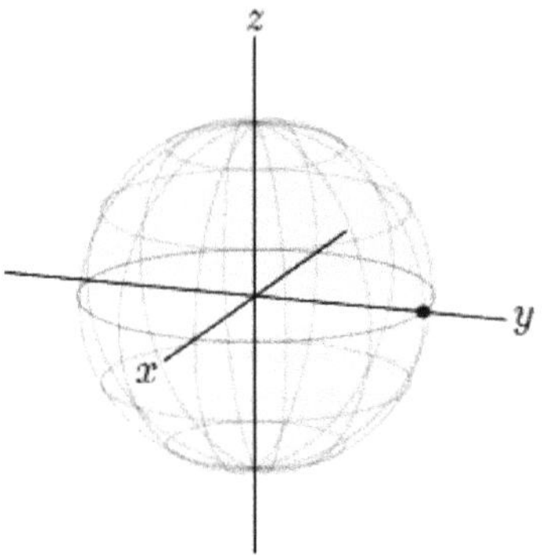

We see that imaginary and complex numbers are used in quantum computing. In case it has been a while since you have used them, in the next section, we will review complex numbers in detail. Continuing, to reach the -y-axis at (0,-1,0), we use a phase of -i:

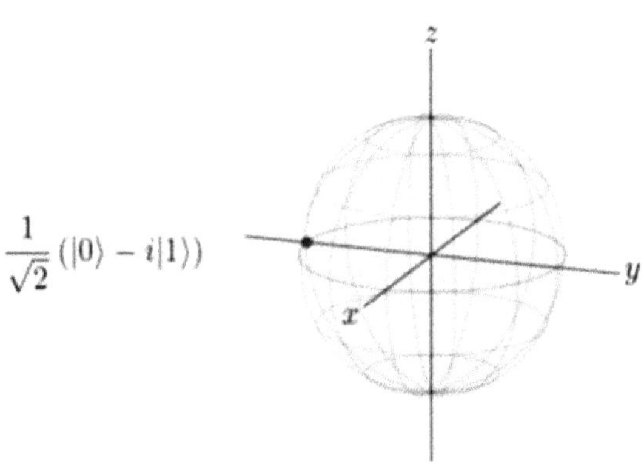

These states appear frequently enough that they have names: "plus," "minus," "i," and "minus i":

$|+\rangle = 1/\sqrt{2}\ (|0\rangle + |1\rangle),$

$|-\rangle = 1/\sqrt{2}\ (|0\rangle + |1\rangle),$ 1.1

$|i\rangle = 1/\sqrt{2}\ (|0\rangle + i|1\rangle),$

$|-i\rangle = 1/\sqrt{2}\ (|0\rangle + -i|1\rangle),$

Drawing them together with |0⟩ and |1⟩ on the Bloch sphere, we get the following, which also appears on the back of every action card in Qubit Touchdown:

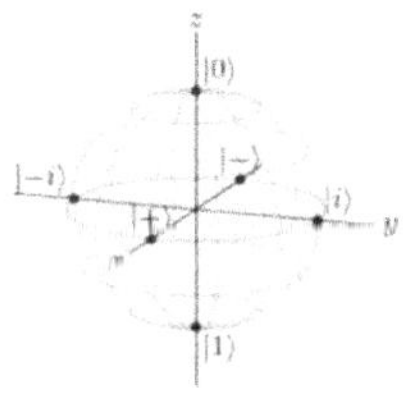

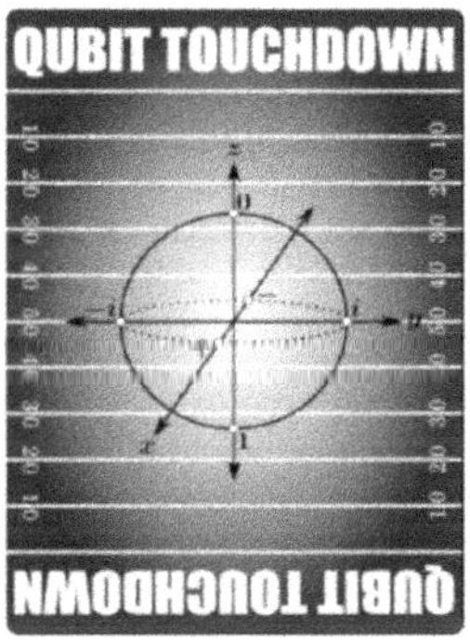

In Qubit Touchdown, these six states correspond to the six positions on the game board in Fig. 2.2a. The football token corresponds to a qubit, so the ball moving around the game board corresponds to a qubit changing between these states (more on this later).

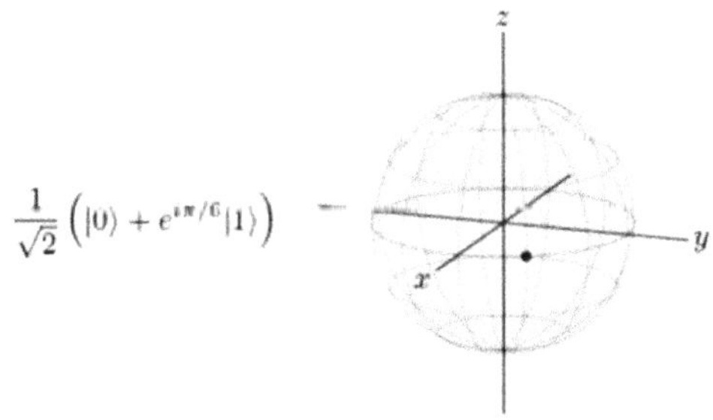

Of course, there are many other points on the equator of the Bloch sphere. We can reach them using other complex phases, such as

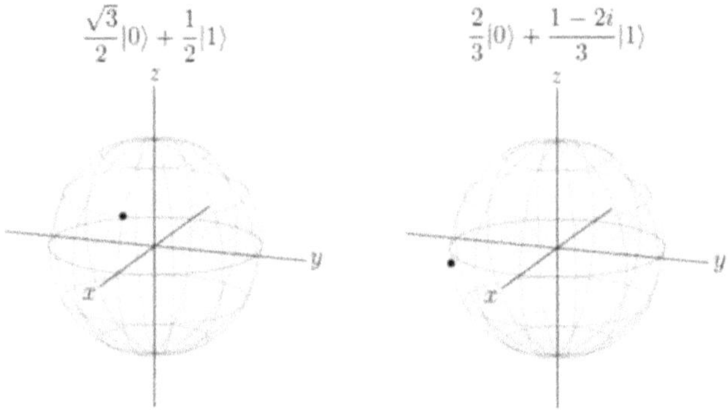

Superpositions are not restricted to the equator, either. They can favor $|0\rangle$ or $|1\rangle$ by being in the northern or southern hemisphere, such as:

Superposition of Qubits in Quantum Computers

Superposition is a fundamental property of quantum mechanics that allows quantum particles to exist in multiple states at the same time. This is in contrast to classical physics, where particles can only exist in one state at a time. Classical physics is a successful description of the macroscopic world, but it breaks down when applied to the microscopic world. This is because classical physics assumes that objects have well-defined positions and momenta, but this is not the case for microscopic objects. For this reason, classical physics is sometimes called "non-relativistic physics" to distinguish it from relativistic physics and quantum mechanics, which are more accurate descriptions of the microscopic world.

In quantum computing, qubits are the basic unit of information. Qubits can exist in a superposition of both 0 and 1, which means that they can be both 0 and 1 at the same time. This is what allows quantum computers to perform calculations that are impossible for classical computers.

For example, a quantum computer could be used to solve the traveling salesman problem, which is a problem that is considered to be NP-complete. NP-complete problems are a class of computationally difficult problems. They are called NP-complete because they are in the complexity class NP, which stands for "nondeterministic polynomial time". This means that there exists a nondeterministic algorithm that can solve the problem in polynomial time. However, a nondeterministic algorithm is an algorithm that can guess the correct answer to the problem. The problem of travelling salesman is so difficult that it would take a classical computer billions of years to solve, but a quantum computer could solve it in a fraction of a second.

The superposition of qubits is a very fragile state, and it can be easily disturbed by noise. This is one of the challenges that need to be addressed before quantum computers can be widely used. However, as quantum computing technology continues to develop, it is likely that these challenges will be overcome.

The states in a quantum bit, or qubit, are in superposition, which can be expressed mathematically as:

$$|\Psi\rangle = \alpha|0\rangle + \beta|1\rangle$$

Where:

- $|\Psi\rangle$ is the state of the qubit
- α and β are complex numbers that represent the probability of the qubit being in state $|0\rangle$ and state $|1\rangle$, respectively
- $|0\rangle$ and $|1\rangle$ are the basis states of the qubit, which represent the states where the qubit is 0 and 1, respectively

The sum of $|\alpha|^2$ and $|\beta|^2$ must always be equal to 1, which represents the fact that the qubit must be in one of the two states $|0\rangle$ or $|1\rangle$.

$$|\alpha|^2 + |\beta|^2 = 1$$

In a complex two-dimensional vector space, a qubit can be represented as a unit vector.

This means that a qubit can exist between the $|0\rangle$ and $|1\rangle$ states in a continuum of states, or in other words, it can exist in a superposition of both states at the same time.

When a qubit is measured, the superposition collapses and the qubit is found to be in either state $|0\rangle$ or $|1\rangle$ with a probability given by the absolute value of the square of the coefficients of the vector.

This property of quantum bits, called superposition, allows them to perform calculations that are impossible for classical computers. For example, quantum computers can be used to factor large numbers, break encryption codes, and design new drugs.

Let a qubit is in a state

$$1/(-3)\ |0\rangle + \sqrt{(2/3)}\ |1\rangle$$

This equation represents the state of a qubit that is in a superposition of the $|0\rangle$ and $|1\rangle$ states.

The probability of the qubit being in the $|0\rangle$ state is $|1/(\sqrt{3})|^2$ or 1/3 or 33%, and the probability of the qubit being in the $|1\rangle$ state is $|\sqrt{(2/3)}|^2$ or 2/3 or 66%.

The equation also shows that the qubit is a unit vector in a complex two-dimensional vector space. This means that the qubit can exist between the $|0\rangle$ and $|1\rangle$ states in a continuum of states, or in other words, it can exist in a superposition of both states at the same time.

When a qubit is measured, the superposition collapses and the qubit is found to be in either state $|0\rangle$ or $|1\rangle$ with a probability given by the absolute value of the square of the coefficients of the vector. In this case, the qubit has a 33% chance of being measured as $|0\rangle$ and a 66% chance of being measured as $|1\rangle$.

The superposition of qubits is one of the key properties that allows quantum computers to perform calculations that are impossible for classical computers. For example, quantum computers can be used to factor large numbers, break encryption codes, and design new drugs.

Entanglement of Q-bit States

Entanglement is a physical phenomenon in which the states of two or more particles are correlated in such a way that they cannot be described independently of each other, even when the particles are separated by a large distance.

For example, if two electrons are entangled, and one electron is measured to be in a spin-up state, the other electron must be in a spin-down state, regardless of how far apart they are. This is because the two electrons share a single wavefunction, and any change to the state of one electron instantaneously affects the state of the other electron.

The equation for two qubits in an entangled state is:

$$|\Psi\rangle = 1/\sqrt{2}\ (|00\rangle + |11\rangle)$$

This equation represents the state of two qubits that are in a superposition of the $|00\rangle$ and $|11\rangle$ states. The $|00\rangle$ state represents the case where both qubits are in the $|0\rangle$ state, and the $|11\rangle$ state represents the case where both qubits are in the $|1\rangle$ state.

The probability of the two qubits being in the $|00\rangle$ state is $|1/\sqrt{2}|^2 = 1/2$, and the probability of the two qubits being in the $|11\rangle$ state is also $|1/\sqrt{2}|^2 = 1/2$.

When the two qubits are measured, they will collapse into either the $|00\rangle$ state or the $|11\rangle$ state, with equal probability. However, the important thing to note is that the two qubits will always collapse into the same state, regardless of which qubit is measured first.

This property of entanglement is what makes it so powerful for quantum computing. For example, quantum computers can use entanglement to perform calculations that are impossible for classical computers.

Entanglement

Product States

Some quantum states can be factored into (the tensor product of) individual qubit states. For example,

$$\frac{1}{2}(|00\rangle - |01\rangle + |10\rangle - |11\rangle) = \underbrace{\frac{1}{\sqrt{2}}(|0\rangle + |1\rangle)}_{|+\rangle} \otimes \underbrace{\frac{1}{\sqrt{2}}(|0\rangle - |1\rangle)}_{|-\rangle}$$
$$= |+\rangle \otimes |-\rangle$$
$$= |+\rangle|-\rangle.$$

To confirm this to yourself, work it out in reverse order by multiplying out the states and showing that you get the original state. Such factorizable states are called product states or simply separable states. Each single-qubit state can be visualized on the Bloch sphere, so |+⟩|”⟩ would be two Bloch spheres, with the first at the x-axis, and the other at the “x-axis:

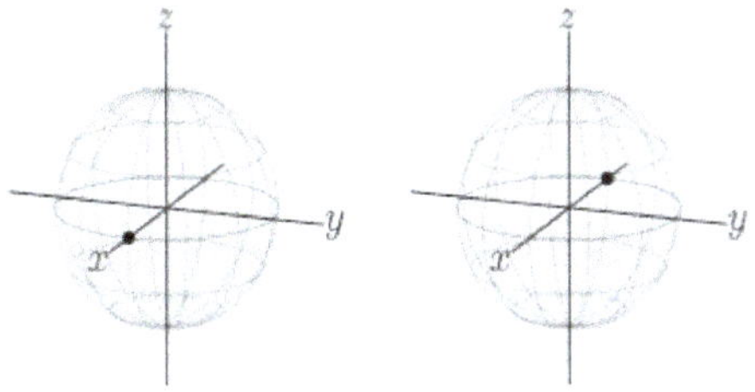

Let us work through an example of how to factor a state. Say two qubits are in the state

$$\frac{1}{2\sqrt{2}}\left(\sqrt{3}|00\rangle - \sqrt{3}|01\rangle + |10\rangle - |11\rangle\right).$$

We want to write this as the product of two single-qubit states,

$|\Psi_1\rangle|\Psi_0\rangle$

Whcrc

$|\Psi_1\rangle = \alpha_1|0\rangle + \beta_1|1\rangle,$

$|\Psi_0\rangle = \alpha_0|0\rangle + \beta_0|1\rangle,$

Then

$|\Psi_1\rangle\,|\Psi_0\rangle \quad = (\alpha_1|0\rangle + \beta_1|1\rangle)\,(\alpha_0|0\rangle + \beta_0|1\rangle)$

$\quad\quad = \alpha_1\alpha_0|00\rangle + \alpha_1\beta_0|01\rangle + \beta_1\alpha_0|10\rangle + \beta_1\beta_0|11\rangle$

Matching up the coefficients with our original state

$$\alpha_1\alpha_0 = \frac{\sqrt{3}}{2\sqrt{2}}, \quad \alpha_1\beta_0 = \frac{-\sqrt{3}}{2\sqrt{2}}, \quad \beta_1\alpha_0 = \frac{1}{2\sqrt{2}}, \quad \beta_1\beta_0 = \frac{-1}{2\sqrt{2}}.$$

Using these equations, let us solve for the variables in terms of one of them. Starting with the first equation, we can solve for á1 in terms of α_0:

$$\alpha_1 = \frac{\sqrt{3}}{2\sqrt{2}\alpha_0}.$$

Plugging this into the second equation, we can solve for â0 in terms of $á_0$:

$$\beta_0 = -\alpha_0.$$

For the third equation, we can solve for â1 in terms of $á_0$:

$$\beta_1 = \frac{1}{2\sqrt{2}\alpha_0}.$$

Finally, plugging in $\beta_1 = 1/2\ \sqrt{2}\alpha_0$ and $\beta_0 = -\alpha_0$ into the fourth equation, we get

$$\frac{-1}{2\sqrt{2}} = \frac{-1}{2\sqrt{2}},$$

which is a true statement, so it is satisfied, although it does not tell us anything new. So, we have solved for α_1, β_1, and β_0 in terms of α_0, and this is actually sufficient. Plugging into the product state,

$$|\Psi_1\rangle|\Psi_0\rangle = (\alpha_1|0\rangle+\beta_1|1\rangle)\ (\alpha_0|0\rangle + \beta_0|1\rangle)$$

$$= \left(\frac{\sqrt{3}}{2\sqrt{2}\alpha_0}|0\rangle + \frac{1}{2\sqrt{2}}\frac{1}{\alpha_0}|1\rangle\right)(\alpha_0|0\rangle - \alpha_0|1\rangle).$$

We see that α_0 cancels, yielding

$$|\psi_1\rangle|\psi_0\rangle = \left(\frac{\sqrt{3}}{2\sqrt{2}}|0\rangle + \frac{1}{2\sqrt{2}}|1\rangle\right)(|0\rangle - |1\rangle).$$

Moving the factor of 1/ " 2 to the right qubit so that both qubits are normalized,

$$|\psi_1\rangle|\psi_0\rangle = \left(\frac{\sqrt{3}}{2}|0\rangle + \frac{1}{2}|1\rangle\right)\left(\frac{1}{\sqrt{2}}|0\rangle - \frac{1}{\sqrt{2}}|1\rangle\right).$$

Thus, the left qubit is in the state $\sqrt{3}/2|0\rangle + ½\ |1\rangle$, and the right qubit is in the state $|-\rangle$.

In general, a product state of n qubits can be written

$(\alpha n\text{-}1|0\rangle+\beta n\text{-}1|1\rangle) \otimes \ldots \otimes (\alpha_1|0\rangle+\beta_1|1\rangle) \otimes (\alpha_0|0\rangle + \beta_0|1\rangle)$.

This only has 2n amplitudes, so a classical computer can efficiently store the amplitudes of product states. If quantum computers only used product states, they would be efficiently simulated by classical computers.

QUANTUM PARALLELISM

Computer scientists sometimes put forth a second definition of quantum parallelism. In the absence of quantum entanglement, operations can still be performed on all qubits at the same time. Using the same 10 qubits as before allows 10 simultaneous operations with each time step. However, this is more analogous to a supercomputer with many, many processors than it is to the massive quantum parallelism previously described. Nonetheless, in principle, a quantum computer with a thousand qubits could act like a classical computer with a thousand processors. That's a far cry from 2^{1000} processors, but it still gets mentioned from time to time.

It is worth noting that although there are no quantum advantages to it, parallel quantum computing is currently being researched. The notion is to divide problems wherever entanglement is weak, execute operations on multiple quantum processors, and then classically merge the results. However, this is meant to be a solution to having quantum computers that are too small to solve real-world problems. Execution of the same algorithm on a single, large, fault-tolerant quantum computer, if it were possible, would be both simpler and faster.

Applications of Quantum Parallelism

Quantum computers are remarkably inefficient at solving simple problems. However, they can be remarkably efficient at solving classically intractable problems – problems that cannot be solved efficiently with classical computers. This means that the applications of quantum computing are going to be limited to extremely challenging problems. Examples of such challenging-to-intractable problems include:

- **Speed.** Problems that grow in complexity exponentially may be solvable with exponentially greater efficiency, resulting in exponential speedups in computation time.
- **Scale.** Problems that grow in memory requirements, such as simulating molecules in quantum chemistry, beyond the capacities of supercomputers, can be solved with relatively small quantum computers.
- **Randomness.** Problems that require humanlike decision making – such as generating art, language, and music – are already being prototyped.
- **Search.** Problems with massive search spaces can have all possible solutions found at the same time and with mathematically-proven optimality.
- **Security.** Cryptographic schemes that rely on the multiplication of prime numbers will become vulnerable to decryption.

A good rule of thumb is that most applications that are possible today will continue to be solved classically in the future. The applications that are not possible today, or otherwise require tremendous time and classical resources, are the applications fueling investments into quantum computing.

The Challenges of Quantum Parallelism

Although quantum computation has the potential to disrupt entire industries, the path to achieving such breakthroughs is not a simple one. Just a few of the challenges that must be addressed along the way include:

- *Control*. Achieving quantum computational advantages is going to require large numbers of qubits, and yet controlling relatively small numbers of qubits is currently difficult.
- *Timing*. Realizing accurate results will require the precise timing of quantum operations, to a degree of precision beyond the capabilities of traditional clocks.
- *Coherence*. Realizing accurate results will require qubits that maintain their quantum states without errors for much longer durations than is currently possible.
- *Efficiency*. Quantum algorithms, such as amplitude encoding, need to become classically feasible to implement, due to their complexity and memory requirements.

Solutions to all of these problems are currently being researched. And while the road to fault-tolerant quantum computing is a long one, steps toward this goal are happening every day.

QUANTUM GATES AND CIRCUITS

Quantum computing is a rapidly growing field of research and development that has the potential to revolutionize the way we process and analyze data. Unlike classical computing, which relies on bits to represent data and perform logical operations, quantum computing uses quantum bits, or qubits, which can represent multiple states simultaneously. One of the key components of quantum computing is the use of quantum gates and circuits, which are the building blocks of quantum algorithms.

Quantum Gates

Boolean Function which was invented by George Boole, is a function that takes logical values True or False as input and returns other logical values as output.

By replacing the logical value True and false to 1 and 0 respectively, the boolean algebra can be used in computers. And by weaving the functions meticulously, we can solve much more complicated computational problems.

This logical function used at basic design of the algorithm is called Logical Gate. There are main examples of the gates; And,Or,Not,Nand etc.

Quantum gates are the basic building blocks of quantum circuits, and they are used to manipulate the quantum state of qubits. A quantum gate is a mathematical operation that acts on the state of one or more qubits, and it can be represented by a matrix. In classical computing, logical gates such as AND, OR, and NOT are used to manipulate the state of bits. In quantum computing, the most commonly used gates are the Pauli gates, the Hadamard gate, the CNOT gate, and the T gate.

The Pauli gates are named after physicist Wolfgang Pauli, and they include the X, Y, and Z gates. The X gate flips the state of a qubit from 0 to 1, or from 1 to 0. The Y gate flips the state of a qubit from 0 to I, or from 1 to -I, where i is the imaginary unit. The Z gate leaves the state of a qubit unchanged if it is in state 0, and flips it to state 1 if it is in state 1.

The Hadamard gate is another commonly used gate in quantum computing, and it is used to create superpositions. The Hadamard gate transforms the state of a qubit from either 0 or 1 to a superposition of both 0 and 1. This gate is useful for performing operations on multiple qubits simultaneously.

The CNOT gate, or Controlled-NOT gate, is a two-qubit gate that is used to create entanglement between qubits. The CNOT gate operates on two qubits, one of which is called the control qubit and the other is called the target qubit. If the control qubit is in state 1, then the CNOT gate flips the state of the target qubit.

Finally, the T gate is a single-qubit gate that is used to create phase shifts. The T gate rotates the state of a qubit by an angle of π/4 radians, which can be useful for performing certain quantum algorithms.

There is a quantum gate named Pauli Transformation Gate, Rotation Gate and Hadamard Gate which takes one qubit and returns one qubit. For gates which take two qubits and return two qubits, there are CNOT gates and SWAP gates. There are tremendous examples of the gates but the most important gates are above. Let's figure them out.

Single Qubit GatesPermalink

Pauli Transformation Gates

Pauli Transformation Gates are four kind of gates which take one qubit and are

$$I=\begin{bmatrix}1&0\\0&1\end{bmatrix}, X=\begin{bmatrix}0&1\\1&0\end{bmatrix}, Y=\begin{bmatrix}0&-i\\i&0\end{bmatrix}, Z=\begin{bmatrix}1&0\\0&-1\end{bmatrix}$$

We can understand X gate somehow, but it is hard to understand Y and Z intuitively. Fortunately, we can understand them easily by using Bloch Sphere.

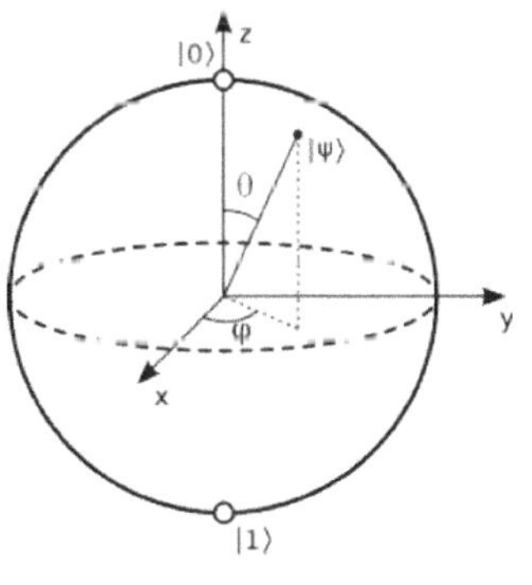

By substituting the vectors and results above, we can know that each matrix works as a rotating operator which rotates each vector as 180' degree along with each axis.

For the rotation along the Z-axis, the vertical direction is not changed. Thus the probabilities are unchanged but the amplitudes in it turn opposite.

Like them, the pauli gates make qubit's state opposite along each axis.

Hadamard Gate

Hadamard Gate is an essential gate of the quantum computer and expressed as below.

$$H = \frac{\sqrt{2}}{2}\begin{bmatrix} 1 & 1 \\ 1 & -1 \end{bmatrix}$$

Or, it can be interpreted as 90' degree rotation along the Y-axis.

For the other gates, there is a θ-Rotation Gate which rotates the state θ' degree with each axis.

Two and Three Qubit GatesPermalink

To represent two or more qubits, the quantum computers use Tensor Product which accounts for every possible case.

$$|\Psi_1\rangle \otimes |\Psi_2\rangle = \begin{bmatrix} \psi_{11} \\ \psi_{12} \end{bmatrix} \otimes \begin{bmatrix} \psi_{21} \\ \psi_{22} \end{bmatrix}$$

$$= \begin{bmatrix} \psi_{11} \begin{bmatrix} \psi_{21} \\ \psi_{22} \end{bmatrix} \\ \psi_{12} \begin{bmatrix} \psi_{21} \\ \psi_{22} \end{bmatrix} \end{bmatrix}$$

For general linear algebra, Dot product is the main operator. So if the operator between subjects is emitted, then it is regarded as a Dot product. However, in quantum physics, the Tensor product is the main operator. So if the operator between subjects is emitted, then it is regarded as a Tensor product like below.

$$|\Psi_1\rangle \otimes |\Psi_2\rangle = |\Psi_1\rangle|\Psi_2\rangle = |\Psi_1\Psi_2\rangle$$

With this notation, let's see 2- qubit gates

CNOT Gate

CNOT gate is abbreviation of Controlled Not Gate and it can be called as CX gate because the X gate is equal with not gate

It takes two inputs and if the first input is 1, then it applies an X gate to the second input and if the first input is 0, then it returns the second input as it is.

The matrix form of the gate is below.

$$CX = \begin{bmatrix} 1\,0\,0\,0 \\ 0\,1\,0\,0 \\ 0\,0\,0\,1 \\ 0\,0\,1\,0 \end{bmatrix}$$

For this gate, the name Controlled X qubit is named because the first input controls the second input. Like the CX gate, there are gates in the quantum computer that one input controls the other qubit. Therefore, there are CZ or CY gates too.

One of the important usages of the CX gates is that it can make a bell's circuit.

SWAP Gate

Swap Gate literally interchanges states of two qubits with each other. The matrix form of the gate is below.

$$SWAP = \begin{bmatrix} 1\,0\,0\,0 \\ 0\,0\,1\,0 \\ 0\,1\,0\,0 \\ 0\,0\,0\,1 \end{bmatrix}$$

Toffoli Gate

Toffoli Gate is also called CCNOT gate or CCX gate. It takes three inputs and returns three outputs.

It apply NOT gate to the third input when all of the first and second inputs are one

Fredkin Gate

Fredkin Gate is also called CSWAP gate. It takes three inputs and returns three outputs.

It apply SWAP gate to the second and third qubit when the first input is one

Like above, the gates can be made with these ways. By combining rotation, swap and control, we can make a lot of gates.

Quantum Circuits

Basic of Quantum Circuit

As a combination of the above gates, we can make some circuits called Quantum Circuit which take specific roles.

IBM provides several quantum computers as open source and lets people use them with a Python package called Qiskit.

Even though Google and Microsoft also makes the quantum computer language called as Q# or circQ, but the IBM Qiskit becomes dominant role in the quantum computer and canon,

In the qiskit, the quantum circuits are depicted as figure below:

Quantum circuits are composed of quantum gates and are used to perform quantum algorithms. A quantum circuit is a series of quantum gates that act on one or more qubits. The gates are arranged in a specific order, and the circuit is executed in a specific sequence. Quantum circuits are similar to classical circuits, but they operate on quantum states rather than classical bits.

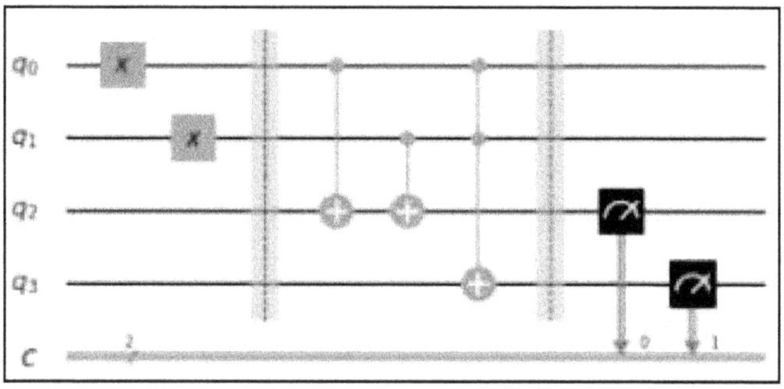

Inputs move into the left side of the circuit and they flow to the right and pass through the gates. For some hardware reasons, all of the input qubits are in the $|0\rangle$ state. The rightmost gates with the instrument panel are measuring the input qubits.

For the single qubit gates. The English character written above directly represents the gate. That is, X means X gate. For the two qubit gates, they are represented below.

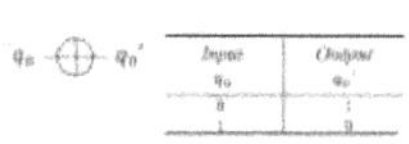

(a) NOT gate

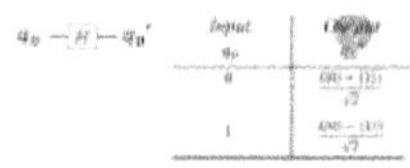

(b) Hadamard Gate

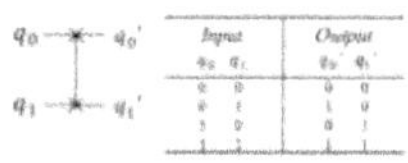

(c) SWAP Gate

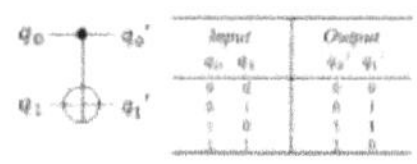

(d) CNOT Gate

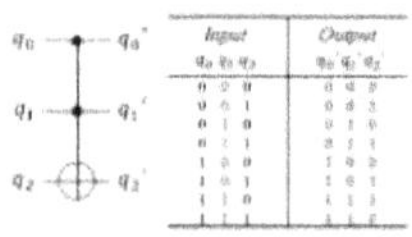

(e) Toffoli Gate

Therefore, we can build custom circuits by using them.

The circuits can do some realistic action. But to understand the quantum machine learning algorithm, it is inevitable to use complex numbers. For example, in quantum machine learning, there are circuits named as quantum fourier transformation or variational quantum circuits in which the phase and complex number do essential roles.

Therefore, let's see them after understanding the basics of complex numbers in a later posting. Instead, let's see a more simple circuit which can be dealt with only real numbers.

Quantum circuits are composed of three main types of gates: single-qubit gates, two-qubit gates, and measurement gates. Single-qubit gates operate on a single qubit and can be used to create superpositions or perform rotations. Two-qubit gates operate on two qubits and are used to create entanglement between qubits. Measurement gates are used to extract information from the quantum state of a qubit.

To create a quantum circuit, the user specifies the initial state of the qubits and then applies a series of quantum gates to manipulate the quantum state. The final state of the qubits is then measured, and the measurement result is used to extract information about the quantum state.

Circuit Diagrams Just like we can draw a classical circuit diagram consisting of bits and logic gates, we can draw quantum circuit diagrams consisting of qubits and quantum gates. For example, HST H|0⟩ is

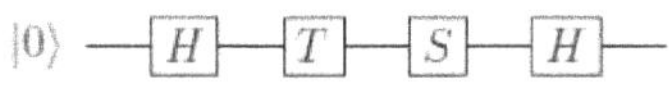

The circuit is read left-to-right, just like a classical circuit diagram. So, we start with a single qubit in the |0⟩ state and apply a Hadamard gate H to it, followed by a T gate, then a phase gate S, and finally another H gate. It is implied that we measure the qubit at the end of the circuit. We can also explicitly draw the measurement as a meter:

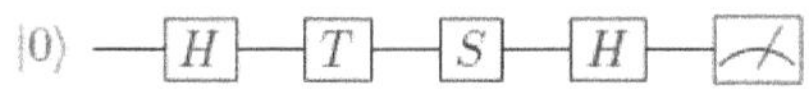

Quirk

A great web-based tool for simulating quantum circuits is Quirk at https://algassert.com/quirk:

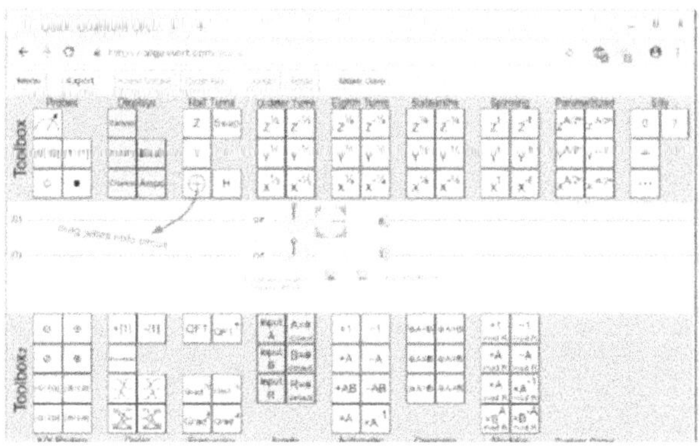

There are a variety of quantum gates that users can drag and drop onto the circuit, and users can also make custom gates. Each qubit is initially a $|0\rangle$, as shown below:

The state of each qubit is visualized a couple ways. First, the probability that a measurement of the qubit yields $|1\rangle$ is zero, and this is labeled as "Off." Second, the Bloch sphere representation of the qubit is shown, and the state is a point at the north pole, as expected. Now if we apply the X gate, Quirk shows the following:

Note Quirk uses ⊗ to denote a single X gate, whereas we use X (later, we will also use ⊗ when the X gate is controlled by another qubit). Since $X|0\rangle = |1\rangle$, the probability of measuring $|1\rangle$ is 1. This is labeled as "On," and the Bloch sphere now shows the state at the south pole, as expected.

Now consider $H|0\rangle = |+\rangle$:

In Quirk, it shows a 50% chance of being $|1\rangle$ when measured in the Z-basis, and it lies on the x-axis of the Bloch sphere, as expected.

Finally, let us simulate HST $H|0\rangle$, which we earlier computed by hand to have a 0.146 probability of being $|0\rangle$ and a 0.854 probability of being $|1\rangle$. Simulating it in Quirk,

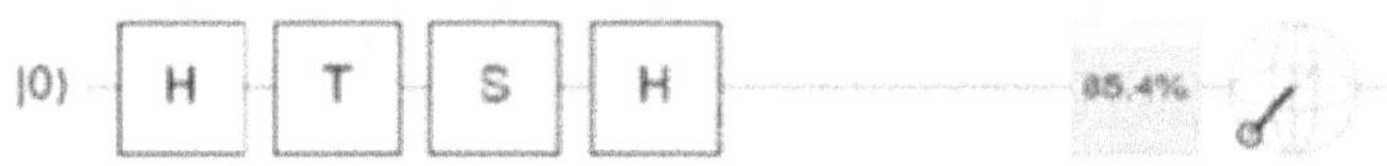

Quirk displays that the probability of measuring $|1\rangle$ is 85.4% = 0.854

CHAPTER-2
QUANTUM MECHANICS PRIMER

Everything in this world works using quantum physics -every particle, atom, and molecule. Quantum mechanics is what makes the Sun work, allows all living things including ourselves be alive, and makes up the actions that make everything every thing. When you look at a waterfall, see a bunny run, watch light hit the ground, or throw a rock, it's all working on quantum mechanics.

The difference is that in order to see only quantum properties and physics laws in a way to understand them, we must see and experiment with them at the sub-atomic level with as few particles as possible. By the time they get combined with a trillion other things (e.g. other particles, light, dust, etc.) and end up being something big enough to be seen by the naked eye (a size called macroscopic in the science world), the individual quantum properties and behaviors get lost among all the "noise". So, in order for scientists to view, experiment, and figure out quantum behaviors, they use only single to a handful or so of individual quantum particles. Any elementary particle, such as an election or photon, readily displays quantum behaviors that can be seen (with the aid of scientific equipment) and experimented with.

Note: An elementary particle is any particle which cannot be subdivided into even smaller components.

If you've heard about the weirdness of quantum mechanics, it is because that much of behavior seems very strange and contrary to what we've previously believed. It's so strange and weird that it's hard to bclicvc for most people hearing about it for the first (or sometimes hundredth) time. The truth is that we just don't know how to appropriately describe it in the simplest possible terms, at least not yet. When we figure out how it works and why, it's likely to be something that we understand as naturally as we understand gravity, the air we breathe, and the concept that the Earth evolves around the Sun (instead of the other way around).

But right now, we are having a hard time describing it using our current frame of reference and understanding. Imagine how the Aztecs felt and described

Spanish troops invading their country in 1519. The Aztecs, never having seen guns or gunpowder, described the Spanish firearms as something akin "sticks which shoot fire". It's important to understand that why we don't know how or why about a particular quantum behavior or attribute, quantum physics is among some of the most proven science in the world. When you understand the many incredible, wonderous things about quantum mechanics, it's not speculation or theory. Someone didn't just make up an imaginary story that we are still trying to prove. It's really does exist, it's been proven to exist, and it really does result in what we are seeing. We just don't always know how or why it does it.

QUANTUM MECHANIC BASICS

There are dozens of quantum laws and attributes which can be used to explain quantum physics. They cannot all be covered here. In fact, none of the books on quantum physics in existence cover all quantum physics laws, so I'm not going to be able to cover them all here. In fact, I'm only going to cover three. But these three are fundamental to all the others and are central to all the quantum behavior which seems so different to our traditional understanding. There are at least a dozen other very, very important quantum behaviors which anyone interested in quantum physics should understand, but these three are a great starting point: quantum measurement, the observer effect, and entanglement.

Quantum Measurement

Perhaps no quantum attribute has more to do with all the other quantum strangeness that we see than how quantum behaviors and outcomes are measured. And in order to do that we need to understand how "classical", non-quantum, traditional physics is seen, predicted, and measured. With traditional physics, if you understand all involved parts and actions, you cannot only accurately describe any outcome of the involved parts at any time, but without seeing them describe what will happen and what the answer will be every single time.

For example, you might have heard that anytime you randomly flip a coin that the coin has a 50% chance of landing on its "heads" side and 50% chance of landing on its "tails" side, and that over many, many flips, say a thousand, that the outcomes from the random flips would be 500-500 for any non-biased coin and coin flip. And this is true.

But from a classical physics perspective, if you flipped the coin the exact same way every time beginning with the same side facing up and applying the exact same upward force every time (including the same environmental conditions, wind, humidity, etc.) then the coin would land the exact same way every time. If it landed heads-side up the first time, it would land heads-side up every time. It wouldn't be a 50-50 outcome. It would be 100% the same side every flip. In fact, it would be strange if even a single flip was a different answer. Not only that, but without seeing the coin or any apparatus, if you told any physicist all the parts involved, they would do a little math and tell you exactly what the coin flip outcome would be every time. The outcome is called "deterministic". If A + B = C, then it will every time.

At the quantum level, the outcome of any single coin flip, even when done 100% the same way is random and always will be random. And all possible answers are the answer (known as *superposition* in the physics world). Even if the coin flip was performed identically every time, what side it landed on would be random, and if you asked a quantum physicist to predict the answer they would correctly say the answer is heads and tails and also heads and tails at the same time. What?

Yes, at the quantum level a measurement of anything results in a random answer and the answer is all possible answers. The answer must be one of the possible answers. But which answer it will be when measured at any particular time will always be random. Over a large number of measurements of the same thing, the random answer will still fit into a probability of possible answers. For example, if flipping a coin a bunch of times randomly results in 50% of the landings being heads and 50% of the landings being tails, then even though each individual landing's result is random, over many tries, the "random" landings will still end up being 50-50. Quantum answers are *probabilistic*, not deterministic.

As another macroscopic example comparison. Suppose we were trying to determine where throwing a rock would make the rock be during a particular part of the rock's travelled pathway. Using classical physics, if you tell me everything about the parts and actions involved in throwing the rock (e.g. the rock's weight, physical characteristics, wind direction and speed, direction and angle the rock was thrown, and with how much force), any physicist could tell you where the rock was while being thrown, and where it was and its speed during any moment in time during the rock's traveled pathway. At the beginning it would be near the beginning. At the end it would be near the end and landing, and everywhere else somewhere along the rock's thrown arc leaving its origination point more and more behind as it traveled through time. And to be clear, this is also true of quantum physics at the macroscopic level of seeing a thrown rock.

But at the subatomic level, the quantum level, any single measurement results in a random answer from a setting of possible probabilities. If (incorrectly) applying those same measurements at the macroscopic, rock-throwing level, the rock could be anywhere along its pathway arc during any moment in time. If you measured the rock near the beginning of its take-off time, at the quantum level, the rock's quantum equivalent, could be near the end of its pathway, near the beginning, or anywhere along the its pathway. In an ordered series of events, any single event could be randomly measured as first, middle, or last. And if you ask a quantum physicist where the rock is, a quantum physicist will say that it is everywhere along it's thrown arc all at the same time. And the answer of what side a coin will land on, from a quantum physics level is that it is both heads and tails at the same time. A quantum answer is always all possible answers.

Again, don't start thinking that thrown rocks don't act like thrown rocks at the quantum level. Quantum physics says that the random answer must still be a possible answer from a set of possible probabilities. If you throw a rock in your front yard in the United States, it's not going to randomly appear in someone's backyard in China. All the other laws of physics, such as those governing motion, energy, and gravity, still apply. But of any of the possible answers, controlled by physics, any single answer can be any of the possible answers. And if you throw a rock, its possible answers at the end of its traveling time (versus at the beginning of its time of being thrown) of its pathway are far higher than the possibilities of the rock still being at the beginning of its pathway. But at the quantum level, any single measurement is not guaranteed to be at the beginning, middle, or end, when you think it should be from a classical viewpoint.

Don't let macroscopic allegories that are often used to try and explain quantum attributes make you think that quantum particles act one way and larger things act another. That isn't true. Everything is quantum. Everything that happens in the observable world only happens because of what happens at the quantum level. The allegories everyone, including me, uses to demonstrate a particular quantum property aren't truly complete. Because if we described it completely and accurately, it would also always correctly describe what we see at the macroscopic level.

We, used to believe that the physics world was looking for some grand, unifying theory to explain how something (seemingly so strange appearing) at the quantum level ends up behaving rather ordinary and classical at the macroscopic level. But quantum mechanics is classical physics. Quantum mechanics makes the classical macroscopic things we observe happen. And if we completely understood and described all the particles and actions and all their probabilities accurately, it would absolutely explain what we see at the macroscopic observable level.

If we flipped a coin in exactly the same way every time, it would, because of quantum properties and behaviors, land the same way every time. Each individual answer would still be random from the list of possibilities, but because the coin was flipped exactly the same way each time, the list of possible probabilities ends up with the same answer. But if, at the quantum level, you measured any particular outcome of any attribute or property, it would be random from a list of possible outcomes according to their probabilities.

Quantum computers operate using qubits, not bits. Unlike traditional bits which can only be 0 **or** 1, a qubit can exist in a 'superposition' of 0 **and** 1. This ability to exist in multiple states at once gives quantum computers tremendous power.

But a qubit is useless unless you can use it to carry out a quantum calculation. And these quantum calculations are achieved by performing a series of fundamental operations, known as quantum logic gates.

There are lots of types of quantum gates. There are single-qubit gates, which can flip a qubit from 0 to 1 as well as allowing superposition states to be created.

Then there are also two-qubit gates. These allow the qubits to interact with each other and can be used to create quantum entanglement: a state of two or more qubits that are correlated in a way that can't be explained by classical physics.

You may have heard of entanglement. It can lead to counterintuitive quantum phenomena that Einstein once famously called "spooky action at a distance", although the logic behind that statement is more complicated than it appears.

An example of a gate is the controlled-NOT (CNOT) gate. It's a two-qubit operation where the first qubit is labelled the control qubit and the second one is the target qubit. If the control qubit is |1> then it will flip the target's qubit state from |0> to |1>or vice versa.

Similar to traditional computers, quantum algorithms with many qubits can be broken down into a sequence of single and two-qubit quantum gates, forming a universal quantum gate set. Therefore, if we can get these quantum gates to work in a reliable way that scales to many qubits, we can use them to run all possible algorithms on our quantum computer.

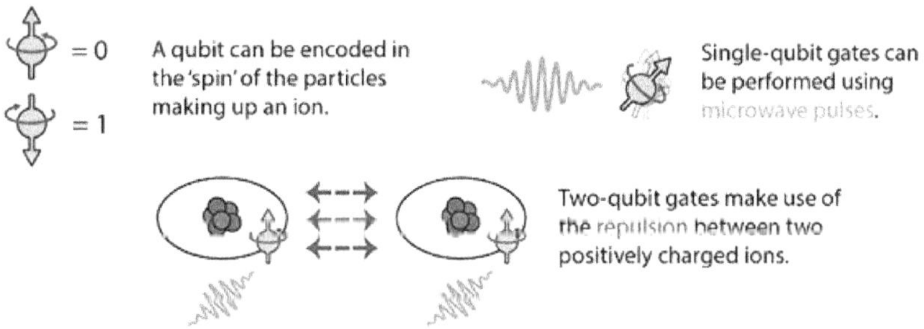

Quantum gates in trapped ions

Trapped ions (charged atoms) are one of the leading platforms for quantum computing.

Each ion can store a single qubit, which is encoded in two atomic states related to a uniquely quantum property of the particles making up the ion (electrons, protons and neutrons) called 'spin'. These spin states are well isolated from the outside world, protecting them from any noise that could destroy the fragile qubit states.

So how do we implement the required quantum logic gates on these trapped-ion qubits?

For single-qubit gates, it's actually quite straightforward: we apply a short pulse of microwave radiation. If the frequency of the microwave exactly matches the resonant frequency of the qubit, it will cause the qubit state to flip. We can also create superposition states in the same way by adjusting how long the pulse lasts.

For the two-qubit gate, things are not so easy, since the spin states used to store the qubits don't naturally interact with one another. The ions themselves do interact, however — they repel each other due to both having a positive electric charge, in a similar way to the repulsion between two bar magnets with their north poles facing each other.

We can use this repulsion to engineer an artificial interaction between the qubits. This can be achieved in a few different ways, including using high-power lasers or using specially shaped magnetic fields combined with microwave pulses.

At Universal Quantum, we use the latter approach, which means all of our gates are laser free — an attribute that we believe makes it easier to scale to millions of qubits.

TECHNIQUES TO IMPROVE QUANTUM GATES

As you've hopefully gathered from the previous sections, quantum gates are an essential part of quantum computers.

Therefore, as we scale up to millions of qubits, it's crucial that they work extremely reliably.

The reliability of quantum gates can be improved using so-called 'quantum control methods', which modify the microwave pulses to make the interaction more protected from noise in the environment.

A recent paper from the University of Sussex (the research group of Universal Quantum's co-founders) unites a number of quantum control methods under a single framework, allowing their effect against different noise sources commonly encountered in the lab to be directly compared.

This paper helps scientists better understand how we can build and compare quantum computers. It's an important feat because there are many ways to make a quantum computer - and no one truly understands which design will succeed and reach the million-qubit scale. So, we need to compare designs to understand how different ideas measure up.

The quantum gate discussed in the paper (the Mølmer-Sørensen gate) is the two-qubit gate that's used in the majority of ion trap groups (like us).

Since it's the workhorse of trapped ion two-qubit gates, it's vital to understand how we can improve this quantum gate to continue moving this technology forward.

FUNDAMENTAL PRINCIPLES OF QUANTUM MECHANICS

There is nothing special about the transmission and absorption of photons through a polarizing film. Exactly the same conclusions as those outlined above are obtained by studying other simple experiments, such as the interference of photons, and the Stern-Gerlach experiment. The study of these simple experiments leads us to formulate the following fundamental principles of quantum mechanics:

- *Dirac's Razor.* Quantum mechanics can only answer questions regarding the outcome of possible experiments. Any other questions lie beyond the realms of physics.
- *Principle of the Superposition of States.* Any microscopic system (i.e., an atom, molecule, or particle) in a given state can be regarded as being partly in each of two or more other states. In other words, any state can be regarded as a superposition of two or more other states. Such superpositions can be performed in an infinite number of different ways.
- *Principle of Indeterminacy.* An observation made on a microscopic system causes it to jump into one or more particular states (which are related to the type of observation). It is impossible to predict into which final state a particular system will jump. However, the probability of a given system jumping into a given final state can be predicted.

The first of these principles was formulated by quantum physicists (such as Dirac) in the 1920's to fend off awkward questions such as "How can a system suddenly jump from one state into another?", or "How does a system decide which state to jump into?". As we shall see, the second principle is the basis for the mathematical formulation of quantum mechanics. The final principle is still rather vague. We need to extend it so that we can predict which possible states a system can jump into after a particular type of observation, as well as the probability of the system making a particular jump.

History of Quantum Mechanics

The history of quantum mechanics is an important part of the history of modern physics. The term "Quantum Mechanics" was coined by a group of physicists including Max Born, Wolfgang Pauli and Werner Heisenberg in the early 1920s at the University of Göttingen. Both matter and radiation have characteristics of waves and particles at the fundamental level. The gradual acknowledgment by scientists that matter has wave-like properties and radiation has particle-like properties provided the momentum for the development of quantum mechanics.

Quantum Mechanics

Quantum mechanics is the branch of physics that deals with the behavior of matter and light on a subatomic and atomic level. It attempts to explain the properties of atoms and molecules and their fundamental particles like protons, neutrons, electrons, gluons, and quarks. The properties of particles include their interactions with each other and with electromagnetic radiation. So below mentioned are those two pointers one should know necessarily before tackling quantum mechanics.

Quantum Mechanics Formulas

Quantum Mechanics is Everywhere

It's extremely difficult to notice the quantum effects when large bodies come into play. All things obey the quantum mechanics laws. This was the reason why quantum physics was explored later in theoretical chemistry. Until the physicist had to find an explanation for the shells in which the electron sits around the nucleus, they had no use for quantum mechanics.

It is an Area of Active Research

Dismissing quantum mechanics as a thing of the past will be a mistake. Agreed that the theory was coined a century before but due to the lack of modern instruments, research into it was at a primitive state. Quantum mechanics has been applied and accepted into many fields such as optics, computers, thermodynamics, cryptography, and also meteorology. Research in these fields is still active.

Information is Never Conveyed Non-Locally

Things appear and disappear at random, but they don't just travel over stretches of space without going through all the things in between. In the hay-days of quantum mechanics, this confusion was a great one but now it has been proved that this theory fits in perfect compatibility with the theory of special relativity. This tells us that entanglement, although a non-local phenomenon, does not have any action.

It was not Denied by Einstein

Quantum mechanics was not denied as a theory by Einstein, although many people have the misconception. He could not have denied the theory as it was successful on such a large scale. What Einstein said was that the theory was incomplete and it was his belief that the random processes of quantum mechanics may have an explanation to them.

Schrodinger's Cat is either Alive or Dead. Surely not both

Macroscopic bodies lose their quantum behavior very fast. This was never well understood by the scientists of that time. This happens because of the regular interactions the body would have to endure. Quantum mechanics has been exceptionally successful in explaining microscopic phenomena in all branches of physics.

Quantum Mechanics Definition Explained

Defining quantum mechanics can be a tad challenging due to its abstract, counter-intuitive nature. It is the fundamental theory in physics that describes the properties of particles, atoms, and photonic systems including their interactions with each other at scales of atomic and subatomic dimensions. The realm of quantum mechanics is characterized by principles of superposition, wave-particle duality, uncertainty, and entanglement.

- **Superposition:** This principle implies that a physical system—such as an electron in an atom—can exist in multiple states or configurations simultaneously, thus allowing the system to be in multiple places at the same time.
- **Wave-Particle Duality:** This is the concept that every particle exhibits both wave and particle properties. An electron, for instance, can behave like a wave (spread out over space) or a particle (localized at a specific point).
- **Uncertainty Principle:** This is Heisenberg's famous principle that states it is impossible to simultaneously measure the exact position and momentum of a particle. In simpler terms, the more precisely one knows a particle's location, the less precise the knowledge of its momentum, and vice versa.
- **Entanglement:** This is a quantum phenomenon where two or more particles become interconnected and the state of one can instantly affect the state of the other, no matter how far apart they are.

The Origins and Development of Quantum Mechanics

The birth of quantum mechanics harks back to the early 20th century, a period marked by a myriad of scientific revolutions. Failure of classical physics to explain certain phenomena—such as black-body radiation, the photoelectric effect, and the stability of electron orbits in atoms—led to its challenge and eventual overhaul with the emergence of quantum theories.

Then came the significant contributors, Niels Bohr and Werner Heisenberg. Bohr introduced the concept of quantized energy levels for electrons in an atom in 1913. Heisenberg, in 1925, formulated the first version of quantum mechanics known as matrix mechanics. The introduction of wave mechanics by Erwin Schrödinger and the subsequent formulation of the uncertainty principle by Heisenberg carved the path for the development of modern quantum mechanics.

The following timeline shows the critical events that shaped quantum mechanics:

1900	Planck's quantum hypothesis
1905	Einstein's photoelectric effect
1913	Bohr's model of the atom
1925	Heisenberg's matrix mechanics
1926	Schrödinger's wave mechanics
1927	Heisenberg's uncertainty principle

In the realm of quantum mechanics, it is the superposition that allows Schrödinger's infamous cat to be both dead and alive until observed. The uncertainty principle hijacks the concept of simultaneous measurement of conjugate properties. The entanglement enables two entangled particles to 'communicate' instantaneously over any distance, seemingly defying the speed limit set by light speed—a concept Einstein famously termed as 'spooky action at a distance'.

Delving into Quantum Mechanical Models

When you delve deeper into the world of quantum mechanics, you encounter an array of models that attempt to describe and predict the behaviour of physical systems. These quantum mechanical models assert a new perspective of physical reality that both elucidates and mystifies scientists even to this day.

An Introduction to the Quantum Mechanical Model

The Quantum Mechanical Model, often represented by Schrödinger's Wave Equation, is the elementary depiction of an atom's electron configuration. Distinct from the traditional Bohr model, which predicts definite orbits for electrons, this quantum model reckons with the natural uncertainty inherent in atomic systems.

At the heart of this model lies the concept of the wave function, often denoted by the Greek letter ýÿ. This function provides indispensable information about the electron's state.

Examples of Quantum Mechanical Models in Practice

The principles elucidated by Quantum Mechanical Models go far beyond just predicting the mysterious motion of an electron. It has, in fact, tipped the domino chain of scientific discoveries in fields as diverse as chemistry, computing, and cryptography.

In **chemistry**, the quantum mechanical model of the atom enables you to predict chemical reactivity and the strength of chemical bonds. For example, the shared electron model—an immediate consequence of quantum theory—has eliminated much of the mysticism surrounding covalent bonding. Quantum mechanics unravels the ability of atoms to share electrons and form strong bonds that constitute molecules, leading to matter's varied forms on Earth and beyond.

In **Information Technology**, quantum mechanics has paved the way for quantum computing—a revolutionary leap in computation power. By exploiting quantum superposition and entanglement, quantum computers can process remarkably complicated computations rapidly, outstripping classical computers' functionality.

In the **world of cryptography**, quantum mechanics offers a new paradigm known as quantum cryptography or quantum encryption. Quantum principles ensure the security of communication channels by enabling the detection of eavesdroppers. Quantum Key Distribution (QKD) systems are an application of quantum encryption, holding grand potential for secure communication.

Limitations and Achievements of Quantum Mechanical Models

While quantum mechanics consistently offers accurate predictions and has opened up new vistas of research, it's also important to identify its fallibilities—it is far from a complete theory.

Despite these limitations, quantum mechanics has remained the cornerstone of modern physics. Its achievements are staggering, having rightfully earned multiple Nobel prizes for ground-breaking practical applications and theoretical advancements. From explaining the minutiae of atomic spectra to predicting the existence of antimatter, from enabling the development of lasers and semiconductors to laying the foundation for quantum field theories, quantum mechanics has reshaped your understanding of the natural world in unprecedented ways.

Unpicking the Principles of Quantum Mechanics

The foundations of Quantum Mechanics rest on several distinctive principles that set it apart from classical physics. These principles challenge the conventional notions of reality, leading to the bizarre and counterintuitive nature of the quantum realm.

The Guiding Principles of Quantum Mechanics

Quantum mechanics operates under a set of guiding principles that contribute to its uniqueness and complexity. First among these is the Wave-Particle Duality Principle. According to this principle, every quantum entity exhibits both wave-like and particle-like characteristics. This is based on the de Broglie hypothesis, which links the wavelength of a particle to its momentum through the equation:

$$\lambda = (h/p)$$

where λ is the wavelength, h is Planck's constant, and p is the momentum of the particle. Such an equation suggests, for instance, that moving particles like electrons have an associated wave function that defines their behaviour.

Next in line is the Principle of Uncertainty, introduced by Werner Heisenberg. This principle asserts that certain pairs of physical quantities, notably position and momentum, cannot simultaneously be known to infinite precision. The more precisely one measures the momentum of a particle, the less precisely its position can be determined, and vice versa. Mathematically, this is expressed as:

$$\Delta x \cdot \Delta p \geq \frac{\hbar}{2}$$

where Δx and Δp are the uncertainties in position and momentum respectively, and h is the reduced Planck's constant.

Additional guiding principles include the Principle of Superposition and the Principle of Entanglement. Superposition establishes that a quantum system can exist in multiple states simultaneously, its final state only being determined upon measurement. Entanglement, on the other hand, describes an instantaneous connection between quantum systems, irrespective of the distance separating them.

Breaking Down Quantum Mechanics Principles and Their Applications

Classical principles are insufficient in the quantum territory, hence Quantum Mechanics established its own set of principles. These principles, though tricky to comprehend, find numerous applications in various domains of science and technology.

Quantum Mechanics Principles: The Uncertainty Principle

The Heisenberg's Uncertainty Principle is one of the most enigmatic and influential principles of Quantum Mechanics, lying at the heart of many of the peculiarities of quantum behaviour. It places a fundamental limit on the precision with which certain pairs of physical properties of a quantum particle can be known simultaneously. The most famous pair being the position and linear momentum of a particle.

The essence of this principle is captured by the following mathematical formulation:

$$\Delta x \cdot \Delta p \geq \frac{\hbar}{2}$$

Here, Δx is the uncertainty in the position and Δy is the uncertainty in the linear momentum. The product of the uncertainties is always at least as large as half of the reduced Planck constant (h/2). This inequality signifies that the more accurately you know the position, the less accurately you can know the momentum, and *vice versa*.

The principles of Quantum Mechanics, including the Uncertainty Principle, are crucial to the functioning of numerous phenomena and devices. For instance, the operation of a scanning tunneling microscope depends on the uncertainty principle. It also explains the stability of atoms and why particles do not simply fall into the atomic nucleus despite the attractive forces thereat.

Quantum Mechanics Principles: Superposition and Entanglement

Superposition and entanglement are two indistinguishable principles of Quantum Mechanics that often appear too fantastical to be true.

The principle of superposition states that a quantum system can be in multiple states, called eigenstates, at the same time. A quantum system in a superposition state does not commit to a particular state until measured. The outcome of the measurement is one of the eigenstates that made up the superposition, and the probability of that outcome is determined by the coefficient of that eigenstate in the superposition state.

Quantum entanglement is perhaps an even more remarkable concept. It describes a situation where multiple particles are connected in such a way that the state of one particle is immediately connected to the state of the other, no matter the distance separating them.

This "spooky action at a distance", as Einstein dubbed it, rests at the heart of Quantum Mechanics and provides the substrate for applications like quantum computing and quantum cryptography.

Comprehension of these principles can be intimidating but, intriguingly, they form the cornerstone for several pioneering technologies. Quantum superposition underlies the extraordinary computational potential in quantum computing.

Quantum entanglement is the key feature that allows quantum computers to perform complex tasks much more quickly than classical computers. Furthermore, quantum entanglement forms the basis of quantum teleportation and quantum cryptography, securing highly sensitive communication.

Techniques in Quantum Mechanics

Quantum mechanics brings a multitude of methodologies and techniques to handle quantum systems efficiently and precisely. It involves the mathematical formalism of quantum states, operators, quantum superposition, and quantum entanglement along with powerful computational techniques. Further, it expands to the application of quantum logic gates and quantum algorithms within the realm of quantum computing.

An Overview of Quantum Mechanics Techniques

The mathematical foundation of Quantum Mechanics is a specialised set of techniques used to define and operate on quantum states. Quantum states are typically represented by a vector in a space known as a Hilbert space. The tools borrowed from linear algebra, such as vectors and operators, become integral in such representation.

An important aspect in the analysis of quantum states involves calculus of probability amplitudes. This involves the calculation of probabilities associated with the possible outcomes of quantum measurements.

- **Quantum operators:** Quantum operators correlate with measurable quantities, such as position, momentum, etc. They act on quantum states to yield another quantum state or its related value.
- **Quantum superposition:** This principle allows a quantum state to exist in multiple states simultaneously until measured.
- **Quantum entanglement:** This phenomenon points to an instantaneous correlation between two or more particles such that the state of one directly influences the state of the others, irrespective of the distance between them.

In addition to these, Quantum Mechanics utilises advanced mathematical techniques like complex analysis and differential equations for the formulation and solution of Schrödinger's equation - a fundamental equation that describes how the quantum state of a quantum system changes over time.

Quantum Mechanics Techniques in Action: A Closer Look

The true power of Quantum Mechanics techniques is manifested in their applications such as in quantum computing and quantum teleportation. Here is a journey into how some of these techniques play out in actual quantum systems and processes:

The wave function: The wave function of a quantum system encapsulates complete information about the state of the quantum system. It typically evolves over time according to the Schrödinger equation:

$$i\hbar \frac{d\left|\psi(t)\right\rangle}{dt} = H\left|\psi(t)\right\rangle$$

where H is the system's Hamiltonian (quantum mechanical total energy operator). The solutions to this equation provide the state of the system at any given time.

Bra-ket notation: Bra-ket notation or Dirac notation is another Quantum Mechanics technique that simplifies the representation of quantum states and the calculation of quantities like probabilities. The technique also offers intuitive descriptions of concepts such as measurement in Quantum Mechanics. The bra (\<|) represents a complex conjugate of a quantum state, and the ket (|>) represents a quantum state. The inner product (i.e., the overlap of these two) gives the probability amplitude for that state.

Quantum gates: In Quantum computing, quantum gates represent the fundamental building blocks. These operations manipulate qubits, the quantum equivalent of classical bits. Unlike classical gates (like AND, OR, NOT), quantum gates are reversible and can be represented by unitary matrices. This is key to exploiting quantum superposition and entanglement to solve complex problems much more efficiently than classical systems can.

Quantum Mechanics techniques may seem abstract and daunting, but they are pivotal to technologies that today stand at the forefront of a revolution. Quantum computing, quantum cryptography, and quantum teleportation - all these cutting-edge technologies are founded on the principles and techniques of Quantum Mechanics. So, understanding these techniques is not just a journey into the heart of nature's most fundamental level, but also a sneak peek into a quantum future.

Theories in Quantum Mechanics

Quantum Mechanics, one of the pillars of modern physics, is grounded in theories that have radically altered our comprehension of the universe. It ventures beyond the realm of everyday experience to investigate phenomena occurring at the atomic and subatomic scale. Understanding the theories of Quantum Mechanics is the key to unlocking the quantum world.

Key Theories in Quantum Mechanics

The cornerstone of Quantum Mechanics lies in a set of theories that express the peculiar behaviour of particles at the quantum level. Below is an exploration of some key theories that have shaped this groundbreaking field of study.

- **The Principle of Wave-Particle Duality**: This concept, introduced by Louis de Broglie, suggests that all particles exhibit both wave-like and particle-like properties. The behaviour they exhibit depends primarily on the nature of the observation.
- **The Uncertainty Principle**: Proposed by Werner Heisenberg, this principle asserts that the simultaneous measurement of a particle's position and momentum (or alternatively, energy and time) cannot both be precisely determined. It is a stark departure from classical physics where such measurements could theoretically be infinitely precise.
- **Superposition and Quantum Entanglement**: These theory concepts, though counterintuitive, have been experimentally proven and form

the basis of many applications of Quantum Mechanics. The concept of superposition allows quantum particles to exist in multiple states at the same time, while quantum entanglement implies an instantaneous link between particles.

These principles and more are encapsulated in the quantum mechanical equation, generously credited to Erwin Schrodinger:

$$-\frac{\hbar^2}{2m}\nabla^2\psi + V\psi = i\hbar\frac{\partial\psi}{\partial t}$$

This equation forecasts the behaviour of a quantum system and underpins the theory of Quantum Mechanics.

Debates and Controversies Around Theories in Quantum Mechanics

The extraordinary nature of the quantum world has prompted many debates and controversies, with several unresolved questions regarding its interpretation. Some noted debates and controversies are worth mentioning.

Another mystery that provokes debate is the phenomenon of **quantum entanglement**. Albert Einstein famously referred to it as "spooky action at a distance" because it seemed to defy the limitation of the speed of light for information flow. It has since been experimentally verified, yet the mechanism underlying it remains a puzzle.

Moreover, there is the question of the true nature of the wave function: whether it is a real entity or a purely mathematical construct. It also relates to the broader question of the ontology of quantum states.

Quantum Mechanics Theories in Modern Physics

Despite their perplexing nature, the theories of Quantum Mechanics have found a multitude of applications in modern physics and beyond. They have become indispensable tools for understanding and manipulating the quantum world.

Quantum field theory, an extension of Quantum Mechanics that incorporates special relativity, has proven incredibly successful in describing fundamental particles and forces. Particularly, quantum electrodynamics (QED), the theory of electrons and photons, and quantum chromodynamics (QCD), the theory of quarks and gluons, have provided a comprehensive framework for describing the microphysical world.

Moreover, Quantum Mechanics has deeply influenced modern cosmology. Quantum fluctuations in the early universe, for instance, are thought to give rise to the large scale structure of the universe we observe today.

Quantum Mechanics theories also paved the way for developing **quantum technologies** like quantum computing, quantum cryptography and quantum teleportation. Particularly, quantum computing, which manipulates quantum superposition and entanglement, has the potential to revolutionise fields like cryptanalysis and artificial intelligence. The impact of Quantum Mechanics theories on modern physics and technology has been profound and is still unfolding, leading us to the portals of an exciting quantum future.

WAVE-PARTICLE DUALITY

Introduction to Wave Particle Duality

Wave-particle duality is the concept in quantum mechanics that quantum entities exhibit particle or wave properties according to the experimental circumstances. It expresses the inability of the classical concepts such as particle or wave to fully describe the behavior of quantum objects. During the 19th and early 20th centuries, light was found to behave as a wave, and then later discovered to have a particulate character, whereas electrons were found to act as particles, and then later discovered to have wavelike aspects. The concept of duality arose to name these contradictions.

De Broglie Wavelength formula is given by $\lambda = h/p$

Where, h is the Planck constant

For a particle of momentum mv, the wavelength is given by $\lambda = h/mv$

This equation is also applicable for photons too.

One can understand wave particle duality via the behaviour of light. Diffraction and interference of light explain that it behaves as a wave. The photoelectric influence explains that it consists of particles. The phenomenon is Wave particle duality. It is also quite relevant for objects as well. The electron to football everything is assumed that it exhibits Wave-particle duality.

The nature of the particle dominates in the case of large objects while wave and particle nature are shown by smaller objects. The electron shows the same interference pattern similar to light when they are passed through the double slit.

Theories of Wave Particle Duality

In chemistry and physics, matter and light have particle-like attributes. The phenomena get focus by physicists. The waves behave the same as particles and particles behave similarly to waves. This Wave-particle duality has many theories. Moreover, we still follow certain theories.

- **The De Broglie wavelength:** This theory was suggested by Louis de Broglie in 1923. The wave-particle is the same for the matter. It is true when the electron and neutron beams were directed on crystal and diffraction patterns were depicted. He said that particle matter has momentum (p) and linked wavelength (^). ^= h/p. The same equation is for photons too. He also said that wave attributes can be observed in small objects.

- **Newton's Corpuscular theory**: Newton said that light composes of corpuscles. These corpuscles travel in straight lines. The law of reflection justifies the wave feature of light if it bounces off from a planar surface after reflection. However, in the case of refraction, the light moves slowly in dense material that tells about the particle-like nature of light.
- **Huygens Wave theory:** It was proposed by Huygens in 1678. The theory states that every point of the light waveform is a source of a spherical wave. It greatly supports the theory by physicists like Kirchhoff and Fresnel.
- **Quantum view of the light**: The light depicting particle properties on a quantum atoms scale is proven by the photoelectric effect. Moreover, the theory said that there will be particle treatment of light refraction by obtaining adequate localization of energy for the ejection of electrons from the surface.
- **Duality of Photons:** A single photon can showcase a distinctive interference fringe. This property is visible when light is in a very weak state due to an extremely high brightness index. Thus, when light projects on a large screen in this state, it creates a scattering towards the border. We refer to this phenomenon as the Duality of Photons.

Wrap up on Wave Particle Duality

The wave-particle duality has been under research for quite many years. Many physicists have derived theories that summarize the existence of wave-particle matter duality. Further, it has been depicted that the larger the wave amplitude the larger is the probability of finding the particle.

Early in this century, De Broglie began to realize the extent to which both models describe the same phenomena. Waves can be described as particles; particles, as waves. Diffraction and interference phenomena reveal a wave-like character in light. Still, the photoelectric effect, absorption and emission by atoms show light to have a particle-like character as well. Electrons have mass but can be diffracted like caves. Nature reveals a particle duality and ambiguity uncharacteristic of science. While the meaning of this wave-particle duality remains a subject of intense debate, many physicists now accept the Bohr complement-yarn principle. The two models exclude one another, yet both are necessary for a complete description of nature.

According to Planck's Hypothesis of the Quantum Theory, the energy is emitted in quanta, which are little packets of energy. He states that energy emitted is related to the frequency of the emitted light, and this can be considered a Wave-Particle Duality definition. According to Planck's hypothesis, the quantum energy is related to the frequency by the equation $\mathbf{E = h\nu}$.

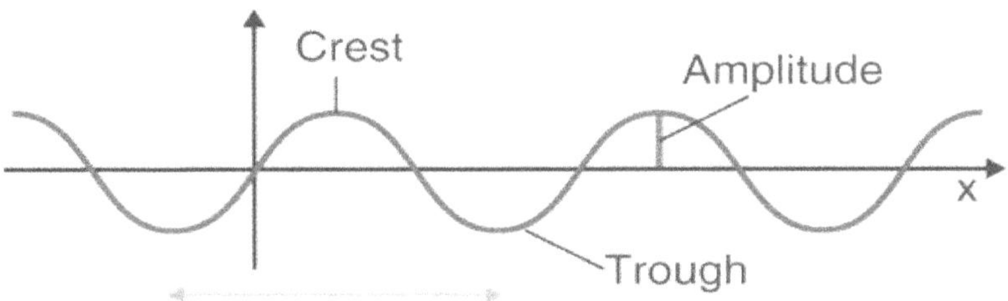

Observing a light is one of the easiest ways to prove the duality between a particle and a wave. Since light is similar to waves, it can diffract, refract, interface, etc.

Albert Einstein's theory of photoelectric effect significantly contributed to De Broglie's Theory and acted as proof that particles and waves could overlap. Light can also be observed in the form of a particle called a photon. When light is seen on certain objects, electrons are released. A certain amount of energy is needed to eliminate an electron from the surface of an object. So, an electron will be emitted when a photon of greater energy than an electron hits a solid.

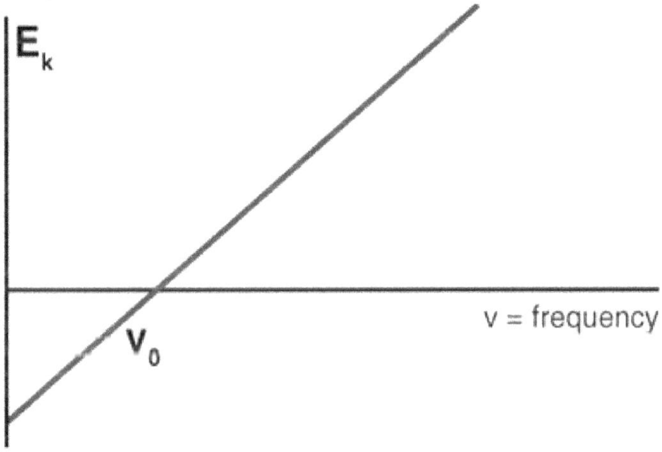

When the electrons are emitted, they also release kinetic energy. According to classical wave theory, the greater the intensity, the greater the energy. Because the energy of a wave is directly proportional to its amplitude, it was complex for scientists to find high-intensity lights that did not affect its overall kinetic energy.

Researchers discovered that light frequency effectively changed the amount of kinetic energy. Since some objects do not emit electrons at particular frequencies, a threshold value V_0 is applied. This threshold is used to describe the amount of kinetic energy required for a photon to eject an electron. The scientists arrived at a linear relationship between frequency and kinetic energy, which can be shown by the rough sketch below.

The slope of this line is known as Planck's Constant, $h = 6.63 \times 10^{-34}$

Since the energy of waves and the energy of light do not coincide, we can say that light is a particle that has the property of waves.

The energy of radiation detected by a radio-signal receiving antenna comes as the energy of an electromagnetic wave. The same energy of radiation detected by a photocurrent in the photoelectric effect comes as the energy of individual photon particles. Therefore, the question arises about the nature of electromagnetic radiation: Is a photon a wave or is it a particle? Similar questions may be asked about other known forms of energy. For example, an electron that forms part of an electric current in a circuit behaves like a particle moving in unison with other electrons inside the conductor.

The same electron behaves as a wave when it passes through a solid crystalline structure and forms a diffraction image. Is an electron a wave or is it a particle? The same question can be extended to all particles of matter—elementary particles, as well as compound molecules—asking about their true physical nature. At our present state of knowledge, such questions about the true nature of things do not have conclusive answers.

All we can say is that **wave-particle duality** exists in nature: Under some experimental conditions, a particle appears to act as a particle, and under different experimental conditions, a particle appears to act a wave. Conversely, under some physical circumstances electromagnetic radiation acts as a wave, and under other physical circumstances, radiation acts as a beam of photons.

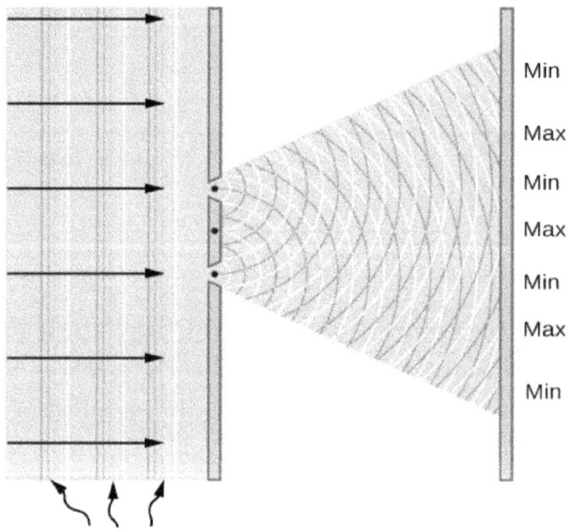

Young's double-slit experiment explains the interference of light by making an analogy with the interference of water waves. Two waves are generated at the positions of two slits in an opaque screen. The waves have the same wavelengths. They travel from their origins at the slits to the viewing screen placed to the right of the slits. The waves meet on the viewing screen. At the positions marked "Max" on the screen, the meeting waves are in-phase and the combined wave amplitude is enhanced. At positions marked "Min," the combined wave amplitude is zero. For light, this mechanism creates a bright-and-dark fringe pattern on the viewing screen.

This dualistic interpretation is not a new physics concept brought about by specific discoveries in the twentieth century. It was already present in a debate between Isaac Newton and Christiaan Huygens about the nature of light, beginning in the year 1670. According to Newton, a beam of light is a collection of corpuscles of light. According to Huygens, light is a wave.

The corpuscular hypothesis failed in 1803, when Thomas Young announced his **double-slit interference experiment** with light (Fig), which firmly established light as a wave. In James Clerk Maxwell's theory of electromagnetism (completed by the year 1873), light is an electromagnetic wave. Maxwell's classical view of radiation as an electromagnetic wave is still valid today; however, it is unable to explain blackbody radiation and the photoelectric effect, where light acts as a beam of photons.

A similar dichotomy existed in the interpretation of electricity. From Benjamin Franklin's observations of electricity in 1751 until J.J. Thomson's discovery of the electron in 1897, electric current was seen as a flow in a continuous electric medium. Within this theory of electric fluid, the present theory of electric circuits was developed, and electromagnetism and electromagnetic induction were discovered.

Thomson's experiment showed that the unit of negative electric charge (an electron) can travel in a vacuum without any medium to carry the charge around, as in electric circuits. This discovery changed the way in which electricity is understood today and gave the electron its particle status. In Bohr's early quantum theory of the hydrogen atom, both the electron and the proton are particles of matter.

Likewise, in the Compton scattering of X-rays on electrons, the electron is a particle. On the other hand, in electron-scattering experiments on crystalline structures, the electron behaves as a wave.

A skeptic may raise a question that perhaps an electron might always be nothing more than a particle, and that the diffraction images obtained in electron-scattering experiments might be explained within some macroscopic model of a crystal and a macroscopic model of electrons coming at it like a rain of ping-pong balls. As a matter of fact, to investigate this question, we do not need a complex model of a crystal but just a couple of simple slits in a screen that is opaque to electrons. In other words, to gather convincing evidence about the nature of an electron, we need to repeat the Young double-slit experiment with electrons. If the electron is a wave, we should observe the formation of interference patterns typical for waves, even when electrons come through the slits one by one. However, if the electron is a not a wave but a particle, the interference fringes will not be formed.

The very first double-slit experiment with a beam of electrons, performed by Claus Jönsson in Germany in 1961, demonstrated that a beam of electrons indeed forms an interference pattern, which means that electrons collectively behave as a wave. The first double-slit experiments with *single* electrons passing through the slits one-by-one were performed by Giulio Pozzi in 1974 in Italy and by Akira Tonomura in 1989 in Japan. They show that interference fringes are formed gradually, even when electrons pass through the slits individually. This demonstrates conclusively that electron-diffraction images are formed because of the wave nature of electrons. The results seen in double-slit experiments with electrons are illustrated by the images of the interference pattern in the Fig below.

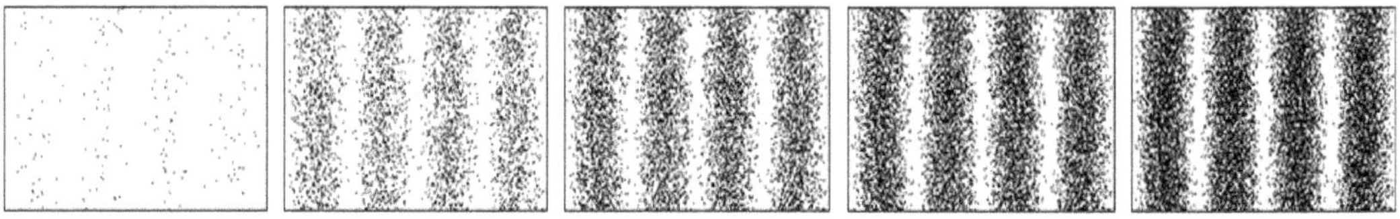

Computer-simulated interference fringes seen in the Young double-slit experiment with electrons. One pattern is gradually formed on the screen, regardless of whether the electrons come through the slits as a beam or individually one-by-one.

The wave-particle dual nature of matter particles and of radiation is a declaration of our inability to describe physical reality within one unified classical theory because separately neither a classical particle approach nor a classical wave approach can fully explain the observed phenomena. This limitation of the classical approach was realized by the year 1928, and a foundation for a new statistical theory, called quantum mechanics, was put in place by Bohr, Edwin Schrödinger, Werner Heisenberg, and Paul Dirac. Quantum mechanics takes de Broglie's idea of matter waves to be the fundamental property of all particles and gives it a statistical interpretation. According to this interpretation, a wave that is associated with a particle carries information about the probable positions of the particle and about its other properties. A single particle is seen as a moving *wave packet* such as the one shown in the figure above.

We can intuitively sense from this example that if a particle is a wave packet, we will not be able to measure its exact position in the same sense as we cannot pinpoint a location of a wave packet in a vibrating guitar string. The uncertainty, Δx, in measuring the particle's position is connected to the uncertainty, Δp, in the simultaneous measuring of its linear momentum by Heisenberg's uncertainty principle:

$$\Delta x \Delta p > \tfrac{1}{2}\hbar \qquad 2.1$$

Heisenberg's principle expresses the law of nature that, at the quantum level, our perception is limited. For example, if we know the exact position of a body (which means that $\Delta x =$ in Eq. 2.1) at the same time we cannot know its momentum, because then the uncertainty in its momentum becomes infinite (because $\Delta p > 0.5$

$\hbar/\Delta x$ in Eq. 2.1). The **Heisenberg uncertainty principle** sets the limit on the precision of *simultaneous* measurements of position and momentum of a particle; it shows that the best precision we can obtain is when we have an equals sign (=) in Equation 2.1, and we cannot do better than that, even with the best instruments of the future. Heisenberg's principle is a consequence of the wave nature of particles.

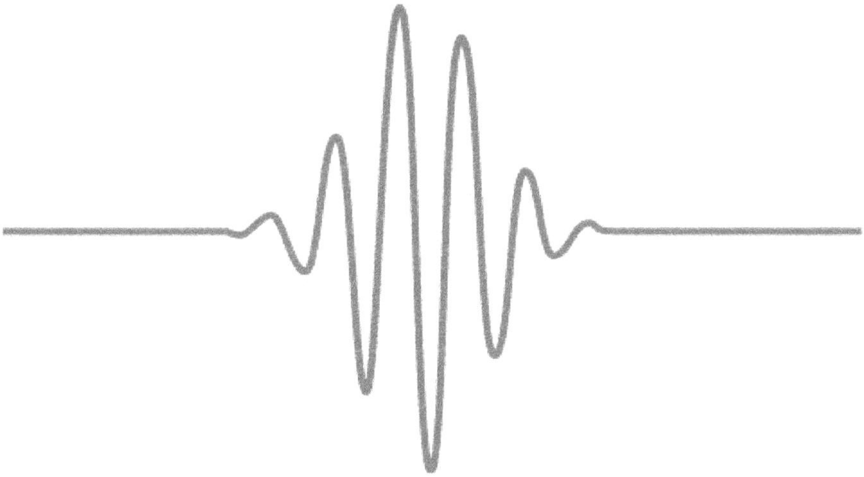

In this graphic, a particle is shown as a wave packet and its position does not have an exact value.

We routinely use many electronic devices that exploit wave-particle duality without even realizing the sophistication of the physics underlying their operation. One example of a technology based on the particle properties of photons and electrons is a charge-coupled device, which is used for light detection in any instrumentation where high-quality digital data are required, such as in digital cameras or in medical sensors. An example in which the wave properties of electrons is exploited is an electron microscope.

In 1931, physicist Ernst Ruska—building on the idea that magnetic fields can direct an electron beam just as lenses can direct a beam of light in an optical microscope—developed the first prototype of the electron microscope. This development originated the field of electron microscopy. In the transmission electron microscope (TEM), shown in Figure below, electrons are produced by a hot tungsten element and accelerated by a potential difference in an electron gun, which gives them up to 400 keV in kinetic energy.]

After leaving the electron gun, the electron beam is focused by electromagnetic lenses (a system of condensing lenses) and transmitted through a specimen sample to be viewed. The image of the sample is reconstructed from the transmitted electron beam. The magnified image may be viewed either directly on a fluorescent screen or indirectly by sending it, for example, to a digital camera or a computer monitor. The entire setup consisting of the electron gun, the lenses, the specimen, and the fluorescent screen are enclosed in a vacuum chamber to prevent the energy loss from the beam.

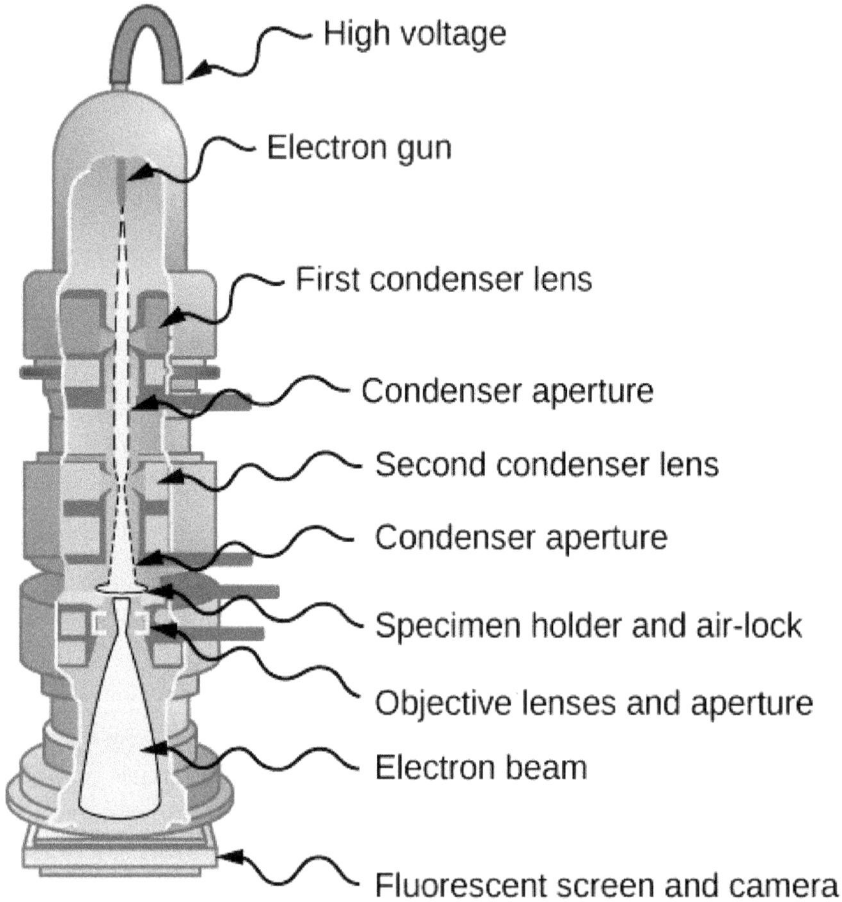

TEM: An electron beam produced by an electron gun is collimated by condenser lenses and passes through a specimen. The transmitted electrons are projected on a screen and the image is sent to a camera.

Resolution of the TEM is limited only by spherical aberration (discussed in a previous chapter). Modern high-resolution models of a TEM can have resolving power greater than 0.5 Å and magnifications higher than 50 million times. For comparison, the best resolving power obtained with light microscopy is currently about 97 nm. A limitation of the TEM is that the samples must be about 100-nm thick and biological samples require a special preparation involving chemical "fixing" to stabilize them for ultrathin slicing.

Such limitations do not appear in the scanning electron microscope (SEM), which was invented by Manfred von Ardenne in 1937. In an SEM, a typical energy of the electron beam is up to 40 keV and the beam is not transmitted through a sample but is scattered off its surface. Surface topography of the sample is reconstructed by analyzing back-scattered electrons, transmitted electrons, and the emitted radiation produced by electrons interacting with atoms in the sample. The resolving power of an SEM is better than 1 nm, and the magnification can be more than 250 times better than that obtained with a light microscope. The samples scanned by an SEM can be as large as several centimeters but they must be specially prepared, depending on electrical properties of the sample.

To expand both the resolution and the types of materials that could be examined, Pratibha L. Gai and Edward D. Boyes invented the environmental transmission electron microscope (ETEM). The device advanced the standard electron microscope by incorporating a gas-filled chamber in which a wider array of substances could be contained. Thus Gai and other researchers could observe reactions taking place at incredible magnifications. Gai later improved on her work by creating the environmental scanning transmission electron microscope (ESTEM), which has even greater resolving power.

High magnifications of the TEM and SEM allow us to see individual molecules. High resolving powers of the TEM and SEM allow us to see fine details, such as those shown in the SEM micrograph of pollen at the beginning of this chapter. Users of ETEM and ESTEM can see even smaller objects: Gai herself was the first person to ever see individual atoms. The devices are used for biological, materials, nanotechnology, fuel cell, catalysis, and a range of other applications.

THE UNCERTAINTY PRINCIPLE

Heisenberg's uncertainty principle states that it is impossible to measure or calculate exactly both the position and the momentum of an object. This principle is based on the wave-particle duality of matter. Although Heisenberg's uncertainty principle can be ignored in the macroscopic world (the uncertainties in the position and velocity of objects with relatively large masses are negligible), it holds significant value in the quantum world. Since atoms and subatomic particles have very small masses, any increase in the accuracy of their positions will be accompanied by an increase in the uncertainty associated with their velocities.

In the field of quantum mechanics, Heisenberg's uncertainty principle is a fundamental theory that explains why it is impossible to measure more than one quantum variable simultaneously. Another implication of the uncertainty principle is that it is impossible to accurately measure the energy of a system in some finite amount of time.

Heisenberg's uncertainty principle imposes a restriction on the accuracy of simultaneous measurement of position and momentum. The more precise our measurement of position is, the less accurate will be our momentum measurement and vice-versa. The physical origin of Heisenberg's uncertainty principle is with the quantum system. Determination of position by performing a measurement on the system disturbs it sufficiently to make the determination of q imprecise and vice-versa. We will learn about the principle in detail below.

Heisenberg's uncertainty principle states that for particles exhibiting both particle and wave nature, it will not be possible to accurately determine both the position and velocity at the same time. The principle is named after German physicist Werner Heisenberg, who proposed the uncertainty principle in the year 1927. This principle was formulated when Heisenberg was trying to build an intuitive model of quantum physics. He discovered that there were certain fundamental factors that limited our actions in knowing certain quantities.

This principle basically highlights that simultaneous measurement of position and the velocity or momentum of microscopic matter waves will have an error such that the product of the error in measurement of position and momentum is equal or more than an integral multiple of a constant.

Origin of the Uncertainty Principle

One of the crucial points for the genesis of the uncertainty principle is solely due to the dual nature of a wave-particle. Every particle is said to have a wave nature, and the probability of finding particles is maximum, where the waveforms are the greatest. If the particle has greater undulation, the wavelength becomes more indistinct or vague. However, we are able to determine the momentum of the particle. From what we have learnt so far, we can say that the particles that have definite positions will have no fixed velocity. On the other hand, a particle with a well-defined wavelength will show a definitive or precise velocity. All in all, if we get an accurate reading of one quantity, it will only lead to large uncertainty in the measurement of the other.

Heisenberg Uncertainty Principle Formula and Application

If Δx is the error in position measurement and Δp is the error in the measurement of momentum, then

$$\Delta x \times \Delta p > h/4\pi$$

Since momentum, $p = mv$, Heisenberg's uncertainty principle formula can be alternatively written as,

$$\Delta X \times \Delta mv > h/4\pi$$

or

$$\Delta X \times \Delta m \times \Delta v > h/4\pi$$

Where, ΔV is the error in the measurement of velocity, and assuming mass remains constant during the experiment,

$$\Delta X \times \Delta V > h/xm\pi.$$

Accurate measurement of position or momentum automatically indicates larger uncertainty (error) in the measurement of the other quantity.

Applying the Heisenberg principle to an electron in an orbit of an atom, with h = 6.626×10^{-34}Js and m= 9.11×10^{-31}Kg,

$$\Delta X \times \Delta V > (6.626 \times 10^{-34}/4 \times 3.14 \times 9.11 \times 10^{-31}) = 10^{-4}\ m^2\ s^{-1}$$

If the position of the electron is measured accurately to its size (10^{-10}m), then the error in the measurement of its velocity will be equal to or larger than 10^6m or 1000 km.

Heisenberg's principle applies to only dual-natured microscopic particles and not to macroscopic particles whose wave nature is minimal.

Explaining Heisenberg Uncertainty Principle with an Example

Electromagnetic radiations and microscopic matter waves exhibit a dual nature of mass/momentum and wave character. The position and velocity/momentum of macroscopic matter waves can be determined accurately and simultaneously. For example, the location and speed of a moving car can be determined simultaneously with minimum error. But, in microscopic particles, it will not be possible to fix the position and measure the velocity/momentum of the particle simultaneously.

An electron in an atom has a mass of 9.91×10^{-31} kg. Naked eyes cannot see such small particles. A powerful light may collide with the electron and illuminate it. Illumination helps in identifying and measuring the position of the electron. The collision of the powerful light source, while helping in identification, increases the momentum of the electron and makes it move away from the initial position. Thus, when fixing the position, the velocity/momentum of the particle would have changed from the original value. Hence, when the position is exact, the error occurs in measuring velocity or momentum. In the same way, the measurement of momentum, accurately, will change the position.

Hence, at any point in time, either position or momentum can only be measured accurately.

Simultaneous measurement of both of them will have an error in both position and momentum. Heisenberg quantified the error in the measurement of both position and momentum simultaneously.

Heisenberg's γ-ray Microscope

A striking thought experiment illustrating the uncertainty principle is Bohr's/ Heisenberg's Gamma-ray microscope. To observe a particle, say an electron, we shine it with the light ray of wavelength λ and collect the Compton scattered light in a microscope objective whose diameter subtends an angle è with the electron, as shown in the figure below

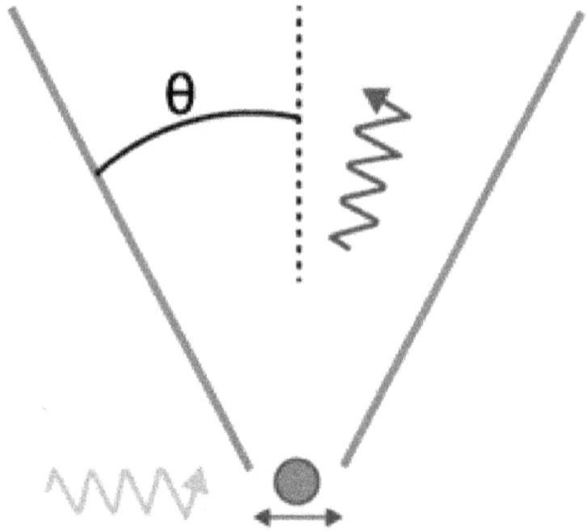

The precision with which the electron can be located, Delta x, is defined by the resolving power of the microscope,

$$\sin\theta = \frac{\lambda}{\Delta x} \Rightarrow \Delta x = \frac{\lambda}{\sin\theta}$$

It appears that by making λ small, we choose γ-ray, and by making sin è large, Delta x can be made as small as desired. But, according to the uncertainty principle, we can do so only at the expense of our knowledge of the x-component of electron momentum.

In order to record the Compton scattered photon by the microscope, the photon must stay in the cone of angle è, and hence its x-component of the momentum can vary within ±(h/λ) sin θ. This implies that the magnitude of the recoil momentum of the electron is uncertain by

$$\Delta p_z = \frac{2h}{\lambda}\sin\theta$$

The product of the uncertainty yields,

$$\Delta x \Delta p_z = \frac{\lambda}{\sin\theta}\frac{2h}{\lambda}\sin\theta = 4\pi h$$

Is Heisenberg's Uncertainty Principle Noticeable in All Matter Waves?

Heisenberg's principle is applicable to all matter waves. The measurement error of any two conjugate properties, whose dimensions happen to be joule sec, like position-momentum, the time-energy will be guided by Heisenberg's value.

But, it will be noticeable and of significance only for small particles like an electron with very low mass. A bigger particle with a heavy mass will show the error to be very small and negligible.

Heisenberg Uncertainty Principle Equations

Heisenberg's uncertainty principle can be considered as a very precise mathematical statement that describes the nature of quantum systems. As such, we often consider two common equations related to the uncertainty principle, and they are as follows:

Equation 1: $\Delta X . \Delta p \sim \hbar$

Equation 2: $\Delta E . \Delta t \sim \hbar$

Where,

$\hbar$ = value of Planck's constant divided by 2*pi

ΔX = uncertainty in the position

Δp = uncertainty in momentum

ΔE = uncertainty in the energy

Δt = uncertainty in time measurement

QUANTUM STATES AND OBSERVABLES

Quantum states

Introduction Quantum mechanics describes the behaviour of matter and light at the atomic scale (i.e. at distances $d \sim 10^{-10}$m), where physical objects behave very differently from what we experience in everyday's life. Because the atomic behaviour is so unusual, we need to develop new, abstract tools that allow us to compute the expected values of physical observables starting from the postulates of the theory. The theory can then be tested by comparing theoretical predictions to experimental results. In this course we will focus on presenting the basic postulates, and in developing the computational tools needed to study elementary systems. As we venture on this journey, we can only develop some intuition by practice; solving problems is an essential component for understanding quantum mechanics. Experimental results at the beginning of the 20th century first highlighted behaviours at atomic scales that were inconsistent with classical mechanics. It took a lot of effort until the combined efforts of many physicists – Planck, Bohr, Schrodinger, Heisenberg, Born (who has been a professor in Edinburgh) amongst others– led to a consistent picture of the new dynamics

Despite its unintuitive aspects, quantum mechanics describes very concrete features of the world as we know it, like e.g. the stability of the hydrogen atom. Many of its predictions have now been tested to great accuracy.

In fact, there are numerous experimental results that provide evidence in favour of quantum mechanics, e.g.

- double-slit experiments,
- photoelectric effect,
- stability of the H atom,
- black-body radiation.

Some of these experiments have been discussed already in previous courses, and we do not want to review them here. You can find exhaustive discussions in most textbooks of Quantum Mechanics.

We shall introduce the basic ideas of quantum mechanics by discussing briefly the doubleslit experiment, which was first performed by Young in 1801, in order to resolve the question of the corpuscular nature of light. As we shall see some of the key concepts emerged from the comparison of the quantum behaviour of electrons with the more familiar behaviour of classical particles and waves.

Experiment with classical particles

Let us consider first a source of classical particles, emitting projectiles (bullets) in random directions. In front of the source we have a wall with two holes that are denoted 1 and 2. A detector is placed behind the wall, counting the bullets that pass through the holes. The apparatus is schematically represented in figure below. We do not want to get into the details of the experiment here, neither into a precise computation of the probability distributions. We should focus instead on the logical steps.

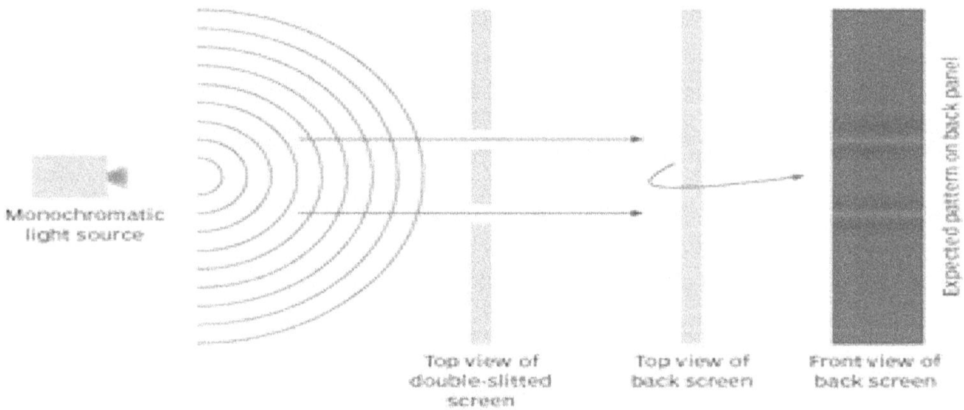

Expected results of double silt experiment

When both holes are open the distribution of bullets on the detector is given by a function that resembles the curve P_{12} in (A). When 2 is closed, and therefore the bullets can only pass through 1, we obtain the distribution labelled P_1 in (B). Similarly, when the bullets can only go through 2, the distribution is given by P_2. The important feature, which is typical of classical mechanics, is that $P_{12} = P_1 + P_2$. We call this result an observation of no interference, particles that go through 1 do not interfere with those that pass through 2, and the probabilities add in an intuitive way. Each electron that arrives into the detector must have gone through either hole 1 or 2. Therefore the chance of arrival at some position x on the detector must be the sum of the probability of getting to x via 1 plus the probability of getting to x via 2.

EDouble slit experiment with light

Figure below shows the double slit experiment with light, whereby the light source is monochromatic. Both slits create circular light waves which overlap, as seen in the example with water. On the right side of figure below there is a yellow curve which represents the intensity of the light when it hits a screen. Three typical characteristics of wave interference occur:

The highest light intensity on the screen is behind the middle section of the double slit which hides the view of the source.

There are areas on the screen which have a direct view of the source but no light hits this area.

There are more intensity maxima than there are slits.

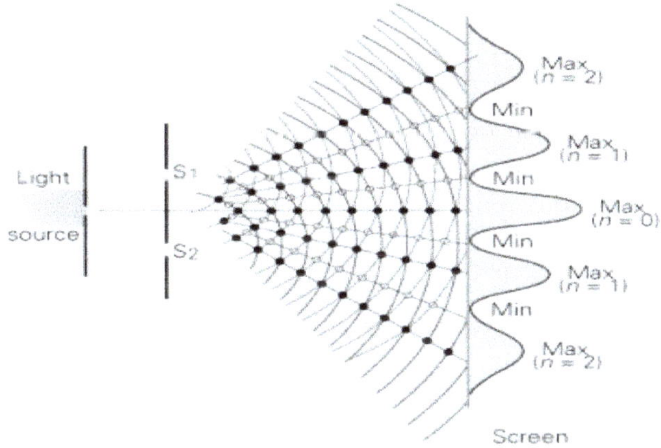

Double slit experiment with monochromatic light

Clearly in the case of diffracted waves $I_{12} \neq I_1 + I_2$. The two waves interfere. The maxima of I_{12} correspond to constructive interference, and viceversa for the minima. The height of the waves at time t can be represented as (the real part of) a complex amplitude $h1e^{i\omega t}$, where h_1 is a complex number, and the intensity is given by $I_1 = |h_1|^2$. In the case of wave interference, the complex amplitudes add up, so that $I_{12} = |h_1 + h_2|^2$.

Experiment with electrons

A conclusive double-slit experiment with electron beams was performed by Tonomura et al. at Hitachi (Japan). This experiment confirmed the observation of an interference pattern similar to the one observed for waves. This experiment shows that the dynamics of the electrons, that can be considered as single indivisible particles, is influenced by the presence of both slits; a single particle at the atomic scale "behaves like a wave". This property is know as wave-particle duality. We can find the correct probability distribution by identifying P_{12} with the absolute square of a complex quantity ψ_{12}, the so-called probability amplitude. The probability amplitudes satisfy the following relations:

$$P_{12}(x) = |\psi_{12}(x)|^2, \quad (2.1)$$

$$P_1(x) = |\psi_1(x)|^2,\ P_2(x) = |\psi_2(x)|^2, \quad (2.2)$$

$$\psi_{12}(x) = \psi_1(x) + \psi_2(x). \quad (2.3)$$

Wave-particle duality was first formulated by De Broglie in 1925, who stated that a particle with momentum p behaves like a wave with wavelength $\lambda = h/p$, where h is Planck's constant:

$$h = 6.62606896(33) \times 10^{-34}\,\mathrm{J \cdot s} \quad (2.4)$$

Planck's constant is a fundamental constant of Nature; it has units [h] = Energy × Time; as we shall see in more details later it defines the scale where quantum phenomena become relevant. We will often encounter the constant $\hbar = h/(2\pi)$.

In order to avoid contradictions that may arise from this dual use of wave and particle languages, we must be very careful to define properly the statements that are permitted about a given experimental situation. In other words, we need to specify carefully the laws of the new quantum theory. As we will see, there are some crucial differences between the quantum and the classical world.

One-dimensional systems

We shall now proceed to summarize the laws of quantum mechanics for one-dimensional systems. Before entering into the details, it is worthwhile to quote Feynman's lectures:

"In this subject we have, of course, the difficulty that the quantum mechanical behavior of things is quite strange. Nobody has an everyday experience to lean on to get a rough, intuitive idea of what will happen. So there are two ways of presenting the subject: We could either describe what can happen in a rather rough physical way, telling you more or less what happens without giving the precise laws of everything; or we could, on the other hand, give the precise laws in their abstract form. But, then because of the abstractions, you wouldn't know what they were all about, physically. The latter method is unsatisfactory because it is completely abstract, and the first way leaves an uncomfortable feeling because one doesn't know exactly what is true and what is false. [...] Here, we will try to find a happy medium between the two extremes".

Quantum states

Let us begin with the fundamental law of quantum mechanics which summarizes the idea of wave-particle duality. The quantum state of a system is described by a complex function ψ, which depends on the coordinate x and on time:

$$\text{quantum state} \sim \psi(x, t) \quad (2.5)$$

The wave function does not depend on the momentum of the particle. Compared to classical mechanics, we seem to have lost the symmetry between coordinates and momenta. We shall revisit this issue later. The wave function encodes all the information about the system, albeit in a probabilistic sense. This is a peculiarity of Quantum Mechanics: as postulated by Born, the theory can only predict the probability of the outcome of an experiment. This probability can be computed from the wave function. There are cases where a complicated computation is needed, and there are cases where this probability can be obtained very easily. For instance,

$|\psi(x, t)|^2\, dx$ is the probability that a measurement of the position of the particle yields a result in the interval $x \rightarrow x + dx$.

Thus $|\psi(x, t)|^2$ is a probability per unit length or probability density. The total probability of finding the particle somewhere along the real axis must be unity, thus:

$$||\psi||^2 = \int dx\, |\psi(x, t)|^2 = 1. \tag{2.6}$$

Any function such that its integral along the real axis is finite can be normalized by multiplying by an appropriate constant. In practice two wave functions that differ by an arbitrary factor $c \in C$ describe the same physical system.

Observables

One of the most difficult and controversial problems in quantum mechanics is the socalled measurement problem. Opinions on the significance of this problem vary widely. At one extreme the attitude is that there is in fact no problem at all, while at the other extreme the view is that the measurement problem is one of the great unsolved puzzles of quantum mechanics. The issue is that quantum mechanics only provides probabilities for the different possible outcomes in an experiment – it provides no mechanism by which the actual, finally observed result, comes about.

Of course, probabilistic outcomes feature in many areas of classical physics as well, but in that case, probability enters the picture simply because there is insufficient information to make a definite prediction. In principle, that missing information is there to be found, it is just that accessing it may be a practical impossibility. In contrast, there is no 'missing information' for a quantum system, what we see is all that we can get, even in principle, though there are theories that say that this missing information resides in so-called 'hidden variables'. But in spite of these concerns about the measurement problem, there are some features of the measurement process that are commonly accepted as being essential parts of the final story.

What is clear is that performing a measurement always involves a piece of equipment that is macroscopic in size, and behaves according to the laws of classical physics. The process of decoherence was mentioned as playing a crucial role in giving rise to the observed classical behaviour of macroscopic systems, and so it is not surprising to find that decoherence plays an important role in the formulation of most modern theories of quantum measurement. Any quantum measurement then appears to require three components: the system, typically a microscopic system, whose properties are to be measured, the measuring apparatus itself, which interacts with the system under observation, and the environment surrounding the apparatus whose presence supplies the decoherence needed so that, 'for all practical purposes (FAPP)', the apparatus behaves like a classical system, whose output can be, for instance, a pointer on the dial on the measuring apparatus coming to rest, pointing at the final result of the measurement, that is, a number on the dial.

Of course, the apparatus could produce an electrical signal registered on an oscilloscope, or bit of data stored in a computer memory, or a flash of light seen by the experimenter as an atom strikes a fluorescent screen, but it is often convenient to use the simple picture of a pointer. The experimental apparatus would be designed according to what physical property it is of the quantum system that is to be measured. Thus, if the system were a single particle, the apparatus could be designed to measure its energy, or its position, or its momentum or its spin, or some other property. These measurable properties are known as observables. But how do we know what it is that a particular experimental setup would be measuring? The design would be ultimately based on classical physics principles, i.e., if the apparatus were intended to measure the energy of a quantum system, then it would also measure the energy of a classical system if a classical system were substituted for the quantum system. In this way, the macroscopic concepts of classical physics can be transferred to quantum systems.

We will not be examining the details of the measurement process in any great depth here. Rather, we will be more concerned with some of the general characteristics of the outputs of a measurement procedure and how these general features can be incorporated into the mathematical formulation of the quantum theory.

Observables and Hermitean Operators

One crucial feature of any output of a measurement is that the result is usually, or at least can be, expressed as a real number. For instance, in the Stern-Gerlach experiment with the magnetic field oriented in the z direction, the outcomes of the measurement are that a spin-half particle will be observed to have a z component of spin with one or the other of the values $S_z = \pm\frac{1}{2}\hbar$.

It is here that we make a very important connection. We have been consistently saying that if an atom emerges in the S_z = ½! beam, then we have assigned the spin state $|+\rangle$ to the atom, and similarly we associate the outcome S z = -½ħ with the state $|-\rangle$. We therefore have a natural pairing off between measurement outcomes (two real numbers, ±½ħ) and the states $|\pm\rangle$. Moreover, these states are orthogonal in that if the atom is in state $|+\rangle$ for instance, there is zero probability of observing it in state $|-\rangle$, i.e. $\langle -|+\rangle = 0$: the two states are mutually exclusive. Finally, we note that we never see an atom emerge from the apparatus in other than the two beams associated with the two spins ±½ħ. Thus, if an atom is prepared in an arbitrary initial state $|S\rangle$, the probability amplitude of finding it in some other state $|S'\rangle$ is

$$\langle S'|S\rangle = \langle S'|+\rangle \langle +|S\rangle + \langle S'|-\rangle\langle -|S\rangle$$

which leads, by the cancellation trick to

$$|S\rangle = |+\rangle\langle +|S\rangle + |-\rangle\langle -|S\rangle$$

which tells us that any spin state of the atom can be expressed as a linear combination of the states $|\pm\rangle$. Thus the states $|\pm\rangle$ constitute a complete set of basis states for the state space of the system. It is useful to note the distinction between a quantum mechanical observable and the corresponding classical quantity. The latter quantity, say the position x of a particle, represents a single possible value for that observable – though it might not be known, it in principle has a definite, single value at any instant in time. In contrast, a quantum observable such as S z is an operator which, through its eigenvalues, carries with it all the values that the corresponding physical quantity could possibly have. In a certain sense, this is a reflection of the physical state of affairs that pertains to quantum systems, namely that when a measurement is made of a particular physical property of a quantum systems, the outcome can, in principle, be any of the possible values that can be associated with the observable, even if the experiment is repeated under identical conditions.

The Measurement Postulate

This procedure of associating a Hermitean operator with every observable property of a quantum system can be readily generalized. The generalization takes a slightly different form if the observable has a continuous range of possible values, such as position and momentum, as against an observable with only discrete possible results. We will consider the discrete case first.

Measurement of Observables with Discrete Values

Suppose we have an observable Q of a system that is found to have the values $q_1, q_2, \ldots$ through an exhaustive series of measurements. If we furthermore represent by $|q_1\rangle, |q_2\rangle, \ldots$ those states of the system for which we are guaranteed to get the results $q_1, q_2, \ldots$ respectively on measuring Q, we can then claim the following:

The states $\{|q_n\rangle; n = 1, 2, 3, \ldots\}$ form a complete set of orthonormal basis states for the state space of the system.

That the states form a complete set of basis states means that any state $|\psi\rangle$ of the system can be expressed as

$$|\psi\rangle = \sum_n c_n |q_n\rangle$$

while orthonormality means that #qn | qm! = änm from which follows cn = $\langle q_n | \psi\rangle$. The completeness condition can then be written as

$$\sum_n |q_n\rangle\langle q_n| = \hat{1}$$

CHAPTER- 3
QUANTUM HARDWARE

Quantum hardware is an emerging technology that uses quantum bits (qubits) instead of bits as the smallest units of data. Qubits can exist in multiple states at the same time, which allows quantum computers to perform many tasks simultaneously and work faster than traditional computers.

In quantum computing, the development of quantum algorithms is much more progressive. The advancement of these algorithms is very rigorous, involving extensive analysis seeking to determine the time it would take to run the algorithm and if it would be an advantage over its classical counterpart. But the problem is that all of this effort is only being put into the purely *theoretical* aspects of quantum computing and computational complexity theory. However, quantum algorithms that tackle real-world problems cannot yet be run on a scale that offers actual speedup over their classical counterparts since we don't currently have the physical hardware to run them. Therefore, the development of *efficient quantum hardware* is just as crucial as developing efficient quantum algorithms.

There are many proposals and ideas for the development of quantum computers, the most common ones being superconducting qubits, neutral atoms, and photonics. But these are not the only two ways of building a quantum computer. We'll go into some much more diverse possibilities (such as topological qubits), but before we get into that craziness, let's first take a step back and put ourselves in the shoes of the pioneers of classical computing. Researchers bet many of them thought that transistors had no future in the computing industry, but now approximately 400 billion of them are within the cellphones we use every day. Therefore, we shouldn't overlook any proposal of building a quantum computer. Since you never know what technology will be the "transistor" of this fascinating technology.

This section will attempt to briefly overview the most studied methods of building quantum computers. Which by no means a complete explanation of every technology mentioned here, but it should give you a good idea of how these work. Some things may not be as easy to get the first time, so researchers advise you to reread any parts that seem confusing and do further research on any technology that interests you. With that, let's get started!

Quantum hardware can be implemented using many different physical realizations of qubits, including:

Trapped ions, superconducting, neutral atoms, electron spin, light polarization, and topological qubits.

Quantum hardware implementation methods are categorized into five groups: Nuclear Magnetic Resonance (NMR), Ion traps, All optical, Super conducting, and Quantum dots.

Some leading qubit-type approaches include: Photonic.

Quantum computers use quantum algorithms to solve problems more efficiently than classical algorithms. Quantum algorithms exploit the principles of quantum mechanics, such as superposition, entanglement, and interference.

Quantum hardware has applications in many fields, including: Medical imaging, Life sciences, Dental imaging, Industrial equipment, Analytical equipment, Color measurement, Infrared measurement, Food sorting and inspection, and Astronomy.

Nuclear Magnetic Resonance

In this technology, an NMR spectrometer is used to measure and control the magnetic field in the nuclei of molecules. The spectrometer has a powerful magnet cooled at a shallow temperature using liquid Nitrogen and Helium. Inside the magnet, there is a crystal of Malonic acid $CH_2(COOH_3)_2$, whose Carbon nuclei act as the qubits. These nuclei behaving like a tiny magnet, align with the magnet's magnetic field placed inside the spectrometer to provide the initial computation stage. Electromagnetic pulses are used to manipulate these qubits. They align with the magnetic field to create the state $|0\rangle$ and against the magnetic field to create the state $|1\rangle$. States between $|0\rangle$ (aligned) and $|1\rangle$ (against) are superposition states. Due to having magnetic properties, nuclei affect one another, which results in entanglement. Any desired quantum algorithms can be implemented by controlling the pulses and interaction between nuclei. After implementing an algorithm, a coil wrapped around the crystal measures the magnetic fields of the nuclei to complete the computation.

Two Coupled 3 Josephson junctions Flux Qubits

Superconducting Qubits

Superconducting qubits consist of a micro scale electrical circuit with some nonlinear element, typically a Josephson junction. This element, essentially a capacitor that allows the tunneling of Cooper pairs, offers incredible possibilities. However, there are multiple ways in which several Josephson Junctions, as well as coils and capacitors can be combined to form a qubit. Some examples are: charge qubits, three Josephson junction flux qubits, fluxonion qubits...

This flexibility in the design, together with the possibility of using circuit elements to mediate interactions between them, makes superconducting circuits one of the most promising platforms for the realization of quantum computing devices. In fact, it is nowadays the supporting platform of most of the state-of-the-art implementations of quantum devices such as IBM's gate-based quantum computer, Google's gate-based quantum computer, or D-wave's quantum annealer.

In this context, our group takes part in the project AVaQus (Annealing-based Variational Quantum Processors) which aims at a radical upgrade of present quantum annealing technology by engineering novel superconducting quantum circuits. AVaQus is a European project funded in the FET-Open 2019 call and brings together research groups and companies to develop a quantum processor that demonstrates coherent quantum annealing and its potential to solve real-life optimization problems. Our work here consists of theoretically designing and analyzing novel circuit architectures for quantum computing and optimization. In particular, we study the possibility of finding strong tunable interactions between three Josephson junction flux qubits and with other circuit elements for its later implementation on the construction of a real quantum annealer.

Quantum Links

We believe that superconducting circuits are a promising platform for quantum information processing, however, they have a very specific drawback: the temperatures at which they operate. Whereas with current technologies, the needed temperatures of a few miliKelvin are easily and cheaply reached, the size of the refrigerators becomes a problem when we aim to scale up the setup.

Two quantum nodes, each consisting of a qubit and a microwave resonator, connected by a superconducting microwave link

The solution that we propose for this is to implement a local area network in which we connect several refrigerators via quantum links. This ambitious idea is tackled within the context of the european collaboration SuperQulan (Superconducting Quantum Local Area Network). Quinfog is in the theory division of this interdisciplinary project designing protocols for distributed quantum information processing. Among these are:

- Shaping of individual photons for state transfer and high fidelity data writing and retrieval by means of time dependent couplings.
- Implementation of a controlled phase gate and eventually of a universal set of gates between distant nodes of the network.
- Entanglement distribution.

For all of this we use quantum optical techniques such as Input-Output formalism and master equation modelization. Our mid term goal is to find a theory that takes full account of the phenomenology for both short and long links and develop a python library that can be used as a toolbox to solve problems related with any distributed setup.

QUANTUM PROCESSORS: QUBITS AND QUANTUM GATES

Introduction

The quantum computers in the case of practical realization can outreach from the best modern computers, in quantum world there are phenomena in a different and amazing kink and so using them in making quantum computers for the process of information is suitable. Engineers that design the quantum computers and the experts of mechanic quantum hope that use from one of the most basic quantum theories principles for design of system (machines) that are able to do parallel computation concurrently, this computations provide the possibility of easy and logical solution of some of the problem that are insoluble in classical computers and also this computations provide the extant difficulty in ground of cry photography.

The memory of a quantum computer is quantum states, quantum computers are mode from qubit.qubit can have zero bit and one bit concurrently i.e. they are equality with superposition of classical bits. So quantum states can be consider as quantum computer bits.in regard to that quantum states are mode from phenomena of quantum mechanics, so computation of quantum computers are found on the base of physics process and quantum principles.

Qubit

In quantum computing, a qubit or quantum bit is a basic unit of quantum information—the quantum version of the classic binary bit physically realized with a two-state device. A qubit is a two-state (or two-level) quantum-mechanical system, one of the simplest quantum systems displaying the peculiarity of quantum mechanics. Examples include the spin of the electron in which the two levels can be taken as spin up and spin down; or the polarization of a single photon in which the two spin states (left-handed and the right-handed circular polarization) can also be measured as horizontal and vertical linear polarization. In a classical system, a bit would have to be in one state or the other. However, quantum mechanics allows the qubit to be in a coherent superposition of multiple states simultaneously, a property that is fundamental to quantum mechanics and quantum computing.

A qubit (or quantum bit) is the quantum mechanical analogue of a classical bit. In classical computing the information is encoded in bits, where each bit can have the value zero or one. In quantum computing the information is encoded in qubits. A qubit is a two-level quantum system where the two basis qubit states are usually written as $|0\rangle$ and $|1\rangle$. A qubit can be in state $|0\rangle$, $|1\rangle$ or (unlike a classical bit) in a linear combination of both states. The name of this phenomenon is superposition.

A general-pure-qubit state is expressed as: $\psi = \alpha|0\rangle + \beta|1\rangle$

where α and β are the complex probability amplitudes for each basis state. Note that the choice of basis states is arbitrary, each set of orthogonal states can be used as basis states.

Below it is shown that a general pure qubit state is described by two real numbers, while above we stated that a generic qubit state is described by two complex parameters (probability amplitudes). This apparent contradiction is solved by the following: First of all, the sum of the probabilities of measuring any of the states should always add to 1. This condition constraints the description already to three real parameters. Another aspect from quantum mechanics is that scaling of a qubit state by a scaling vector does not change the measureable properties (observables) of a quantum state. This means that all probability amplitudes can always be scaled by an arbitrary (real) factor without changing any of the observable properties of the system. This is also known as scaling by a global phase factor. This condition constraints the system to a state which can be defined by two real parameters.

Qubit is the smallest part of a system (memory unit) in quantum computers that is analog bit in classical computers. Each quantum state that is superposition of

$$|\psi\rangle = \alpha|0\rangle + \beta|1\rangle \quad , \quad |\alpha|^2 + |\beta|^2 = 1 \qquad (1)$$

$$\{|0\rangle, |1\rangle\}$$

In regard to the condition of norm there are number of infinity amounts for ,and infinity concurrently state for qubit. The main works of quantum computers are in a way that processes concurrently the qubits that are include infinity state.

In the base on basic principles of quantum mechanics theory , a qubit can has zero state and one state concurrently , so it is possible that a qubit take a part in more them one computation instantly , because of this the quantum computers are able to do a lot of parallel computation.

Bolch sphere representation

Bolch used from a sphere with unit rudius that are shown the angle points on sphere.opposite figure and the following connection are know as bolch sphere representation.

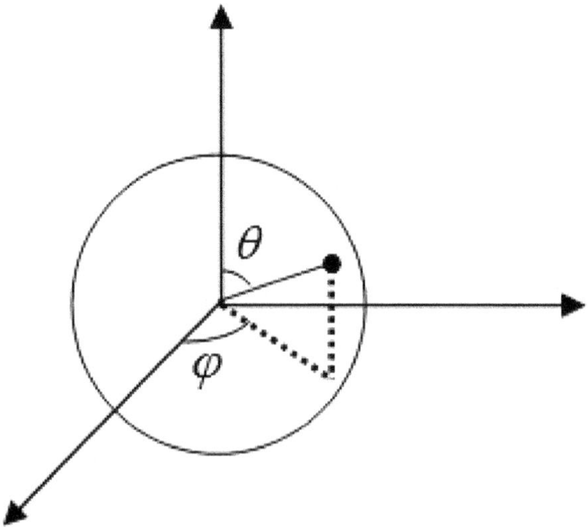

Bolch sphere representation Qubit

Qubit technologies

Several different physical implementations of qubits are possible. A number of examples are the polarizations of a photon, two of the (multiple) discrete energy levels of an ion, a superconducting Transmon qubit, the nuclear spin states of an atom or the spin states of an electron. Quantum Inspire is designed to control different qubit technologies. Its modular design allows it to re-use components that are technology independent while replacing components (software and hardware) that are technology dependent.

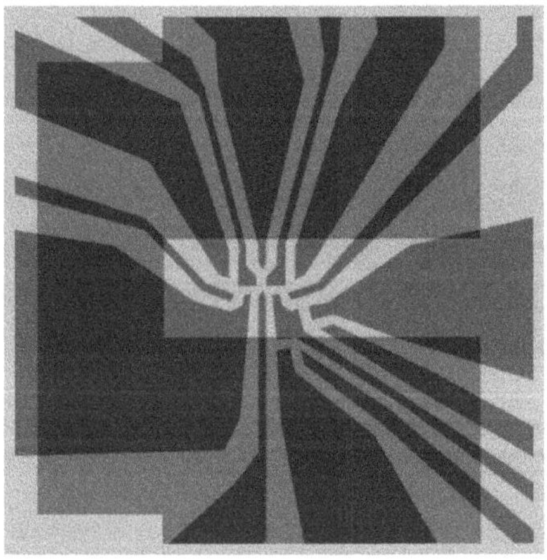

Impression (stylized SEM image) of Spin-2

Quantum Computing

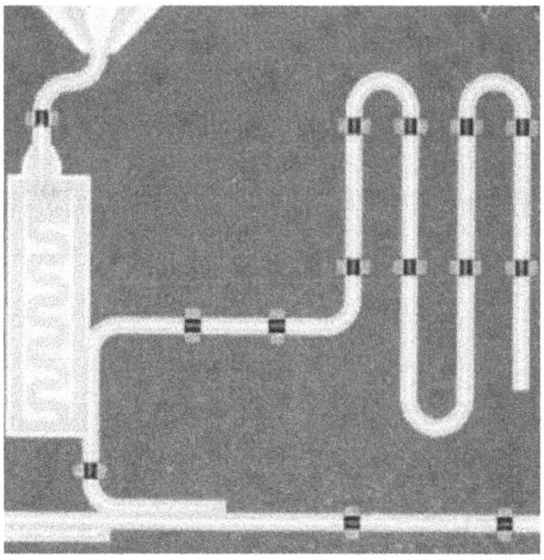
Impression of a transmon qubit

Quantum computing is an emerging technology that aims to revolutionize the way we process information. Unlike classical computers that use bits to represent information as either 0 or 1, quantum computers use quantum bits or qubits that can exist in multiple states simultaneously. This ability gives quantum computers the potential to solve problems that are infeasible for classical computers. The field of quantum computing is rapidly evolving, and there are many exciting developments taking place in academia and industry.

Here are some key points to help you understand the basics of quantum computing:

- **Superposition:** Quantum bits can exist in multiple states simultaneously, a phenomenon known as superposition. For example, a classical bit can be either 0 or 1, while a qubit can be in a state that is both 0 and 1 at the same time.
- **Entanglement:** Quantum entanglement is a phenomenon where two qubits become linked in such a way that the state of one qubit affects the state of the other, regardless of the distance between them. This property is essential for many quantum algorithms.
- **Quantum Gates:** Quantum gates are the building blocks of quantum circuits. They are analogous to classical logic gates, but they operate on qubits instead of classical bits. Examples of quantum gates include the Hadamard gate, which puts a qubit into superposition, and the CNOT gate, which performs a controlled NOT operation.
- **Quantum Algorithms:** Quantum algorithms are a set of instructions that are executed on a quantum computer to solve specific problems. One of the most famous quantum algorithms is Shor's algorithm, which can factor large numbers exponentially faster than classical algorithms. This algorithm has significant implications for cryptography and data security.
- **Quantum Hardware:** Building a quantum computer is a challenging task because of the fragility of qubits. The hardware required to implement a quantum computer is still in its infancy, and there are many different approaches being explored. Some of the leading approaches include superconducting qubits, trapped ions, and topological qubits.

Quantum computing is a fascinating field that has the potential to transform many industries, from finance to drug discovery. As the technology develops, we can expect to see many new algorithms and applications emerge, which will undoubtedly change the way we think about computing.

The Basics of Quantum Gates

Quantum computing is an emerging field that has the potential to revolutionize the way we process information. One of the key components of quantum computing is the quantum gate. A quantum gate is a fundamental building block of a quantum circuit, which is a series of quantum gates applied to a set of qubits, or quantum bits. These gates manipulate the state of the qubits, and by combining them in different ways, complex computations can be performed. In this section, we will explore the basics of quantum gates, including their types, operations, and applications.

Gate Operations

Quantum gates operate in a fundamentally different way than classical gates. While classical gates operate on bits, quantum gates operate on qubits. A qubit can exist in a superposition of two states, which allows quantum gates to perform multiple operations simultaneously. The most common operations performed by quantum gates include:

- **Rotation:** Rotation gates are used to rotate the state of a qubit around the X, Y, or Z axis.
- **Phase shift:** Phase shift gates are used to shift the phase of a qubit by a certain amount.
- **Measurement:** Measurement gates are used to measure the state of a qubit, collapsing it to either |0 or |1.

Applications of Quantum Gates

Quantum gates are essential for many quantum algorithms, including Shor's algorithm for factoring large numbers and Grover's algorithm for searching unsorted databases. Additionally, quantum gates are used in quantum error correction, which is essential for making quantum computers practical for real-world applications.

Quantum gates are an essential component of quantum computing. They allow us to manipulate the state of qubits, which allows for complex computations that would be impossible with classical computers. By understanding the basics of quantum gates, we can begin to explore the exciting possibilities of quantum computing.

The Different Types of Quantum Gates

Quantum gates are the fundamental building blocks of quantum circuits that perform operations on qubits, the quantum equivalent of classical bits. These gates allow us to manipulate the quantum states of qubits and perform complex computations that classical computers are not capable of. There are different types of quantum gates, each with its unique functionality and set of properties. Understanding the different types of quantum gates is crucial in designing quantum algorithms and building quantum computers. In this section, we will explore the different types of quantum gates and their applications.

- **Pauli Gates:** The Pauli gates are the most fundamental type of quantum gates that operate on a single qubit. They include the Pauli-X, Pauli-Y, and Pauli-Z gates. The Pauli-X gate acts as a classical NOT gate, flipping the state of the qubit from |0 to |1 or vice versa. The Pauli-Y gate rotates the qubit state by 90 degrees around the Y-axis of the Bloch sphere, while the Pauli-Z gate rotates the qubit state by 180 degrees around the Z-axis of the Bloch sphere. These gates are essential in building quantum circuits and are used in various quantum algorithms, such as the Deutsch-Jozsa algorithm.
- **Hadamard Gate:** The Hadamard gate is a single-qubit gate that transforms the basis states |0 and |1 into equal superpositions of these states, represented by |+ and |, respectively. The Hadamard gate is widely used in quantum algorithms, such as the famous quantum algorithm, Grover's search algorithm. It is also used in the construction of quantum error-correcting codes.
- **Phase Shift Gates:** Phase shift gates, also known as rotation gates, are single-qubit gates that rotate the qubit state by a certain angle around the Z-axis of the Bloch sphere. The most common phase shift gate is the R gate, which rotates the qubit state by an angle. These gates are widely used in quantum algorithms, such as the quantum phase estimation algorithm.
- **Controlled Gates:** Controlled gates are two-qubit gates that operate on two qubits, where the first qubit acts as a control qubit and the second qubit acts as a target qubit. The most common controlled gates are the Controlled-NOT (CNOT) gate and the Controlled-Z (CZ) gate. The CNOT gate flips the second qubit if the first qubit is in the state |1, while the CZ gate applies a phase shift of to the target qubit if the control qubit is in the state |1. These gates are essential in building quantum circuits and are used in various quantum algorithms, such as the Shor's algorithm.

The different types of quantum gates have their unique functionality and set of properties that make them suitable for various quantum applications. Understanding the properties and applications of these gates is essential in designing quantum algorithms and building quantum computers.

Quantum Entanglement and Superposition

Quantum Entanglement and Superposition are two fundamental concepts in quantum mechanics that have significant implications in quantum computing. The idea behind quantum entanglement is that two particles can become entangled in such a way that the state of one particle is dependent on the state of the other particle, regardless of the distance between them. This means that when one particle is measured, the state of the other particle can be determined instantaneously, even if they are light-years apart. Superposition, on the other hand, is the idea that a quantum system can exist in multiple states at once until it is measured.

Understanding quantum entanglement and superposition is crucial to the development of quantum computing. Here are some in-depth insights into these concepts:

- Entanglement is a unique property of quantum mechanics that has no classical analog. When two particles are entangled, their properties are correlated in such a way that the state of one particle is dependent on the state of the other. Imagine two coins that are entangled, one is always heads and the other is always tails. If you flip one of the coins, the other coin automatically flips to the opposite side, regardless of the distance between them.
- Superposition is a fundamental concept in quantum mechanics that allows a quantum system to exist in multiple states at once. For example, a quantum bit, or qubit, can exist in a superposition of both 0 and 1 at the same time until it is measured. This means that a quantum computer can perform multiple calculations simultaneously, making it much faster than a classical computer.
- Quantum entanglement and superposition are closely related. In fact, quantum entanglement is often used to create superposition. By entangling two particles and then measuring one of them, the other particle can be put into a superposition of states.
- One of the most exciting applications of entanglement and superposition is quantum teleportation. In quantum teleportation, a quantum state is transferred from one particle to another using entanglement. This means that information can be transmitted instantaneously over any distance, making it a potentially powerful tool for communication and cryptography.

Quantum entanglement and superposition are two fundamental concepts in quantum mechanics that have significant implications in quantum computing. Understanding these concepts is crucial to the development of quantum technologies, and their potential applications are vast and exciting.

Building Quantum Circuits

As we venture deeper into the world of quantum computing, one of the most fundamental components that we come across is the quantum circuit. Quantum circuits are the building blocks of quantum computing, and they are used to perform operations on quantum bits (qubits). Building quantum circuits requires a thorough understanding of quantum mechanics and a solid grasp of the mathematical concepts that underlie quantum computing.

From the perspective of computer science, quantum circuits can be thought of as a series of gates that manipulate the state of qubits. Each gate represents a specific operation that can be performed on qubits, and they can be combined to create more complex circuits. In this section, we will explore the intricacies of building quantum circuits and the different types of gates that are used to perform quantum operations.

- **Quantum Gates:** Quantum gates are the basic building blocks of quantum circuits. They are used to manipulate the state of qubits and perform operations on them. Each quantum gate corresponds to a specific operation that can be performed on a qubit. Some of the most commonly used quantum gates include the Pauli-X gate, the Hadamard gate, and the CNOT gate.
- **Circuit Construction:** In order to build a quantum circuit, we need to know the sequence of gates that we need to apply to our qubits. This requires an understanding of the mathematical concepts that underlie quantum computing. For example, the sequence in which gates are applied can have a significant impact on the final state of the qubits. Circuit construction involves selecting the appropriate gates and arranging them in the correct sequence.
- **Error Correction:** Quantum computing is prone to errors due to the fragile nature of qubits. Errors can occur due to a variety of factors, including environmental noise and imperfections in the hardware. To mitigate these errors, quantum circuits are designed with error correction in mind. One common technique for error correction is to use redundant qubits and error correcting codes.
- **Applications:** Quantum circuits have a wide range of applications in quantum computing. For example, they can be used for quantum teleportation, quantum error correction, and quantum cryptography. In addition, quantum circuits are used in a variety of quantum algorithms, such as Shor's algorithm for factoring large numbers and Grover's algorithm for searching unstructured databases.

Building quantum circuits is an essential part of quantum computing. It requires a deep understanding of quantum mechanics and a solid grasp of the mathematical concepts that underlie quantum computing. By combining different types of gates, we can create complex circuits that perform a wide range of quantum operations. The potential applications of quantum circuits are vast, and they are at the forefront of the development of quantum computing.

Challenges in Quantum Computing

Quantum computing is a rapidly evolving field that has gained a lot of attention in recent years. It promises to revolutionize the way we solve complex problems that are currently impossible for classical computers to solve. However, the development of quantum computing is not without its challenges. In this section, we will explore some of the challenges that researchers and developers face in the field of quantum computing.

Noise and Decoherence

One of the biggest challenges in quantum computing is the issue of noise and decoherence. Quantum bits or qubits are extremely sensitive to their environment, making it difficult to maintain the coherence necessary for quantum computation. Even small perturbations can cause qubits to lose their quantum states, leading to errors in calculations. Researchers are working on developing error-correcting codes and quantum error correction techniques to overcome this challenge.

Scalability

Another challenge in quantum computing is scalability. While current quantum computers can perform a few quantum operations, they are still far from being able to perform complex computations. Scaling up quantum computers requires overcoming a number of technical challenges, such as developing more efficient quantum gates and improving qubit control.

Hardware Limitations

Quantum computing hardware is still in its infancy, and there are many limitations that need to be overcome. For example, the number of qubits in a quantum computer is limited by the physical size of the device, as well as the amount of noise and decoherence that occurs. Additionally, quantum hardware is very expensive to develop and maintain, making it difficult for smaller organizations to invest in quantum computing research.

Quantum Algorithms

Developing quantum algorithms is another challenge in quantum computing. While many classical algorithms have been developed over the past few decades, quantum algorithms are still in their early stages. Researchers are working on developing new algorithms that can take advantage of the unique properties of quantum computers, but this is a time-consuming and challenging process.

Interoperability

Finally, interoperability is a challenge in quantum computing. There are currently many different quantum computing platforms and programming languages, making it difficult for researchers to collaborate and share information. Developing standards for quantum computing could help to overcome this challenge and accelerate the development of quantum computing.

In summary, quantum computing is a promising field that has the potential to revolutionize the way we solve complex problems. However, there are many challenges that need to be overcome before quantum computers can become a reality. Researchers and developers are working hard to address these challenges, and it will be exciting to see what the future holds for quantum computing.

QUANTUM REGISTERS AND QUANTUM MEMORY

The Quantum Memory Register Class

The qureg class, my quantum memory register, is defined in qureg.C. When a quantum memory register is constructed it takes as input the number of qubits which it will contain. In my implementation quantum memory register of n bits requires 2^n complex numbers to represent. This is because a register of n bits can exist in any one of 2^n base states, and a quantum register may exist in any superposition of those base states. I use one complex number per base state to describe the probability of that state being measured.

For example, if a quantum register has 3 bits it can exist in any one of the following states:

$|0, 0, 0\rangle$

$|0, 0, 1\rangle$

$|0, 1, 0\rangle$

$|0, 1, 1\rangle$

$|1, 0, 0\rangle$

$|1, 0, 1\rangle$

$|1, 1, 0\rangle$

$|1, 1, 1\rangle$

If I take these values to be binary numbers where the most significant bit is the left most bit then these states correspond to the numbers 0,1,2,3,4,5,6,7. There are $2^3 = 8$possible base states.

We follow the convention that the probability of measuring the j'th state whose complex amplitude is w_j is

$$|w_j|^2 / \sum_j |w_j|^2$$

We also ensure throughout that algorithm that the $\Sigma_j|w_j|^2$ are equal to 1, so the probability of measuring the *j*'th state is $|w_j|^2$. Since my qureg class is only being used in Shor's algorithm, any given base state that is measured will correspond to an integer value, for example, in steps 7 and 9 we will measure only integer values. These the base states of our *n* bit quantum register can be thought of as being the integers 0 through 2^{n-1}. In my code a quantum register of size *n* will be represented by an array of complex numbers of size 2^n. The value stored at the *j*'th array position is the complex probability amplitude associated with measuring the number *j*. For example, in a quantum memory register of size 2 that contains an equal superposition of the numbers 0-3 would be represented by:

$State[0] = 1/2 + i*0$

$State[1] = 1/2 + i*0$

$State[2] = 1/2 + i*0$

$State[3] = 1/2 + i*0$

Observe that the probability of measuring any given state is $|w_j|^2 = ½ +0^2 = ¼$

If we attempt to measure this register, we will with equal probability get the number 0,1,2,3. Let us assume we measure the state and get the value 2, this has the effect of collapsing all probabilities not measured to 0, so the new state of our quantum register is:

$State[0] = 0 + i*0$

$State[1] = 0 + i*0$

$State[2] = 1 + i*0$

$State[3] = 0 + i*0$

If we were to measure this register again we would measure the value 2 without fail.

Sometimes during the course of operation we cause a state to exist in the quantum memory register where the sum over the squares of the probability amplitudes is not 1, for example a quantum register could be in the state:

$State[0] = 1 + i*0$

$State[1] = 1 + i*0$

We would expect that when measured 0 and 1 would be equally likely outcomes, however we would also like for simplicity to have $|w_j|^2$ be the probability of measuring the *j*'th state. To accommodate this desire the qureg class contains a subroutine which will normalize the probability amplitudes, such that sum of the $|w_j|^2$ over all *j*'s is one.

The qureg class also allows the state of the register to be set to any arbitrary state. This functionality is used in steps 5, 6, 7, and 8 of Shor's algorithm as described above. The quantum memory register class has two member functions which do things that a real quantum memory register could not do.

The first such function is the Dump() function which dumps the entire state information of the register without collapsing it, and is included for debugging. The reason why a real quantum memory register could not do such a thing is that to detect the state information of a real quantum memory register without applying some measurement, which would collapse the state vector of the quantum memory register into one of the base states.

The second such function is the GetProb(state) which gets the probability amplitude of any given state. This function suffers from the same problems as the Dump function, it is impossible to attain information about the state vector without causing it to collapse into one of the base states. The GetProb function is used in the main program to calculate the discrete Fourier transform in step 8. While a real quantum computer could not use this information in step 8, a real quantum computer would not need to. In a real quantum computer the Fourier transformation would take place in one step, and the transform function would take as its argument a state which could in general be any superposition of base states. This function is used to simulate this use of a function which takes a superposition of states as its argument.

Quantum memory

In quantum computing, **quantum memory** is the quantum-mechanical version of ordinary computer memory. Whereas ordinary memory stores information as binary states (represented by "1"s and "0"s), quantum memory stores a quantum state for later retrieval. These states hold useful computational information known as qubits. Unlike the classical memory of everyday computers, the states stored in quantum memory can be in a quantum superposition, giving much more practical flexibility in quantum algorithms than classical information storage.

Quantum memory is essential for the development of many devices in quantum information processing, including a synchronization tool that can match the various processes in a quantum computer, a quantum gate that maintains the identity of any state, and a mechanism for converting predetermined photons into on-demand photons. Quantum memory can be used in many aspects, such as quantum computing and quantum communication. Continuous research and experiments have enabled quantum memory to realize the storage of qubits.

Types

Atomic Gas Quantum Memory

Normal, classical optical signals are transmitted by varying the amplitude of light. In this case, a piece of paper, or a computer hard disk, can be used to store information on the lamp. In the quantum information scenario, however, the information may be encoded according to the amplitude and phase of the light. For some signals, you cannot measure both the amplitude and phase of the light without interfering with the signal. To store quantum information, light itself needs to be stored without being measured. An atomic gas quantum memory is recording the state of light into the atomic cloud. When light's information is stored by atoms, relative amplitude and phase of light is mapped to atoms and can be retrieved on-demand.

Solid Quantum Memory

In classical computing, memory is a trivial resource that can be replicated in long-lived memory hardware and retrieved later for further processing. In quantum computing, this is forbidden because, according to the no clone theorem, any quantum state cannot be reproduced completely. Therefore, in the absence of quantum error correction, the storage of qubits is limited by the internal coherence time of the physical qubits holding the information. "Quantum memory" beyond the given physical qubit storage limits will be a quantum information transmission to "storing qubits" not easily affected by environmental noise and other factors. The information would later be transferred back to the preferred "process qubits" to allow rapid operations or reads.

Research and application

Quantum memory is an important component of quantum information processing applications such as quantum network, quantum repeater, linear optical quantum computation or long-distance quantum communication.

Optical data storage has been an important research topic for many years. Its most interesting function is the use of the laws of quantum physics to protect data from theft, through quantum computing and quantum cryptography unconditionally guaranteed communication security.

They allow particles to be superimposed and in a superposition state, which means they can represent multiple combinations at the same time. These particles are called quantum bits, or qubits. From a cybersecurity perspective, the magic of qubits is that if a hacker tries to observe them in transit, their fragile quantum states shatter. This means it is impossible for hackers to tamper with network data without leaving a trace. Now, many companies are taking advantage of this feature to create networks that transmit highly sensitive data. In theory, these networks are secure.

Microwave storage and light learning microwave conversion

The nitrogen-vacancy center in diamond has attracted a lot of research in the past decade due to its excellent performance in optical nanophotonic devices. In a recent experiment, electromagnetically induced transparency was implemented on a multi-pass diamond chip to achieve full photoelectric magnetic field sensing. Despite these closely related experiments, optical storage has yet to be implemented in practice. The existing nitrogen-vacancy center (negative charge and neutral nitrogen-vacancy center) energy level structure makes the optical storage of the diamond nitrogen-vacancy center possible.

The coupling between the nitrogen-vacancy spin ensemble and superconducting qubits provides the possibility for microwave storage of superconducting qubits. Optical storage combines the coupling of electron spin state and superconducting quantum bits, which enables the nitrogen-vacancy center in diamond to play a role in the hybrid quantum system of the mutual conversion of coherent light and microwave.

Orbital angular momentum is stored in alkali vapor

Large resonant light depth is the premise of constructing efficient quantum-optical memory. Alkali metal vapor isotopes of a large number of near-infrared wavelength optical depth, because they are relatively narrow spectrum line and the number of high density in the warm temperature of 50-100°C. Alkali vapors have been used in some of the most important memory developments, from early research to the latest results we are discussing, due to their high optical depth, long coherent time and easy near-infrared optical transition.

Because of its high information transmission ability, people are more and more interested in its application in the field of quantum information. Structured light can carry orbital angular momentum, which must be stored in the memory to faithfully reproduce the stored structural photons. An atomic vapor quantum memory is ideal for storing such beams because the orbital angular momentum of photons can be mapped to the phase and amplitude of the distributed integration excitation. Diffusion is a major limitation of this technique because the motion of hot atoms destroys the spatial coherence of the storage excitation.

Early successes included storing weakly coherent pulses of spatial structure in a warm, ultracold atomic whole. In one experiment, the same group of scientists in a caesium magneto-optical trap was able to store and retrieve vector beams at the single-photon level. The memory preserves the rotation invariance of the vector beam, making it possible to use it in conjunction with qubits encoded for maladjusted immune quantum communication.

The first storage structure, a real single photon, was achieved with electromagnetically induced transparency in rubidium magneto-optical trap. The predicted single photon generated by spontaneous four-wave mixing in one magneto-optical trap is prepared by an orbital angular momentum unit using spiral phase plates, stored in the second magneto-optical trap and recovered. The dual-orbit setup also proves coherence in multimode memory, where a preannounced single photon stores the orbital angular momentum superposition state for 100 nanoseconds.

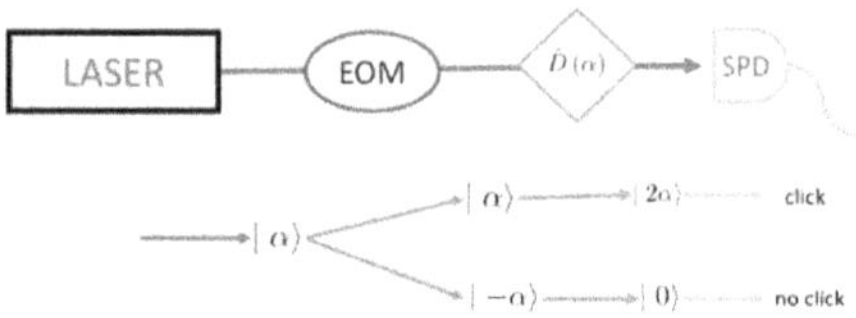

Optical Quantum

GEM

GEM (Gradient Echo Memory) is a protocol for storing optical information and it can be applied to both atomic gas and solid-state memories. The idea was first demonstrated by researchers at ANU. The experiment in a three-level system based on hot atomic vapor resulted in demonstration of coherent storage with efficiency up to 87 per cent.

Electromagnetically induced transparency

Electromagnetically induced transparency (EIT) was first introduced by Harris and his colleagues at Stanford University in 1990. The work showed that when a laser beam causes a quantum interference between the excitation paths, the optical response of the atomic medium is modified to eliminate absorption and refraction at the resonant frequencies of atomic transitions. Slow light, optical storage, and quantum memories can be achieved based on EIT.

In contrast to other approaches, EIT has a long storage time and is a relatively easy and inexpensive solution to implement. For example, electromagnetically induced transparency does not require the very high power control beams usually needed for Raman quantum memories, nor does it require the use of liquid helium temperatures. In addition, photon echo can read EIT while the spin coherence survives due to the time delay of readout pulse caused by a spin recovery in non-uniformly broadened media. Although there are some limitations on operating wavelength, bandwidth, and mode capacity, techniques have been developed to make EIT-based quantum memories a valuable tool in the development of quantum telecommunication systems.

In 2018, a highly efficient EIT-based optical memory in cold atom demonstrated a 92% storage-and-retrieval efficiency in the classical regime with coherent beams and a 70% storage-and-retrieval efficiency was demonstrated for polarization qubits encoded in weak coherent states, beating any classical benchmark. Following these demonstrations, single-photon polarization qubits were then stored via EIT in a ^{85}Rb cold atomic ensemble and retrieved with an 85% efficiency and entanglement between two cesium-based quantum memories was also achieved with an overall transfer efficiency close to 90%.

Crystals doped with rare earth

The mutual transformation of quantum information between light and matter is the focus of quantum informatics. The interaction between a single photon and a cooled crystal doped with rare earth ions is investigated. Crystals doped with rare earth have broad application prospects in the field of quantum storage because they provide a unique application system Li Chengfeng from the quantum information laboratory of the Chinese Academy of Sciences developed a solid-state quantum memory and demonstrated the photon computing function using time and frequency.

Based on this research, a large-scale quantum network based on quantum repeater can be constructed by utilizing the storage and coherence of quantum states in the material system. Researchers have shown for the first time in rare-earth ion-doped crystals. By combining the three-dimensional space with two-dimensional time and two-dimensional spectrum, a kind of memory that is different from the general one is created. It has the multimode capacity and can also be used as a high fidelity quantum converter. Experimental results show that in all these operations, the fidelity of the three-dimensional quantum state carried by the photon can be maintained at around 89%.

Raman scattering in solids

Diamond has very high Raman gain in optical phonon mode of 40 THz and has a wide transient window in a visible and near-infrared band, which makes it suitable for being an optical memory with a very wide band. After the Raman storage interaction, the optical phonon decays into a pair of photons through the channel, and the decay lifetime is 3.5 ps, which makes the diamond memory unsuitable for communication protocol.

Nevertheless, diamond memory has allowed some revealing studies of the interactions between light and matter at the quantum level: optical phonons in a diamond can be used to demonstrate emission quantum memory, macroscopic entanglement, pre-predicted single-photon storage, and single-photon frequency manipulation.

Future development

For quantum memory, quantum communication and cryptography are the future research directions. However, there are many challenges to building a global quantum network. One of the most important challenges is to create memories that can store the quantum information carried by light. Researchers at the University of Geneva in Switzerland working with France's CNRS have discovered a new material in which an element called ytterbium can store and protect quantum information, even at high frequencies.

This makes ytterbium an ideal candidate for future quantum networks. Because signals cannot be replicated, scientists are now studying how quantum memories can be made to travel farther and farther by capturing photons to synchronize them. In order to do this, it becomes important to find the right materials for making quantum memories. Ytterbium is a good insulator and works at high frequencies so that photons can be stored and quickly restored.

QUANTUM ERROR CORRECTION

Quantum error correction requires that we encode quantum information into more qubits than we would otherwise need. However, achieving quantum error correction in a scalable and fault-tolerant way has, to this point, been out of reach without considering scales of one million or more physical qubits. Our new result published today greatly reduces that overhead, and shows that error correction is within reach.

Quantum error correction requires that we encode quantum information into more qubits than we would otherwise need. However, achieving quantum error correction in a scalable and fault-tolerant way has, to this point, been out of reach without considering scales of one million or more physical qubits. Our new result published today greatly reduces that overhead, and shows that error correction is within reach.

The motivation is that although QEC is now quite a well established subject, it remains only vaguely understood by many people interested in quantum information and computing, or little studied by students learning it, because it appears to require mathematical knowledge they do not possess, and to be limited in application. Introductions tend to stay at the level of singleerror-correcting codes, and single-qubit encoding codes, but this is a mistake because some of the essential properties only emerge when multiple errors and encoding of multiple qubits are considered. The mathematical methods are elegant and fairly easy to acquire, they are probably essential tools for anyone wishing to think of good ways to manipulate multi-qubit systems.

An important area only briefly touched on in this tutorial is the physics of noise, and the fidelity that can be achieved via QEC methods. This is important because it underlies much of what we think can actually be achieved by quantum information processing in the future. A further important subject closely connected to QEC is that of fault-tolerant methods.

Error correction is especially important in quantum computers, because efficient quantum algorithms make use of large scale quantum interference, which is fragile, i.e. sensitive to imprecision in the computer and to unwanted coupling between the computer and the rest of the world. This makes large scale quantum computation so difficult as to be practically impossible unless error correction methods are used. Indeed, before quantum error correction was discovered, it seemed that this fragility would forbid large scale quantum computation. The ability to correct a quantum computer efficiently without disturbing the coherence of the computation is highly non-intuitive, and was thought more or less impossible. The discovery of powerful error correction methods therefore caused much excitement, since it converted large scale quantum computation from a practical impossibility to a possibility.

Three bit code

We will begin by analysing in detail the workings of the most simple quantum error correcting code. Exactly what is meant by a quantum error correcting code will become apparent. Suppose a source A wishes transmit quantum information via a noisy communication channel to a receiver B. Obviously the channel must be noisy in practice since no channel is perfectly noise-free. However, in order to do better than merely sending quantum bits down the channel, we must know something about the noise. For this introductory section, the following properties will be assumed: the noise acts on each qubit independently, and for a given qubit has an effect chosen at random between leaving the qubit's state unchanged (probability 1 - p) and applying a Pauli óx operator (probability p < ½). This is a very artificial type of noise, but once we can correct it, we will find that our correction can also offer useful results for much more realistic types of noise.

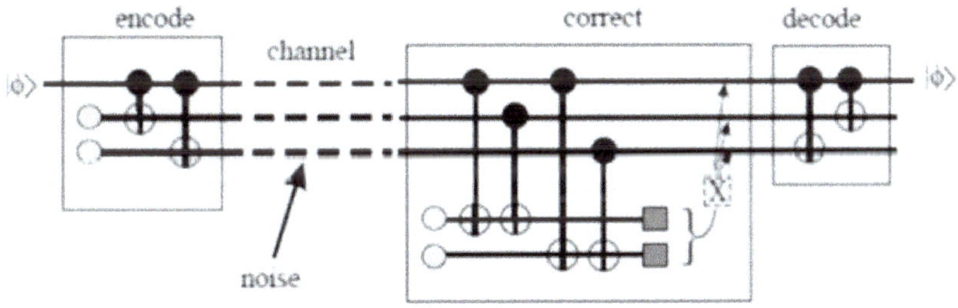

Simple example illustrating the principles of quantum error correction.

The simplest quantum error correction method is summarised in fig. below. We adopt the convention of calling the source Alice and the receiver Bob. The state of any qubit that Alice wishes to transmit can be written without loss of generality a |0i + b |1i. Alice prepares two further qubits in the state |0i, so the initial state of all three is a |000i + b |100i. Alice now operates a controlled-not gate from the first qubit to the second, producing a |000i + b |110i, followed by a controlled-not gate from the first qubit to the third, producing a |000i + b |111i. Finally, Alice sends all three qubits down the channel.

Bob receives the three qubits, but they have been acted on by the noise in the channel. Their state is one of the following:

state probability

a |000i + b |111i $(1 - p)^3$

a |100i + b |011i $p(1 - p)^2$

a |010i + b |101i $p(1 - p)^2$

a |001i + b |110i $p(1 - p)^2$

a |110i + b |001i $p^2(1 - p)$

a |101i + b |010i $p^2(1 - p)$

a |011i + b |100i $p^2(1 - p)$

a |111i + b |000i p^3

Bob now introduces two more qubits of his own, prepared in the state |00i. This extra pair of qubits, referred to as an ancilla, is not strictly necessary, but makes error correction easier to understand and becomes necessary when fault-tolerant methods are needed. Bob uses the ancilla to gather information about the noise. He first carries out controlled-nots from the first and second received qubits to the first ancilla qubit, then from the first and third received qubits to the second ancilla bit. The total state of all five qubits is now

state probability

(a |000i + b |111i)|00i $(1 - p)^3$

(a |100i + b |011i)|11i $p(1 - p)^2$

(a |010i + b |101i)|10i $p(1 - p)^2$

(a |001i + b |110i)|01i $p(1 - p)^2$ 2

(a |110i + b |001i)|01i $p^2(1 - p)$

(a |101i + b |010i)|10i $p^2(1 - p)$

(a |011i + b |100i)|11i $p^2(1 - p)$

(a |111i + b |000i)|00i p^3

Bob measures the two ancilla bits in the basis {|0i, |1i}. This gives him two classical bits of information. This information is called the error syndrome, since it helps to diagnose the errors in the received qubits. Bob's next action is as follows:

Suppose for example that Bob's measurements give 10 (i.e. the ancilla state is projected onto |10⟩). We see that the state of the received qubits must be either a |010⟩+b |101⟩ (probability p(1 - p) 2} or a |101⟩ + b |010⟩ (probability p^2 (1 - p)). Since the former is more likely, Bob corrects the state by applying a Pauli óx operator to the second qubit. He thus obtains either a |000⟩ + b |111⟩ (most likely) or a |111⟩+b |000⟩.

measured syndrome	action

00	do nothing
01	apply σ_x to third qubit
10	apply σ_x to second qubit
11	apply σ_x to first qubit

Finally, to extract the qubit which Alice sent, Bob applies controlled-not from the first qubit to the second and third, obtaining either $(a |0\rangle + b |1\rangle)|00\rangle$ or $(a |1\rangle + b |0\rangle)|00\rangle$. Therefore Bob has either the exact qubit sent by Alice, or Alice's qubit operated on by σ_x. Bob does not know which he has, but the important point is that the method has a probability of success greater than 1 - p. The correction is designed to succeed whenever either no or just one qubit is corrupted by the channel, which are the most likely possibilities. The failure probability is the probability that at least two qubits are corrupted by the channel, which is $3p\ 2\ (1 - p) + p^3 = 3p^2 - 2p^3$, i.e. less than p (as long as $p < 1/2$).

To summarise, Alice communicates a single general qubit by expressing its state as a joint state of three qubits, which are then sent to Bob. Bob first applies error correction, then extracts a single qubit state. The probability that he fails to obtain Alice's original state is $O(p^2)$, whereas it would have been $O(p)$ if no error correction method had been used. We will see later that with more qubits the same basic ideas lead to much more powerful noise suppression, but it is worth noting that we already have quite an impressive result: by using just three times as many qubits, we reduce the error probability by a factor $\sim 1/3p$, i.e. a factor ~ 30 for $p = 0.01$, ~ 300 for $p = 0.001$, and so on.

SUPERCONDUCTING QUBITS, TRAPPED LONS, AND TOPOLOGICAL QUBITS

Superconducting qubits

Superconducting qubits, trapped ions, and topological qubits are all types of qubits used in quantum computing, but they differ in their physical implementation and characteristics. Here are the key differences:

Superconducting Qubits:

- **Physical Implementation:** Superconducting qubits are typically fabricated using superconducting materials, such as niobium, that exhibit zero electrical resistance below a critical temperature.
- **Operation:** They operate by creating superposition and entanglement states through the manipulation of microwave pulses.
- **Connectivity:** They can be interconnected using superconducting resonators, allowing for the implementation of multi-qubit gates.

- **Error Rates:** Superconducting qubits are susceptible to errors from various sources, such as microwave leakage and thermal fluctuations.

Trapped Ions

- **Physical Implementation:** Trapped ions are individual ions (charged atoms) that are trapped using electromagnetic fields.
- **Operation:** They operate by using laser beams to manipulate the internal energy levels of the ions, creating superposition and entanglement states.
- **Connectivity:** Trapped ions can be interconnected using laser beams to create entanglement between ions in different traps.
- **Error Rates:** Trapped ions have relatively low error rates compared to other qubit types, making them attractive for error-corrected quantum computing.

Topological Qubits

- **Physical Implementation:** Topological qubits are based on anyons, which are exotic quasiparticles that arise in certain two-dimensional materials.
- **Operation:** They encode quantum information in the non-local properties of the anyons, making them highly resilient to local errors.
- **Connectivity:** Topological qubits can be interconnected by braiding the anyons, which changes the quantum state of the system.
- **Error Rates:** Topological qubits have the potential for very low error rates due to their topological protection, but practical implementations are still in development.

In summary, superconducting qubits are based on superconducting circuits, trapped ions use individual ions trapped in electromagnetic fields, and topological qubits rely on exotic quasiparticles called anyons. Each type has its own advantages and challenges, and researchers are actively exploring all three approaches to quantum computing.

Trapped-Ion

Trapped-ion technology emerges as a favoured approach among several up-and-coming quantum startups, including Quantinuum, IonQ, and Oxford Ionics. At the heart of this technique lies the manipulation of individual ions suspended within an electromagnetic field to serve as qubits. By harnessing laser or microwave radiation, interactions between these ions are meticulously controlled, facilitating the execution of logic gates crucial for quantum computation.

One of the standout features of trapped-ion systems is their remarkable coherence times—the duration a system maintains its quantum state.These coherence times often surpass those of superconducting qubits by orders of magnitude, significantly reducing the need for error correction. This extended coherence allows for the storage and manipulation of quantum information over longer durations, enabling high-fidelity operations. Quantinuum and other companies have leveraged these advantages to demonstrate impressive quantum volume and performance metrics, positioning trapped-ion technology at the forefront of quantum computing advancements.

However, scaling trapped-ion systems presents a formidable challenge. Managing, controlling, and maintaining a larger number of ions within the system introduces complexities that must be addressed. Nevertheless, companies are making strides in overcoming these hurdles through innovations such as improved ion traps and more efficient laser technologies.

While trapped ions themselves can operate at room temperature without the need for supercooling, the surrounding infrastructure requires temperature control to maintain optimal conditions. Maintaining a high vacuum and stable electromagnetic field is essential for the system's operation, necessitating temperature regulation. Additionally, managing the heat generated by the lasers poses another consideration, requiring cooling mechanisms to prevent overheating—a crucial detail unless one fancies a charred lab coat as a fashion statement.

In conclusion, trapped-ion technology offers tantalizing prospects for quantum computing, boasting exceptional coherence times and high-fidelity operations. Despite scalability challenges and temperature control requirements, ongoing innovations and advancements promise to propel trapped-ion systems towards realizing their full potential in revolutionizing computational capabilities. With companies at the forefront of this technology pushing boundaries, the future of trapped-ion quantum computing appears bright and promising.

Diamond quantum

Diamond quantum computing represents a cutting-edge approach to quantum technology, capitalizing on the unique properties of a defect found in diamond crystals—the nitrogen-vacancy (NV) center—to form qubits. These NV centers occur naturally when a nitrogen atom replaces one of the carbon atomsin a diamond lattice, leaving behind a vacancy. This defect creates what is known as a "color center," giving the diamond its distinctive light color compared to the clear, colorless diamonds used in jewellery.

What sets NV centers apart is their ability to absorb and emit light, making them ideal candidates for qubit implementation.Additionally, NV centers possess an electron spin state, which can serve as the basis for encoding quantum information. This spin state, with its binary up or down configuration, can be manipulated and read using laser light, allowing for data processing and computation.

Similar to photonic qubits, diamond qubits can maintain their quantum state at room temperature, offering practical advantages for deployment in various settings. Companies like Quantum Brilliance are exploring the potential of diamond quantum devices for edge computing applications, envisioning their use in scenarios like driverless cars.

However, scalability remains a challenge for diamond qubits.While a single NV center functions excellently as a qubit, entangling multipleNV centers over long distances proves to be complex. Moreover, controlling NV centers can be complicated by variations in their orientation within the diamond lattice, necessitating the fabrication of synthetic diamonds to achieve desired properties and orientations.

Despite these scalability hurdles, diamond quantum computing holds promise for driving innovation in quantum technology. With ongoing research and development efforts aimed at overcoming scalability challenges and harnessing the unique properties of NV centers, diamond qubits may pave the way for groundbreaking advancements in quantum computation and edge computing applications. As companies and researchers continue to explore this exciting frontier, the future of diamond quantum computing appears bright and full of potential.

Topical Qubits

Among the various types of qubits, topological qubits standout as the most experimental and intriguing. Still in the research phase, these qubits rely on a unique form of particle capable of being braided, offering resistance to noise and errors. This distinct feature stems from their reliance on a non-Abelian quantum phase of matter, known as a topological state of matter. While initially theoretical, recent breakthroughs by researchers fromMicrosoft and Quantinuum have demonstrated the feasibility of this concept.

Given its recent emergence from theory to practice, the full range of pros and cons associated with topological qubits remains unclear. Unlike more established qubit types such as superconducting, photonic, and trapped-ion qubits, topological qubits have yet to undergo rigorous testing.However, the inherent braided nature of the anyons used in these qubits suggests inherent noise and error mitigation capabilities, potentially requiring fewer qubits to achieve practical utility.

Despite the promise of topological quantum computing, challenges remain. Similar to superconducting qubits, topological qubits may still necessitate supercooling to maintain the delicate topological state of matter, which could be susceptible to thermal fluctuations. Moreover, questions regarding coherence times and scalability linger. Anyons, essential for topological qubits, exist only in two-dimensional systems and require complex braiding manoeuvres for computation—a feat thus far demonstrated only in two-dimensional electron gas stored in a strong magnetic field.

Nevertheless, topological qubits hold significant potential as a pathway toward fault-tolerant quantum computing. Researchers are actively exploring these elusive particles, driven by the vision of achieving groundbreaking advancements in quantum technology. Microsoft, for example, aims to unveil a topological quantum supercomputer in the coming years, underscoring the momentum behind this promising avenue of research.

Power of Topological Qubits

Quantum computing, with its promise of exponentially faster processing power, has captivated researchers and tech enthusiasts alike. Traditional quantum bits, or qubits, are susceptible to noise and errors, which pose significant challenges to the stability and scalability of quantum systems. However, a new breed of qubits, known as topological qubits, has emerged as a potential solution. With their robustness against environmental disturbances and errors, topological qubits have the power to revolutionize the field of quantum computing.

Understanding Topological Qubits

To comprehend the power of topological qubits, it's important to delve into their fundamental properties. Topological qubits are based on the principles of topological physics, a branch of science that studies the properties of matter that remain unchanged under continuous deformations. These qubits exploit exotic quantum states known as anyons, which are particles that can store and process information. Unlike traditional qubits that rely on fragile physical properties like electron spins or superconducting circuits, topological qubits encode information in the collective behavior of anyone. These anyons exist as quasiparticles that emerge from the complex interactions within a two-dimensional material, such as a superconducting surface or a fractional quantum Hall system. The robust nature of anyons makes topological qubits highly resistant to errors caused by noise or imperfections in the hardware.

Error Correction and Fault Tolerance

One of the key advantages of topological qubits is their inherent error-correction capabilities. Traditional qubits require a significant amount of resources to correct errors, often through the use of redundant qubits and complex error-correcting codes. In contrast, topological qubits possess built-in error correction mechanisms due to the topological protection afforded by anyone. Topological qubits benefit from the phenomenon known as non-Abelian braiding, where anyone can be manipulated by swapping their positions. By skillfully manipulating anyons, researchers can create logical operations that are fault-tolerant against errors caused by local perturbations. This fault tolerance allows for the development of large-scale quantum computers that can perform complex computations reliably, even in the presence of noise and imperfections.

Scalability and Quantum Supremacy

The robustness and error-correcting capabilities of topological qubits make them highly scalable. As quantum computers increase in size and complexity, the occurrence of errors becomes more prevalent. Traditional qubits face significant challenges in maintaining coherence and stability in such scenarios. In contrast, topological qubits, through their intrinsic protection against errors, offer a viable path toward building large-scale, fault-tolerant quantum computers. Moreover, topological qubits hold the potential to achieve quantum supremacy, a milestone where a quantum computer can perform computations that surpass the capabilities of classical computers. Quantum supremacy has already been demonstrated by Google's Sycamore processor, which utilized superconducting qubits. With topological qubits, the quest for quantum supremacy could be taken to the next level, unlocking even greater computational power and enabling breakthroughs in fields such as cryptography, optimization, and drug discovery.

Conclusion

In conclusion, while uncertainties persist, topological qubits represent a captivating frontier in quantum computing. As research progresses and technology evolves, the true capabilities and limitations of topological qubits will become clearer, potentially paving the way for transformative advancements in computation and beyond.

Topological qubits have the potential to revolutionize quantum computing by addressing the significant challenges of noise, errors, and scalability faced by traditional qubits. These robust qubits, based on the principles of topological physics, offer inherent error correction capabilities, fault tolerance, and scalability. With topological qubits, quantum computers can push the boundaries of computational power and open up new possibilities in various fields. As research and development in this area continue to progress, we can expect topological qubits to play a pivotal role in shaping the future of quantum computing.

CHAPTER-4
QUANTUM ALGORITHMS

An algorithm is a step-by-step procedure to perform a calculation, or a sequence of instructions to solve a problem, where each step can be performed on a computer. Therefore, an algorithm is a quantum algorithm when it can be performed on a quantum computer. In principle it is possible to run all classical algorithms on a quantum computer. However, the term quantum algorithm is applied to algorithms of which at least one of the steps is distinctly 'quantum', using superposition or entanglement.

Quantum algorithms leverage the unique properties of qubits to perform parallel computations on all possible inputs simultaneously. Some well-known quantum algorithms include Shor's algorithm, which can factor large numbers exponentially faster than the best-known classical algorithms, and Grover's algorithm, which can search an unsorted database quadratically faster than classical methods. These algorithms demonstrate the potential for quantum computing to revolutionize areas such as cryptography and database search.

Designing quantum algorithms is a complex task that requires a deep understanding of quantum mechanics and computational theory. The development of new quantum algorithms often leads to insights into the fundamental nature of computation and can reveal new connections between physics and computer science.

However, implementing quantum algorithms on current quantum hardware is challenging due to issues like error rates, decoherence, and the limited number of qubits available. Research into error correction, fault tolerance, and hardware optimization is essential to make quantum algorithms practical for real-world applications.

Quantum algorithms are at the heart of the promise of quantum computing, offering new ways to tackle problems that are intractable for classical computers. They are a vibrant area of research and development, with potential applications across various fields, including finance, medicine, logistics, and cyber-security.

Examples

Simon's Algorithm

Simon's problem was one of the first computational problems to prove that a quantum algorithm could solve a problem exponentially faster than a classical algorithm.

This algorithm, although not providing much practical value on its own, inspired the Quantum Fourier Transforms in Shor's algorithm, one of the most famous quantum algorithms of all time!

Shor's Algorithm

Shor's algorithm is by far one of the most famous quantum algorithms of all time, as it can factor integers in polynomial time. It was invented in 1994 by Peter Shor to solve the problem of finding the prime factors of a given number, N.

Shor's algorithm even has the potential to break modern public-key cryptography, like the widespread RSA cryptosystem, on an **ideal** quantum computer. RSA relies on the impossible nature of factoring the product of two prime numbers for a large enough number. However, this scenario is unlikely to happen in the near future because we still have a lot more progress to make in lowering quantum noise and quantum decoherence in current quantum computers.

Still, Shor's algorithm is an extremely efficient project in giving you a hands-on experience with using a quantum Fourier transform especially for those that are interesting in the intersection of QC and Cryptography!

Deutsch-Jozsa Algorithm

The Deutsch-Jozsa Algorithm was proposed by David Deutsch and Richard Jozsa in 1992 to showcase how quantum algorithms can be exponentially faster than any possible deterministic classical algorithm.

The algorithm itself doesn't provide much practical use besides being specifically designed to be easy for a quantum algorithm and hard for any deterministic classical algorithm.

The Deutsch-Jozsa problem consists of an oracle that implements a hidden boolean function, which takes as input a string of bits, and returns either 0 or 1. The Deutsch-Jozsa quantum algorithm produces an answer that is always correct with a single evaluation of the function.

Grover's Algorithm

Lov Grover created this algorithm to solve the problem of an unstructured search. It can find the unique input to a black box function that produces a particular output value, using just O(sqrt N) evaluation of the function, N being the function's domain.

In other words, let's say we had a shuffled deck of cards and were tasked with finding 1 specific card. The *classical* algorithm would solve this by going through all the cards in the deck one by one, or *N* evaluations. On the other hand, Grover's algorithm would only require O(sqrt N) evaluation to do the same job.

Unlike the previous quantum algorithms mentioned, Grover's algorithm only provides a quadratic speedup in evaluation time for unstructured searches, compared to their exponential speedup. Still, the amplitude amplification trick employed in Grover's algorithm is extremely useful when trying to obtain quadratic run time improvements for a variety of other algorithms.

Bernstein-Vazirani Algorithm

The Bernstein-Vazirani Algorithm was invented by Ethan Bernstein and Umesh Vazirani in 1992. It is a restricted version of the Deutsch–Jozsa algorithm.

So, let's just say that we are given a **box**. Hidden in the box is a secret number. This "secret number" is represented by six bits made up of 0's and 1's. We need to figure out what the "secret number" is.

Classically, a computer would find it most efficient to calculate the "secret number" by evaluating the function *n* times, where x = 2^i and i is the summation of 0, 1, . . ., n-1.

Now imagine if you could find out what the secret number is in **one try,** no matter its size. That's exactly what running the Bernstein-Vazirani algorithm on a **quantum computer** allows you to do.

QUANTUM FOURIER TRANSFORM AND SHOR'S ALGORITHM

Quantum Fourier Transform

Quantum Fourier transform (QFT) is a key tool for quantum algorithms, such as Shor's algorithm for factoring large numbers and quantum phase estimation for finding eigenvalues of operators. But what is QFT and how can you understand it intuitively and effectively? In this article, we will explain the basics of QFT, how it differs from the classical Fourier transform, and some of its applications in quantum computing.

QFT works by applying a series of quantum gates, such as Hadamard gates and controlled phase shift gates, to a register of qubits. Each qubit represents a binary digit of the input state, and each gate modifies the qubit's amplitude and phase according to a certain formula. The result is a quantum state that has the same number of qubits as the input state, but each qubit's amplitude and phase correspond to a coefficient of the Fourier series of the input state.

QFT is different from classical Fourier transform in several ways. First, QFT operates on quantum states, which can be in superposition of multiple values, whereas classical Fourier transform operates on discrete or continuous signals or functions. Second, QFT is reversible, meaning that it can be undone by applying the inverse QFT operation, whereas classical Fourier transform is not reversible, meaning that some information is lost in the process. Third, QFT is more efficient than classical Fourier transform, meaning that it requires fewer operations and resources to perform.

Here we will present a quantum algorithm for computing the discreet Fourier transform which is exponentially faster than the famous Fast Fourier Transform of classical computers. However, this algorithm is an example of the tension between exponentially faster quantum algorithms and the problems of measurement.

While we can carry out the QFT algorithm to transform the n qubit state vector $|\alpha\rangle = \alpha_0 |0\rangle + \alpha_1 |1\rangle + \cdot \quad \cdot \quad \cdot + \alpha_n |n\rangle$ to its Fourier transform $|\beta\rangle = \beta_0 |0\rangle + \beta_1 |1\rangle + \cdot \quad \cdot \quad \cdot + \beta_n |n\rangle$, a measurement on $|\beta\rangle$ will only return one of its n components, and we are not able to recover all the information of the Fourier transform. For this reason, we describe this algorithm as quantum Fourier sampling.

The Quantum Fourier Transform is a generalization of the Hadamard transform. It is very similar, with the exception that QFT introduces phase. The specific kinds of phases introduced are what we call primitive roots of unity, ù. Before defining the Fourier Transform, we will take a quick look at these primitive roots of unity.

Recall that in the complex numbers, there exist n solutions to the equation $z^n = 1$. For example if n = 2, z could be 1 or -1. If n = 4, z could be 1, i, -1, or -i. You can easily check that these roots can be written as powers of $\omega = e^{2\pi i/n}$. This number ω is called a primitive nth root of unity. In the figure below ù is drawn along with the other complex roots of unity for n=5.

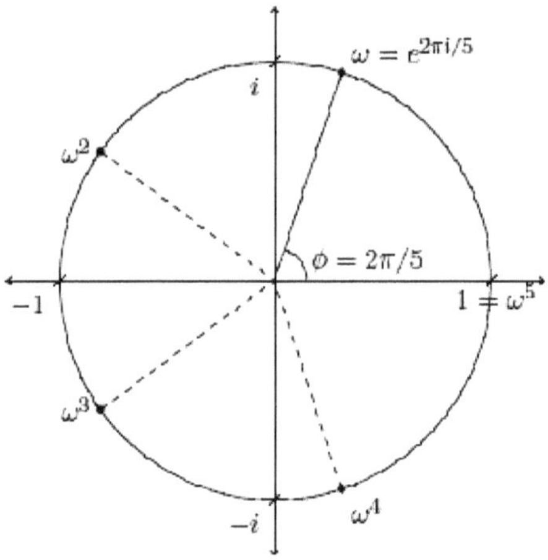

The 5 complex 5th roots of 1.

In this figure, we see that ù lies on the unit circle so | ù |= 1, and the line from the origin to ù makes the angle ö = 2ð/M with the real line. If we square ù, we double the angle. Furthermore, if we raise ù to the jth power, ùj has phase angle ö = 2jð/M and is still an Mth root of unity.

Now, we can move in to the Fourier Transform itself. The discreet Fourier transform is defined by

$$QFT_M = \frac{1}{\sqrt{M}} \begin{pmatrix} 1 & 1 & 1 & 1 & \cdots & 1 \\ 1 & \omega & \omega^2 & \omega^3 & \cdots & \omega^{M-1} \\ 1 & \omega^2 & \omega^4 & \omega^6 & \cdots & \omega^{2M-2} \\ 1 & \omega^3 & \omega^6 & \omega^9 & \cdots & \omega^{3M-3} \\ \vdots & \vdots & \vdots & \vdots & \ddots & \vdots \\ 1 & \omega^{M-1} & \omega^{2M-2} & \omega^{3M-3} & \cdots & \omega^{(M-1)(M-1)} \end{pmatrix}$$

Another way of writing this is to say that the jkth entry of QF TM is ùjk.

The transform takes the vector

$$\begin{pmatrix} \alpha_0 \\ \alpha_1 \\ . \\ . \\ . \\ \alpha_n \end{pmatrix}$$

to its Fourier transform

$$\begin{pmatrix} \beta_0 \\ \beta_1 \\ . \\ . \\ . \\ \beta_n \end{pmatrix}$$

as specified by the above matrix.

Properties of QFT

Studying the properties of a mathematical object gives us insight into the way it works. These properties will not only be important to our use of the Fourier transform later on, but they also provide a foundation of how to understand the discreet Fourier transform.

QF TM is unitary

Proof It is well known that an operator is unitary if its columns are orthonormal. Denote the ith and jth columns of QF TM as Fi and Fj .

Then

$$F_i = \frac{1}{\sqrt{M}}\begin{pmatrix}1\\ \omega^{i*1}\\ \vdots\\ \omega^{i*(M-1)}\end{pmatrix} \text{ and } F_j = \frac{1}{\sqrt{M}}\begin{pmatrix}1\\ \omega^{i*j}\\ \vdots\\ \omega^{j*(M-1)}\end{pmatrix}.$$

Thus

$$\langle F_i|F_j\rangle = \frac{1}{M}\sum_{n=0}^{M-1}\omega^{ni}\overline{\omega^{nj}} = \frac{1}{M}\sum_{n=0}^{M-1}(\omega^{i-j})^n$$

From here it is easy to see that if i = j, $\langle F_i|F_j\rangle = 1$.

For the case $i \neq j$, we will notice that

$$\left(\frac{1}{M}\right)\sum_{n=0}^{M-1}(\omega^{i-1})^n$$

is a geometric series, and expand the sum. Thus

$$\frac{1}{M}\sum_{n=0}^{M-1}(\omega^{i-j})^n = \frac{1}{M}\frac{\omega^{M(i-j)}-1}{\omega^{i-j}-1} = \frac{1}{M}\frac{1-1}{\omega^{i-j}-1} = 0$$

where $\omega^{M(idj)} = 1$ because ù is an Mth root of unity.

Because the Fourier transform is a unitary operator, we can implement it in a quantum circuit. Thus if $N = 2^n$, we can apply the Fourier transform QFT_N to a n-qubit system.

Linear Shift. This, property exemplified above, states that a linear shift of a state-vector causes a relative phase shift of its Fourier transform. This is expressed mathematically by saying if $|f(x)\rangle$, $x \in Z_M$ has Fourier transform

$$|\hat{f})x)\rangle,$$

then $|f(x + j)\rangle$ has Fourier transform

$$|\hat{f}(x)\rangle e^{\frac{2\pi}{M}xj}.$$

Furthermore, because QFT_M is unitary and $QFT_M QF_T^{\dagger} M = I$, the converse is true. A linear phase shift on $|f\rangle$ produces a linear shift in $|\hat{f}\rangle$

So if

$$QFT_N\begin{pmatrix}\alpha_0\\ \alpha_1\\ \vdots\\ \alpha_{N-1}\end{pmatrix} = \begin{pmatrix}\beta_0\\ \beta_1\\ \vdots\\ \beta_{N-1}\end{pmatrix}, \text{ then } QFT_N\begin{pmatrix}\alpha_1\\ \alpha_2\\ \vdots\\ \alpha_0\end{pmatrix} = \begin{pmatrix}\beta_0\\ \omega\beta_1\\ \vdots\\ \omega^{N-1}\beta_{N-1}\end{pmatrix}$$

and

$$QFT_N \begin{pmatrix} \alpha_0 \\ \omega\alpha_1 \\ \vdots \\ \omega^{N-1}\alpha_{N-1} \end{pmatrix} = \begin{pmatrix} \beta_1 \\ \beta_2 \\ \vdots \\ \beta_0 \end{pmatrix}.$$

If you have never seen this property before, it should be shocking. We will not offe … that N = 4.

$$\left|\hat{\Theta}\right\rangle = \frac{1}{2}\begin{pmatrix} 1 & 1 & 1 & 1 \\ 1 & i & -1 & -i \\ 1 & -1 & 1 & -1 \\ 1 & -i & -1 & i \end{pmatrix}\begin{pmatrix} \alpha_0 \\ \alpha_1 \\ \alpha_2 \\ \alpha_3 \end{pmatrix} = \frac{1}{2}\begin{pmatrix} \alpha_0+\alpha_1+\alpha_2+\alpha_3 \\ \alpha_0+i\alpha_1-\alpha_2-i\alpha_3 \\ \alpha_0-\alpha_1+\alpha_2-\alpha_3 \\ \alpha_0-i\alpha_1-\alpha_2+i\alpha_3 \end{pmatrix} = \begin{pmatrix} \beta_0 \\ \beta_1 \\ \beta_2 \\ \beta_3 \end{pmatrix}$$

$$\left|\hat{\Phi}\right\rangle = \frac{1}{2}\begin{pmatrix} 1 & 1 & 1 & 1 \\ 1 & i & -1 & -i \\ 1 & -1 & 1 & -1 \\ 1 & -i & -1 & i \end{pmatrix}\begin{pmatrix} \alpha_1 \\ \alpha_2 \\ \alpha_3 \\ \alpha_0 \end{pmatrix} = \frac{1}{2}\begin{pmatrix} \alpha_0+\alpha_1+\alpha_2+\alpha_3 \\ -i\alpha_0+\alpha_1+i\alpha_2-\alpha_3 \\ -\alpha_0+\alpha_1-\alpha_2+\alpha_3 \\ i\alpha_0+\alpha_1-i\alpha_2-\alpha_3 \end{pmatrix} = \begin{pmatrix} \beta_0 \\ -i\beta_1 \\ -\beta_2 \\ i\beta_3 \end{pmatrix}$$

The important point here is that the only difference between $\left|\Theta\right\rangle$ and $|\Phi\rangle$ is a relative phase shift. But does this matter?

If we are going to measure a state, then the phases don't matter at all, because if the phase is ϕ, $\langle\phi\,|\phi\rangle = 1$. Therefore the phase of a given state does not effect the probability of measuring that state. However, there is a way we can gather information about the pahses.

We won't be able to tell by measuring the difference between

$$\frac{1}{2}\begin{pmatrix} 1 \\ 1 \\ 1 \\ 1 \end{pmatrix} \text{ and } \frac{1}{2}\begin{pmatrix} 1 \\ i \\ -1 \\ -i \end{pmatrix}$$

by making a measurement. However, if we apply QFT, we see that

$$QFT_4\,\frac{1}{2}\begin{pmatrix} 1 \\ 1 \\ 1 \\ 1 \end{pmatrix} = \begin{pmatrix} 1 \\ 0 \\ 0 \\ 0 \end{pmatrix} \text{ and } QFT_4\,\frac{1}{2}\begin{pmatrix} 1 \\ i \\ -1 \\ i \end{pmatrix} = \begin{pmatrix} 0 \\ 0 \\ 0 \\ 0 \end{pmatrix}.$$

Thus, measuring the Fourier Transform of the states will reveal the relative phases.

Period/Wavelength Relationship. Suppose f is periodic with period r, for example

Then $\hat{f}$ (the Fourier transform of f) is periodic with period M/r. Thus, $\hat{f}$ would look something like below figure.

If r is the period of f, we can think of M/r as the wavelength of f. If you already have intuition for Fourier transform this should come as no surprise. In general,

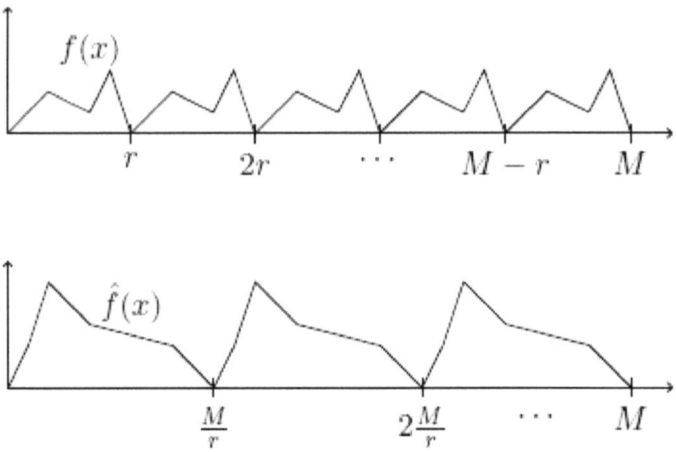

the wider the range of a function, the sharper the range in the Fourier domain; and vice versa. In example, the Fourier transform of a delta function is an even spread, while the transform of an even spread is a delta function.

We will prove this in a special case, where

$$f(x)\begin{cases}\sqrt{\frac{r}{M}} & \text{if } x = 0(\text{mod } r)\\ 0 & \text{otherwise.}\end{cases}$$

While this is a very special case, it is actually the only case that we will need to develop Shor's algorithm. Furthermore this property can be proved in general.

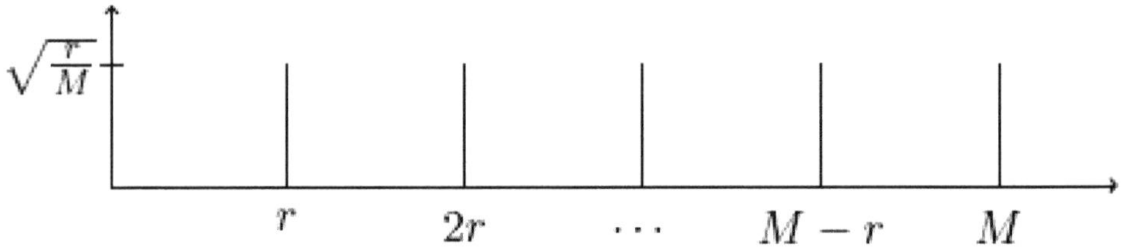

Figure f(x)

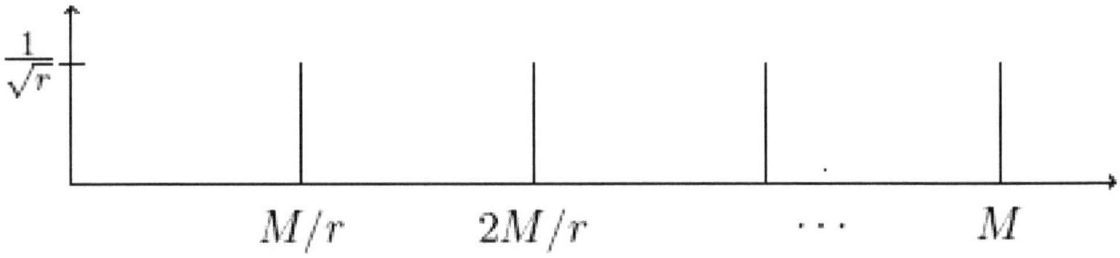

Figure $\hat{f}$ ˆf(x)

Because this function is relatively simple, we can prove the desired relationship by brute force. Suppose

$$|\alpha\rangle = \begin{pmatrix} \alpha_0 \\ \alpha_1 \\ . \\ . \\ . \\ \alpha_N \end{pmatrix} \text{ has Fourier transform } |\beta\rangle = \begin{pmatrix} \beta_0 \\ \beta_1 \\ . \\ . \\ . \\ \beta_N \end{pmatrix},$$

then the jth component of its Fourier transform is given by

$$\beta_j = \frac{1}{\sqrt{M}} \sum_{i=0}^{N=1} \alpha_i \varpi^{ij} \tag{1}$$

This expression comes from matrix multiplication, you should take a look at FN to verify this if it looks unfamiliar. In our special case,

$$f(x) = \begin{cases} \sqrt{\frac{r}{M}} \text{ if } x = 0 \text{ (mod r) otherwise.} \\ 0 \end{cases}$$

Using (1) we can calculate its Fourier transform

$$\hat{f}(x) = \frac{\sqrt{r}}{M} \sum_{i=0}^{\frac{M}{r}=1} \omega^{rix} \tag{2}$$

Where we have written $\hat{f}$ (x) instead of $\hat{f}_j$ because the $\hat{f}_j$ is equal to the value of the Fourier transform evaluated at x = j.

We have seen sums like this before. It is just a geometric series, and it is not too difficult to compute.

$$\sum_{i=0}^{\frac{M}{r}-1} \omega^{rix} = \frac{\omega^{Mx} - 1}{\omega^{rx} - 1}$$

But $\omega^{Mj} = 1$ (recall $\omega^M = 1$), so the numerator is always equal to 0. The only time the denominator can equal zero is when rx = kM, or x = kM/r ≡ 0 (mod (M/r). In this case, the numerator and the denominator are equivalently 0, so we must compute the limit using l'Hospitals rule.

Notice that the normalization factor makes good sense.

To get a look at how we could prove this property in general, imagine periodic functions (in r) of this type as a basis for any periodic function. Allow the possibility of relative phase shifts, and you can prove this property in general.

SHOR'S QUANTUM FACTORING ALGORITHM

One of the most celebrated algorithms for quantum computers is Shor's Algorithm for factoring. The time it takes for a classical computer to factor some number N grows as a polynomial in N, while the time it takes a quantum computer grows as a polynomial in log(N).

The reason we focused so much attention on period finding is because the problem of factoring can be reduced to the problem of period finding by using modular arithmetic. This isn't obvious, but we can understand it with the following two lemmas.

Setup

In modular arithmetic, we call a number x a non-trivial square root of 1 modulo N if $x^2 \equiv 1 \pmod N$ and $x \neq \pm 1$. For example, 2 is a non-trivial square root of unity modulo 3 because $2^2 = 4 \equiv 1 \pmod 3$. It turns out that if we can find such an x, we can factor N. Furthermore, we can use period finding to find x. This idea is summed up in the following lemmas.

Lemma Factoring is equivalent to finding a nontrivial squareroot of 1 mod N.

Proof Let $x \neq \pm 1$ mod N and $x^2 = 1$ mod N. Then $x^2 - 1 = 0 \pmod N$ so that $x^2 - 1$ is a multiple of N. Factoring, we see that N |(x + 1)(x - 1), but because $x \neq \pm 1 \pmod N$, N ! (x ± 1).

Therefore, gcd(N,x + 1) and gcd(N,x - 1) are factors of N, and greatest common divisor is easy to compute with Euclid's algorithm. **Example:** Suppose we want to factor the number 15. It is easy to see that $4^2 = 16 \equiv 1$ mod 15, but $4 \neq \pm 1$ mod 15. So 4 is a non-trivial square root of unity modulo 15. Then gcd(15,5) and gcd(15,3) are factors of 15. Sure enough we see that 5 • 3 = 15.

Now, all we need to do is find this nontrivial squareroot of unity, and we can factor whatever number we need. As promised, we can do this with period finding, specifically by computing the order of a random integer.

The order of some integer x modulo N is the smallest integer r such that xr = 1 mod N. For example, the order of 2 modulo 3 is 2 since 22 ≡ 1, the order of 3 modulo 5 is 4 since 32 = 9 ≡ 4; 33 = 25 ≡ 2; and 34 = 81 ≡ 1 (mod 5). Another way to say this is that the order of x is just the period of the function f(i) = xi mod N.

Lemma Suppose N = p • q, and x ∈ ZN , x ≠ p, q. Then with probability ≥ ½, the order s of x is even, and $x^{s/2}$ is a nontrivial square root of 1 mod N.

The proof of this statement requires results from number theory (Fermat's little Theorem, Chinese remainder Theorem) that are outside the scope of this course, so we will state it without proof. However, it should be intuitive: if you imagine the order of a number to vary randomly from one number to the next, you expect the order of a number to be even with probability about half.

Example: Find the order of 2a (mod 63), and use it to factor 63.

1. 2=2

2. $2^2 = 4$

3. $2^3 = 8$

4. $2^4 = 16$

5. $2^5 = 32$

6. $2^6 = 64$ ad 1 (mod 63)

so that the order of 2 is 6. Note that a quantum computer wouldn't have to compute each of these powers, it would simply use the period finding algorithm described earlier. Now we compute $2^3 = 8 \neq \pm 1$, so that gcd(63, 8 + 1) = 9 and gcd(63, 8 d 1) = 7 are factors of 63.

The Algorithm

When finding order using the period finding algorithm, it is important to use enough qubits. A sensible rule is that you need to use m qubits so that $2^m >> N^2$, where N is the number we are trying to factor, because the order of a random number might be as large as N.

We now have all the necessary tools to carry out Shor's algorithm. Start by picking a random number, then use the period finding algorithm to compute its order. If the order is even, we can use it to find a nontrivial square root of unity. If the order is odd or $x^{s/2}$ = d1, throw it out and start with a new number.

Because we know that the order of x will be even and $x^{s/2}$ will be a nontrivial square root with probability at least 1/2, we can be confident that we will be able to factor N in just a few runs of the algorithm. Because the time it takes to find the period grows as a polynomial in the number of bits, and the number of bits grows like 2 log N(by the above requirement), we expect the time it takes to factor N to grow as a polynomial in log N.

Here is the circuit for Shor's Algorithm. It relies heavily on period finding, and so the circuit looks a lot like the circuit for period finding. The key difference is that we are finding the period of $f(i) = x^i$, and the number of bits we need to input is very large.

Example

Here's an example that's a little more fun. Lets factor 119. Suppose we pick the number 16 to start with.

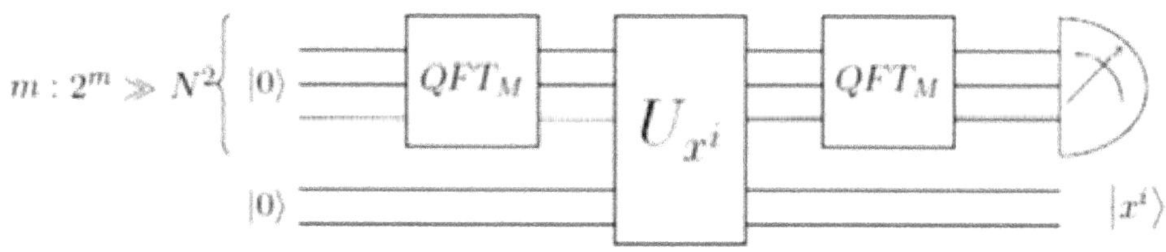

Circuit for factoring

First, we compute it's order.

- $16 = 16$
- $16 \quad \cdot 16 = 256 \equiv 18$
- $18 \quad \cdot 16 = 288 \equiv 50$
- $50 \quad \cdot 16 = 800 \equiv 86$
- $86 \quad \cdot 16 = 1376 \equiv 67$
- $67 \quad \cdot 16 = 1072 = 119 \qquad \cdot 7{+}1 \equiv 1$

so that the order of 16 mod 119 is 6. Now, we compute $16^3 \equiv 50$. Gcd(49,119) = 7, so 7 is a factor of 119, and gcd(51, 119) = 17 which is another factor of 119.

GROVER'S SEARCH ALGORITHM

Grover's algorithm is a quantum algorithm that can find a marked item in an unsorted database with high probability, using only O(sqrt(N)) queries, where N is the size of the database. This is much faster than the O(N) queries required by a classical algorithm, which gives Grover's algorithm a quadratic speedup. The algorithm uses quantum superposition, interference, and amplitude amplification to create a state that is close to the marked item, and then measures it to obtain the result.

Quantum computing has battered classical computers, in terms of their acceleration in solving complex problems. Quantum computers harness the phenomenon of quantum physics to store data and to perform computations. The basic unit of quantum memory is the quantum bit or qubit, similar to the bits 0's and 1's in classical computers. But still, there are problems where the classical ones beat the quantum computer, so using both of them according to the computational need will be a superior combination of accelerated computing.

Let us dive into one of the most significant algorithms in quantum computing by Lov Kumar Grover, who discovered Grover's searching algorithm in 1996, An Indian scientist known as one of the most prominent computer scientists in India.

Algorithm

Grover's algorithm i.e the quantum algorithm solves one of the complex scenarios in the area of computing. It's the second major algorithm proposed for quantum computing. It solves the problem of searching through unstructured data. Let's go a bit deeper into it.

Let's consider a situation where you have a list of unsorted numbers N as shown in the below diagram, where you want to find a value w from it that possesses some unique properties. So how could you find w?

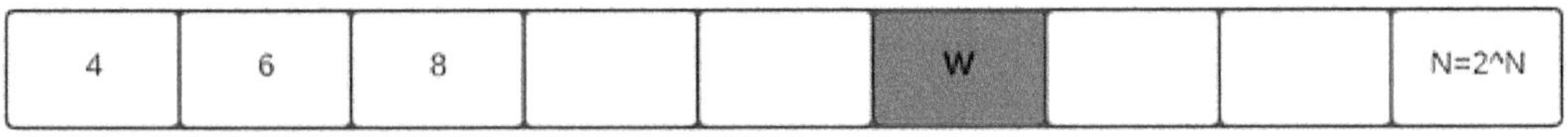

List on n numbers

Classical approach: In classical computing, we would have to check on average N/2 of these items in the list. In simple terms you would have to verify each of them one by one, In which you will require N steps i.e O(N). if random access and pre-sort are added to implement binary search on ordered data, it will require log(N) steps i.e O(log(N)). however, using a quantum algorithm will just roughly take √N steps i.e O(√N) for finding w, for instance, let's take a list of 25 elements and we want to search for a value from the list so classically it will take N steps and with the quantum algorithm, it will take √N steps i.e classically it will take 25 steps and quadratically it will take √25=5 steps.

It utilizes superposition and phase interference to improve the search. It's the amplitude amplification that plays a very spatial role in searching the element we want. let's visualize the amplitude amplification.

The amplitude amplification is a procedure that increases the probability amplitude of the value to be searched and decreased the rest of the probability amplitudes consider the below Kets ($k_1, k_2, k_3, \ldots .k_n$) in a balanced superposition, we want to hunt kw so by performing amplitude amplification we and when the kets are sent for amplification process, the first oracle flips the kw ket upside down to negative phase from the probability of .0 to -.5 which separates it from other kets.

The second oracle inverts all the amplitude by calculating its mean i.e the average. This leads to a decrease in the amplitude $A \notin kw$. And increases the kw ket such that the kw becomes 1 and the rest of the kets becomes 0.

At the final stage, the states from the second oracle are measured with encoded values relating to the item in the list. And it maps the resulting state back to the database. If the answer is incorrect the steps are repeated. the error probability is O(1/N).

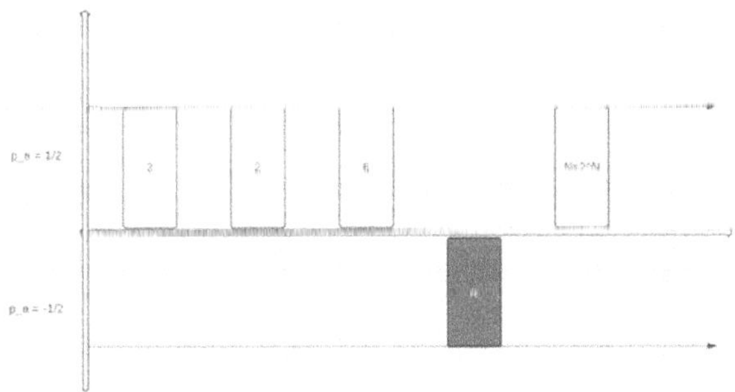

Oracle

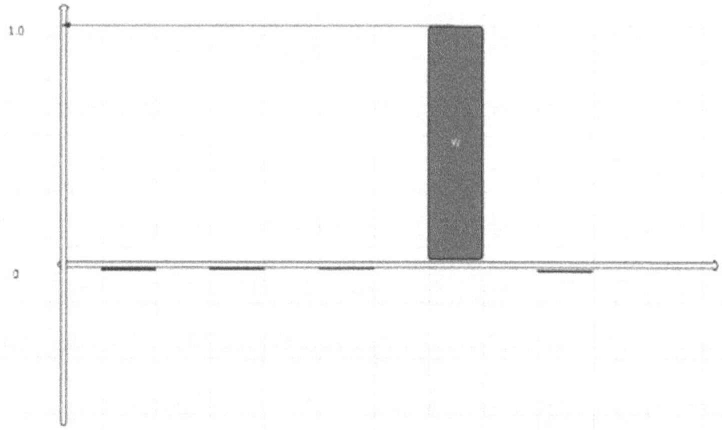

Diffuser

- Here you can assume oracle and diffuser are simply two black boxes that perform certain operations on the qubits.

Firstly, oracle is denoted as Uf and the second one as Uö, which is Grover's diffusion operator. These oracles are repeated dN times. If the matches are multiple m, then the oracles are repeated d(N/t) times. Grover search can also be used to search multiple elements.

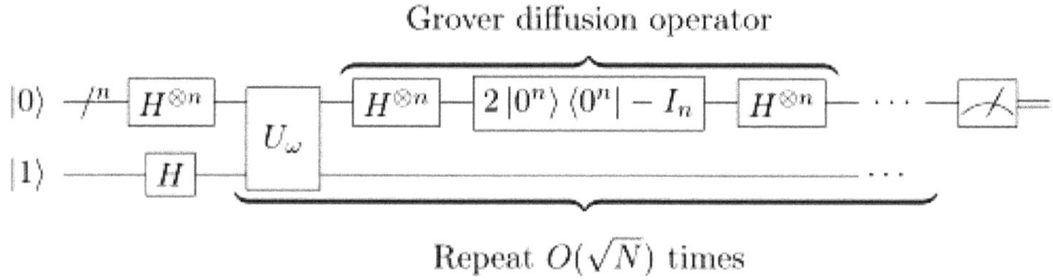

Grover's algorithm circuit [source]

The above figure is Grover's algorithm circuit that follows the below algorithm.

Let's take a quick look over Grover's Quantum algorithm

The algorithm is summarized as follows:

- Pick a random value you wanna search from the qubits.
- Put all the qubits to superposition by passing it to Hadamard gate H.

$$|s\rangle = \frac{1}{\sqrt{N}} \sum_{x=0}^{N-1} |x\rangle$$

- Construct oracle f that flips the amplitude of the object to be searched.
- Construct the Diffuser that inverts around the mean.

$$U_s = 2|s\rangle\langle s| - I.$$

- Repeat the oracle "N times for a single target and √(N/t) for multiple targets.
- finally, validate the states with the values in the database.
- And take a sip of coffee. you're done.

Superposition is the ability of a quantum system to be in multiple states at the same time

Facts

- Quantum circuits are sensitive to electromagnetic fields, collisions, air molecules, and heat that causes a qubit to lose its quantum properties
- Quantum computers are kept in extremely cold environments, as sub-atomic particles must be as close as possible to a stationary state.

Conclusion

Grover's algorithm has been outperforming the classical searching method by the quadratic acceleration. Quantum computers are embedded with the tendency to perform complex computations within an extremely short span, which will take years in comparison to classical computers.

QUANTUM APPROXIMATION AND OPTIMIZATION ALGORITHMS

As a consequence of the widely-believed P ≠ NP conjecture, there is a broad classification of NP-hard optimization problems for which precise solutions cannot be found in polynomial time. Approximation algorithms are a class of algorithms, born from theoretical computer science, that efficiently find approximate, provably near-optimal solutions to these optimization problems. Together, approximation and randomized algorithms arose as possible solutions to intractability.

The first challenge of approximation algorithms is to approximate solutions to problems as close as possible to the optimal solutions while remaining within polynomial time. The second challenge is to guarantee the closeness of the approximations through mathematical proofs of the worst-case results.

These mathematical proofs are crucial, because they distinguish approximation algorithms from heuristics, which are not guaranteed to succeed. Examples of heuristics include annealing and genetic algorithms.

It is import to note that approximation is not limited to numerical problems. The approximate string matching algorithm, also known as fuzzy string searching, finds strings of characters that approximately match patterns, as opposed to finding only exact matches. Another example is the successive approximation algorithm, which converts continuous analog waveforms into discrete digital representations within analog-to-digital converters (ADCs).

What are Approximation Algorithms?

Not all approximation algorithms are classical algorithms. Quantum approximation algorithms are a classification of quantum algorithms that, like their classical counterparts, find approximate solutions for combinatorial optimization problems. They consist of parameterized quantum circuits alongside classical neural networks which determine the optimal parameters within these quantum circuits. While the term "advantage" is often applied to potential speed advantages using quantum computers, another possible advantage could be providing higher-quality approximations, which is what these quantum algorithms aim to do.

The most popular quantum approximation algorithms are QAOA and VQE, although both have become families of algorithms, rather than just individual algorithms. As we note in our article titled "Quantum Approximate Optimization Algorithm (QAOA)," QAOA seeks to find approximate solutions to NP-hard combinatorial optimization problems, which become more and more challenging to solve precisely as problem sizes grow. As we further note in our article titled "Variational Quantum Algorithm," this hybrid classical-quantum approach can be used to approximate eigenvalue problems in addition to optimization problems.

Quantum Approximation Algorithms in Action

Quantum approximation algorithms have steadily grown in popularity due to their practicality relative to quantum algorithms that require large, fault-tolerant quantum computers that do not yet exist. As a result of their ability to be executed on current quantum computers, the number of use cases being researched has grown considerably in recent years. At a high-level, a sampling of these applications include:

- Financial portfolio optimization, which leverages QAOA to optimize allocations of assets so as to minimize risk and maximize profits for investment portfolios
- Credit scoring, which determines the credit worthiness of individuals or organizations so as to help make lending decisions
- Infrastructure optimizations, which leverage QAOA to optimize times, costs, or even safety for such things as delivery routes, air traffic routes, and shipping routes
- Scheduling, which may seek such benefits as minimizing manufacturing times or minimizing associated labor costs
- Placement, maximizing coverage and minimizing overlap for locations such as cellular towers, coffee shops, restaurants, and electric vehicle (EV)

recharging stations

- Cargo, which involves maximizing the total value of the contents in a container considering the volumes and weights of the individual items that may be selected
- Combinatorial optimization problems, which leverage QAOA to find optimal solutions within very large sets of solutions, such as Maximum Cut (MaxCut) and Maximum Independent Set (MIS) problems

It is important to note that quantum approximation algorithms, such as QAOA, are not the only possible solvers for these classes of problems. For example, Rydberg blockades naturally and efficiently solve MIS and Maximum Clique problems on neutral atom quantum computers. The relative popularity of QAOA is due to it being around longer, but acceleration can be observed in neutral atom research as it relates to optimization and other problems.

Approximation Algorithms Challenges and Limitations

Like the NP-hard problems they try to solve, approximation algorithms have their own challenges and limitations:

- Whether classical or quantum, algorithms must have mathematical proofs showing that their performance is near-optimal even when the optimal solutions are not known
- For many specific, important problems, there might not be any known approaches to finding precise solutions within polynomial time
- If approximations are acceptable in lieu of precise solutions, a determination needs to be made as to how close approximations need to be in order to be acceptable

Quantum approximation algorithms have additional challenges and limitations:

- The approximations are not guaranteed to be the best possible results, they're only guaranteed to be within the range of acceptably close results
- This means that an algorithm such as QAOA may be run again, and the results might be either closer or farther away from the optimal results
- QAOA and VQE both rely on classical machine learning algorithms, which introduce their own challenges and limitations
- Current quantum computers are too error-prone to be of any usefulness today, and the fault-tolerant quantum computers of tomorrow will run different classes of algorithms
- The problem with errors is that it can take longer to converge at solutions as the values occasionally diverge away from the optimal solutions

One of the major challenges of the third point is the integration of classical neural networks with parameterized quantum circuits. As the quantum circuits grow to tackle larger optimization problems, the number of parameters grows. The complexity of optimizing larger numbers of parameters, paradoxically, becomes its own optimization problem. This is an ongoing area of research.

One such research project is "Approximation Algorithms Quantum Information & Semidefinite Optimization" by Centrum Wiskunde & Informatica (CWI), which is the Netherlands' national research institute for mathematics and computer science. This group of researchers seeks to maximize the efficiency of approximation considering both classical and quantum computational resources.

Combinatorial Optimization

Combinatorial optimization generally involves finding an optimal object from a finite set of objects. Classical methods quickly reach their limits here, as enumerating all objects and checking their optimality soon exceeds capacity limits. The problems in combinatorial optimization are typically NP-hard.

Examples include the Traveling Salesman, Maximum Cut, and Minimum Spanning Tree problems. QAOA belongs to a class of hybrid quantum algorithms that solve such and more general optimization problems exponentially faster than known classical algorithms.

Maximum Cut

Let's examine the Maximum Cut, or MaxCut (a graph problem), as an example of optimization problems. Unlike the minimum cut, this problem is NP-complete.

Imagine a graph whose nodes are divided into black and white. The goal is to maximize the number of edges with endpoints in different node groups through a cut (Cut).

We define a cut as a partition of the node set K of an undirected graph into two disjoint sets S and T = K d S, with T being the complementary set of S. The cut edge set is then all edges

$$\{(u, v) \mid u \in S \text{ und } v \in T\}$$

The size (or weight) of a cut is the cardinality of the cut edge set, meaning the number of edges affected by the cut. Here, we distinguish between weighted graphs, where the size is the sum of the weights of the edges, and unweighted graphs, where each edge has a weight of 1. Furthermore, in connected graphs, a cut is uniquely determined by its cut edge set.

Why is it an Optimization Problem?

Consider a graph G = (K, E) with n nodes. Let S and T be a cut of K. We define a function z:K ® {+1,-1}, which assigns each node a value of +1 and -1.

$(x(u) = +1 \Leftrightarrow u \in S, (z(u) = -1 \Leftrightarrow u \in T)$

This means:

- If i and j, the endpoints of an edge, are in the same node set, it's not a cut edge
- If i and j, the endpoints of an edge, are in different node sets, it is a cut edge

VARIATIONAL QUANTUM ALGORITHMS

The variational method in quantum theory is a classical method for finding low energy states of a quantum system. The rough idea of this method is that one defines a trial wave function (sometimes called an *ansatz*) as a function of some parameters, and then one finds the values of these parameters that minimize the expectation value of the energy with respect to these parameters. This minimized ansatz is then an approximation to the lowest energy eigenstate, and the expectation value serves as an upper bound on the energy of the ground state.

In the last few years, it has been realized that quantum computers can mimic the classical technique and that a quantum computer does so with certain advantages. In particular, when one applies the classical variational method to a system of η qubits, an exponential number (in η) of complex numbers is necessary to generically represent the wave function of the system. However, with a quantum computer, one can directly produce this state using a parameterized quantum circuit with less than exponential parameters, and then use repeated measurements to estimate the expectation value of the energy.

This idea has led to a class of algorithms known as variational quantum algorithms. Indeed this approach is not just limited to finding low energy eigenstates, but minimizing any objective function that can be expressed as a quantum observable. It is an open question to identify under what conditions these quantum variational algorithms will succeed, and exploring this class of algorithms is a key part of the research for noisy intermediate scale quantum computers.

The classical problem we will focus on is the 2D +/- Ising model with transverse field (ISING). This problem is NP-complete. It is highly unlikely that quantum computers will be able to efficiently solve it across all instances because it is generally believed that quantum computers cannot solve all NP-complete problems in polynomial time. Yet this type of problem is illustrative of the general class of problems that Cirq is designed to tackle.

Algorithms based on the quantum Fourier transform

The quantum Fourier transform is the quantum analogue of the discrete Fourier transform, and is used in several quantum algorithms. The Hadamard transform is also an example of a quantum Fourier transform over an n-dimensional vector space over the field $\mathbf{F}_2$. The quantum Fourier transform can be efficiently implemented on a quantum computer using only a polynomial number of quantum gates.

Deutsch–Jozsa algorithm

The Deutsch–Jozsa algorithm solves a black-box problem that requires exponentially many queries to the black box for any deterministic classical computer, but can be done with a single query by a quantum computer. However, when comparing bounded-error classical and quantum algorithms, there is no speedup, since a classical probabilistic algorithm can solve the problem with a constant number of queries with small probability of error. The algorithm determines whether a function *f* is either constant (0 on all inputs or 1 on all inputs) or balanced (returns 1 for half of the input domain and 0 for the other half).

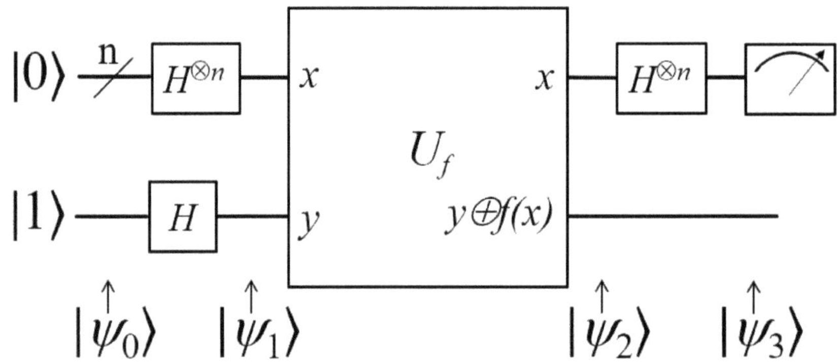

Deutsch-Jozsa algorithm

Bernstein–Vazirani algorithm

The Bernstein–Vazirani algorithm is the first quantum algorithm that solves a problem more efficiently than the best known classical algorithm. It was designed to create an oracle separation between BQP and BPP.

Simon's algorithm

Simon's algorithm solves a black-box problem exponentially faster than any classical algorithm, including bounded-error probabilistic algorithms. This algorithm, which achieves an exponential speedup over all classical algorithms that we consider efficient, was the motivation for Shor's algorithm for factoring.

Quantum phase estimation algorithm

The quantum phase estimation algorithm is used to determine the eigenphase of an eigenvector of a unitary gate, given a quantum state proportional to the eigenvector and access to the gate. The algorithm is frequently used as a subroutine in other algorithms.

Shor's algorithm

Shor's algorithm solves the discrete logarithm problem and the integer factorization problem in polynomial time, whereas the best known classical algorithms take super-polynomial time. These problems are not known to be in P or NP-complete. It is also one of the few quantum algorithms that solves a non-black-box problem in polynomial time, where the best known classical algorithms run in super-polynomial time.

Hidden subgroup problem

The abelian hidden subgroup problem is a generalization of many problems that can be solved by a quantum computer, such as Simon's problem, solving Pell's equation, testing the principal ideal of a ring R and factoring. There are efficient quantum algorithms known for the Abelian hidden subgroup problem.

The more general hidden subgroup problem, where the group isn't necessarily abelian, is a generalization of the previously mentioned problems, as well as graph isomorphism and certain lattice problems. Efficient quantum algorithms are known for certain non-abelian groups. However, no efficient algorithms are known for the symmetric group, which would give an efficient algorithm for graph isomorphism and the dihedral group, which would solve certain lattice problems.

Estimating Gauss sums

A Gauss sum is a type of exponential sum. The best known classical algorithm for estimating these sums takes exponential time. Since the discrete logarithm problem reduces to Gauss sum estimation, an efficient classical algorithm for estimating Gauss sums would imply an efficient classical algorithm for computing discrete logarithms, which is considered unlikely. However, quantum computers can estimate Gauss sums to polynomial precision in polynomial time.

Fourier fishing and Fourier checking

Consider an oracle consisting of n random Boolean functions mapping n-bit strings to a Boolean value, with the goal of finding n n-bit strings $z_1, \ldots, z_n$ such that for the Hadamard Fourier transform, at least 3/4 of the strings satisfy

$$|\hat{f}(z_i)| \geq 1$$

and at least 1 / 4 satisfy

$$|\hat{f}(z_i)| \geq 2$$

This can be done in bounded-error quantum polynomial time (BQP).[14]

Algorithms based on amplitude amplification

Amplitude amplification is a technique that allows the amplification of a chosen subspace of a quantum state. Applications of amplitude amplification usually lead to quadratic speedups over the corresponding classical algorithms. It can be considered as a generalization of Grover's algorithm.

Quantum counting

Quantum counting solves a generalization of the search problem. It solves the problem of counting the number of marked entries in an unordered list, instead of just detecting whether one exists. Specifically, it counts the number of marked entries in an ýÿ-element list with an error of at most ýÿ by making only

$$\Theta\left(\varepsilon^{-1}\sqrt{N/k}\right)$$

Deutsch-Jozsa algorithm

queries, where k is the number of marked elements in the list. More precisely, the algorithm outputs an estimate k' for k, the number of marked entries, with accuracy $|k-k'|<\varepsilon k$.

Algorithms based on quantum walks

A quantum walk is the quantum analogue of a classical random walk. A classical random walk can be described by a probability distribution over some states, while a quantum walk can be described by a quantum superposition over states. Quantum walks are known to give exponential speedups for some black-box problems. They also provide polynomial speedups for many problems. A framework for the creation of quantum walk algorithms exists and is a versatile tool.

Boson sampling problem

The Boson Sampling Problem in an experimental configuration assumes an input of bosons (e.g., photons) of moderate number that are randomly scattered into a large number of output modes, constrained by a defined unitarity. When individual photons are used, the problem is isomorphic to a multi-photon quantum walk. The problem is then to produce a fair sample of the probability distribution of the output that depends on the input arrangement of bosons and the unitarity.

Solving this problem with a classical computer algorithm requires computing the permanent of the unitary transform matrix, which may take a prohibitively long time or be outright impossible. In 2014, it was proposed that existing technology and standard probabilistic methods of generating single-photon states could be used as an input into a suitable quantum computable linear optical network and that sampling of the output probability distribution would be demonstrably superior using quantum algorithms.

In 2015, investigation predicted[26] the sampling problem had similar complexity for inputs other than Fock-state photons and identified a transition in computational complexity from classically simulable to just as hard as the Boson Sampling Problem, depending on the size of coherent amplitude inputs.

Element distinctness problem

The element distinctness problem is the problem of determining whether all the elements of a list are distinct. Classically, $\Omega(N)$ queries are required for a list of size N; however, it can be solved in $\Theta(N^{2/3})$ queries on a quantum computer. The optimal algorithm was put forth by Andris Ambainis, and Yaoyun Shi first proved a tight lower bound when the size of the range is sufficiently large. Ambainis and Kutin independently (and via different proofs) extended that work to obtain the lower bound for all functions.

Triangle-finding problem

The triangle-finding problem is the problem of determining whether a given graph contains a triangle (a clique of size 3). The best-known lower bound for quantum algorithms is $\Omega(N)$, but the best algorithm known requires $O(N^{1.297})$ queries, an improvement over the previous best $O(N^{1.3})$ queries.

Formula evaluation

A formula is a tree with a gate at each internal node and an input bit at each leaf node. The problem is to evaluate the formula, which is the output of the root node, given oracle access to the input.

A well studied formula is the balanced binary tree with only NAND gates. This type of formula requires $\Theta(N^c)$ queries using randomness, where

$$c = \log_2(1+\sqrt{33})/4 \approx 0.754$$

With a quantum algorithm, however, it can be solved in $\Theta(N^{1/2})$ queries. No better quantum algorithm for this case was known until one was found for the unconventional Hamiltonian oracle model. The same result for the standard setting soon followed.

Fast quantum algorithms for more complicated formulas are also known.

Group commutativity

The problem is to determine if a black-box group, given by k generators, is commutative. A black-box group is a group with an oracle function, which must be used to perform the group operations (multiplication, inversion, and comparison with identity). The interest in this context lies in the query complexity, which is the number of oracle calls needed to solve the problem. The deterministic and randomized query complexities are $\Theta(k^2)$ and $\Theta(k)$, respectively.[37] A quantum algorithm requires $\Theta(k^{2/3})$ queries, while the best-known classical algorithm uses $O(k^{2/3}$loga ýÿ) queries.[38]

BQP-complete problems

The complexity class BQP (bounded-error quantum polynomial time) is the set of decision problems solvable by a quantum computer in polynomial time with error probability of at most 1/3 for all instances. It is the quantum analogue to the classical complexity class BPP.

A problem is BQP-complete if it is in BQP and any problem in BQP can be reduced to it in polynomial time. Informally, the class of BQP-complete problems are those that are as hard as the hardest problems in BQP and are themselves efficiently solvable by a quantum computer (with bounded error).

Computing knot invariants

Witten had shown that the Chern-Simons topological quantum field theory (TQFT) can be solved in terms of Jones polynomials. A quantum computer can simulate a TQFT, and thereby approximate the Jones polynomial, which as far as we know, is hard to compute classically in the worst-case scenario.

Quantum simulation

The idea that quantum computers might be more powerful than classical computers originated in Richard Feynman's observation that classical computers seem to require exponential time to simulate many-particle quantum systems, yet quantum many-body systems are able to "solve themselves." Since then, the idea that quantum computers can simulate quantum physical processes exponentially faster than classical computers has been greatly fleshed out and elaborated.

Efficient (i.e., polynomial-time) quantum algorithms have been developed for simulating both Bosonic and Fermionic systems,[42] as well as the simulation of chemical reactions beyond the capabilities of current classical supercomputers using only a few hundred qubits. Quantum computers can also efficiently simulate topological quantum field theories. In addition to its intrinsic interest, this result has led to efficient quantum algorithms for estimating quantum topological invariants such as Jones and HOMFLY polynomials, and the Turaev-Viro invariant of three-dimensional manifolds.

Solving a linear systems of equations

In 2009, Aram Harrow, Avinatan Hassidim, and Seth Lloyd, formulated a quantum algorithm for solving linear systems. The algorithm estimates the result of a scalar measurement on the solution vector to a given linear system of equations.

Hybrid quantum/classical algorithms

Hybrid Quantum/Classical Algorithms combine quantum state preparation and measurement with classical optimization. These algorithms generally aim to determine the ground-state eigenvector and eigenvalue of a Hermitian operator.

QAOA

The quantum approximate optimization algorithm takes inspiration from quantum annealing, performing a discretized approximation of quantum annealing using a quantum circuit. It can be used to solve problems in graph theory. The algorithm makes use of classical optimization of quantum operations to maximize an "objective function."

Variational quantum eigensolver

The variational quantum eigensolver (VQE) algorithm applies classical optimization to minimize the energy expectation value of an ansatz state to find the ground state of a Hermitian operator, such as a molecule's Hamiltonian. It can also be extended to find excited energies of molecular Hamiltonians.

Contracted quantum eigensolver

The contracted quantum eigensolver (CQE) algorithm minimizes the residual of a contraction (or projection) of the Schrödinger equation onto the space of two (or more) electrons to find the ground- or excited-state energy and two-electron reduced density matrix of a molecule. It is based on classical methods for solving energies and two-electron reduced density matrices directly from the anti-Hermitian contracted Schrödinger equation.

CHAPTER-5

QUANTUM SOFTWARE AND PROGRAMMING LANGUAGES

Quantum computing is a field that is rapidly evolving and has the potential to transform the way we solve problems in areas such as chemistry, finance, and cryptography. While there has been a significant amount of progress in the hardware development of quantum computers, the software and programming languages required to harness their power have lagged.

Quantum computing software

Quantum computing software is responsible for performing computations on quantum hardware. Unlike classical computing, quantum computing is not based on classical bits but instead uses quantum bits or qubits. These qubits can be in a superposition of states, allowing quantum computers to perform certain calculations much faster than classical computers.

One of the main challenges of quantum computing software is to write programs that can take advantage of the properties of qubits. This requires a different way of thinking about algorithms, as many classical algorithms do not translate well to the quantum world.

There are several different approaches to quantum computing software, each with its strengths and weaknesses. One approach is to use a high-level programming language that abstracts away some of the complexities of quantum computing. Examples of such languages include Q# from Microsoft and Qiskit from IBM.

Another approach is to use a low-level programming language that provides more control over the quantum hardware. Examples of such languages include Quil from Rigetti and OpenQASM from IBM.

Quantum programming languages

Quantum programming languages are used to write quantum algorithms and programs. These languages are designed to work with the unique properties of qubits, such as superposition and entanglement.

There are several quantum programming languages available today, each with its syntax and semantics. Some of the most popular quantum programming languages include Q#, Qiskit, and PyQuil.

One of the challenges faced by quantum programming languages is that they are still relatively new and evolving rapidly. As a result, there are not yet established best practices and coding standards, making it difficult for developers to write reliable and efficient code.

The future of quantum computing software and programming languages

The field of quantum computing software and programming languages is rapidly evolving, and there are many promising developments on the horizon. One of the most exciting developments is the emergence of quantum machine learning, which combines quantum computing with classical machine learning techniques to solve complex problems.

Another promising development is the use of quantum error correction codes, which can help overcome the challenges of noise and decoherence in quantum hardware. This will require the development of new algorithms and programming languages that can take advantage of these error-correction techniques.

QUANTUM ASSEMBLY LANGUAGE

Introduction

A natural question that arises when one considers quantum computers is whether a quantum machine language exists and what its nature might be. The question about of higher level languages is also relevant. Can we develop a quantum assembly language and exist there equivalents to the languages as C, C++, Java, or C#?

The classical (non – quantum) computer can be viewed in a simplified model as a system having a main memory, register and a central processing unit (CPU) that executes program instructions step by step. A set of data and program (set of instructions) is stored in memory. The CPU executes the program step by step using the data to produce an output set of data. The basic instructions of assembly language moves data values between memory and the registers and provides basic arithmetic and logical operations. A computer has another register called the program counter. The value in the program counter is the memory location of the next instruction to execute. In this article we discuss some aspects of quantum assembly languages with position their algebraic representation.

Algebraic Representation of Assembly Language

The view of assembly language is that it has a word consisting number of bits (64-bit computer). Some assembly language programmers would even say that assembly language is english-like oriented to make them easier for programmers.

In this section we follow the opposite course and show that the computer language can be reduced to an algebraic representation. It means that computer language can be represented with creation and annihilation operators. We can develop the algebraic representation for the case of the simple assembly language. It provides better understanding of computer language and quantum computers.

The algebraic representation can be used develop a representation for words consisting of some number of bits using commuting harmonic oscillator-like raising and lowering operators. To establish the algebraic representation we associate a creation operator a^{+}_{i} and annihilation operator a_i with each memory location. These operators satisfy the commutation relations

$$[a_i, a_j^*] \equiv a_i a_j^* - a_j^* \delta_i = a_i = d_{ij}, [a_i, a_j] = 0, [a_i^+, a_j^+] = 0, \quad (1)$$

where $ä_{ij}$ is 1 if i = j and zero otherwise. We also define a pair of creation and annihilation operators for the register r and r^+, respectively. To develop a simple algebraic representation of assembly language we will assume the size of a word is so large that it can be viewed as infinitive.

The ground state of the computer is the state with the values at all memory locations set to zero. It is represented by the state vector. A state of the computer will be represented by a vector of the form

$$|n, m, p, \ldots > \equiv N(r^+)^n(a_0^+)^m(a_1^+)^p \ldots |0, 0, \ldots > \quad (2)$$

where N is a normalization constant and with the first number being the value in the register, the second number the value at memory location 1, and so on. We can set a computer state to have certain initial values in memory a then it evolve by execution a program to a final computer state with a different set of computer values in memory. The program is mapping of the instructions of a assembly language program to algebraic expression by the creation and annihilation operators.

We can define M and P operators to express the algebraic equivalent of assembly language instructions. For example, if we want load the value at memory location m into register, then operators have expression $P_r^m M_r$. Store the value in the register at memory location m will be $P_m^r M_m$. Assembly language instructions could be combined to form an assembly language program. It means, that the following an assembly language program

1 INPUT a

2 INPUT b

3 LOAD c

4 ADD b

5 STORE c

6 OUTPUT c

7 HALT

can be translated to the algebraic equivalent

$$(P_{out}{}^{c}M_{out})_6(P_c^rM_c)_5((a_r^+)^{N_b}\frac{\sqrt{N_r!}}{\sqrt{(N_r+N_b)!}})_4(P_r^aM_r)_3(P_b^{in}M_b)_2(P_a^{in}M_a)_1\,|\ldots> \tag{3}$$

If we will not to consider superposition of computer states we get classical computer and in the opposite regime we have quantum computer – it depends on a hardware realization.

To create a quantum computer we need have a material which approximates a lattice with spins at each lattice site that we can oriented electromagnetically at the beginnig of a program. The electromagnetic fields implement a set of interaction between spins that simulate the calculation to be performed. The interaction are specified with some Hamiltonian.

However, from a practical point of view may be difficult to create such hardware that would serve to implement the quantum version of the assembly language. We can use a simplified version of the quantum computer, when we have only two parts, the first part is called *register*, where are located qubits and the second part is counter instructions –*program counter*. The every instruction could be represented by a system of laser pulses that act defined way on the system ions located in the linear ion trap.

Let G be some sort of operation for example on three ions a, b, and c, which converts the original state |a, b, c> into a next state |a‘, b‘, c‘>. We are not trying to move data from one position to another – we are going *to change it*. It means

$$|a',b',c'> = G|a,b,c> \tag{4}$$

G is an operator or a matrix.

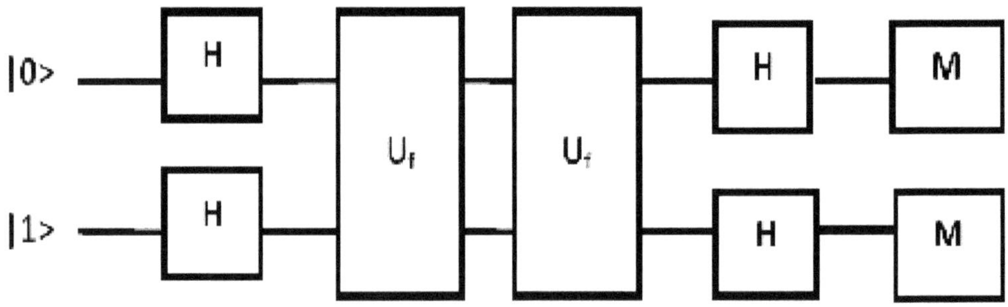

The quantum circuit as a sequence of the primitives.

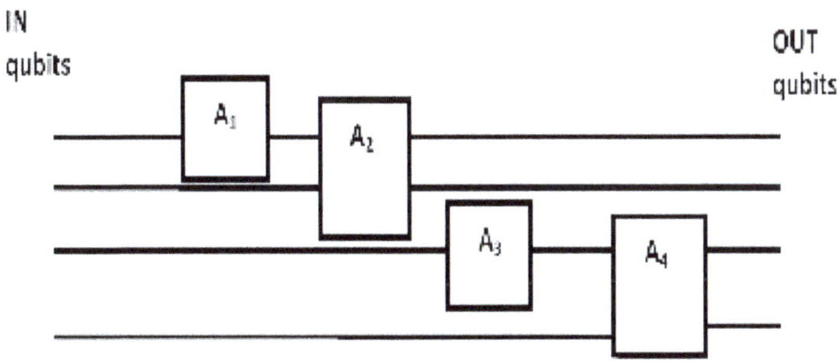

Application of operators to input qubits can be expressed as a sequence of primitive 1- and 2-qubit operators

The operator G can be expressed in the form of the product of one- and two-qubit operators as it is shown in the figure above.

$G|IN> = A_4, A_3, A_2, A_1, |IN>$ (5)

Let take to consider as an example a quantum circuit shown in fig. below:

The operátor is tensor product and the operator corresponds to the XOR operations. If the function f has properties: f(0) = f(1) = 0 we get the following result |F> = |0>|1>. This means that the final state is such that the first qubit with probability p = 1 can be found in the state | 0>.

A quantum computer can be built using single qubit operation and two-qubit CNOT gates because any computation can be decomposed into a sequence of these basic gate operations. It is possible to create primitive gates so that their combined give effect to quantum calculations. In this sense quantum computer is made up of primitive gates which sequentially acts on the qubits in the register.

Quantum computation is a new computational model based on the principles of quantum mechanics. Its goal is to solve problems that cannot be solved classicaly efficiently. Quantum computers are the next generation computers. They can perform complex engineering, mathematical and other computations in much less time. Due to certain disadvantages and high price, quantum computers may not currently replace the traditional computers. We believe that after the ongoing researches and developments in the field, we may soon get handy quantum computers.

QUANTUM CIRCUIT DESIGN

uantum arithmetic circuits have attracted extensive attention recently since it plays fundamental roles in many applications of quantum computing. Specifically, quantum circuits for integer multiplication are of great significance to various quantum algorithms, including Shor's integer factorization and discrete logarithm algorithm. In this article, we design a family of quantum circuits for integer multiplication based on the famous classical integer multiplication algorithm, Schönhage–Strassen algorithm. We have made slight modifications to the algorithm to simplify its quantum circuit implementation. As a result, the quantum circuit we designed has gate depth $O(\log^2 n)$.

To the best of our knowledge, this is the first poly-logarithmic depth quantum circuit for integer multiplication which keeps the circuit size and the number of ancillary qubits subquadratic. Our design has size $O(n \log n \log \log n)$ counted by elementary quantum gates which is the same as the time complexity of the Schönhage–Strassen algorithm, and it consumes $O(n \log n \log \log n)$ clean ancillary qubits. In addition, we also utilize a weaker version of Schönhage–Strassen algorithm to give a family of circuits which has depth at the same order $O(\log^2 n)$ but with significantly smaller constants, while still keeping the size and number of ancillary qubits subquadratic.

Simulating quantum mechanical evolutions in general is difficult on classical computers because the size of the Hilbert space grows exponentially with the number of particles involved in the simulations.

However, a quantum computer, which obeys the laws of quantum mechanics, is believed to perform such simulations more efficiently. The time evolution operator, a unitary matrix, of a quantum system acts as a quantum gate changing the state of the system in time.

Therefore, any computation on quantum computers can be interpreted as a unitary transformation on quantum state vectors. Generally, quantum gates are sufficiently simple operations so as to avoid difficulty in the physical implementation. The implementation of a general given computation represented by a unitary matrix on quantum computers requires finding an array of elementary quantum gates describing the desired computation. This describes a matrix decomposition problem known as the quantum circuit design problem.

Quantum Computation

Quantum computation is an emerging area of study, which considers the processing of quantum information, rather than the familiar classical information. The state of a quantum computer is defined as a superposition of qubits. A computation on such a computer is the unitary evolution of this state, i.e. the action of a unitary matrix operator U upon the state $|\psi\rangle$.

Quantum Gates and Circuits

Much recent work has been devoted to the construction of unitary transformations from sequences of more primitive ones. Deutsch introduced the notion that such simple unitary operators can be thought of as elementary gates performing logical operations, and more sophisticated operators can be thought of as circuits composed of gates, in analogy to the standard formalism for classical Boolean electrical circuits.

This is sometimes called the network model of computation. Following the classical computation line of analysis, in which certain small sets of gates (as small as one gate) are known to be sufficient to represent all possible circuits, several researchers have proposed such universal gate sets (as small as a single parametrized gate family) for quantum circuits. Besides the identification of such sets, some attempts have been made to characterize the minimal number of gates drawn from a given universal set required to implement a given operator U.

Circuit Design

Now assume we would like build a circuit to implement a certain computation, represented by U. Most likely our mechanisms for manufacturing quantum computers will begin with allowing us to implement certain very specific primitive quantum operations more effectively than others, for a variety of reasons which will be peculiar to the technology.

Searching the Space of Circuit Designs

Automated Circuit Design

In this section we are concerned not with the theoretical analysis of minimality of representation, but rather with the practical automated discovery of a correct circuit for a target unitary transformation U. We characterize the problem as a search over the space of possible circuit designs. We focus foremost on demonstrating a search algorithm which finds a correct circuit in less time than it would take to try every possibility. Parsimony of representations will be encouraged through the thoughtful definition of heuristics in the search procedure. It is useful to state here that to avoid exhaustive enumeration, we give up any worst-case guarantee of finding a correct circuit design; so far this is the state of the art in combinatorial optimization.

Future Directions in Quantum Circuit Design

The field of quantum computing has witnessed remarkable advancements in recent years, with researchers and engineers striving to design efficient and reliable quantum circuits. These circuits form the backbone of quantum information processing (QIP) systems, enabling the execution of logical operations on qubits. As we delve into the future directions of quantum circuit design, it becomes evident that there are several exciting avenues to explore. In this section, we will discuss some key insights from different perspectives and highlight potential areas of focus for researchers in the field.

- **Fault-tolerant Quantum Circuits:** One of the primary challenges in quantum computing is dealing with errors caused by noise and decoherence. To overcome these obstacles, fault-tolerant quantum circuit design aims to develop techniques that can detect and correct errors during computation. Various error-correcting codes, such as surface codes or color codes, have been proposed to protect qubits from errors. These codes involve redundant encoding of qubits, allowing for error detection and correction. For instance, the surface code employs a two-dimensional lattice structure where each qubit is surrounded by neighboring qubits forming a stabilizer measurement pattern. By measuring these stabilizers, errors can be detected and corrected.
- **Optimized Compilation Techniques:** Quantum circuits are typically implemented using a set of elementary gates, such as single-qubit rotations and two-qubit entangling gates. However, physical implementations may have limitations in terms of gate availability or gate fidelity. Therefore, optimizing the compilation process becomes crucial to minimize resource requirements while maintaining circuit accuracy. Techniques like gate synthesis aim to find efficient decompositions of complex gates into elementary gates that are available in a given hardware platform. Additionally, mapping algorithms help determine an optimal placement of logical qubits onto physical qubits in a quantum device to minimize gate overheads and improve circuit performance.
- **Quantum Circuit Verification:** As quantum circuits become more complex, ensuring their correctness becomes increasingly challenging. Verification techniques play a vital role in guaranteeing the accuracy of quantum circuits. Formal methods, such as model checking or theorem proving, can be employed to verify the correctness of quantum circuits against desired properties. For example, one can verify that a circuit implementing a specific algorithm satisfies the expected output for all possible inputs. Additionally, simulation-based approaches can be used to validate the behavior of quantum circuits by comparing their outputs with classical simulations for a range of input states.
- **Quantum Circuit Synthesis:** Quantum circuit synthesis involves finding an optimal sequence of gates that implements a given quantum operation or algorithm.

Future of Quantum Circuit Design and QIP

Quantum Circuit Design and QIP are two of the most important aspects of quantum computing, both of which are essential to building quantum computers. Quantum Circuit Design is the process of designing circuits that can perform quantum operations, while QIP (Quantum Information Processing) is the field of study that deals with the processing of quantum information. The future of both Quantum Circuit Design and QIP is very bright, as researchers are constantly finding new ways to improve these fields.

Quantum Circuit Design

Quantum Circuit Design is one of the most important aspects of quantum computing. It involves designing circuits that can perform quantum operations, such as quantum gates, which are the building blocks of quantum circuits. There are several different approaches to Quantum Circuit Design, including the use of quantum algorithms, quantum error correction, and quantum simulation.

- **Quantum Algorithms:** Quantum algorithms are algorithms that are designed to run on a quantum computer. These algorithms are typically designed to solve problems that are difficult or impossible to solve on classical computers. One example of a quantum algorithm is Shor's algorithm, which can be used to factor large numbers. Quantum algorithms are essential to Quantum Circuit Design because they provide a framework for designing circuits that can perform specific quantum operations.
- **Quantum Error Correction:** Quantum Error Correction is the process of detecting and correcting errors in quantum circuits. Errors can occur in quantum circuits due to decoherence, which is the loss of coherence in quantum systems over time. Quantum Error Correction is essential to Quantum Circuit Design because it allows quantum circuits to be more reliable and accurate.
- **Quantum Simulation:** Quantum simulation is the process of simulating quantum systems using classical computers. Quantum Simulation is essential to Quantum Circuit Design because it allows researchers to design and test quantum circuits before they are implemented on a quantum computer.

QIP (Quantum Information Processing):

QIP (Quantum Information Processing) is the field of study that deals with the processing of quantum information. QIP is essential to Quantum Circuit Design because it provides a framework for designing circuits that can process quantum information. There are several different approaches to QIP, including the use of quantum algorithms, quantum error correction, and quantum communication.

- **Quantum Algorithms:** Quantum algorithms are essential to QIP because they provide a framework for processing quantum information. Quantum algorithms can be used to perform tasks such as quantum teleportation, quantum cryptography, and quantum key distribution.

- **Quantum Error Correction:** Quantum Error Correction is essential to QIP because it allows quantum information to be processed more reliably and accurately. Without Quantum Error Correction, quantum information would be susceptible to errors due to decoherence.
- **Quantum Communication:** Quantum Communication is the process of communicating quantum information over long distances. Quantum Communication is essential to QIP because it allows quantum information to be shared between distant quantum computers.

Future of Quantum Circuit Design and QIP:

The future of Quantum Circuit Design and QIP is very bright, as researchers are constantly finding new ways to improve these fields. One of the most promising areas of research is the development of new quantum algorithms, which can be used to solve problems that are difficult or impossible to solve on classical computers. Another promising area of research is the development of new quantum error correction techniques, which can be used to make quantum circuits more reliable and accurate.

- **New Quantum Algorithms:** The development of new quantum algorithms is essential to the future of Quantum Circuit Design and QIP. One example of a new quantum algorithm is the Variational Quantum Eigensolver (VQE), which can be used to find the ground state of a quantum system. VQE is a promising algorithm because it can be used to solve problems in quantum chemistry, which is important for developing new materials and drugs.
- **New Quantum Error Correction Techniques:** The development of new quantum error correction techniques is essential to the future of Quantum Circuit Design and QIP. One example of a new quantum error correction technique is the Surface Code, which is a type of quantum error correction code that is more efficient than previous codes. The Surface Code is promising because it can be used to make quantum circuits more reliable and accurate.

The future of Quantum Circuit Design and QIP is very promising, as researchers are constantly finding new ways to improve these fields. The development of new quantum algorithms and quantum error correction techniques will be essential to the future of these fields, and will help to make quantum computing a reality.

Challenges in the Quantum Computing Field

Quantum computing is a revolutionary field that has the potential to solve problems that classical computers are unable to address. However, despite the immense potential of quantum computing, the field is still in its infancy, and there are significant challenges that must be overcome before we can fully harness its power. Some of the most significant challenges in the quantum computing field include the following:

- **Hardware limitations:** One of the biggest challenges in the field of quantum computing is the hardware limitations. Quantum computers are incredibly sensitive to their environment, and even a small disturbance can cause the system to collapse. Moreover, quantum computers require a tremendous amount of resources, including high-quality qubits, precise control mechanisms, and powerful cooling systems. These hardware limitations make it incredibly challenging to build and operate quantum computers, and there is still much work to be done before we can create a practical quantum computer.
- **Error correction:** Another significant challenge in the field of quantum computing is error correction. Quantum systems are inherently noisy, and errors can occur at any point in the computation. These errors can quickly accumulate, leading to incorrect results. Developing effective error correction mechanisms is critical to the success of quantum computing, and there is still much work to be done in this area.
- **Software development:** In addition to the hardware limitations and error correction challenges, software development is also a significant challenge in the quantum computing field. Developing software for quantum computers requires a fundamentally different approach than classical computing, and there are still many open questions about how to best develop software for quantum computers. Moreover, quantum algorithms are often complex and difficult to design, and there is still much research to be done in this area.
- **Expertise:** Finally, another significant challenge in the quantum computing field is the lack of expertise. Quantum computing is a highly specialized field, and there are relatively few experts in the field. Moreover, quantum computing requires expertise in a wide range of fields, including physics, computer science, and electrical engineering. As a result, there is a shortage of skilled professionals to develop and operate quantum computers.

Despite these challenges, the potential benefits of quantum computing are enormous, and there is a significant effort underway to overcome these challenges. For example, researchers are developing new hardware architectures that are more robust and scalable, and they are exploring new error correction mechanisms to mitigate the impact of noise. Moreover, researchers are working to develop new quantum algorithms that can take advantage of the unique properties of quantum systems. As these efforts continue, we can expect to see significant progress in the field of quantum computing in the coming years.

Limitations and Challenges of Quantum Annealing

When it comes to quantum computing, quantum annealing is a popular technique that is gaining a lot of attention for its potential to solve complex optimization problems more efficiently than classical computing. However, like any technology, quantum annealing has its limitations and challenges that need to be addressed. It is important to gain a deeper understanding of these limitations and challenges to fully appreciate the potential of quantum annealing and to anticipate any problems that may arise. From the perspective of quantum hardware, quantum annealing is limited by the number of qubits available and the coherence time of these qubits. The number of qubits available determines the size of the problems that can be solved, and the coherence time determines how long the qubits can remain in a superposition state before they decohere. From the perspective of software, the limitations are more related to the complexity of the problems that can be solved and the algorithms that can be used to solve them.

To provide a more in-depth understanding of the limitations and challenges of quantum annealing, here are some key points to consider:

- **Limited qubit connectivity**: In quantum annealing, qubits are connected together to form a network that can be used to solve optimization problems. However, the connectivity between qubits is often limited, which can make it difficult to find solutions to certain types of problems. For example, problems that require long-range interactions between qubits may be difficult or impossible to solve using current quantum annealing hardware.
- **Limited precision**: The precision of quantum annealing is limited by the number of qubits available, which can make it difficult to find optimal solutions to some problems. For example, in some cases, the optimal solution may require a large number of qubits, but the available hardware may not have enough qubits to find the optimal solution.
- **Noise and errors**: Quantum annealing relies on the delicate manipulation of qubits, which can be affected by noise and errors. These errors can arise from a variety of sources, including environmental factors, imperfections in the hardware, and errors in the algorithms used to manipulate the qubits. These errors can reduce the accuracy of the results and make it difficult to find the optimal solution to a problem.
- **Limited algorithmic flexibility**: Quantum annealing is designed to solve a specific type of problem, namely optimization problems. While there are many types of optimization problems, quantum annealing may not be well-suited to solving other types of problems, such as simulation or cryptography problems. This limits the flexibility of the technology and may make it less appealing to some users.

Overall, quantum annealing has the potential to revolutionize the field of optimization and solve complex problems that are beyond the reach of classical computing. However, it is important to be aware of the limitations and challenges of the technology, and to work to overcome these limitations as the technology continues to develop. By doing so, we can unlock the full potential of quantum annealing and develop new solutions to some of the world's most challenging problems.

QUANTUM SOFTWARE DEVELOPMENT KITS (SDKS)

Introduction

Quantum Software Development Kit is a tool for developing quantum algorithms that can be used in quantum computers or simulators and emulators.

A quantum simulator is an implementation of quantum gates by using classical gates. For example, Intel provides a Quantum Simulator that can simulate general quantum gates in order to test their software in simulation.

Some companies like Microsoft, IBM, Google and Rigetti, are developing open-source development kits. They provide the tools necessary for software developers to solve their own problems and enable them to access to simulators or quantum computers to implement their quantum algorithms through the cloud.

These kits often allow the use of classic programming languages, such as Python, or quantum software languages, such as Q# developed by Microsoft.

Quantum development kits

Here are some examples of quantum development kits:

- D-Wave-Ocean
- Rigetti- Forest
- IBM- Qiskit
- Google-Cirq
- Microsoft- Quantum Development Kit (QDK)
- Zapata- Orquestra
- 1QBit- 1QBit SDK
- Amazon- Braket SDK
- ETH Zurich- ProjectQ
- Xanadu- Strawberry Fields
- Riverlane- Anian

Export Circuit Board

Click on the tab with the generated circuit board to make it the active window. On the right side of the tab bar there will be an export button. This gives the user the option to export to an svg or png. The file will then appear as title.(chosen extension) in the directory opened in VS Code.

Note: Exported images will be light or dark based on your VS Code theme. To change your theme in VS Code press Ctrl + Shift + P and enter Color Theme.

Note: There is an issue where exported images do not contain Intel's custom font.

Understanding the json

IntelQuantumID: Tells the extension that this json represents a quantum circuit board

"IntelQuantumID": "Circuit-v1",

title: Sets the title of the circuit board

"title" : "Teleport |1é'",

gateColorMethod: Chooses one of a few styles that describes how the gates should be colored

Note: Gate color methods include default, clifford, axis, and simple

"gateColorMethod": "simple",

numQbits: Defines the size of the y-axis and the number of qbits to display

"numQbits" : 3,

qbitNames: Defines the name of each qbit. The drawer will dynamically size the circuit to accommodate longer names. Empty strings will be converted to |0é'.

```
"qbitNames" : [
    "example_0",
    "example_1",
    ""
],
```

gates: Defines the gates that will be displayed on the circuit board. Gates require a name and a list of qbits to act upon. There is also an option to add attributes which will be displayed when the user hovers over that specific gate. Notice that some gates such as MeasZ have a custom gate icon.

```
"gates" : [
    {
            "name" : "Prep",
            "qubits" : [0]
    }, ...
    {
            "name" : "H",
```

```
            "qubits" : [1],
            "attributes" : ["Gate: Hadamard", "Test: 1"]
    },
    {
            "name" : "X",
            "qubits" : [1,2]
    }, ...
    {
            "name" : "Z",
            "qubiWts" : [0,2]
    }, ...
    {
            "name" : "MeasZ",
            "qubits" : [0]
    }, ...
]
```

Generate Histogram (Beta)

With a valid Intel Quantum Histogram Json file the user can generate a histogram to view the given state of a quantum system in graphical form.

The compiler does not print the json required to use this feature so the user must create the json themselves and the layout of the json is subject to change

This feature is still being developed and does not yet allow for exporting

Writing New Algorithms

Writing a new algorithm is as easy as writing C++ code. A basic template and example file can be found in new_algo_- start_here.cpp. For a new .cpp file, the only additions needed to access quantum-specific functionality are:

- Add the #include header which defines the quantum gates listed in Supported Quantum Logic Gates, and add the header which defines the FullStateSimulator class.
- Declare the variable(s) that represent your quantum algorithm's qubits as globally defined qubit data types.
- Before invoking any function containing quantum instructions, prepare the backend that will serve as the quantum hardware by instantiating an object of the desired class. The FullStateSimulator class provides access to both IQS and QD Simulator as backends.

- Place all calls to quantum gates inside a function or method, not raw in main(). Add the function specifier quantum_- kernel to the definition of functions and methods including quantum gates or other quantum_kernel functions. Thesefunctions can declare and operate on classical (non-quantum) data types using typical scope rules. The compiler will move the classical calculation to have it available to a quantum_kernel while also preventing the classical instruction from being sent to quantum hardware. A quantum_kernel function can have parameters of qbit type as long as the logic ultimately resolves unambiguously to a globally defined qbit variable.
- Just like any C++ program, use the int main() function to run your primary computation. Conceptually, your program is a hybrid of traditional or "classical" components and quantum components. The quantum components are sent to the quantum backend/device.

Supported Quantum Logic Gates

Below is a list of quantum logic gates and their signatures. To see the matrix definitions for these gates, refer the file

```
/<path>/<to>/<IntelQuantumSDK>/LLVM-10.0.0-Linux/include/clang/Quantum/quintrinsics.h
1. Hadamard (H)
void H(qbit q);
2. Pauli X (X)
void X(qbit q);
3. Pauli Y (Y)
void Y(qbit q);
4. Pauli Z (Z)
void Z(qbit q);
5. Phase (S)
void S(qbit q);
phase shift with phi = pi / 2.
6. Phase Inverse (Sdag)
void Sdag(qbit q);
conjugate transpose of S.
7. T
void T(qbit q);
phase shift with phi = pi / 4.
8. T Inverse (Tdag)
void Tdag(qbit q);
conjugate transpose of T.
9. X axis Rotation (RX)
void RX(qbit q, double angle);
10. Y axis Rotation (RY)
void RY(qbit q, double angle);
```

11. Z axis rotation (RZ)
void RZ(qbit q, double angle);
12. Controlled Z (CZ)
void CZ(qbit ctrl, qbit target);
13. CNOT
void CNOT(qbit ctrl, qbit target);
14. SWAP
void SWAP(qbit ctrl, qbit target);
15. Toffoli
void Toffoli(qbit ctrl0, qbit ctrl1, qbit tgt);
Two controls Toffoli gate.
16. PrepX
void PrepX(qbit q);
initializes/resets qubit to the '+' computational state.
17. PrepY
void PrepY(qbit q);
initializes/resets qubit to the 'R' computational state.
18. PrepZ
void PrepZ(qbit q);
initializes/resets qubit to the '0' computational state.
19. MeasX
void MeasX(qbit q, cbit c);
measures the qubit q in the '+' or '-' computational states and stores the result in c.
20. MeasY
void MeasY(qbit q, cbit c);
measures the qubit q in the 'R' or 'L' computational states and stores the result in c.
21. MeasZ
void MeasZ(qbit q, cbit c);
measures the qubit q in the '0' or '1' computational states and stores the result in c.
22. CPhase
void CPhase(qbit ctrl, qbit target, double angle);
Controlled Phase gate.
23. XY-plane Rotation
void RXY(qbit q, double theta, double phi);
Define a rotation in the XY-plane of the Bloch sphere.
24. Swap Alpha
void SwapA(qbit q1, qbit q2, double angle);
Rotation in the Span{|01e' |10e'} subspace.

Language Extensions

The Intel® Quantum SDK defines a number of data types, keywords, and classes to facilitate expressing quantum algorithms as well as some common tasks associated with working with quantum qubit simulators. A complete list of the methods is provided in Provided Classes & Methods.

1 Built-in Types & Intrinsic Functions

qbit data type for variables to represent qubits.

cbit data type for variables to represent a classical bit returned by a quantum measurement.

quantum_kernel attributefor afunction that will contain quantum logic, e.g. a gate acting on a qubit or another quantum_- kernel.

release_quantum_state() An intrinsic function that once invoked in a quantum_kernel, indicates that the quantum state is unconstrained from that point onwards. Quantum variables can be re-used in a new quantum_kernel, but they must be re-initialized using PrepX, PrepY, or PrepZ. Calling release_quantum_state facilitates optimizations when compiled using the -O1 flag, which can lead to a more efficient execution of the quantum algorithm. For an example of the effects of optimization on a quantum_kernel using release_quantum_state().

7.1.1 Known Limitations

All qbit type variables must be declared in the global namespace.

Placing variable of cbit type in STL containers can create a bug. You can instead use a STL container of bool or int type and convert measured cbit values for storage as a workaround.

7.2 Namespace

iqsdk a namespace providing access to the classes and methods of the Intel® Quantum SDK.

7.3 Includes & Classes

<clang/Quantum/quintrinsics.h> This header file is required, and provides access to the supported quantum gates as well as the instructions to prepare the state of a qubit and perform a measurement on a qubit. See Supported

Quantum Logic Gates and Intel Quantum Dot Qubit Gates for additional details about the gates. <quantum.hpp> This header file is required, and provides access to the FullStateSimulator class as well as auxiliary helper classes.

IqsConfig configuration data specifically used to configure the FullStateSimulator class.

FullStateSimulator class with API calls to both set up a quantum simulator device and access the underlying quantum state during simulation. See Configuring the FullStateSimulatorfor a quick explanation or Provided

Classes & Methods for a complete description of the class' methods.

<qrt_errors.hpp> This header file is included by quantum.hpp. It defines the data type for communicating success or failure from the quantum runtime.

QRT_ERROR_T data type representing potential errors in setting up a quantum device. Either QRT_ERROR_SUCCESS, QRT_ERROR_WARNING, or QRT_ERROR_FAIL.

This header file is included by quantum.hpp. It defines the data types for facilitating access to the data of the FullStateSimulator.

QssIndex data type for representing quantum basis elements. Used for indexing into data structures representing quantum state spaces (QSS).

QssMap a map from QssIndex values to type T values. Used for representing total or partial quantum state spaces where T is double for probabilities or complex for amplitudes.

Additional features include:

- Code in familiar patterns: Intel has extended the industry-standard LLVM with quantum extensions and developed a quantum runtime environment that is modified for quantum computing, and the IQS provides a state-vector simulation of a universal quantum computer.

- Efficient execution of hybrid classical-quantum workflows: The compiler extensions allow developers to integrate results from quantum algorithms into their C++ project, opening the door to the feedback loops needed for hybrid quantum-classical algorithms like the quantum approximate optimization algorithm (QAOA) and quantum variational eigen-solver (VQE).
- High-performance simulation: Intel DevCloud users can build executables capable of simulating applications and algorithms with up to 32 qubits on a single computational node and more than 40 on multiple nodes.
- How Intel is Building a Quantum Ecosystem: Intel is committed to advancing the quantum computing field and is working to build a community of developers. As a starting point for this effort, Intel has provided grants to five universities to develop quantum course curricula to share with additional universities and proliferate its use across academia: the University of Pennsylvania, Technische Hochschule Deggendorf, Keio University, The Ohio State University and Pennsylvania State University.
- Deggendorf Institute of Technology in Munich, Germany, is utilizing the SDK to explore a fluid dynamics problem important for aerodynamics and hydrodynamics. In January 2023, Intel hosted an Intel Quantum Computing Challenge at Deggendorf Institute of Technology. Submissions explored quantum use cases using the beta version of the Intel Quantum SDK, including image denoising and realistic image generation, and solving unstructured search problems. Leidos, another beta user, is exploring applications like quantum machine learning, simulation of materials and astrophysics problems like quantum teleportation, black holes and wormholes.

Here's what beta testers are saying:

- **University of Pennsylvania**: "The Intel Quantum SDK is easy to start, and since everything is on the cloud, all we need is a secure shell client and the simulator will generate very detailed reports so that I can analyze and debug the kernels we write," said Gushu Li, assistant professor, Computer and Information Science Department.
- **Deggendorf Institute of Technology**: "The Intel Quantum SDK is a game-changer in the quantum development space because it readily allows the developer to operate at a level closer to the hardware for better resource utilization," said Yaknan John Gambo, graduate student.
- **Penn State University**: "Intel's Quantum SDK offered a unique way to apply my knowledge of C to the quantum domain," said Jeremie Pope, a student in the Computer Engineering Department. It's helped me adopt quantum programming as if it were a classical language."

- **Leidos Innovation Center**: "Leidos has enjoyed the versatility of their hardware-agnostic simulation for software development and comparative analysis," said Elizabeth Iwasawa, Ph.D., quantum technology lead and research scientist. Even with the beta version, we explored a broad variety of research topics from materials modeling and quantum machine learning to theoretical research into thermofield double states.

QUANTUM CLOUD COMPUTING

Cloud-based quantum computing is the invocation of quantum emulators, simulators or processors through the cloud. Increasingly, cloud services are being looked on as the method for providing access to quantum processing. Quantum computers achieve their massive computing power by initiating quantum physics into processing power and when users are allowed access to these quantum-powered computers through the internet it is known as quantum computing within the cloud.

In 2016, IBM connected a small quantum computer to the cloud and it allows for simple programs to be built and executed on the cloud. In early 2017, researchers from Rigetti Computing demonstrated the first programmable cloud access using the pyQuil Python library. Many people from academic researchers and professors to schoolkids, have already built programs that run many different quantum algorithms using the program tools. Some consumers hoped to use the fast computing to model financial markets or to build more advanced AI systems. These use methods allow people outside a professional lab or institution to experience and learn more about such a phenomenal technology.

Quantum cloud computing is the advanced way to analyze, stockpile, and remotely control huge amounts of information. In its essence, cloud-based quantum computing is made up of quantum simulators, emulators or processors that are available for use via the cloud. It can be used to connect powerful quantum computer systems to complete compound tasks.

In 2016, IBM connected a small quantum computer to the cloud. This allowed for simple programs to be built and executed on the cloud. A year later, researchers from Rigetti Computing demonstrated the first programmable cloud access using the pyQuil Python library.

Still in the early days of the industry, we are yet to see the true benefits quantum cloud computing could manifest in our everyday lives. One thing is for sure, though: cloud-based quantum computing has empowered the masses to get involved with the nascent industry — and maybe it won't be too long before we see some major breakthroughs in such sectors like finance and logistics because of it.

Quantum Cloud Computing Solutions

The Quantum Insider will now list thirteen of the top companies offering quantum cloud computing services in 2024. We have listed these companies in no particular order of merit and is by no means exhaustive. GCP, AWS and Azure provide access to other companies' quantum computers which is starting to be known as Quantum Computing as a Service.

IBM Q EXPERIENCE: IBM (QUANTUM CLOUD PROVIDER)

Let's start off today's post with one of the giants of the quantum computing industry in IBM and its IBM Q Experience. This company provides access to quantum hardware as well as HPC simulators. These can be accessed programmatically using the Python-based Qiskit framework, or via a graphical interface with the IBM Q Experience GUI.

Launched in May 2016 as the IBM Quantum Experience, both Qiskit and the graphical interface with the IBM Q Experience GUI are based on the OpenQASM standard for representing quantum operations. There is also a tutorial and online community. Currently available simulators and quantum devices are multiple transmon qubit processors. Those with five and 16 qubits are publicly accessible. However, devices up to 65 qubits are available through the IBM Q Cloud Network.

GOOGLE QUANTUM AI: GOOGLE (QUANTUM CLOUD PROVIDER)

Another major player in the space, Google Quantum AI is advancing the state of the art of quantum computing and developing the tools for researchers to operate beyond classical capabilities.

The Quantum AI Lab was established by Google Research in May 2013. Its Quantum Computing Service offers a platform that enables researchers to access beyond-classical computational resources by providing chaperoned access to NISQ processors and simulators for researchers who aim to advance the state-of-the-art in quantum cloud computing and publicly share their results in algorithms, applications, tools, and processor characterizations.

XANADU QUANTUM CLOUD: XANADU (QUANTUM CLOUD PROVIDER)

The first startup on the list, Canada-based Xanadu's Quantum Cloud consists of cloud-based access to three fully programmable photonic quantum computers.

The company's full-stack Python library, codename Strawberry Fields, is for designing, optimizing and utilizing photonic quantum computers and makes access to a unique set of near-term applications possible within quantum chemistry, finance, logistics, and cloud based quantum machine learning (ML).

FOREST: RIGETTI COMPUTING (QUANTUM CLOUD SERVICES)

Another startup, Rigetti Computing — a Berkeley, California-based company — offers its Quantum Cloud Services (QCS), Rigetti's quantum-first cloud computing platform. With QCS, its quantum processors (QPUs) are tightly integrated with classical computing infrastructure and made available to you over the cloud.

Its Forest SDK is a set of software tools that allow individuals to write quantum programs in Quil, then compile and run them via QCS or a simulator.

The SDK comprises of pyQuil, a Python library for building and executing Quil programs, quilc, an optimizing Quil compiler and QVM, a quantum virtual machine (quantum computer simulator).

AMAZON BRAKET: AWS (CLOUD SYSTEM PROVIDER)

Back to one of the big guns now with AWS Amazon Braket, a fully managed service that helps users get started with quantum computing by providing a development environment to explore and design quantum algorithms, test them on simulated quantum computers and run them on your choice of different quantum system hardware technologies.

Amazon Braket empowers users to research quantum computing algorithms, test different quantum hardware, build quantum software faster, as well as explore industry applications.

With beginnings that date back to the early 2000s, by the mid-2010s AWS had become the market leader in the sector.

AZURE QUANTUM: MICROSOFT

Microsoft is a large company in the tech space whose Azure Quantum cloud service brings together the most innovative quantum computing and optimization solutions into a single cloud service.

Microsoft Azure

Designed as an open ecosystem to write and run code on a diverse selection of today's quantum hardware, Azure Quantum gives people the flexibility to use their preferred development tools with support for Cirq, Qiskit, and Q#.

Anyone can get started with quantum cloud software by writing code and running it on the quantum hardware of their choice — and can even take advantage of the very generous $500 in free credit per provider.

QUANTUM INSPIRE: QUTECH (QUANTUM CLOUD SERVICES)

Quantum Inspire by Qutech was launched in May 2020 by Minister Ingrid van Engelshoven and European Commissioner Mariya Gabriel and is probably the least known quantum cloud computing supplier offering services that can proudly boast as being the first platform in Europe to provide cloud based quantum computing to two hardware chips.

Qutech itself, however, was founded in 2014 as a collaboration between Delft University of Technology (TU Delft) and the Netherlands Organisation for Applied Scientific Research (TNO).

Quantum Inspire is a prototype full-stack quantum computer. It serves as a training and education platform, a test-bed for application development and as an invitation for co-development and collaborative R&D of quantum computers.

Quantum Inspire is the first platform in the world to provide online access to a fully programmable two-qubit electron spin quantum processor called Spin-2, a two-qubit quantum processor hosting two single electron spin qubits in a double quantum dot in isotopically purified 28Si.

Along with the Spin-2 is the Starmon-5, which consists of five superconducting transmon qubits in an X configuration.

Next to the quantum chips, the platform gives access to QX, a quantum emulator backend. Two instances of the QX emulator are available, emulating up to 26 qubits on a commodity cloud-based quantum server and up to 31 qubits using one 'fat' nodes on Cartesius, the Dutch national supercomputer of SurfSara. Circuit-based quantum machine learning algorithms can be created through a graphical user interface or through the Python-based Quantum Inspire SDK, providing a backend for the projectQ framework, the Qiskit framework. Quantum Inspire provides a knowledge base with user guides and some example algorithms written in cQASM.

FORGE: QC WARE (QUANTUM CLOUD PLATFORM)

QC Ware is a Palo Alto, California-based startup founded in 2014. Its Forge cloud platform, which provides access to D-Wave hardware as well as Google and IBM simulators, offers a 30-day free trial including one minute of quantum computing time. During the trial, you can test free cloud based quantum machine learning software.

Built for turn-key algorithm implementations for data scientists, financial analysts, and engineers, its circuit building blocks system also allows for the creation of users' own algorithms.

D-WAVE

Founded in 1999, D-Wave is a Canadian company based in Burnaby, British Columbia, Canada. Taking pride in the fact it was the world's first company to sell computers to exploit quantum effects in their operation, D-Wave's The Leap™ quantum cloud service delivers immediate, real-time access to its Advantage quantum computer and quantum hybrid solver service, all with enterprise-class performance and scalability.

Leap provides access to a portfolio of hybrid solvers, enabling enterprises to address all kinds of business problems that range in size and complexity. Its solvers include the binary quadratic model solver, the discrete quadratic model solver and the constrained quadratic model solver.

AQT (QUANTUM CLOUD SERVICES)

AQT is an Innsbruck, Austria-based quantum cloud computing company founded in 2018 and supported by the Federation of Austrian Industries Tyrol, the FFG Austrian Research Promotion Agency and the University of Innsbruck.

Working on general-purpose quantum information processors, that will support a broad range of applications in various industries, AQT uses a scalable trapped-ion approach combining unmatched physical performance, extraordinary qubit control, and demonstrated optical networkability, they provide quantum cloud computing services.

Based on the versatile ion-trap platform, a growing number of quantum computers are being set up for users' convenience. These devices — the quantum simulator without noise (free and available online), the quantum simulator with noise (free and available online), the IBEX (available to partners), and PINE (in preparation) — operate at room temperature in a normal office environment, are installed in standard 19" racks, and are powered from an ordinary wall-mounted power-plug.

OXFORD QUANTUM CIRCUITS (OQC)

Founded in 2017 and based in Reading, the UK, OQC is building quantum computers and using quantum cloud software to help its customers solve some of humanity's most significant challenges, from climate change to new drug discoveries.

Last summer OQC also launched the UK's first Quantum Computing as-a-Service (QCaaS), bringing the quantum cloud computing system to the enterprise, at the fingertips of its customers and partners. OQC's platform takes its proprietary quantum technology to the market through a private cloud, where it will be used by strategic partners and customers to further experiment with quantum until ultimately they make breakthrough discoveries and tackle some of the world's most intractable.

ALIBABA GROUP

Founded by Chinese business magnate, investor and philanthropist Jack Ma in 1999, 2017 saw Alibaba release its cloud service subsidiary Aliyun ("Alibaba Cloud") and the Chinese Academy of Sciences jointly launched an 11-qubit quantum cloud computing service, which was at the time available to the public on the Quantum Computing Cloud Platform.

Its Quantum Lab — a member of the international quantum computing community — currently offers the Alibaba Cloud Quantum Development Platform (ACQDP) — a simulator-driven development tool for quantum algorithms and quantum computers.

QUANTINUUM (QUANTUM CLOUD SERVICES)

Formed when Honeywell Quantum Solutions and Cambridge Quantum Computing came together in late 2021, Quantinuum is a quantum cloud computing supplier offering, hardware-diverse software development platform, an operating system, real-world applications, and high-performing quantum systems.

The Quantinuum AI platform incorporates Quantum Natural Language Processing, Cloud-Based Quantum Machine Learning services, and Quantum Deep Learning - all of which will exponentially increase processing speed over today's classical solutions.

The company's TKET - an advanced quantum computing software development kit for the creation and execution of programs for gate-based quantum computers - is platform-inclusive, and its state-of-the-art circuit optimization routines allow users to extract as much power as possible from any of today's Noisy Intermediate-Scale Quantum (NISQ) devices. TKET is open source and easily accessible through the PyTKET Python package, with extension modules providing compatibility with many quantum computers, classical simulators, and popular quantum software libraries.

Applications of Quantum Computing in the Cloud

By harnessing the power of quantum algorithms and resources, researchers and businesses can tackle complex problems and unlock new frontiers of knowledge. Let's explore some of the key applications of quantum computing in the cloud.

Optimization and Operations Research

Quantum algorithms, like Quantum Approximate Optimisation Algorithm (QAOA) and the Quantum Annealing Algorithm, can solve complex optimisation problems at an unprecedented speed. Cloud-based quantum computing platforms allow users to test and develop these algorithms, enabling businesses to optimize their operations and take informed decisions based on quantum-optimised solutions.

Quantum Machine Learning

Quantum machine learning is an emerging field that combines the power of quantum computing with the principles of machine learning. In the cloud, researchers can explore quantum machine learning algorithms that leverage the unique properties of quantum systems to enhance data analysis and pattern recognition tasks. QML algorithms have the potential to outperform classical machine learning algorithms in domains like quantum chemistry, cryptography, financial modelling and natural language processing, enabling the discovery of new insights from complex datasets.

Drug Discovery and Material Science

Quantum computing holds tremendous promise for drug discovery and material science. Quantum simulations can accurately model molecular interactions, which are essential for understanding chemical reactions, predicting the properties of materials, and designing new drugs. In the cloud, researchers can leverage the power of quantum computing to accelerate the simulation of complex molecules, significantly reducing the time and cost involved in drug discovery and material science research. This enables scientists to explore novel compounds, optimise drug candidates, and discover materials with tailored properties, paving the way for groundbreaking advancements in healthcare and material engineering.

Future of Quantum Computing in the Cloud

As advancements in hardware, algorithms, and software continue, quantum computing holds immense potential for advancements and breakthroughs and will impact various industries and sectors, driving innovation, enabling breakthroughs, and transforming the way we solve complex problems. Through tackling challenges and capitalizing on opportunities, we can unleash the complete potential of cloud-based quantum computing, heralding a fresh age of technological progress.

Advancements in Quantum Computing

As the field continues to evolve, several emerging trends are shaping the future of quantum computing:

- **Increasing Qubit Counts**: Quantum hardware is rapidly advancing, with efforts focused on increasing the number of qubits in quantum processors. As qubit counts increase, quantum computers will become more powerful, capable of solving larger and more complex problems.
- **Error Correction and Noise Mitigation**: Research in error correction techniques and noise mitigation is crucial for improving the reliability and stability of quantum computations. Advancements in error correction codes and error mitigation strategies will enable quantum computers to deliver more accurate and reliable results.
- **Hybrid Quantum-Classical Architectures**: Hybrid quantum-classical architectures combine the strengths of classical and quantum computing to solve complex problems efficiently. These architectures leverage classical computers to perform preprocessing and post-processing tasks while offloading computationally intensive tasks to quantum processors. This approach opens up new opportunities for solving problems that are beyond the reach of classical computing alone.

Advantages of Quantum Computing

Quantum computing platforms hosted in the cloud offer users availability, removing the necessity for substantial upfront investments in infrastructure. Nevertheless, every revolutionizing technology has its share of benefits and drawbacks. Thus, let us delve into the merits and hurdles of cloud-based quantum computing and uncover the strategies employed by quantum computing providers to address them.

- **Accessibility:** Cloud-based Quantum computing democratises access to this cutting-edge technology. Previously, quantum computing was limited to specialised research institutions and organisations with significant resources. Cloud-based quantum computing platforms, such as AWS Quantum Computing, Google Quantum Computing, IBM Quantum Experience and Microsoft Azure Quantum, provides a user-friendly interface and infrastructure to experiment with quantum algorithms and run quantum simulations. This accessibility allows researchers, developers, and businesses to explore the potential of quantum computing without requiring substantial investments in hardware and infrastructure.
- **Scalability:** Cloud providers can dynamically scale their quantum infrastructure to accommodate increased demand and advancements in quantum hardware. As quantum computers evolve and qubit counts increase, cloud users can leverage these advancements without needing to make significant upgrades to their own infrastructure.
- **Flexibility and Experimentation:** Cloud-based quantum simulators allow users to simulate quantum circuits and test algorithms without the need for physical quantum hardware. This flexibility enables rapid prototyping, algorithm development, and the exploration of new use cases, fostering innovation and discovery.
- **Collaboration and Community:** Cloud-based quantum computing platforms facilitate collaboration among researchers, developers, and enthusiasts, allowing users to share knowledge and ideas as well as collaborate on quantum projects. This collaborative environment helps to accelerate advancements in quantum computing, fostering a vibrant community that pushes the boundaries of the emerging technologies.

Ethical and Societal Implications of Quantum Computing

Quantum computing, with its immense power and potential, brings forth a range of ethical and societal considerations. As this technology advances, it is crucial to examine the ethical implications, address potential risks, and ensure responsible and ethical use of quantum computing technology.

- **Privacy and Data Security:** Quantum computing has the potential to break traditional cryptographic algorithms, raising concerns about data privacy and security. As quantum-resistant encryption algorithms are developed, it is important to ensure the protection of sensitive information and safeguard privacy rights.
- **Fairness and Bias:** As quantum machine learning algorithms evolve, it is vital to address issues of fairness, bias, and transparency. Efforts should be made to prevent the propagation of biases present in training data and ensure that quantum machine learning models are fair, transparent, and accountable.
- **Intellectual Property and Patenting:** Quantum computing advancements may lead to breakthroughs that could have significant intellectual property implications. Questions arise regarding patentability, ownership, and the sharing of quantum computing inventions. Developing fair and inclusive policies is crucial to promote innovation while safeguarding intellectual property rights.
- **Ethical Frameworks and Regulations:** Establishing ethical frameworks, guidelines, and regulations for the development, deployment, and use of quantum computing is essential. These frameworks should address issues such as privacy, fairness, accountability, and the responsible handling of sensitive data.
- **International Collaboration:** Global collaboration and coordination among governments, organizations, and researchers are crucial to address ethical and societal implications at an international level. Collaborative efforts can result in development of ethical standards, policies, and best practices that promote responsible use of quantum computing technology.
- **Ethical Education and Public Awareness:** Promoting public awareness and education about quantum computing and its ethical implications is vital. Encouraging open dialogue and public engagement can help foster a better understanding of the technology and its potential impact, empowering individuals to make informed decisions and shape ethical policies.

CHAPTER-6

QUANTUM CRYPTOGRAPHY AND QUANTUM COMMUNICATION

QUANTUM CRYPTOGRAPHY

Quantum cryptography is a method of encryption that uses the naturally occurring properties of quantum mechanics to secure and transmit data in a way that cannot be hacked.

Cryptography is the process of encrypting and protecting data so that only the person who has the right secret key can decrypt it. Quantum cryptography is different from traditional cryptographic systems in that it relies on physics, rather than mathematics, as the key aspect of its security model.

Quantum cryptography is a system that is completely secure against being compromised without the knowledge of the message sender or the receiver. That is, it is impossible to copy or view data encoded in a quantum state without alerting the sender or receiver. Quantum cryptography should also remain safe against those using quantum computing as well.

Quantum cryptography uses individual particles of light, or photons, to transmit data over fiber optic wire. The photons represent binary bits. The security of the system relies on quantum mechanics. These secure properties include the following:

- particles can exist in more than one place or state at a time;
- a quantum property cannot be observed without changing or disturbing it; and
- whole particles cannot be copied.

These properties make it impossible to measure the quantum state of any system without disturbing that system.

Photons are used for quantum cryptography because they offer all the necessary qualities needed: Their behavior is well understood, and they are information carriers in optical fiber cables. One of the best-known examples of quantum cryptography currently is quantum key distribution (QKD), which provides a secure method for key exchange.

Unlike traditional cryptography, which is built on mathematics, quantum cryptography is built on the laws of physics. Specifically, quantum cryptography relies on the unique principles of quantum mechanics:

- **Particles are inherently uncertain:** On a quantum level, particles can simultaneously exist in more than one place or in more than one state of being at the same time. And it is impossible to predict their exact quantum state.
- **Photons can be measured randomly in binary positions:** Photons, the smallest particles of light, can be set to have specific polarities, or spins, which can serve as a binary counterpart for the ones and zeros of classical computational systems.
- **A quantum system cannot be measured without being altered:** According to the laws of quantum physics, the basic act of measuring or even observing a quantum system will always have a measurable effect on that system.
- **Particles can be partially, but not totally cloned:** While the properties of some particles can be cloned, a 100% clone is believed to be impossible.

How Quantum Cryptography Works

Quantum cryptography, or quantum key distribution (QKD), uses a series of photons (light particles) to transmit data from one location to another over a fiber optic cable. By comparing measurements of the properties of a fraction of these photons, the two endpoints can determine what the key is and if it is safe to use.

Breaking the process down further helps to explain it better.

- The sender transmits photons through a filter (or polarizer) which randomly gives them one of four possible polarizations and bit designations: Vertical (One bit), Horizontal (Zero bit), 45 degree right (One bit), or 45 degree left (Zero bit).
- The photons travel to a receiver, which uses two beam splitters (horizontal/vertical and diagonal) to "read" the polarization of each photon. The receiver does not know which beam splitter to use for each photon and has to guess which one to use.
- Once the stream of photons has been sent, the receiver tells the sender which beam splitter was used for each of the photons in the sequence they were sent, and the sender compares that information with the sequence

of polarizers used to send the key. The photons that were read using the wrong beam splitter are discarded, and the resulting sequence of bits becomes the key.

If the photon is read or copied in any way by an eavesdropper, the photon's state will change. The change will be detected by the endpoints. In other words, this means you cannot read the photon and forward it on or make a copy of it without being detected.

Example of how quantum encryption works

Imagine you have two people, Alice and Bob, who want to send a secret to each other that no one else can intercept. With QKD, Alice sends Bob a series of polarized photons over a fiber optic cable. This cable doesn't need to be secured because the photons have a randomized quantum state.

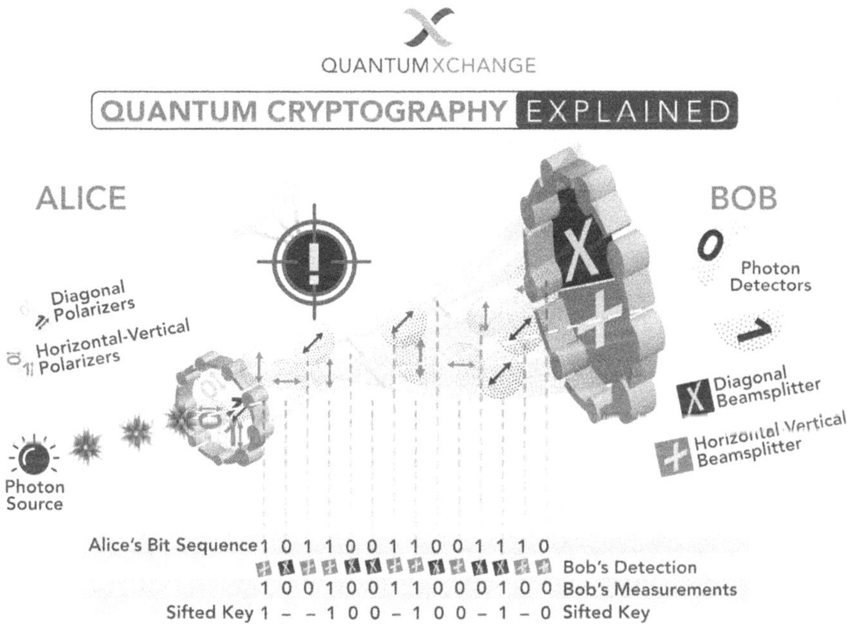

Quantum Cryptography: Explained

If an eavesdropper, named Eve, tries to listen in on the conversation, she has to read each photon to read the secret. Then she must pass that photon on to Bob. By reading the photon, Eve alters the photon's quantum state, which introduces errors into the quantum key. This alerts Alice and Bob that someone is listening and the key has been compromised, so they discard the key. Alice has to send Bob a new key that isn't compromised, and then Bob can use that key to read the secret.

History

Quantum cryptography was first proposed by Stephen Weisner in his work "Conjugate Coding" in the early 1970s. The proposal was published in 1983 in Sigact

News, and by that time two scientists Bennet and Brassard, who were familiar with Weisner's ideas, were ready to publish their own ideas. In 1984, they produced the first quantum cryptography protocol, the "BB84." The first experimental prototype based on this was made in 1991. It operated over a distance of 32 centimeters. Over time, the technology has been refined and the distance increased to kilometers.

More recently, in June 2003, a team at the University of Vienna transmitted entangled photons across the river Danube, through free space. In April 2004, the first money transfer encrypted by quantum keys occurred between two Austrian banks. The two buildings were 500 meters apart, yet fibre optics were fed through 1.5 kilometers of sewage system to link them together. Then on June 4th, 2004 the following excerpt was published in newscientist.com:

The first computer network in which communication is secured with quantum cryptography is up and running in Cambridge, Massachusetts. Chip Elliott, leader of the quantum engineering team at BBN Technologies in Cambridge, sent the first packets of data across the Quantum Net (Qnet) on Thursday. The project is funded by the Pentagon's Defense Advanced Research Projects Agency. Currently the network only consists of six servers, but they can be integrated with regular servers and clients on the internet. Qnet's creators say the implementation of more nodes in banks and credit card companies could make exchanging sensitive data over the internet more secure than it is with current cryptography systems. The data in Qnet flows through ordinary fibre optic cables and stretches the 10 kilometers from BBN to Harvard University... Qnet is the first network consisting of more than two nodes to use quantum cryptography - a more complex challenge [than the transfer of keys between two banks]... In Qnet, software-controlled optical switches made of lithium niobate crystals steer photons down the correct optical fibre.

The process of quantum coding

Quantum cryptography is not replacing traditional cryptography; rather, it allows for a more secure transfer of the keys used in encoding and decoding. The amount of information which can be transferred using quantum cryptography is not very large or very fast, but it is very secure.

The maximum speed, scale and security of the transfer is achieved by sending the secret key using quantum coding, but encoding and sending the data itself using traditional methods and algorithms. This way the users can ensure more privacy by making sure their key is as secure as modern technology can make it, while still transferring the information as quickly as possible.

Thus note than in the discussion that follows, "information exchange" refers just to the secret key, which is later used to decode the bulk of the information, not to the information itself. Many algorithms of encoding and decoding information using a given key have been created already, many years before quantum cryptography came into existence, and so they will not be discussed here.

Outline of the process

In quantum cryptography, data is converted to bits of 0s and 1s, and then transferred using polarized photons. Photons are put into a particular quantum state by the sender and are observed by the recipient. A photon can be in one of four polarizations: 90, 0, 45 and -45 degrees, and can be measured using three different bases: rectilinear (horizontal or vertical), circular (left-circular or right-circular), and diagonal. Only the rectilinear and circular bases are used here. The receiver can distinguish between a 0 and 90 degrees, or -45 and 45 degrees polarizations. Due to the physical principles, a measurement destroys the photon, so it is impossible to carry out both observations.

Thus the receiver not only needs to receive the signals, but also measure them with respect to the correct bases. This information can not be transferred between the sender and the receiver because, if intercepted, would allow a third party to obtain the secret key. Instead, the receiver randomly chooses one of the two: it either distinguishes between a 0 and 90, or -45 and 45 degree polarizations for each signal.

Then the receiver contacts the sender, and publicly discusses which type of measurement was done for each bit. The sender confirms which types were correct, and the sender and the receiver both discards the bits that weren't measured accurately. This constitutes the key.

Accuracy and security

Now the two parties must make sure that their keys are the same, but do so in a way that wouldn't violate the security of the transfer. This is a crucial step because there might be errors introduced into the transfer by random noise or by eavesdroppers. To ensure the maximum accuracy without revealing the specific bits received, the sender and the receiver can discuss groups of bits instead of individual ones, and can compare the parity (the remainder when the sum is divided by 2) within those groups.

This can even be done in public, as long as the individual bits remain secret. Groups with discrepancies in parity can then be discarded, or broken down into other groups (still ensuring that they are sufficiently large as to not reveal too much), one or more of which is discarded or corrected. In the end this process, if repeated enough times, guarantees that the keys are arbitrarily similar.

Furthermore, if after comparing their groups of bits this way, the sender and the receiver discard an agreed-upon bit, such as the last one, the parity revealed becomes useless to any eavesdroppers. Also, if desired, a publicly chosen hash function, h, can be used to map the string of received bits, x, into h(x), which can now be used as the key instead of x. It can be shown that by doing so, the eavesdropper's expected knowledge of h(x) can get arbitrarily small.

Step-by-step example

A very nice online demonstration of the process of transferring information using quantum cryptography methods, created by Fred Henle, is located at http://monet.mercersburg.edu/henle/bb84/. The following is a specific step-by-step outline of the process, paraphrased and augmented from (3). Staying with the convention, Alice is used to refer to the sender, Bob to the receiver, and Eve to the eavesdropper in this description.

Sending

- Alice determines the polarization (horizontal, vertical, left-circular or right-circular) of each burst of photons which she's going to send to Bob. Since a lot of this information will later be discarded, this can probably be done randomly. The goal is not to transfer a specific key, but to agree on a key that is common to both parties.
- A light source from a light-emitting diode (LED) or from a laser is filtered to produce the desired polarized photons. Ideally, each pulse consists of a single photon. However, in real life it actually has to be a beam of light with very low intensity. If the intensity is too low, a pulse may be undetectable for the receiver, yet if it's too high, then the polarization of the photons can be detected discreetly (i.e. a photon from the beam can be measured by the eavesdropper with respect to both bases without any noticeable difference to the beam). Both cases are undesireable to say the least, so the intensity has to be regulated very carefully.

Receiving and converting

- Bob randomly generates a sequence of bases (rectilinear or circular), and measures the polarization of each photon with respect to one of them.
- Bob tells Alice which sequence of bases he used, without worrying about other people hearing this information.
- Alice publicly responds with which bases were chosen correctly.
- Alice and Bob discard all observations except for those with the correctly-chosen bases.
- The remaining observations are converted on to binary code (left-circular or horizontal is 0, and right-circular or vertical is 1).

Correcting errors - step 1

- Alice and Bob agree on random permutations of bits in the resulting string, to randomize the positions of errors. Two errors next to each other are very hard to detect, yet it is likely that an error with the instruments or because of random noise would alter a sequence of bits one after the other. Randomization helps account for that.
- The strings are partitioned into blocks of size k, with k ideally chosen to make the probability of multiple errors per block very small. Note that if Alice's string contains 101100 and Bob's contains 101111, the parity is the same, 1, even though there are two mistakes in the block. Making k small is one of the steps taken to minimize the chance of this happening, since the chances of having two errors in a block of size 50 is much less than in a block of 500, especially after the errors are randomized.
- Alice and Bob compute and exchange parities for each block. This information can be made public, but, to ensure security, the last bit of each block is then discarded, making the information useless for Eve.
- Any block with different reported is broken down further and a binary search is used to locate and correct the error. Alternatively, if the length of the key is already sufficiently large, those blocks could even be discarded.
- Steps 9-12 are then repeated with increasing block size, k, in an attempt to discover multiple errors that could've gone undetected within original blocks.

Correcting errors - step 2

- Finally, to determine if additional errors remain, Alice and Bob do another randomized check. They publicly agree on a random assortment of half the bit positions in their string, and compare parities, followed discarding the last digit, as always.
- If the strings are different, then there is ýÿ probability of a disagreement of parities. Then a binary search is used to find and eliminate error, as described above.
- After r repetitions of step 13 without disagreements, Alice and Bob can conclude that their strings disagree with probability (1/2)r, which can obviously be made arbitrarily small by increasing r.

Alternate methods of exchanging keys

Actually, the information can be exchanged in a number of ways, not just the one described above. Below is a brief description of two of those.

One-time pad method

- Alice generates two random bits, B1 and B2. She uses B1 to select the basis and B2 to select the polarization of the photon. Bob generates a random bit B3 and sets his detector to that basis. He then reads Alice's signal using that basis, and records B4.
- Alice and Bob compare B1 and B3, the bases they used, over a public channel. These bases will be the same half of the time, since Alice's base can be one of two things, and so can Bob's, so out of the four possibilities, namely (B1, B3) = (0, 0), (0, 1), (1, 0), (1, 1), two match.
- If B1 and B3 don't match, then the bit needs to be resent until they do match. Note that each time the bases should be chosen randomly, to ensure privacy.
- When B1 and B3 match, Alice and Bob record B2 and B4, knowing that they are the same unless Eve is listening, in which case she would be changing the states of the photons. Later comparing the strings using binary search as described in the previous section would allow Alice and Bob to detect any such interventions.

Quantum entanglement

This process uses entangled photons, which can be generated by firing a laser through a crystal and splitting a single photon into two. The most interesting thing about them is that, by the laws of physics, disturbing the state of one will instantly disturb the other, no matter how far apart they are. This is extremely useful in detecting eavesdroppers, as will be discussed below.

The technicalities of such a transfer are similar to the original process described, where Alice sends polarized photons to Bob, who measures them using randomly selected states. However, here a photon generator is placed between Alice and Bob so that pairs of entangled photons with the same polarization go to Alice and Bob at the same time. Then both parties measure the signals with randomly varying bases, and record the result and the time received.

After comparing the bases, they can discard the bits measured with different bases, and keep those that are the same. They can then test for errors using the algorithms described above. Note that while this method is very similar to the original one described, they are different in terms of security and detection of intervention, as described below.

Privacy measures

It is clear that transfers using quantum cryptography are much more secure than those that use traditional cryptography, because quantum methods rely on the laws of physics instead of the impracticality of calculating certain mathematical problems. Given the algorithms that exist today, those problems would required thousands of years to solve, but it is still not an impossible, and no one has proven that there does not exist and efficient algorithm which yields the result sooner, perhaps even in a matter of hours or minutes.

Quantum mechanics provides a way of transferring secret keys over extremely secure channels. After the keys are exchanged, there is very little concern that someone would be able to decode the data without these keys, since they are different every time and are always generated randomly, or at least become random after about half the bits are discarded to match the polarization states measured by Alice and Bob, and after the error-correcting algorithms. So the only real concern in the system is ensuring that Eve does not intercept the secret key during transfer, which is unlikely.

What makes quantum cryptography so secure is the fact that it's easy to detect eavesdroppers and correct the damage they cause. So the two parties are always aware if their channel is not very secure, assuming they take all the necessary percussions. However, due to some practical imperfections of this theoretically perfect system, as well as to the constant improvement of technology, there might still be some small loopholes.

Detecting eavesdropping

The key here is that it is impossible to measure the polarization of the photon without destroying it. So if Eve intercepts the signal and measures the photons, she will have to send new photons onto the receiver if she doesn't want to be detected. However, she will inevitably introduce errors, since she doesn't know which state to measure in, and so in which polarization to send them in. So Alice and Bob can simply check for errors by revealing a random subset of their generated sequence and comparing it publicly. If they are not satisfied with the error rate, they can try to set up a different channel. This ensures that while Alice and Bob can not stop Eve from listening in, they would always know that she is there.

A similar method can be used with entangled photon transfer. By the laws of physics, a change in the polarization of one photon in the pair will affect the other one, no matter how far apart they are. In order to eavesdrop, Eve would have to detect one of the photons and measure it, thus destroying half of the pair. This act will end the quantum relationship of the two members of the pair, which is very easy to detect by Alice and Bob, and impossible to reverse for Eve. Without revealing the specific results of their measurements, the sender and the receiver can talk publicly and see where intervention has taken place.

Possible loopholes

The practical implementation of quantum cryptography is not perfect. For one, it is impossible to use single photons to transmit information, so small bursts of light are used instead. So it could be possible for Eve to isolate single photons from the beam and measure them, only reducing the intensity of the light slightly. This would be virtually impossible to detect, because this reduction could be attributed to the fact that light had to travel over a long distance, and there are possible imperfections in the channel.

These imperfections, or noise, are a big problem in detecting eavesdropping. Intervention by a third party and noise produce identical results as far as Alice and Bob are concerned, so since noise can never be entirely avoided in the physical world, they might have to sacrifice some of their privacy and hope that the interference they are getting is not coming from Eve. This might make eavesdropping without detection possible, as long as the attacker is operating very slowly and carefully; however, various methods have been suggested that could deal with this problem.

Quantum cloning

The techniques of quantum cryptography provide no protection against the so-called "bucket brigade," or "man-in-the-middle," attack, where the eavesdropper can intercept, receive, copy, and resend messages with perfect accuracy and without delay. However, it is believed that the laws of physics will prohibit such an eavesdropper from ever occurring. Nevertheless, while entangled photons are still considered absolutely safe, a group of Oxford researchers led by Antia Lama-Linares considered the possibility of eavesdropping on regular photon transfer, and were able to achieve amazing results.

In 1997, they started wondering how well they can copy a quantum state, or the polarization of the photon, and thus produce a "quantum clone." The theoretical accuracy limit of copying the clone is 5/6, or 83%. The group reported that they copied the quantum state with 81% accuracy. They used the process of stimulated emission, and sent the photon into a crystal with atomic states that have been excited by laser pulses. So when the photons entered, its presence stimulated the emission of the clone photon, which was in the same identical state. The only problem was that the crystal also spontaneously emitted light, which is the noise that prevented the theoretical accuracy from ever achieving 100%.

Potential dangers

There are two possible ways of viewing this result. One, presented by Richard Hughes of the Los Alamos National Laboratory in the US, is that this does not make quantum cryptography more susceptible to eavesdroppers. First, copying a transmission with 83% accuracy is not even close to decoding 5 out of 6 letters in the message. Second, there are various mathematical algorithms which were developed long before quantum cryptography, that allow the users to amplify the privacy of their exchanges even when communicating along non-secure channels. So as long as users are careful and assume the presence of eavesdroppers, they can amplify their privacy beyond Eve's ability to decode.

A different view, however, was presented by Hoi-Kwong Lo from the quantum computing and cryptography firm Magiq Technologies. He is worried that there are many possible technology developments in the near future and many loopholes in the system which are not obvious to anybody today, but may well be discovered tomorrow. Theoretical safety against eavesdroppers is not enough, and mathematical tricks can not fully compensate for the possible danger of cloning. All that matters is the physical safety of the information, which is obviously threatened by the ability to clone photons, which was thought to be impossible earlier.

Prospects

Clearly, quantum cryptography is still a long way from being common in information transfer, because the real world is still a long way from theoretical perfection. However, it's important to keep in mind that the basic foundation for this great technique has been laid, and so now it only needs to be refined.

Current limitations

For now, computers capable to transmitting information using quantum cryptography are very large, custom-made and, thus, expensive. A couple of banks have already taken advantage of this security method, but few other organizations would be able to afford it in the foreseeable future.

With regards to entangled photons, which seem to be absolutely safe, there is also a serious practical problem not only with the cost, but also with keeping them entangled long enough to meet the needs of the real world. While the system is perfect in theory, it is going to be very hard to implement it in practice.

Another problem is that for distances beyond 50 kilometers or so, the noise becomes so great that error rates skyrocket. This not only leaves the channel very vulnerable for eavesdroppers, but also makes it virtually impossible to send information. However, it is potentially possible for quantum keys to be exchanged through the air in the future. Tiny telescopes would then have to be aligned to detect the signal. Some calculations even suggest that photons could be detected by a satellite, which would allow communication between continents!

The future of quantum cryptography

For now, non-quantum cryptography is still very safe, because it relies on algorithms that can't be cracked in less than the lifetime of the universe by all the currently existing computers. So in theory, there is not much need for quantum cryptography yet; however, we never know when technology will take a leap forward and quantum techniques will become necessary to protect our information. When quantum computers will come into play, the computational speeds will increase dramatically, so the mathematical complexity of algorithms will become less of a challenge. It is still debatable whether or not it will be possible to simply increase the numbers use in the algorithms and thus increase the complexity enough to outrun even quantum computer.

Yet there is no debate about the fact that quantum cryptography is a true breakthrough in the field. It is still being refined and developed further. However, already it is clear that even with its current imperfections, it is many steps above everything that was developed before it. All we need is some years, or maybe decades or even centuries, to refine the technique and make it practical in the real world.

QUANTUM COMMUNICATION

- Quantum communication is an amalgamation of quantum mechanics and modern communication and Information Technology to study data transmission and processing. It takes advantage of the laws of quantum physics to protect data and securely transmit data.
- Conventionally, sensitive data is encrypted and sent through fibre optic cables with a digital "key" to decrypt the information. This data is transmitted in classical binary bits (0s and 1s), which makes it vulnerable to hackers who can read and copy it without a trace. Theoretically, this makes these networks ultrasecure.
- However, in a quantum communication network, data is transmitted via quantum bits or qubits. Qubits are particles, usually photons of light, in a superposition state, i.e., they can be in multiple states and represent numerous combinations of 0 and 1. If a hacker tries to read this data, the qubits would "collapse" from their fragile quantum state to either a 0 or 1, thereby leaving a clear trace of external activity.

Definition

Quantum communication is a groundbreaking field that leverages the principles of quantum mechanics to transmit information. Unlike classical communication, which uses classical bits (0 or 1), quantum communication employs quantum bits or qubits. These qubits can exist in a superposition of states, allowing for more complex and secure communication.

Historical Background

The history of quantum communication is intertwined with the development of quantum mechanics itself:

- **Early 1900s:** Pioneers like Max Planck and Albert Einstein laid the foundation of quantum mechanics, challenging classical physics.
- **1980s:** The concept of quantum communication took shape with the proposal of quantum key distribution (QKD) by Stephen Wiesner, Charles Bennett, and others.
- **1990s to Present:** The field has seen rapid advancements, with practical applications emerging and ongoing research exploring new possibilities.

Importance and Applications

Quantum communication's significance lies in its unparalleled security and efficiency:

- **Secure Banking:** Traditional encryption can be vulnerable to attacks, but quantum communication offers a theoretically unbreakable solution.
- **Military Communications:** Governments and defense organizations are investing in quantum communication to protect sensitive information.
- **Healthcare:** Patient data security is paramount, and quantum communication provides a robust safeguard.
- **Scientific Research:** Quantum communication facilitates secure and efficient data sharing among research institutions.

Quantum Bits (Qubits)

Explanation of Qubits

Qubits are the building blocks of quantum information. Unlike classical bits, which are binary, qubits can exist in a superposition of both 0 and 1 states simultaneously. This property allows for more complex computations and data encoding.

Superposition

Superposition is a fundamental quantum principle. A qubit in superposition can be mathematically represented as:

$$|\psi\rangle = \alpha(0)+\beta|1\rangle$$

Where, α and β are complex numbers, and the probabilities of measuring the qubit in state 0 or 1 are given by $|\alpha|^2$ and $|\beta|^2$, respectively.

Entanglement

Entanglement is another unique quantum phenomenon. When qubits are entangled, the state of one qubit is directly related to the state of another, regardless of the distance between them. This property is central to many quantum communication protocols and has been experimentally verified.

Quantum Key Distribution (QKD)

Explanation of QKD

Quantum Key Distribution (QKD) is a method that enables two parties to share a secret cryptographic key securely. It uses the principles of quantum mechanics to detect any eavesdropping attempts, ensuring the integrity and confidentiality of the communication.

Protocols

- **BB84:** Proposed by Bennett and Brassard in 1984, BB84 uses the polarization of photons to create a secure key. It's one of the first and most well-known QKD protocols.
- **E91:** Proposed by Ekert in 1991, E91 uses entangled photon pairs, making it more resilient against certain attacks.

Security Aspects

Quantum Key Distribution (QKD) is renowned for its unparalleled security features, which are rooted in the fundamental principles of quantum mechanics. Below are the key aspects that contribute to the robust security of QKD:

No-Cloning Theorem

The no-cloning theorem states that it is impossible to create an exact copy of an arbitrary unknown quantum state. This principle ensures that any eavesdropping attempt to clone the quantum key will inevitably fail. An eavesdropper cannot make perfect copies of the qubits being transmitted without altering the original state, making unauthorized duplication impossible.

Heisenberg's Uncertainty Principle

Heisenberg's uncertainty principle plays a crucial role in QKD security. It asserts that certain pairs of physical properties, like position and momentum, cannot be simultaneously measured with perfect accuracy. In the context of QKD, any attempt to measure the quantum key's qubits will introduce disturbances, alerting the communicating parties to potential eavesdropping.

Quantum Entanglement

Some QKD protocols, such as the E91, utilize quantum entanglement to enhance security. Entangled qubits share a correlated state, and any measurement on one qubit immediately affects the other, regardless of the distance between them. This property can be used to detect eavesdropping, as unauthorized measurements will disrupt the entanglement.

Privacy Amplification

Privacy amplification is a technique used in QKD to further secure the key. Even if an eavesdropper gains partial information about the key, privacy amplification allows the legitimate parties to distill a shorter key that is virtually unknown to the eavesdropper. This process ensures that the final key remains secure.

Authentication

Authentication protocols are often integrated with QKD to verify the identities of the communicating parties. This ensures that the key is being exchanged between legitimate parties and not an impersonator. Authentication adds an additional layer of security to the quantum key exchange process.

Real-World Implementations and Challenges

While QKD offers theoretical security guarantees, real-world implementations must consider potential vulnerabilities in the physical devices and communication channels. Side-channel attacks, where an attacker exploits physical imperfections in the devices, are a concern. Ongoing research and development are addressing these challenges, ensuring that QKD remains secure in practical applications.

Quantum Teleportation

Explanation of Quantum Teleportation

Quantum teleportation is the process of transferring the state of a quantum system from one location to another. Unlike science fiction teleportation, it doesn't transport matter but rather the information about a quantum state.

Mathematical Representation

The process can be described using the following equation:

$$|\psi\rangle = \alpha(0) + \beta|1\rangle$$

Here, $|\psi\rangle$ represents the quantum state being teleported, and α and β are complex coefficients.

Practical Applications

Quantum teleportation has been experimentally demonstrated over significant distances. It holds promise for quantum networking and could revolutionize long-distance secure communication.

Quantum Repeaters and Networks

Explanation of Quantum Repeaters

Quantum repeaters are devices that extend the range of quantum communication. They reduce the loss of quantum information over long distances, enabling more extensive quantum networks.

Quantum Networks

Quantum networks connect multiple quantum devices, facilitating complex quantum computations and secure communication. They are essential for building a quantum internet, where quantum information can be transmitted globally.

Challenges and Future Prospects

Future Developments

The future of quantum communication is not only promising but also filled with intriguing possibilities:

- **Global Quantum Networks:** The development of quantum repeaters and satellites equipped with quantum technology will enable the creation of global quantum networks. These networks will facilitate secure and efficient communication across continents.
- **Advancements in Quantum Cryptography:** Beyond QKD, new cryptographic protocols are being developed to enhance security further. Quantum-resistant algorithms are being explored to ensure that quantum technology itself doesn't render current cryptographic methods obsolete.
- **Integration with Classical Systems:** Bridging quantum and classical communication systems is vital for the gradual transition to a quantum era. Research is underway to create hybrid systems that leverage the best of both quantum and classical technologies.
- **Quantum Internet:** The concept of a quantum internet goes beyond secure communication. It encompasses quantum-enhanced computation, distributed quantum computing, and more. The quantum internet would revolutionize how we compute, communicate, and secure information.
- **Regulatory and Ethical Considerations:** As quantum communication advances, there will be a need for regulations and ethical guidelines. Balancing security, privacy, and accessibility will be key challenges to address.

QUANTUM KEY DISTRIBUTION (QKD)

Quantum cryptography is a technology that relies on quantum physics to secure the distribution of symmetric encryption keys. A more accurate name for it is quantum key distribution (QKD). It works by sending photons, which are "quantum particles" of light, across optical links. Today, these links are based on optical fibers, with a corresponding distance limitation caused by loss. Work is also underway to leverage trusted quantum satellites to enable end-to-end global coverage.

The principles of quantum physics stipulate that observation of a quantum state causes perturbation. The various QKD protocols are designed to ensure that any attempt by an eavesdropper to observe the transmitted photons will indeed perturb the transmission. This perturbation will lead to transmission errors, which can be detected by the legitimate users. This is used to verify the security of the distributed keys.

QKD implementation therefore requires interactions between the legitimate users. These interactions need to be authenticated. This can be achieved through various cryptographic means.

The end-result is that QKD can utilize an authenticated communication channel and transform it into a confidential communication channel.

Note that, in classical information theory, a provably secure (also known as Information Theoretically Secure or ITS) authenticated channel only requires a short secret key, regardless of the amount of data, while a provably secure confidential channel requires a secret key that is as long as the transmitted data. QKD, which precisely provides a provably secure confidential channel with a short initial secret key, is therefore a first example of a quantum advantage, which cannot be achieved classically.

In order to achieve ITS, QKD should be combined with One-Time Pad (OTP) encryption. However, an OTP requires keys, which are as long as the data to be encrypted and can be used only once.

This would impose strong limitations on the available bandwidth because the key distribution rate of QKD is typically 1,000 to 10,000 times slower than conventional optical communications.

Therefore, in practical implementations, QKD is often combined with conventional symmetric encryption, such as AES, and used to frequently refresh short encryption keys. This is sufficient to provide quantum-safe security.

Global Developments

Recently there has been remarkable progress in the deployment of quantum technologies in communication infrastructures, with several quantum key distribution (QKD) networks under construction worldwide. In the UK, metropolitan quantum networks have been built by the Quantum Communications

Hub in Cambridge and Bristol, connected by a long-distance link via London. Quantum digital signatures were demonstrated in the NICT metro network in Tokyo. Meanwhile a 2000 km backbone connects Beijing and Shanghai in China, while the Micius satellite will extend QKD to global distances. The current high level of activity in quantum communications means that there is a pressing need to develop industry standards for the technology.

Unique Advantages of Quantum Cryptography Interest in quantum cryptography stems from its unique security properties derived directly from the Laws on Nature, rather than assumptions about the diûculty of certain mathematical operations. It will allow networks that are more resilient to technological advances in the future. There is a concern that network communications that are encrypted using conventional public-key cryptography may be stored today and decrypted in the future when more powerful processors or new cryptanalysis methods are available. In contrast, quantum cryptographic protocols should be resilient to all advances in computing and mathematics.

The first applications of quantum cryptography are likely to be those requiring long-term secrecy, such as encryption of sensitive government or corporate data or individuals' health records. Recently demonstrated examples include secure communication of human genome sequences and inter-site data replication in the financial sector.

The Threat of Quantum Computers

Quantum cryptography will also be secure from a quantum computer. Quantum computers can process the inputs of a calculation in parallel and can therefore solve certain numerical problems much more eûciently than a "classical" processor. We know that a quantum computer can factorise large integers very eûciently. As the factorization problem is the basis of conventional public-key cryptography, this would significantly weaken many of the techniques that we rely on today. As such there is a pressing need to develop cryptography that will remain secure when large scale quantum computers become available. The solution to these new threats is likely to involve quantum cryptography and new quantum-resistant algorithms, with improved resilience to number-crunching by a quantum computer.

The Need for Industrial Standards

Standards are essential for ensuring the interoperability of equipment and protocols in complex systems and stimulating a supply chain for components, assemblies, and applications through the definition of common interfaces. Without standards, there would be no global networks for fibre optic and mobile communications or low-cost consumer electronics based on reliable and widely available components from multiple suppliers. New standards are required to integrate quantum communications into networks and stimulate their commercialization.

Several Group Specification documents have been published on QKD Use Cases:

- Application Interfaces
- Security Proofs
- Module Specification
- Characterization of Components
- A standard interface to deliver key material to applications
- Device and communication channel parameters for QKD deployments

ETSI Industry Specification Group (ISG) QKD is now working on various specifications:

- Protection Profile for QKD systems
- Protection against Trojan horse attacks in one-way QKD systems
- Characterization of the optical output of QKD transmitter modules
- A control interface for SDN (Software Defined Networks)
- A review of network architecture
- Application Interface (API) in response to new network developments

QKD: Concept and Protocol

QKD is used to distribute an encryption key for symmetric and asymmetric ciphers, and it is not to transmit any plain data between communication parties (usually called master and slave). In this era, a lot of QKD protocols have been created, nevertheless, few are used in practice . The QKD is merely used to negotiate secret quantum keys among parties through two communication channels, classical and quantum channels, like Unshielded Twisted Pair (UTP) and fiber optic channels. In a sense, QKD comes as an alternative to the existing "public/secret key distribution system.

The first invented protocol was BB84. This protocol, based on photon polarization (states aided to transmit classical information over a quantum channel), is the most reputable solution in practice quantum cryptographic environment. Others protocol, such as B92 or E91 are modified versions of the BB84 protocol. Both communication parties must have devices or simulators that can generate and detect pulses of light in different polarization. As shown in figure1, secure privacy of the BB84 protocol stemmed from encoding the classical information in non-orthogonal states (vertical-V, horizontal-H, left diagonal-LD and right diagonal-RD. The characteristic of quantum physics, the state cannot be measured without discarding or disturbing it, is a central feature that bolstered the strength of quantum cryptographic key.

In order to generate a secret quantum cryptographic key depending on BB84 protocol, two primary phases must be implemented.

- **Transmission**: a qubit randomly selected and sent based on photon polarization (Master side).
- **Negotiation**: two communication parties check the degree of compatibility between their key obtained.

In order to produce a final secret key in this phase, four primary stages must be achieved. These stages are:

Raw Key Extraction (RK)

The central purpose of RK is to eliminate all possible errors which occurred through qubits discussion over a quantum channel. Negotiated communication parties compare their photon polarizations are selected, then, nonvalent qubits will be eliminated, otherwise, the qubit will be considered.

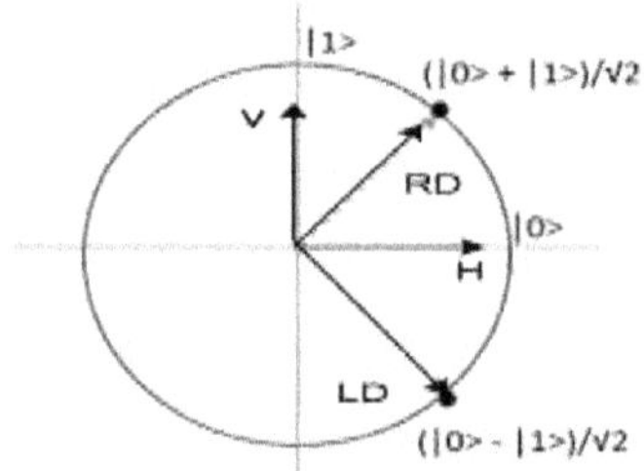

Photon states (P_s) orthogonal state

Error Estimation (EE)

The negotiation process is to resolve a quantum key might occur over a noisy-unsecured classical channel. Such channel can cause a partial key damage or unmet conditions due to physical noise of transmission medium. Therefore, in order to avoid this dilemma, both master and slave determine an error threshold value "E_{max}" when they are sure that there is no attacks on transmission medium. Then, after each QKD round, they compare some qubits of their RK in order to compute a transmission error rate "E". In a nutshell, if $E > E_{max}$ they can be sure about existence of an attack.

Key Reconciliation (KR)

In case of $E < E_{max}$, errors might/can be found within the non-valent parts of the raw key. KR is provided to minimize those errors within the key as possible. This stage consists of a number of sub-stages. Such dividing the raw key into blocks of length K bits, computing the parity bits for each block and parity comparison. Finally, those sup-stage are repeatedly executed by communication parties for N number of rounds.

PA is the final stage of quantum key extraction protocol (BB84) which applied to minimize the number of bits that an attack might know the raw resolved key from KR. Communication parties apply a shrinking method to their qubits sequences in a way that reduces the authentication cost and reduces an attacker presence.

Experimental Environment

In order to create an innovative system capable to simulate the processes of QKD system and quantum computation, the illustration and description of physical processes must be achieved. Any process of quantum mechanics can be depicted as an operator (operator is formalized as multiplication by a matrix). Consequently, the logic gates (circuits), embrace the operator as a square matrix, are given in matrices of vectors. Drastically, matrices illustration is a delightful topic in scientific quantum computing. Furthermore, many tools and random algorithms are considered in the simulation of QKD.

Generally, Master and Slave must be guaranteed an acceptance secure communication without the presence of the attack. Consequently, in order to obtain the quantum cryptographic key, two communication parties going to be executed the stages of the QKD-BB84 (RK, EE, KR and PA).

As shown in figure below, the main hardware requirements for the deployment of BB84 simulation are at least two computers machines connected by switches. Each machine has a static IP (computer join to domain) to communicate over the switch and on each machine will implement assigned software (Master, Slave). The simulation is performed using a Core i5 (4.8 GHz) processor associated with 8GB of RAM as a Master hardware and a Core i3 (2.4 GHz) processor associated with 4GB of RAM as a Slave hardware.

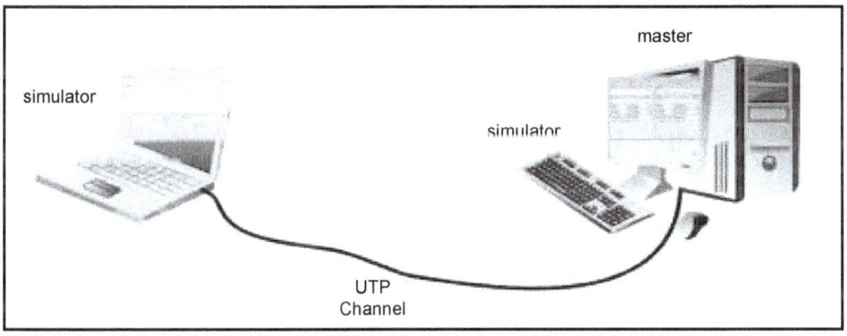

Experimental environment for QKD –BB84

In addition, the main parameter for system development (simulation environment) such as states, mathematics operations, randomness algorithms, etc.

Thus, an important feature of the quantum key distribution is that two communicating users can find out whether a third party has tried to gain knowledge of the key, and in that case, the key distribution can be aborted. The feature of QKD is that any intervention or tampering in quantum channel will get detected and leads to destruction of key. QKD solution consists of "Alice" (QKD Transmitter) and "BOB" (QKD Receiver) nodes which are connected to each other through a Quantum Channel and Classical Channel, both implemented using Single Mode Optical Fibers.

The following figure shows typical deployment scenario of QKD solution.

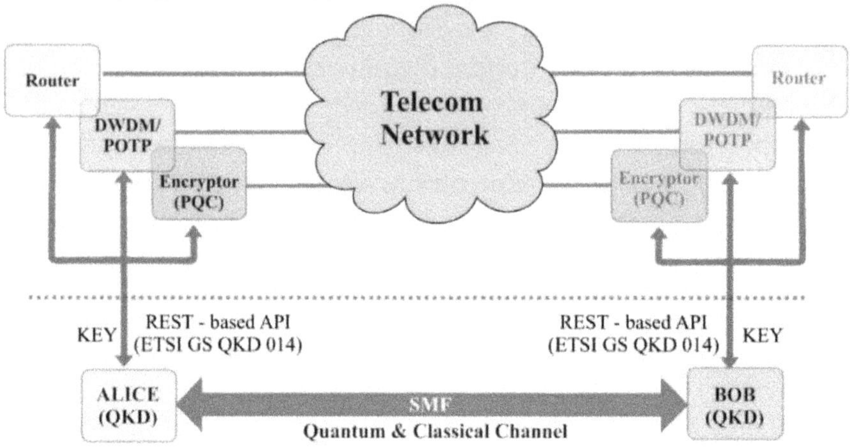

The secured keys are provided to other Network Elements (like Encryptor, Router, DWDM – Dense Wavelength Division Multiplexing equipment, POTP – Packet Optical Transport Platform etc.) over a standardized interface. In the figure, Post-Quantum-Cryptography (PQC) refers to the new upcoming cryptography techniques that can be used to protect future communication systems from the threat of Quantum Computers. This is an alternate approach to address the threat posed by the advancement in Quantum Computing and both QKD and PQC can be combined to offer maximum security. NIST (National Institute of Standards & Technology), USA is in the process of standardizing the Post-Quantum Cryptographic algorithms.

C-DOT has its own in-house developed PQC encryptor which can be used as shown in the figure above for enhanced security requirements.

It has become imperative both for government and industries to be prepared to develop and deploy these emerging and disruptive technologies in order to secure critical communication infrastructure, financial transactions, strategic & defense networks etc.

System Features

- Any intervention or tempering in quantum channel will get detected and leads to destruction of the key at both Alice and Bob Nodes.
- Supports DPS (Differential Phase Shift) and COW (Coherent One Way) protocols.
- Hardware-based (FPGA) key processing for high key distribution rate
- True Random Number Generator (TRNG) in both Alice & Bob nodes
- Performance monitoring and Alarm generation for errors

- Provide Variable Key Length on request
- RESTful API for Key distribution
- Key exchange through Ethernet & USB interfaces
- Supports > 100 Km Single Mode Fiber (SMF) for the Quantum Channel
- Support Local Management Interface (LMI)
- Compact & Standard 19" Rack mountable
- Graphical User Interface (GUI) to control and operate the CDOT-QKD solution

QUANTUM TELEPORTATION

Quantum teleportation is a technique to transfer quantum information from source to destination by employing the entangled states. Namely, in quantum teleportation, entanglement in the Bell state (EPR pair) is used to transport arbitrary quantum state $|\psi\rangle$ between two distant observers A and B (often called Alice and Bob). The quantum teleportation system employs three qubits: qubit 1 is an arbitrary state to be teleported, while qubits 2 and 3 are in the Bell state $|B_{00}\rangle(|00|11\rangle/2$. The operation principle is shown in Fig. below for an input state $|x\rangle$, where $x = 0,1$. Evaluation of the three-qubit state in five characteristic points of the quantum circuit is shown as well. The input three-qubit state at point (1) can be written as:

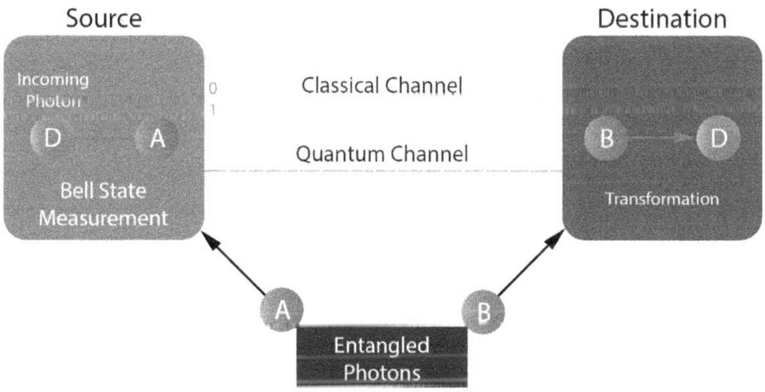

The quantum teleportation principle.

Quantum teleportation is a technique for transferring quantum information from a sender at one location to a receiver some distance away. While teleportation is commonly portrayed in science fiction as a means to transfer physical objects from one location to the next, quantum teleportation only transfers quantum information. The sender does not have to know the particular quantum state being transferred. Moreover, the location of the recipient can be unknown, but to complete the quantum teleportation, classical information needs to be sent from sender to receiver. Because classical information needs to be sent, quantum teleportation cannot occur faster than the speed of light.

The Quantum Teleportation Process

The process of quantum teleportation is a complex, multi-step procedure that, when broken down, can be understood in simpler terms.

- **Entanglement Creation:** Quantum teleportation begins with creating an entangled pair of particles, typically called a Bell pair. These particles are separated and each one is assigned a specific role.
- **Preparation of the Quantum State:** The sender, who wishes to teleport information, prepares a quantum state using a third particle. This state contains the information to be teleported.
- **Bell Measurement:** The sender then performs a special type of measurement on both the quantum state to be teleported and their part of the entangled Bell pair.
- **Transmission of Information:** The results of the measurement are sent to the receiver via classical communication. This information is crucial to completing the teleportation process.
- **Receiver's Operation:** Armed with the measurement results, the receiver performs a quantum operation on their entangled particle.
- **Completion of Teleportation:** The receiver's entangled particle takes on the quantum state of the sender's original particle, effectively teleporting the quantum information.

The Importance of Quantum Teleportation

Quantum teleportation might sound like a fascinating party trick, but its significance goes far beyond the realm of science fiction. It's a critical component of quantum communication and quantum computing, two fields poised to revolutionize the way we process and transmit information.

- **Quantum Communication:** Secure communication is a pressing concern in the digital age, and quantum teleportation plays a pivotal role in quantum cryptography. By teleporting quantum states, it's possible to create unbreakable encryption keys, as any attempt to intercept the information would alter the quantum state and be immediately detectable.
- **Quantum Computing:** Quantum computers have the potential to solve problems that are currently intractable for classical computers. Quantum teleportation is essential for quantum computation because it allows qubits, the basic units of quantum information, to be transmitted between different parts of a quantum computer.

Current Challenges and Future Prospects

Implementing quantum teleportation in practical scenarios requires precise control over entanglement, accurate measurements, and error-free classical communication. Research continues to focus on improving the efficiency, reliability, and scalability of quantum teleportation, as well as integrating it into emerging quantum technologies.

Quantum teleportation is more than a fascinating theoretical concept; it represents a fundamental building block of quantum information processing. Its discovery has deepened our understanding of quantum entanglement and has paved the way for advances in quantum communication and quantum networking, as well as in quantum computation; it forms the basis for certain quantum algorithms and protocols.

Quantum teleportation is a remarkable demonstration of the unique properties of quantum systems. It showcases the power of entanglement and provides a practical tool for transmitting quantum information. As technology advances, quantum teleportation may play a vital role in the development of global quantum networks and secure communication systems. The Quantum Insider titled "The Mysteries Of Quantum Teleportation Explained" lists its top three applications:

- A teleportation-based quantum Internet may connect quantum computers for the secure transmission of quantum information, as well as to enable distributed quantum computation
- Teleportation-based quantum sensors could enable higher precision measurements for both sensing and metrology applications
- Teleportation-based networks could use quantum key distribution (QKD) to secure communications between remote parties

A novel application, related but different, is quantum energy teleportation. At a high level, teleporting energy and information seems quite similar, after all measuring a qubit reveals which energy level it has been found in. The distinctions between teleporting energy and teleporting information, however, is beyond the scope of this definition.

QUANTUM COMMUNICATION NETWORKS

The next-generation technology has paved the way for the realization of quantum networking, enabling efficient communication between quantum devices to solve complex problems more effectively than traditional computing algorithms. In the realm of next-generation quantum networking, researchers have explored harnessing quantum computer features such as circuit design, entanglement, and superposition to accelerate specific calculations.

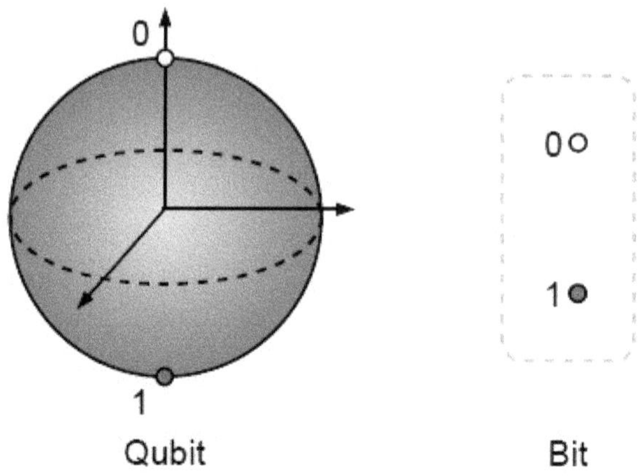

Graphical representation of qubit and a traditional binary digit (bit).

This section begins by defining quantum computing and its inherent features, such as quantum design, entanglement, and superposition, among other attributes that enhance specific communications. We delve into the concept of quantum entanglement, a distinctive trait of quantum computing involving quantum bits, or qubits (Fig. above), that exhibit strong correlation. Furthermore, the paper demonstrates how measuring a qubit leads to its collapse into one of two potential values, similar to a classical binary digit. Our discussion highlighting the coordination of entangled quantum bits and their correlated movement. Ultimately, the paper provides a comprehensive view of performance measures for evaluating quantum networks, encompassing quantum routing, scheduling, reliability, security, and standards for Quantum Key Distribution (QKD) protocols.

Figure below illustrates a generalized quantum network comprising both quantum and classical communication channels. The showcases a teleportation technique that establishes end-to-end entanglement between quantum computers, a pivotal operation for constructing basic quantum networks. Multiple quantum repeaters integrated along quantum channels extend the entanglement range, enabling connectivity over greater distances. As seen in the Fig., teleportation is crucial in quantum networking, allowing quantum circuits to extend across computers. This entails entangling qubits across the network, interconnecting qubits between computers. These interlinked qubits, referred to as "flying qubits," encode photon spin or polarization, traversing optical fibers or wireless mediums. Thoughtfully sequenced flying qubits facilitate quantum state transfer across extended distances.

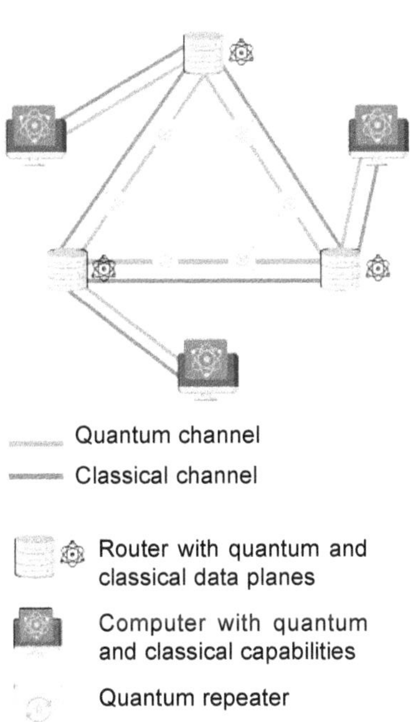

Quantum Network with quantum and classical channels. Quantum repeaters are used to extend the range of quantum entanglement

At the core of a quantum computer lies the quantum bit (qubit), analogous to the classical binary digit (bit). Unlike classical bits that represent only 0 or 1, qubits span the full range between 0 and 1, justified by the principles of quantum mechanics. In classical computing, a bit can exist in one of two discrete states, 0 or 1. However, in quantum computing, qubits can exist in a state of superposition, meaning they can represent a combination of both 0 and 1 simultaneously, as well as any value between these two states. This property is a fundamental aspect of quantum mechanics and serves as a foundation for quantum computation. The concept that qubits can exist in a superposition of states between 0 and 1 is a fundamental principle of quantum mechanics. This idea is often explained through Schrodinger's ¨ equation, which describes how quantum states evolve over time. In quantum computing, qubits leverage this property to perform multiple calculations simultaneously, leading to the potential for exponential speedup in certain computations compared to classical computers.

Quantum Design

Implementing quantum algorithms within quantum-based computers requires designing quantum circuits for executing arithmetic operations, including addition, subtraction, and multiplication. Our journey into quantum algorithms, covering tasks such as integer factoring, searching, and quantum mechanical modeling, begins with the quantum circuit for multiplication.

Quantum bits (qubits) serve as the fundamental unit of quantum information. The distinction between the conventional binary digit (bit) and the qubit. While a bit can only adopt values of 0 or 1, a qubit can represent 0 or 1 as well as any value between them or on the surface of a sphere. A distinctive attribute of the qubit is its superposition property, wherein it exists in multiple states until measured. Following measurement, the qubit collapses to a specific state.

Given the limited availability of qubits in existing quantum computers, researchers often consider the qubit cost, which represents the total number of qubits used in constructing a quantum circuit, as a critical performance measure.

However, quantum computers face a significant challenge in increased susceptibility to noise errors, known as decoherence. This phenomenon deteriorates qubit state functions, reducing the accuracy of quantum calculations. Decoherence arises from entanglement with external factors such as light, vibration, sound, cosmic rays, and interference from wireless devices, as well as internal interactions between qubits within the same system. The task of isolating individual qubits further compounds this challenge.

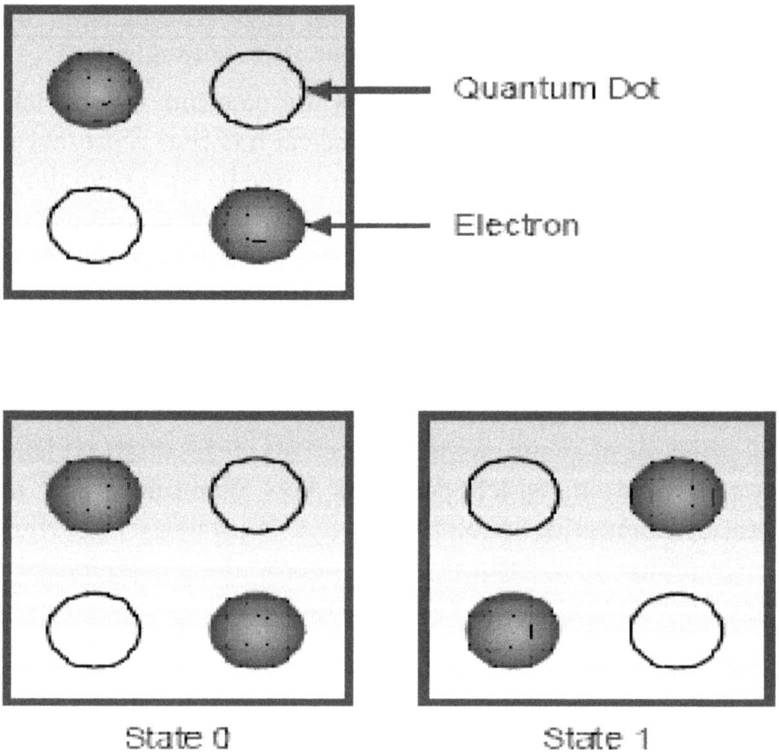

Quantum-dot Cellular Automata (QCA). The shaded dots represent two charged electrons free to move to any part of the cell. Based on the principle of electrostatic repulsion, the charged electrons will attempt to move as far as possible from each other in the cell. The two electrons represent two possible states.

A potential solution involves constructing quantum circuits that incorporate Clifford+T gates, leveraging their inherent fault tolerance capabilities. Clifford gates, which use conjugation to normalize qubits, offer a means of error mitigation. When combined with T gates, these circuits gain resilience through the application of error-correcting codes, a vital technique for safeguarding quantum information from noise-induced errors.

The introduction of fault tolerance brings with it additional challenges of computational overhead. Unlike classical bits with discrete "1" or "0" states, qubits exist in superposition. Maintaining fault tolerance necessitates resources to restore qubit states, which extends to the complexity of T gate implementation. Managing this supplementary layer of overhead is crucial for ensuring the reliability and robustness of quantum computations. Quantum-dot Cellular Automata (QCA) offers an energy-efficient solution for circuits with limited resources. QCA utilizes quantum circuits and internal connections to interlink building blocks, enabling the design of low-power circuits and high-throughput networks. In Figure below, you can see an overview of a typical QCA configuration, with shaded dots representing two charged electrons capable of tunnelling across the cell.

Governed by electrostatic repulsion, these electrons strive to position themselves as far apart as possible within the cell, representing two distinct states. Recent research highlights QCA's potential to replace conventional integrated circuits, making it a compelling option for low-power circuit design.

In the realm of digital circuits, an adder is responsible for performing addition operations. Among these, the carry look-ahead adder (CLA) stands out as a pivotal component in digital arithmetic processing. The CLA excels in its ability to perform addition with higher efficiency and speed compared to alternatives such as the ripple carry adder (RCA). This efficiency stems from its capability to predict carry bits before determining the sum, effectively reducing computation time. The quantum carry look-ahead adder (QCLA) serves as the quantum counterpart to the CLA, executing addition with a time complexity of O(log(n)). The QCLA leverages ripple carry adders and is characterized by a linear depth equivalent to its input bit count. This results in significantly improved speed compared to RCAs, which require O(n) time for similar operations. Quantum-dot Cellular Automata (QCA) offers an energy-efficient solution for circuits with limited resources. By utilizing quantum circuits and internal connections, QCA can interlink building blocks, enabling the design of low-power circuits and high-throughput networks. The general QCA setup, features charged electrons capable of tunnelling across the cell. Governed by electrostatic repulsion, these electrons assume positions that maximize their separation within the cell, representing distinct states.

Recent research underscores QCA's potential to replace conventional integrated circuits, making it a compelling avenue for achieving low-power circuit design. In digital circuits, the task of addition is typically performed by an adder. The carry look-ahead adder (CLA) stands out as a pivotal component in digital arithmetic processing. It excels in performing addition with higher efficiency and speed compared to alternatives like the ripple carry adder (RCA). This efficiency stems from its ability to predict carry bits before determining the sum, effectively reducing computation time. The quantum carry look-ahead adder (QCLA) serves as the quantum counterpart to the CLA, executing addition with a time complexity of O(log(n)).

Leveraging ripple carry adders, the QCLA's linear depth corresponds to its input bit count, resulting in significantly improved speed compared to RCAs, which require O(n) time for similar operations. Direct connections between inputs and outputs of a quantum circuit often introduce complexities, necessitating ancillae (auxiliary) qubits and producing output garbage. Ancillae are involved when a constant input is applied to the quantum circuit, while garbage output arises when a quantum circuit's work doesn't contribute as input to another circuit. Removing garbage output is crucial for reducing the quantum circuit's overall qubit and T gate costs. QCLAs can be categorized as in-place and out-of-place. An in-place QCLA replaces a direct input with the sum, while an outof-place QCLA returns the sum on ancillae. For quantum computing applications, QCLAs should ideally produce no garbage output without significantly impacting qubit and T gate costs. Achieving this goal requires efficient utilization of T-gate-efficient Toffoli gates, which serve as reversible logic building blocks.

Quantum Network Routing

Efficiently constructing quantum-based network topologies necessitates the creation and optimization of network routing. Quantum routing is centered around identifying the optimal channel for teleporting qubits, a process crucial for extending quantum circuits beyond individual computers. Unlike classical bits, qubits cannot be copied, but they can be teleported between quantum systems, establishing quantum entanglement. This unique feature, characterized by strong correlations among specific groups of qubits, demands a holistic consideration of potential qubit values due to interdependent probabilities.

Entangling qubits is facilitated by 'flying qubits,' which encode states in photon spin or polarization for transmission through fiber optic cables or wireless methods. However, flying qubits experience fidelity degradation with increased distance. Quantum repeaters serve as intermediaries to extend their range, utilizing entanglement swapping between two flying qubits to generate end-to-end entanglement.

Challenges such as signal power attenuation and transmission imperfections influence entanglement quality along the chain. Evaluation measures for quantum network quality encompass throughput and entanglement fidelity, reflecting data delivery success rates and the variance between desired and actual quantum states.

Figure below, you can see the illustration of the establishment of end-to-end entanglement between quantum computers via three quantum repeaters. This emphasizes the significance of quantum entanglement and repeaters within networks that integrate both quantum and classical communication.

The efficiency of quantum entanglement relies on the effectiveness of quantum routing strategies, which involve finding the right balance between scheduling and path selection. Scheduling entails selecting quantum couples to establish end-to-end entanglement within specific time slots. The choice of optimal paths or quantum repeater sets plays a vital role in entanglement creation. Effective quantum routing utilizes strategies such as weighted roundrobin or iterative selection for path optimization, enhancing both the entanglement rate and fidelity. Certain quantum routing algorithms pre-allocate qubits to prevent resource conflicts during entanglement swapping. However, resource fragmentation can hinder network efficiency. Strategies like Q-CAST aim to mitigate this issue by considering fragmentation during entanglement and using priority connections for recovery in case of failures. Another approach involves employing entanglement purification techniques to enhance entanglement quality between sets of qubits across nodes. Q-PATH identifies purification choices based on cost considerations, while Q-LEAP minimizes fidelity loss along the shortest route, using efficient purification decision methods to streamline computations.

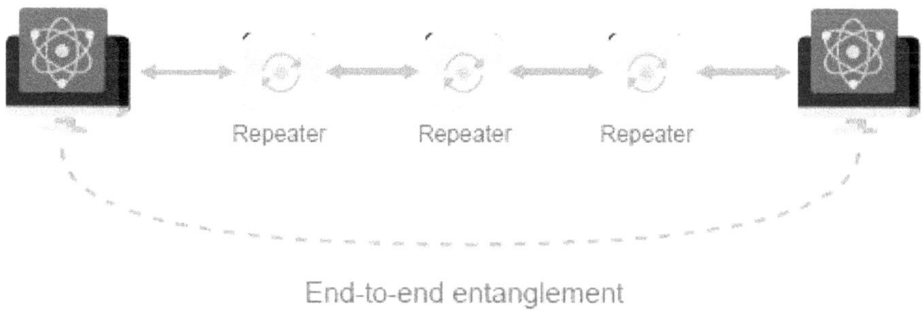

End-to-end entanglement between two quantum computers using a series of three quantum repeaters

Quantum Network Reliability

In the realm of network communications, users and computers often compete for the shortest and quickest paths. However, network reliability becomes a concern when multiple users or computers choose the same route. Navigating network reliability requires a delicate balance between transmission latency and cost. For example, network congestion can be assessed through total transmission time, which combines routing time and travel time.

Travel time represents the duration for a network packet to reach its destination, while routing time signifies the time taken for a packet to select a route. As more packets opt for a common route, the travel time for each packet increases. Therefore, each packet faces two choices: (1) Opt for the shortest path and risk potential delays due to congestion, or (2) choose a longer path with lower congestion-induced delays. Classical approaches treat these options as binary decisions (0 or 1).

In contrast, quantum computing allows for representing various options through multiple states between 0 and 1 within a qubit. Additionally, the impact of noise on qubit states, termed fault tolerance to noise, is a crucial consideration. Novel proposed solutions leverage quantum game theory to address network congestion and reliability concerns. In this paradigm, packets engage in self-interested competition for optimal routes. Initially, quantum states are assigned to represent each possible strategy. Subsequently, each packet adapts its local qubit's state to choose the optimal strategy. Such approaches hold potential to reduce travel and routing times, providing innovative solutions to alleviate network congestion and enhance reliability.

Quantum Communication Security

Security concerns loom over end-to-end quantum networks, encompassing challenges in cybersecurity across cloud and edge computing, privacy and security attacks in fog computing architectures, and vulnerabilities in IoT-based devices. To address these concerns, Quantum Key Distribution (QKD) emerges as a novel security paradigm, harnessing the unique properties of quantum mechanics for cryptographic operations such as encryption and decryption. QKD also provides a means to obtain critical cryptanalysis information, serving as a countermeasure against attempts to exploit quantum-based physical characteristics for constructing distributed symmetric keys.

In Fig. below, you can see a typical QKD scenario where two computers establish a network link via classical and quantum channels. In this illustration, one computer generates a secret key and transmits it to the other computer through the quantum channel, established via end-to-end entanglement and teleportation techniques.

The quantum nature of the channel ensures that any eavesdropping attempt results in the qubit's consumption upon measurement. Upon receiving an intact message containing the secret key, the second computer uses the private and public keys for decryption. If the integrity of the secret key is compromised, the key must be resent, ensuring robust security in the quantum communication network.

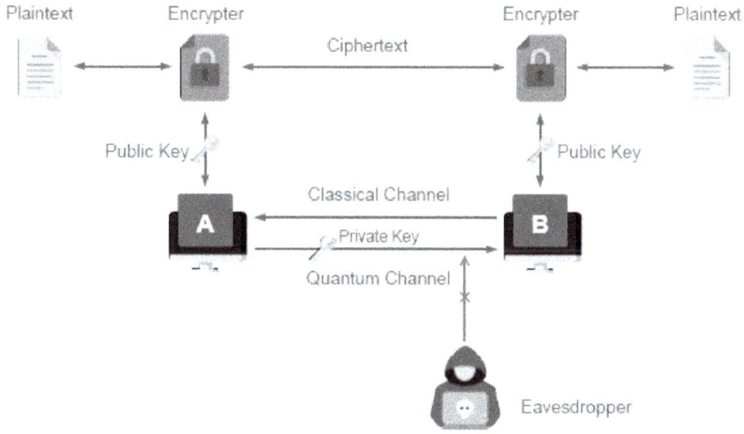

Quantum Key Distribution (QKD). Two computers, A and B, establish a connection via classical and quantum channels. A transmits the secret key to B over a quantum channel established using quantum entanglement and teleportation techniques. An eavesdropper cannot measure the qubits on a quantum channel without disturbing the integrity of the qubits. The loss of integrity of the message sent over the quantum channel is indicative of an eavesdropping attempt. B can use the private and public keys to decrypt if message integrity is good. Otherwise, the secret key needs to be present.

Progress is being made in the realm of multi-domain orchestration, empowering service providers to establish comprehensive network services that span distinct network administration domains. However, this advancement introduces overarching security concerns that encompass the entire end-to-end network. These concerns include potential security threats associated with mobile edge computing (MEC) and Internet of Things (IoT) devices, as well as security and privacy vulnerabilities tied to fog computing architectures. Addressing these security challenges, some proposals advocate the use of Quantum Key Distribution (QKD). For instance, the q-ROADM, a QKD switch-enabled flex-grid architecture, supports classical and quantum data channels across a 5G optical network. qROADM aims to enhance end-to-end security across heterogeneous networks, a significant objective of 5G. Expanding on the 5GUK Exchange orchestrator, the q-ROADM framework demonstrates a quantum-secured diverse multidomain 5G network. This network facilitates the seamless deployment of services by chaining virtual network functions (VNFs) across various domains. The architecture integrates a quantum-secured optical network, catering to both quantum and classical channels, and offers dynamic quantum key switching and inter-domain optical network connectivity. This approach enables efficient VNF chaining while ensuring robust quantum protection.

To bolster security and trust in future quantum and postquantum cryptographic standardization, cryptosystem approaches have emerged. These implementations, including LDPC and MDPC, Reed-Solomon designs, and McEliece, address the security challenges of convolutional cryptography and safeguard quantum systems against cyberattacks. These techniques find applications in consumer electronics, A.I., and blockchain-based technologies like Bitcoin. The approaches involve generating binary codes for system authentication, secure digital signatures, and cryptographic key exchange over untrusted mediums, offering resilience against various attacks. Emerging cyberattacks targeting quantum computing, such as side-channel and power analysis attacks, are also being countered. One unique approach focuses on mitigating side-channel attacks during the implementation of the McEliece cryptosystem on resource-constrained platforms. Utilizing quantum arithmetic benchmarks, this approach evaluates cryptosystem measures benchmarked on FPGA, incorporating error detection mechanisms to thwart fault attacks in quantum computing design.

POST-QUANTUM CRYPTOGRAPHY

Post-quantum cryptography (PQC), sometimes referred to as quantum-proof, quantum-safe, or quantum-resistant, is the development of cryptographic algorithms (usually public-key algorithms) that are thought to be secure against a cryptanalytic attack by a quantum computer. The problem with popular algorithms currently used in the market is that their security relies on one of three hard mathematical problems: the integer factorization problem, the discrete logarithm problem or the elliptic-curve discrete logarithm problem. All of these problems could be easily solved on a sufficiently powerful quantum computer running Shor's algorithm[1][2] or even faster and less demanding (in terms of the number of qubits required) alternatives.

While as of 2023, quantum computers lack the processing power to break widely used cryptographic algorithms, cryptographers are designing new algorithms to prepare for Q-Day, the day when current algorithms will be vulnerable to quantum computing attacks. Their work has gained attention from academics and industry through the PQCrypto conference series hosted since 2006, several workshops on Quantum Safe Cryptography hosted by the European Telecommunications Standards Institute (ETSI), and the Institute for Quantum Computing. The rumoured existence of widespread harvest now, decrypt later programs has also been seen as a motivation for the early introduction of post-quantum algorithms, as data recorded now may still remain sensitive many years into the future.

In contrast to the threat quantum computing poses to current public-key algorithms, most current symmetric cryptographic algorithms and hash functions are considered to be relatively secure against attacks by quantum computers. While the quantum Grover's algorithm does speed up attacks against symmetric ciphers, doubling the key size can effectively block these attacks. Thus post-quantum symmetric cryptography does not need to differ significantly from current symmetric cryptography.

Cryptography in the era of quantum computers

The private communication of individuals and organizations is protected online by cryptography. Cryptography protects our information as it travels over and is stored on the internet—whether making a purchase from an online store, uploading data to the cloud, or accessing work email remotely. Our research and engineering work has focused on protecting private information and communication from the possible threat of future quantum computers.

Quantum Computers will advance human knowledge in many fields. To balance that, we need to update some cryptography. Existing public-key cryptography (also known as asymmetric cryptography) is based on the difficulty of factoring and the difficulty of calculating elliptic curve discrete logarithms. Because those two problems will be readily and efficiently solved by a sufficiently large-scale quantum computer, we have been studying cryptography approaches that appear to be resistant to an attacker who has access to a quantum computer, and we have been developing cryptosystems whose security relies on different, hard mathematical problems that are resistant to being solved by a large-scale quantum computer.

Our work is open, open-source, and conducted in collaboration with academic and industry partners. The goal is robust, trusted, tested and standardized post-quantum cryptosystems.

This work started in 2014, with our first paper published in 2015. In the intervening years we've submitted candidates to the NIST Post-Quantum Project and shepherded them through several rounds. One candidate remains standing, the others are included below as both a record of the work and because perhaps it will inspire future innovations.

The key points: At the end of round 3, NIST picked for standardization CRYSTALS-Kyber for public-key encryption and key establishment, and CRYSTALS-Dilithium and two other algorithms for digital signatures. Meanwhile, ISO has approved FrodoKEM and two other algorithms for standardization.

What's involved in post-quantum cryptography?

Any new cryptography has to integrate with existing internet protocols, such as TLS. A new cryptosystem must weigh:

- The size of encryption keys and signatures
- The time required to encrypt and decrypt on each end of a communication channel, or to sign messages and verify signatures, and

- The amount of traffic sent over the wire required to complete encryption or decryption or transmit a signature for each proposed alternative.

The new cryptosystems also require careful cryptanalysis, to determine if there are any weaknesses that an adversary could exploit. The work of developing new cryptosystems that are quantum-resistant must be done openly, in full view of cryptographers, organizations, the public, and governments around the world, to ensure that the new standards emerging have been well vetted by the community, and to ensure that there is international support.

And lastly, we must keep moving quickly because we don't know exactly when today's classic cryptography will be broken. It's difficult and time-consuming to pull and replace existing cryptography from production software. Add to all that the fact that someone could store existing encrypted data and unlock it in the future once they have a quantum computer, and our task becomes even more urgent.

Crypto libraries, protocol integrations, and other resources

We are proud to participate in the Open Quantum Safe project where we help develop the liboqs library which is designed to further post-quantum cryptography. Additional information, protocol integrations, and related releases can be found on those sites.

Post-Quantum Crypto VPN

A fork of OpenVPN integrated with post-quantum cryptography to enable testing and experimentation with these algorithms.

Post-Quantum TLS

A PQ Crypto enlightened fork of OpenSSL.

Post-Quantum SSH

A fork of OpenSSH 7.7 that adds quantum-resistant key exchange and signature algorithms.

NIST Post-Quantum Project

We focused first on the NIST Post-Quantum Project, which asked for cryptographers around the world to submit candidates for subsequent peer review and analysis. Our team is worked with academia and industry on four candidates for cryptography systems that can both withstand quantum computer capabilities, while still working with existing protocols.

Why four? We worked on two collaborations for key exchange, and one for signatures, as well as providing code in support of a second signature system. Each proposal had different strengths and weaknesses, and each was built upon a different mathematical "hard problem." with different trade-offs regarding performance and key size. Pursuing multiple candidates is also appropriate as the post-quantum cryptography field is young, and many years of cryptanalysis are needed to determine whether any post-quantum proposal is secure.

FrodoKEM

FrodoKEM is based upon the Learning with Errors problem, which is, in turn, based upon lattices.

SIKE

SIKE (Supersingular Isogeny Key Encapsulation) uses arithmetic operations of elliptic curves over finite fields to build a key exchange.

Picnic

Picnic is a public-key digital signature algorithm, based on a zero-knowledge proof system and symmetric key primitives.

qTESLA

qTESLA is a post-quantum signature scheme based upon the Ring Learning With Errors (R-LWE) problem.

The need for post-quantum cryptography is based on four major factors.

- Public-key cryptography is commonly used in online communication where Bob wants to send a message to Alice. To do this privately, Alice generates a public and private key pair. Bob uses the public key to encrypt a message that Alice's private key can only decrypt.
- Classical computers find recognizing a private key quite difficult because only Alice has the private key, but her public key is available to everyone. And classical computers cannot find the current mathematical problems of the link between private and public keys.
- Quantum computers can estimate a private key very quickly because quantum computers process information differently from conventional computers, permitting new types of calculation. That encloses an algorithm that can easily figure out a private key purely from the public key.
- Quantum hackers could sabotage trust and privacy online because, without new public-key cryptography benchmarks, quantum computer-equipped hackers could listen in on lots of online communication and interfere with a system that relies on trust.

TYPES OF POST-QUANTUM CRYPTOGRAPHY

There are four basic types of post-quantum cryptography.

Types of PQC

Code-based cryptography

Code-based cryptography is an approaching opponent for diversifying today's public-key cryptosystems, which depend on the complexness of factorization or discrete logarithm issues.

Unlike public-key algorithms, Code-based cryptography is based on the issue of solving unknown error-correcting codes, assumed to be NP-hard. There are two simple code-based cryptography techniques named after Robert McEliece and Harald Niederreiter.

Hash-based cryptography

A hash-based cryptography scheme is derived from a one-time signature (OTS), i.e., a signature scheme that must only use each key pair to sign a message. If an OTS key pair signs two different notes, this cab threatens the network, and a hacker will effortlessly forge fake signatures that expose the customer's personal details.

Multivariate cryptography

The foundation of **multivariate cryptography** schemes is based upon the challenge of solving non-linear equation structures over finite fields.

The primary layout is used for all Multivariate Public-Key Cryptosystems (MPKC), as they all rely on multivariate polynomials over a limited field.

In most possibilities, the polynomial equations are of degree two, resulting in multivariate quadratic polynomials, which are yet credited with being solved as NP-hard.

Lattice-based cryptography

Lattice-based cryptographic algorithms are mainly established on the problem with the nearest vector or the shortest vector problem.

In most lattice-based cryptographic algorithms, the cryptographic builders are very time-efficient and straightforward while still delivering security guarantees founded on the worst-case hardness.

This method uses both lattices and a generalization of the issue of parity learning. Given an n-dimensional vector space, a lattice is a precise interpretation of points with a periodic structure used in various fields.

CHAPTER-7
QUANTUM MACHINE LEARNING

Quantum machine learning uses algorithms run on quantum devices, such as quantum computers, to supplement, expedite, or support the work performed by a classical machine learning program. Also called *quantum-enhanced machine learning*, quantum machine learning leverages the information processing power of quantum technologies to enhance and speed up the work performed by a machine learning model.

While classical computers are constrained by limited storage and processing capacities, quantum-enabled ones allow for exponentially more storage and processing power. This ability to store and process huge amounts of information means that quantum computers can analyze massive data sets that would take classical methods significantly longer to perform. As a result, quantum machine learning leverages this out-sized processing power to expedite and improve the development of machine learning models, neural networks, and other forms of artificial intelligence (AI).

Machine Learning

Machine learning investigates how computers can learn (or improve their performance) based on data. A main research area is for computer programs to automatically learn to recognize complex patterns and make intelligent decisions based on data. For example, a typical machine learning problem is to program a computer so that it can automatically recognize handwritten postal codes on mail after learning from a set of examples. Machine learning is a fast-growing discipline. Here, we illustrate classic problems in machine learning that are highly related to data mining.

Supervised learning is basically a synonym for classification. The supervision in the learning comes from the labeled examples in the training data set. For example, in the postal code recognition problem, a set of handwritten postal code images and their corresponding machine-readable translations are used as the training examples, which supervise the learning of the classification model.

Unsupervised learning is essentially a synonym for clustering. The learning process is unsupervised since the input examples are not class labeled. Typically, we may use clustering to discover classes within the data.

For example, an unsupervised learning method can take, as input, a set of images of handwritten digits. Suppose that it finds 10 clusters of data. These clusters may correspond to the 10 distinct digits of 0 to 9, respectively. However, since the training data are not labeled, the learned model cannot tell us the semantic meaning of the clusters found.

Semi-supervised learning is a class of machine learning techniques that make use of both labeled and unlabeled examples when learning a model. In one approach, labeled examples are used to learn class models and unlabeled examples are used to refine the boundaries between classes. For a two-class problem, we can think of the set of examples belonging to one class as the positive examples and those belonging to the other class as the negative examples. In Fig. 1, if we do not consider the unlabelled examples, the dashed line is the decision boundary that best partitions the positive examples from the negative examples. Using the unlabeled examples, we can refine the decision boundary to the solid line. Moreover, we can detect that the two positive examples at the top right corner, though labelled, are likely noise or outliers.

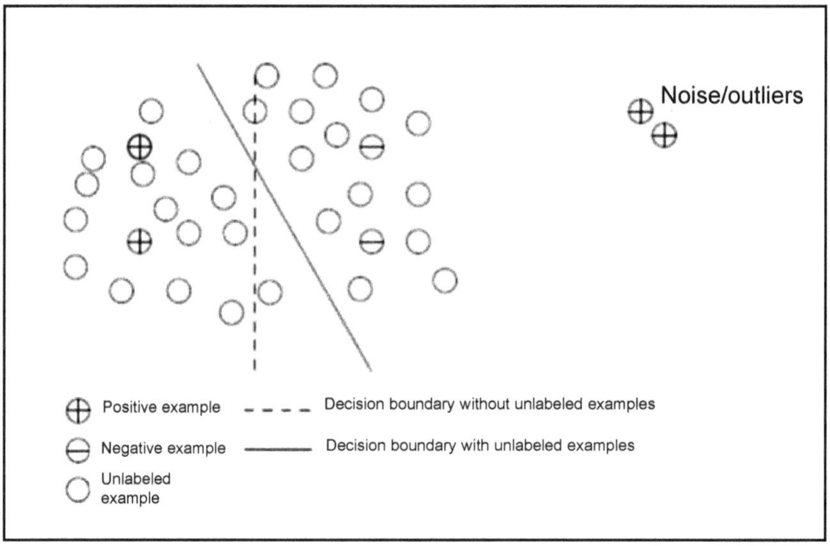

Fig. 1. Semi-supervised learning.

Active learning is a machine learning approach that lets users play an active role in the learning process. An active learning approach can ask a user (e.g., a domain expert) to label an example, which may be from a set of unlabeled examples or synthesized by the learning program. The goal is to optimize the model quality by actively acquiring knowledge from human users, given a constraint on how many examples they can be asked to label.

You can see there are many similarities between data mining and machine learning. For classification and clustering tasks, machine learning research often focuses on the accuracy of the model. In addition to accuracy, data mining research places strong emphasis on the efficiency and scalability of mining methods on large data sets, as well as on ways to handle complex types of data and explore new, alternative methods.

Quantum machine learning has the potential to revolutionize data processing and analysis, but it also raises ethical concerns regarding data privacy, security, and fairness. Efforts are required to address these concerns and establish ethical guidelines for quantum machine learning.

Quantum Machine Learning Standards

The establishment of industry standards for quantum machine learning is necessary to ensure inter-operability and reliability in quantum computing ecosystems.

Standardization efforts should cover software, hardware, and security aspects.

Quantum Cloud Services

Quantum cloud platforms are expected to become more accessible, enabling a broader range of users to experiment with quantum hardware and quantum machine learning. Quantum

Machine Learning Libraries

Quantum machine learning libraries will continue to evolve, providing a wealth of tools and resources for quantum algorithm development and research.

Quantum Advantage in Diverse Fields

Quantum machine learning is poised to make significant contributions to fields like healthcare, finance, climate modelling, and more. Continued research and collaboration will drive advancements in these domains.

Quantum Hardware Innovation

Ongoing innovation in quantum hardware will lead to the development of increasingly powerful and reliable quantum processors, opening new opportunities for quantum machine learning applications.

Quantum Machine Learning Research

Continued interdisciplinary research at the intersection of quantum computing and machine learning will lead to the discovery of novel quantum algorithms and their application in AI and data analysis.

Quantum AI Integration

The integration of quantum machine learning into existing AI systems and infrastructure will become more prevalent, allowing businesses and researchers to harness quantum advantages for improved decision-making and data analysis.

Quantum Machine Learning Start ups

The emergence of quantum machine learning start ups will drive innovation and competition in the quantum technology landscape, potentially accelerating the development and adoption of quantum solutions.

The confluence of quantum computing and AI in the form of quantummachine learningrepresents a promising frontier with transformative potential. While challenges remain, continued research and investment in quantum technology will shape the future of AI anddataanalysis, unlocking new opportunities and solutions for complex problems.

QUANTUM-ENHANCED CLASSICAL MACHINE LEARNING

In quantum-enhanced reinforcement learning, a quantum agent interacts with a classical or quantum environment and occasionally receives rewards for its actions, which allows the agent to adapt its behavior—in other words, to learn what to do in order to gain more rewards.

Quantum computing, a revolutionary technology, holds the promise of transforming the world as we know it. With its ability to harness the peculiarities of quantum mechanics, quantum computing has the potential to solve complex problems at an unprecedented scale. One fascinating application of this emerging technology is its ability to enhance the performance of classical computers in the realm of machine learning. We will explore the inner workings of quantum computing, its potential for boosting classical computer performance, and the implications it holds for the field of machine learning.

Understanding Quantum Computing

To grasp the concept of quantum-enhanced machine learning, it is crucial to first understand the fundamentals of quantum computing. Unlike classical computers that use bits to process information, which represent either a 0 or a 1, quantum computers utilise quantum bits or qubits. These qubits can exist in multiple states simultaneously, thanks to a property called superposition. Moreover, they can also be entangled, meaning the state of one qubit can be instantly correlated with the state of another, regardless of distance.

Quantum computing leverages the principles of superposition and entanglement to perform computations at an exponential scale. While a classical computer's processing power grows linearly with the number of bits, a quantum computer's processing power grows exponentially with the number of qubits. This fundamental difference enables quantum computers to solve problems that are practically infeasible for classical computers.

The Potential of Quantum-enhanced Machine Learning

Machine learning algorithms lie at the heart of many artificial intelligence (AI) systems, enabling computers to learn patterns and make predictions. However, training these algorithms often requires immense computational resources, especially for complex tasks. This is where quantum-enhanced machine learning comes into play. By leveraging the capabilities of quantum computing, machine learning algorithms can be enhanced in various ways.

Quantum computers excel in solving optimisation problems, and this ability can be leveraged to improve optimisation algorithms used in machine learning. Tasks such as clustering, classification, and regression can benefit from the enhanced optimization capabilities offered by quantum computers.

Quantum computing can also accelerate the training of machine learning models. The process of training a model typically involves iterating through massive datasets and adjusting weights and biases based on the observed errors. Quantum computers can speed up this iterative process, enabling faster convergence and reducing training time significantly.

Implications for the Future

Quantum-enhanced machine learning has the potential to revolutionise various industries. Faster and more accurate machine learning algorithms can have profound implications in fields such as healthcare, finance, logistics, and more. For example, drug discovery processes that traditionally take years could be expedited with the help of quantum-enhanced algorithms, leading to faster development of life-saving medications.

However, it is important to note that quantum computing is still in its nascent stages. The technology faces significant challenges, such as qubit stability, error correction, and scalability. Nevertheless, researchers and industry experts are actively working to overcome these obstacles, and the progress made so far is promising.

The Synergy of Quantum Computing and Machine Learning: An Unbeatable Duo

Now, imagine the immense possibilities when these two technologies – quantum computingand machine learning – join forces. As quantum computers become more accessible, they hold the potential to enhance the capabilities of machine learning algorithms significantly. Quantum machine learning combines quantum computing's exponential computing power with machine learning's ability to analyse and learn from data.

But what practical applications can we expect from this dynamic duo? Quantum machine learning can optimise complex processes in areas such as finance, logistics, and drug discovery. It can revolutionise the field of cryptography by developing stronger encryption algorithms that are resistant to attacks by quantum computers themselves. Additionally, quantum machine learning holds promise in improving artificial intelligence systems, enabling smarter decision-making and more accurate predictions.

As the world continues to evolve, there is an increasing need to learn and understand the fascinating realms of quantum computing and machine learning. Together, they have the potential to reshape industries, solve complex problems, and pave the way for a brighter future.

QUANTUM NEURAL NETWORKS

Quantum neural networks (QNNs) are machine learning models that combine artificial neural networks and quantum computing. The concept of QNNs was first introduced in 1995 by Subhash Kak and Ron Chrisley.

Quantum vs. Classical Neural Networks

Classical neural networks are algorithmic models inspired by the human brain that can be trained to recognize patterns in data and learn to solve complex problems. They are based on a series of interconnected nodes, or *neurons*, organized in a layered structure, with parameters that can be learned by applying machine or deep learning training strategies.

The motivation behind quantum machine learning (QML) is to integrate notions from quantum computing and classical machine learning to open the way for new and improved learning schemes. QNNs apply this generic principle by combining classical neural networks and parametrized quantum circuits. Because they lie at an intersection between two fields, QNNs can be viewed from two perspectives:

- From a **machine learning perspective**, QNNs are, once again, algorithmic models that can be trained to find hidden patterns in data in a similar manner to their classical counterparts. These models can **load** classical data (**inputs**) into a quantum state, and later **process** it with quantum gates parametrized by **trainable weights**. Figure 1 shows a generic QNN example including the data loading and processing steps. The output from measuring this state can then be plugged into a loss function to train the weights through backpropagation.

- From a **quantum computing perspective**, QNNs are quantum algorithms based on parametrized quantum circuits that can be trained in a variational manner using classical optimizers. These circuits contain a **feature map** (with input parameters) and an **ansatz** (with trainable weights), as seen in Fig 2.

As you can see, these two perspectives are complementary, and do not necessarily rely on strict definitions of concepts such as "quantum neuron" or what constitutes a QNN's "layer".

Implementation in qiskit-machine-learning

The QNNs in qiskit-machine-learning are meant as application-agnostic computational units that can be used for different use cases, and their setup will depend on the application they are needed for. The module contains an interface for the QNNs and two specific implementations:

- **Neural Network:** The interface for neural networks. This is an abstract class all QNNs inherit from.
- **Estimator QNN:** A network based on the evaluation of quantum mechanical observables.
- **Sampler QNN:** A network based on the samples resulting from measuring a quantum circuit.

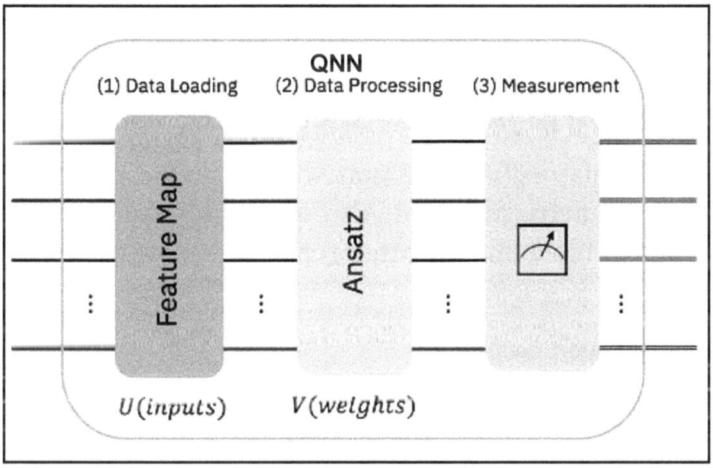

Fig. 2. Generic quantum neural network (QNN) structure.

These implementations are based on the qiskit primitives. The primitives are the entry point to run QNNs on either a simulator or real quantum hardware. Each implementation, EstimatorQNN and SamplerQNN, takes in an optional instance of its corresponding primitive, which can be any subclass of BaseEstimator and BaseSampler, respectively.

The qiskit.primitives module provides a reference implementation for the Sampler and Estimator classes to run statevector simulations. By default, if no instance is passed to a QNN class, an instance of the corresponding reference primitive (Sampler or Estimator) is created automatically by the network. For more information about primitives please refer to the primitives documentation.

The NeuralNetwork class is the interface for all QNNs available in qiskit-machine-learning. It exposes a forward and a backward pass that take data samples and trainable weights as input.

It's important to note that NeuralNetworks are "stateless". They do not contain any training capabilities (these are pushed to the actual algorithms or applications: classifiers, regressors, etc), nor do they store the values for trainable weights.

Let's now look into specific examples for the two NeuralNetwork implementations. But first, let's set the algorithmic seed to ensure that the results don't change between runs.

```
[1]:
from qiskit_algorithms.utils import algorithm_globals
algorithm_globals.random_seed = 42
```

How to Instantiate QNNs

EstimatorQNN

The EstimatorQNN takes in a parametrized quantum circuit as input, as well as an optional quantum mechanical observable, and outputs expectation value computations for the forward pass. The EstimatorQNN also accepts lists of observables to construct more complex QNNs.

Let's see an EstimatorQNN in action with a simple example. We start by constructing the parametrized circuit. This quantum circuit has two parameters, one represents a QNN input and the other represents a trainable weight:

```
[2]:
from qiskit.circuit import Parameter
from qiskit import QuantumCircuit
params1 = [Parameter("input1"), Parameter("weight1")]
qc1 = QuantumCircuit(1)
qc1.h(0)
qc1.ry(params1[0], 0)
qc1.rx(params1[1], 0)
qc1.draw("mpl", style="clifford")
```

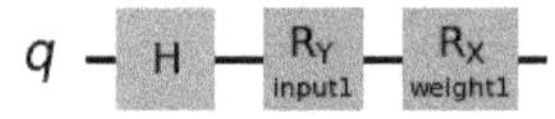

[2]:

We can now create an observable to define the expectation value computation. If not set, then the EstimatorQNN will automatically create the default observable $Z^{\otimes n}$. Here, n is the number of qubits of the quantum circuit.

In this example, we will change things up and use the $Y^{\otimes n}$ observable:

```
[3]: from qiskit.quantum_info import SparsePauliOp
observable1 = SparsePauliOp.from_list([("Y" * qc1.num_qubits, 1)])
```

Together with the quantum circuit defined above, and the observable we have created, the EstimatorQNN constructor takes in the following keyword arguments:

- **estimator:** optional primitive instance
- **input_params:** list of quantum circuit parameters that should be treated as "network inputs"
- **weight_params:** list of quantum circuit parameters that should be treated as "network weights"

In this example, we previously decided that the first parameter of params1 should be the input, while the second should be the weight. As we are performing a local statevector simulation, we will not set the estimator parameter; the network will create an instance of the reference Estimator primitive for us. If we needed to access cloud resources or Aer simulators, we would have to define the respective Estimator instances and pass them to the EstimatorQNN.

```
[4]: from qiskit_machine_learning.neural_networks import EstimatorQNN
estimator_qnn = EstimatorQNN(
    circuit=qc1 observables=observable1, input_params=[params1[0]], weight_params=[params1[1]]
)
estimator_qnn
```

```
[4]: <qiskit_machine_learning.neural_networks.estimator_qnn.EstimatorQNN at 0x7fc3d809fdc0>
```

We'll see how to use the QNN in the following sections, but before that, let's check out the SamplerQNN class.

SamplerQNN

The SamplerQNN is instantiated in a similar way to the EstimatorQNN, but because it directly consumes samples from measuring the quantum circuit, it does not require a custom observable.

These output samples are interpreted by default as the probabilities of measuring the integer index corresponding to a bitstring. However, the SamplerQNN also allows us to specify an interpret function to post-process the samples. This function should be defined so that it takes a measured integer (from a bitstring) and maps it to a new value, i.e. non-negative integer.

(!) It's important to note that if a custom interpret function is defined, the output_shape cannot be inferred by the network, and needs to be provided explicitly.

(!) It's also important to keep in mind that if no interpret function is used, the dimension of the probability vector will scale exponentially with the number of qubits. With a custom interpret function, this scaling can change. If, for instance, an index is mapped to the parity of the corresponding bitstring, i.e., to 0 or 1, the result will be a probability vector of length 2 independently of the number of qubits.

Let's create a different quantum circuit for the SamplerQNN. In this case, we will have two input parameters and four trainable weights that parametrize a two-local circuit.

```
[5]: from qiskit.circuit import ParameterVector
inputs2 = ParameterVector("input", 2)
weights2 = ParameterVector("weight", 4)
print(f"input parameters: {[str(item) for item in inputs2.params]}")
print(f"weight parameters: {[str(item) for item in weights2.params]}")
qc2 = QuantumCircuit(2)
qc2.ry(inputs2[0], 0)
qc2.ry(inputs2[1], 1)
qc2.cx(0, 1)
qc2.ry(weights2[0], 0)
qc2.ry(weights2[1], 1)
qc2.cx(0, 1)
qc2.ry(weights2[2], 0)
qc2.ry(weights2[3], 1)
qc2.draw("mpl", style="clifford")
input parameters: ['input[0]', 'input[1]']
weight parameters: ['weight[0]', 'weight[1]', 'weight[2]', 'weight[3]']          [5]:
```

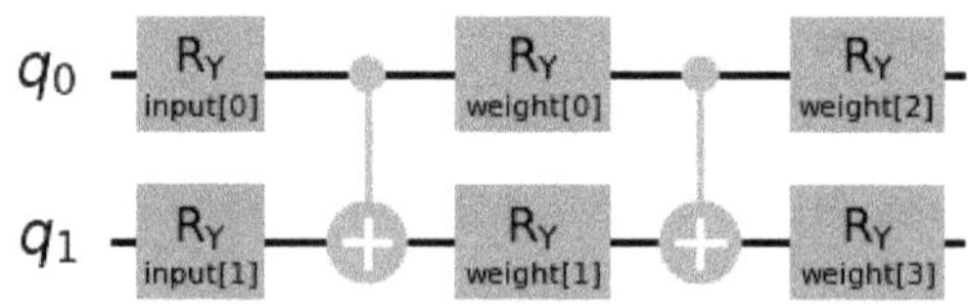

Similarly to the EstimatorQNN, we must specify inputs and weights when instantiating the SamplerQNN. In this case, the keyword arguments will be: - sampler: optional primitive instance - input_params: list of quantum circuit parameters that should be treated as "network inputs" - weight_params: list of quantum circuit parameters that should be treated as "network weights"

Please note that, once again, we are choosing not to set the Sampler instance to the QNN and relying on the default.

```
[6]: from qiskit_machine_learning.neural_networks import SamplerQNN

sampler_qnn = SamplerQNN(circuit=qc2, input_params=inputs2, weight_params=weights2)

sampler_qnn

[6]: <qiskit_machine_learning.neural_networks.sampler_qnn.SamplerQNN at 0x7fc3c75aa5b0>
```

How to Run a Forward Pass

Set-Up

In a real setting, the inputs would be defined by the dataset, and the weights would be defined by the training algorithm or as part of a pre-trained model. However, for the sake of this tutorial, we will specify random sets of input and weights of the right dimension:

EstimatorQNN Example

```
[7]: estimator_qnn_input = algorithm_globals.random.random(estimator_ qnn.num_inputs)

estimator_qnn_weights = algorithm_globals.random.random(estimator_qnn.num_weights)

[8]: print(

  f"Number of input features for EstimatorQNN: {estimator_qnn.num_inputs} \nInput: {estimator_
qnn_input}"

)

print(

   f"Number of trainable weights for EstimatorQNN: {estimator_qnn.num_weights} \nWeights:
{estimator_qnn_weights}"

)

Number of input features for EstimatorQNN: 1

Input: [0.77395605]

Number of trainable weights for EstimatorQNN: 1

Weights: [0.43887844]
```

3.1.2. SamplerQNN Example

```
[9]: sampler_qnn_input = algorithm_globals.random.random(sampler_qnn.num_inputs)
```

```
sampler_qnn_weights = algorithm_globals.random.random(sampler_qnn.num_weights)
[10]: print(
    f"Number of input features for SamplerQNN: {sampler_qnn.num_inputs} \nInput: {sampler_qnn_input}"
)
print(
f"Number of trainable weights for SamplerQNN: {sampler_qnn.num_weights} \nWeights: {sampler_qnn_weights}"
)
Number of input features for SamplerQNN: 2
Input: [0.85859792 0.69736803]
Number of trainable weights for SamplerQNN: 4
Weights: [0.09417735 0.97562235 0.7611397  0.78606431]
```

Once we have the inputs and the weights, let's see the results for batched and non-batched passes.

Non-batched Forward Pass

EstimatorQNN Example

For the EstimatorQNN, the expected output shape for the forward pass is (1, num_qubits * num_observables) where 1 in our case is the number of samples:

```
[11]:
estimator_qnn_forward = estimator_qnn.forward(estimator_qnn_input, estimator_qnn_weights)
print(
   f"Forward pass result for EstimatorQNN: {estimator_qnn_forward}. \nShape: {estimator_qnn_forward.shape}"
)
Forward pass result for EstimatorQNN: [[0.2970094]].
Shape: (1, 1)
```

SamplerQNN Example

For the SamplerQNN (without a custom interpret function), the expected output shape for the forward pass is (1, 2**num_qubits). With a custom interpret function, the output shape will be (1, output_shape), where 1 in our case is the number of samples:

```
[12]:
sampler_qnn_forward = sampler_qnn.forward(sampler_qnn_input, sampler_qnn_weights)
print(
```

```
    f"Forward pass result for SamplerQNN: {sampler_qnn_forward}. \nShape: {sampler_qnn_forward.shape}"
)
Forward pass result for SamplerQNN: [[0.01826527 0.25735654 0.5267981  0.19758009]].
Shape: (1, 4)
```

Batched Forward Pass

Estimator QNN Example

For the EstimatorQNN, the expected output shape for the forward pass is (batch_size, num_qubits * num_observables):

```
[13]:
estimator_qnn_forward_batched = estimator_qnn.forward(
    [estimator_qnn_input, estimator_qnn_input], estimator_qnn_weights
)
print(
    f"Forward pass result for EstimatorQNN: {estimator_qnn_forward_batched}. \nShape: {estimator_qnn_forward_batched.shape}"
)
Forward pass result for EstimatorQNN: [[0.2970094]
 [0.2970094]].
Shape: (2, 1)
```

Sampler QNN Example

For the SamplerQNN (without custom interpret function), the expected output shape for the forward pass is (batch_size, 2**num_qubits). With a custom interpret function, the output shape will be (batch_size, output_shape).

```
[14]: sampler_qnn_forward_batched = sampler_qnn.forward(
    [sampler_qnn_input, sampler_qnn_input], sampler_qnn_weights
)
print(
    f"Forward pass result for SamplerQNN: {sampler_qnn_forward_batched}. \nShape: {sampler_qnn_forward_batched.shape}"
)
Forward pass result for SamplerQNN: [[0.01826527 0.25735654 0.5267981  0.19758009]
 [0.01826527 0.25735654 0.5267981  0.19758009]].
Shape: (2, 4)
```

How to Run a Backward Pass

Let's take advantage of the inputs and weights defined above to show how the backward pass works. This pass returns a tuple (input_gradients, weight_gradients). By default, the backward pass will only calculate gradients with respect to the weight parameters.

If you want to enable gradients with respect to the input parameters, you should set the following flag during the QNN instantiation:

qnn = ...QNN(..., input_gradients=**True**)

Please remember that input gradients are **required** for the use of TorchConnector for PyTorch integration.

Backward Pass without Input Gradients

Estimator QNN Example

For the EstimatorQNN, the expected output shape for the weight gradients is (batch_size, num_qubits * num_observables, num_weights):

```
[15]: estimator_qnn_input_grad, estimator_qnn_weight_grad = estimator_qnn.backward(
    estimator_qnn_input, estimator_qnn_weights
)
print(
    f"Input gradients for EstimatorQNN: {estimator_qnn_input_grad}. \nShape: {estimator_qnn_input_grad}"
)
print(
    f"Weight gradients for EstimatorQNN: {estimator_qnn_weight_grad}. \nShape: {estimator_qnn_weight_grad.shape}"
)
Input gradients for EstimatorQNN: None.
Shape: None
Weight gradients for EstimatorQNN: [[[0.63272767]]].
Shape: (1, 1, 1)
```

Sampler QNN Example

For the SamplerQNN (without custom interpret function), the expected output shape for the forward pass is (batch_size, 2**num_qubits, num_weights). With a custom interpret function, the output shape will be (batch_size, output_shape, num_weights).:

[16]:

```
sampler_qnn_input_grad, sampler_qnn_weight_grad = sampler_qnn.backward(
    sampler_qnn_input, sampler_qnn_weights
)
print(
    f”Input gradients for SamplerQNN: {sampler_qnn_input_grad}. \nShape: {sampler_qnn_input_grad}”
)
print(
    f”Weight gradients for SamplerQNN: {sampler_qnn_weight_grad}. \nShape: {sampler_qnn_weight_grad.shape}”
)
```

```
Input gradients for SamplerQNN: None.
Shape: None
Weight gradients for SamplerQNN: [[[ 0.00606238 -0.1124595  -0.06856156 -0.09809236]
  [ 0.21167414 -0.09069775  0.06856156 -0.22549618]
  [-0.48846674  0.32499215 -0.32262178  0.09809236]
  [ 0.27073021 -0.12183491  0.32262178  0.22549618]]].
Shape: (1, 4, 4)
```

4.2. Backward Pass with Input Gradients

Let’s enable the input_gradients to show what the expected output sizes are for this option.

[17]:

```
estimator_qnn.input_gradients = True
sampler_qnn.input_gradients = True
```

Estimator QNN Example

For the EstimatorQNN, the expected output shape for the input gradients is (batch_size, num_qubits * num_observables, num_inputs):

[18]:

```
estimator_qnn_input_grad, estimator_qnn_weight_grad = estimator_qnn.backward(
    estimator_qnn_input, estimator_qnn_weights
)
print(
    f”Input gradients for EstimatorQNN: {estimator_qnn_input_grad}. \nShape: {estimator_qnn_input_grad.shape}”
```

```
)
print(
    f"Weight gradients for EstimatorQNN: {estimator_qnn_weight_grad}. \nShape: {estimator_qnn_weight_grad.shape}"
)
Input gradients for EstimatorQNN: [[[0.3038852]]].
Shape: (1, 1, 1)
Weight gradients for EstimatorQNN: [[[0.63272767]]].
Shape: (1, 1, 1)
```

SamplerQNN Example

For the Sampler QNN (without custom interpret function), the expected output shape for the input gradients is (batch_size, 2**num_qubits, num_inputs). With a custom interpret function, the output shape will be (batch_size, output_shape, num_inputs).

```
[19]:
sampler_qnn_input_grad, sampler_qnn_weight_grad = sampler_qnn.backward(
    sampler_qnn_input, sampler_qnn_weights
)
print(
    f"Input gradients for SamplerQNN: {sampler_qnn_input_grad}. \nShape: {sampler_qnn_input_grad.shape}"
)
print(
    f"Weight gradients for SamplerQNN: {sampler_qnn_weight_grad}. \nShape: {sampler_qnn_weight_grad.shape}"
)
Input gradients for SamplerQNN: [[[-0.05844702 -0.10621091]
  [ 0.38798796 -0.19544083]
  [-0.34561132  0.09459601]
  [ 0.01607038  0.20705573]]].
Shape: (1, 4, 2)
Weight gradients for SamplerQNN: [[[ 0.00606238 -0.1124595  -0.06856156 -0.09809236]
  [ 0.21167414 -0.09069775  0.06856156 -0.22549618]
  [-0.48846674  0.32499215 -0.32262178  0.09809236]
```

```
[ 0.27073021 -0.12183491  0.32262178  0.22549618]]].
Shape: (1, 4, 4)
```

Advanced Functionality

EstimatorQNN with Multiple Observables

The EstimatorQNN allows to pass lists of observables for more complex QNN architectures. For example (note the change in output shape):

```
[20]: observable2 = SparsePauliOp.from_list([("Z" * qc1.num_qubits, 1)])


estimator_qnn2 = EstimatorQNN(
    circuit=qc1,
    observables=[observable1, observable2],
    input_params=[params1[0]],
    weight_params=[params1[1]],
)
[21]:
estimator_qnn_forward2 = estimator_qnn2.forward(estimator_qnn_input, estimator_qnn_
weights)
estimator_qnn_input_grad2, estimator_qnn_weight_grad2 = estimator_qnn2.backward(
    estimator_qnn_input, estimator_qnn_weights
)
print(f"Forward output for EstimatorQNN1: {estimator_qnn_forward.shape}")
print(f"Forward output for EstimatorQNN2: {estimator_qnn_forward2.shape}")
print(f"Backward output for EstimatorQNN1: {estimator_qnn_weight_grad.shape}")
print(f"Backward output for EstimatorQNN2: {estimator_qnn_weight_grad2.shape}")
Forward output for EstimatorQNN1: (1, 1)
Forward output for EstimatorQNN2: (1, 2)
Backward output for EstimatorQNN1: (1, 1, 1)
Backward output for EstimatorQNN2: (1, 2, 1)
```

SamplerQNN with custom interpret

One common interpret method for SamplerQNN is the parity function, which allows it to perform binary classification. As explained in the instantiation section, using interpret functions will modify the output shape of the forward and backward passes. In the case of the parity interpret function, output_shape is fixed to 2. Therefore, the expected forward and weight gradient shapes are (batch_size,

2) and (batch_size, 2, num_weights), respectively:

```
[22]: parity = lambda x: "{:b}".format(x).count("1") % 2
output_shape = 2 # parity = 0, 1

sampler_qnn2 = SamplerQNN(
   circuit=qc2,
   input_params=inputs2,
   weight_params=weights2,
   interpret=parity,
   output_shape=output_shape,
)
[23]:
sampler_qnn_forward2 = sampler_qnn2.forward(sampler_qnn_input, sampler_qnn_weights)
sampler_qnn_input_grad2, sampler_qnn_weight_grad2 = sampler_qnn2.backward(
   sampler_qnn_input, sampler_qnn_weights
)
print(f"Forward output for SamplerQNN1: {sampler_qnn_forward.shape}")
print(f"Forward output for SamplerQNN2: {sampler_qnn_forward2.shape}")
print(f"Backward output for SamplerQNN1: {sampler_qnn_weight_grad.shape}")
print(f"Backward output for SamplerQNN2: {sampler_qnn_weight_grad2.shape}")
Forward output for SamplerQNN1: (1, 4)
Forward output for SamplerQNN2: (1, 2)
Backward output for SamplerQNN1: (1, 4, 4)
Backward output for SamplerQNN2: (1, 2, 4)
```

QUANTUM FEATURE MAPPING AND QUANTUM SUPPORT VECTOR MACHINE

Introduction

Quantum feature mapping is a technique used in machine learning and quantum computing. It's a function that transforms input data into a Hilbert space. The feature vectors are quantum states.

Although quantum computers are not yet accessible for everyone, Quantum Machine Learning (QML) is a promising field of study as it uses the intrinsic probabilistic nature of quantum systems to develop models. Right now, data scientists around the world are trying to understand how to leverage the quantum paradigm to produce better, scalable models. It is not possible to quantify when this will happen because it also depends on the evolution of quantum hardware, but there is accelerated growth in this matter.

In the last studies we were trying to design Variational Quantum Classifiers (VQCs). This is an interesting case of study if you are starting to study QML.

However, lately researcher also started to study a quantum approach to the Support Vector Machine (SVM) and researcher was intrigued by how SVM could be translated into the quantum world.

As we were studying VQCs, researcher was very biased and was trying to guess how the SVM could be translated into a parameterizable quantum circuit, but researcher found that the quantum enhancement here works differently, which was a nice surprise and helped me to open my mind about this subject.

In this section researcher start with a brief introduction of SVM followed by how to do a Quantum Machine Learning (QML) approach to this technique and finish with an example of quantum enhanced SVM (QSVM) using the Titanic dataset.

SVM and kernels

But what is this hyperplane that separates the classes? Suppose we are working with data in a two-dimensional vector space and we have two classes, as in Figure 3.

In this example we have data points from 2 different classes and we can easily draw a line separating both. Our solid line is the hyperplane that separates our data with the best possible margin, as seen by the dashed lines. Thus, SVM tries to find the best separator.

You may think that my example was too naive and a line is a very particular case of a hyperplane, which is a valid point. What if our two-dimensional data looks like Fig. 4?

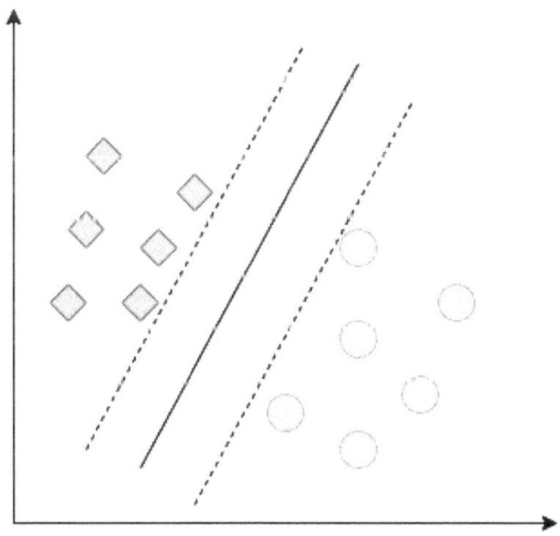

Fig. 3. 2D data with a very clear linear separator

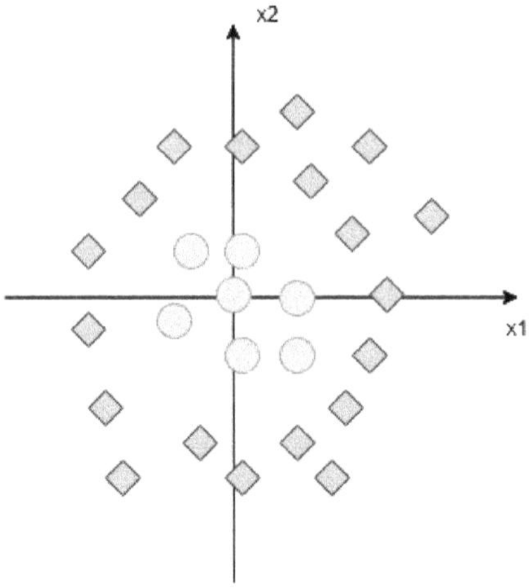

Fig. 4. 2D data with nonlinear separator

In this case we can't draw a line that separates our data correctly. If we look at this figure, we could draw a circle as a good separator. However, this shape is neither a line nor a plane, so SVM isn't able to directly solve this problem. However, this is the coolest SVM trick and the part where a high dimensional hyperplane occurs! What if we have the transformation of this data into a higher dimension vector space? As:

$$x_3 = f(x_1, x_2) = x_1^2 + x_2^2$$

So we would could draw a plane:

$x_3 = k, k \in$ □

Which separates the two classes optimally, as seen in Figure 5:

In our case, the function f is what we call the kernel, which projects data into a higher dimensional space, which makes it easier to find a hyperplane that can correctly identify data from different classes.

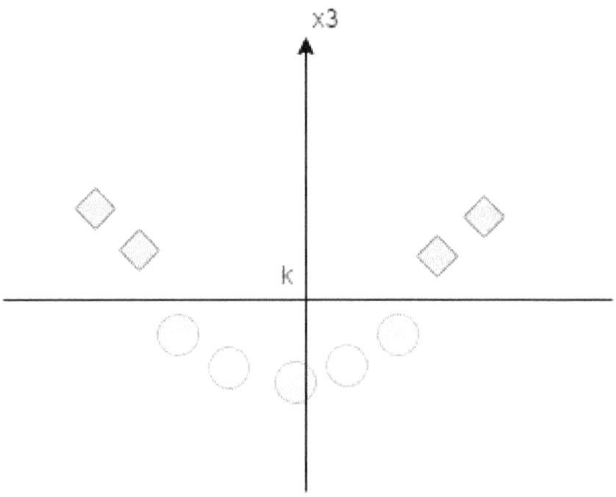

Fig. 5. Plane that separates our data in a higher dimensional space

This was a very brief introduction about kernels and SVM, if you are interested in more explanation about SVM I recommend you to read these two posts (1 and 2), which are really good introductions to SVM and I used both of them as references in this post.

You might be thinking now that my example was very convenient to explain the kernel concept, but how in real life do we find a suitable kernel that solves our problems? There are some kernels that are very flexible and are very helpful to solve a good number of problems, like the Radial Basis Function (RBF), which is the default option of scikit-learn's SVC. If you are interested in learning more about this kernel, researcher recommend this post. An important detail about kernels such as the RBF is that they aren't described by an analytic function, but as a similarity matrix between data points based on the kernel.

However, what if we want to be more creative? If you have read my previous posts you might remember that one of the most interesting properties of quantum computing is the exponential relation between qubits and quantum states. Thus, a quantum system is a very interesting candidate for a good kernel, as it tends to drive our system towards a high-dimensional vector space, depending on the quantity of qubits we are using.

Quantum Kernels

Quantum kernels are usually defined by an similarity matrix based on a quantum circuit, that might be parameterizable or not. Both Pennylane and Qiskit have built-in functions that create kernels that can be used in scikit-learn's SVC.

The project of a quantum kernel has some steps:

Embedding data into quantum states

x - > |x⟩

Designing a quantum circuit that might be parameterizable or not

|y⟩ = U (|x⟩)

x-At this stage, it is highly recommended to work with some degree of superposition and entanglement between states to obtain the best that quantum computing can provide.

Building the similarity matrix

Here we work with the unitary U(|x⟩) that we built in the last step and its adjoint to design a similarity matrix.

Example

Here we are designing a simple quantum kernel with Pennylane to use it with an SVC from scikit-learn for the Titanic Classification dataset, where we want to predict whether a person survived the Titanic tragedy based on variables such as age, gender and boarding class.

In our example we are using the following variables:

- **is_child:** if the age of the person is less than 12 (boolean)
- **Pclass_1:** if the person boarded in the first class (boolean)
- **Pclass_2:** if the person boarded in the second class (boolean)
- **Sex_female:** if the gender of the person is female (boolean)

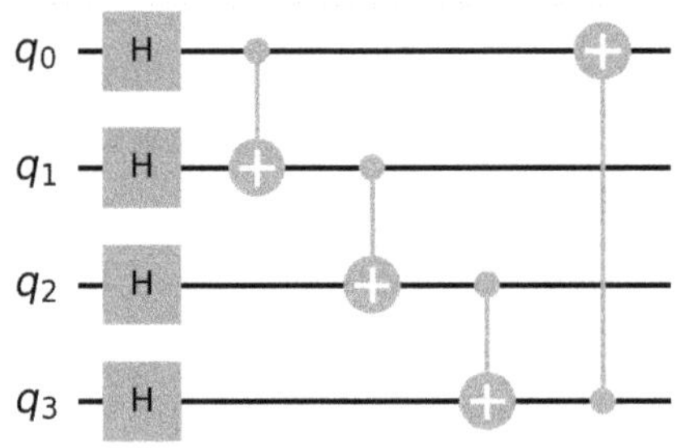

Fig. 6 Ansatz for our kernel example

As you can see, this is a very simple model with four boolean variables. We are embedding our data into quantum states using quantum embedding (Basis Embedding), applying Hadamard gates to apply superposition into our qubits and CNOT gates to generate entanglement.

This is a simple and non-parameterizable ansatz, but it generates superposition and entanglement between our variables.

The code to create the kernel and SVM is here:

```
import pennylane as qml
from pennylane import numpy as np
from sklearn.model_selection import train_test_split
import pandas as pd
from sklearn.metrics import accuracy_score
from sklearn.metrics import f1_score, precision_score, recall_score
from sklearn.svm import SVC
num_qubits = 4
def layer(x):
    qml.BasisEmbedding(x, wires=range(num_qubits))
    for j, wire in enumerate(wires):
    qml.Hadamard(wires=[wire])
```

```
      if j != num_qubits-1:
         qml.CNOT(wires=[j, j+1])
      else:
         qml.CNOT(wires=[j, 0])
def ansatz(x, wires):
   layer(x)
adjoint_ansatz = qml.adjoint(ansatz)
dev = qml.device("default.qubit", wires=num_qubits, shots=None)
wires = dev.wires.tolist()
@qml.qnode(dev, interface="autograd")
def kernel_circuit(x1, x2):
   ansatz(x1, wires=wires)
   adjoint_ansatz(x2, wires=wires)
   return qml.probs(wires=wires)
def kernel(x1, x2):
   return kernel_circuit(x1, x2)[0]
df_train = pd.read_csv('train.csv')
df_train['Pclass'] = df_train['Pclass'].astype(str)
df_train = pd.concat([df_train, pd.get_dummies(df_train[['Pclass', 'Sex', 'Embarked']])], axis=1)
X_train, X_test, y_train, y_test = train_test_split(df_train.drop(columns=['Survived']), df_
train['Survived'], test_size=0.10, random_state=42, stratify=df_train['Survived'])
X_train['Age'] = X_train['Age'].fillna(X_train['Age'].median())
X_test['Age'] = X_test['Age'].fillna(X_test['Age'].median())
X_train['is_child'] = X_train['Age'].map(lambda x: 1 if x < 12 else 0)
X_test['is_child'] = X_test['Age'].map(lambda x: 1 if x < 12 else 0)
cols_model = ['is_child', 'Pclass_1', 'Pclass_2', 'Sex_female']
X_train = X_train[cols_model]
X_test = X_test[cols_model]
X_train = np.array(X_train.values, requires_grad=False)
init_kernel = lambda x1, x2: kernel(x1, x2)
K = qml.kernels.square_kernel_matrix(X_train, init_kernel, assume_normalized_kernel=True)
svm = SVC(kernel=lambda X1, X2: qml.kernels.kernel_matrix(X1, X2, init_kernel)).fit(X_train,
y_train)
X_test = np.array(X_test.values, requires_grad=False)
```

```
predictions = svm.predict(X_test)
accuracy_score(y_test, predictions)
precision_score(y_test, predictions)
recall_score(y_test, predictions)
f1_score(y_test, predictions, average='macro')
svm1 = SVC(gamma='auto', kernel='rbf')
svm1.fit(X_train, y_train)
y_pred = svm1.predict(X_test)
accuracy_score(y_test, y_pred)
precision_score(y_test, y_pred)
recall_score(y_test, y_pred)
f1_score(y_test, y_pred, average='macro')
```

Advantages of Quantum Support Vector Machines

There are several advantages of quantum support vector machines (QSVMs) over classical support vector machines (SVMs):

- **Faster training times:** QSVMs can achieve faster training times than classical SVMs due to the increased computational power of quantum computers. This can be especially useful for large-scale machine learning tasks where training time is a major bottleneck.
- **Better generalization performance:** QSVMs have been shown to have better generalization performance, meaning they are able to make more accurate predictions on unseen data than classical SVMs. This is because QSVMs can capture more complex patterns in the data due to the higher-dimensional feature space used by quantum kernel functions.
- **Ability to handle non-linear data:** QSVMs can handle non-linear data more effectively than classical SVMs because they use quantum kernel functions, which can map the data into a higher-dimensional space where it is linearly separable. This is not possible with classical SVMs, which are limited to linear kernel functions.

Here are a few examples of how QSVMs can outperform classical SVMs:

- In a study published in Nature Communications, QSVMs were able to classify cancer tissue samples with higher accuracy than classical SVMs.
- In another study published in Scientific Reports, QSVMs were able to classify handwritten digits with higher accuracy than classical SVMs.
- In a third study published in Physical Review Letters, QSVMs were able to classify images of faces and buildings with higher accuracy than classical

SVMs.

Overall, these studies demonstrate the potential of QSVMs to outperform classical SVMs in various machine-learning tasks. In the next section, we will discuss the implementation of QSVMs.

Implementing Quantum Support Vector Machines

Several tools and frameworks are available for implementing quantum support vector machines (QSVMs). Some popular options include:

Qiskit

Qiskit is an open-source quantum computing framework developed by IBM. It provides tools for constructing and running quantum circuits and a library of quantum algorithms, including QSVMs. Here is an example of how to implement a QSVM using Qiskit:

Python

```python
from qiskit import Aer, QuantumCircuit, execute
from qiskit.aqua.algorithms import QSVM

# Load the training data
training_data = {'A': [[0,0], [0,1]], 'B': [[1,0], [1,1]]}

# Set up the quantum circuit
feature_map = ZZFeatureMap(feature_dimension=2, reps=2, entanglement='linear')
qsvm = QSVM(feature_map, training_data)

# Execute the quantum circuit
backend = Aer.get_backend('qasm_simulator')
```

```
result = execute(qsvm.construct_circuit(), backend=backend).result()

# Extract the results
predicted_labels = qsvm.predict(result)
print(predicted_labels)  # should output ['A', 'A', 'B', 'B']

```

PennyLane

PennyLane is a library for quantum machine learning that can be used to implement QSVMs and other quantum algorithms. It is designed to be used with popular machine-learning libraries such as PyTorch and TensorFlow. Here is an example of how to implement a QSVM using PennyLane:

Python

```
import pennylane as qml
from pennylane import numpy as np

# Load the training data
training_data = {'A': [[0,0], [0,1]], 'B': [[1,0], [1,1]]}

# Set up the quantum circuit
dev = qml.device('default.qubit', wires=2)

@qml.qnode(dev)
def circuit(weights):
```

```
    qml.SVMCircuit(weights, X=training_data['A'])
    return qml.expval(qml.PauliZ(0))


# Execute the quantum circuit
result = circuit(np.array([0.5, 0.5]))
print(result)  # should output a value between -1 and 1
```

In addition to these tools and frameworks, there are also a few best practices to keep in mind when implementing QSVMs:

- Use quantum computers with high quantum volume: Quantum volume is a measure of the complexity of a quantum computer, and higher quantum volume generally indicates better performance for quantum algorithms.
- Choose the appropriate kernel function: Different kernel functions may perform better for different types of data, so it is important to experiment with different options and choose the one that gives the best results.
- Use appropriate hyperparameters: Hyperparameters such as the learning rate and regularization strength can have a big impact on the performance of the QSVM, so it is important to tune these parameters appropriately.

We hope this helps to give you an idea of how to implement quantum support vector machines. In the next section, we will discuss the applications of QSVMs.

Applications of QSVM

Quantum support vector machines (QSVMs) have the potential to be applied to a wide range of real-world problems. Some examples of applications of QSVMs include:

- **Healthcare:** QSVMs could be used to classify medical images or predict patient outcomes, potentially leading to more accurate diagnoses and better patient care.
- **Finance:** QSVMs could be used to analyze financial data and make investment decisions, potentially leading to more informed investment strategies.

- **Transportation:** QSVMs could be used to predict traffic patterns or optimize routes for self-driving vehicles, potentially leading to more efficient transportation systems.

In addition to these applications, there are also many potential future developments in QSVMs. Some areas of research include improving the scalability and robustness of QSVMs, as well as developing new quantum algorithms specifically designed for machine learning tasks.

Overall, the potential applications of QSVMs are vast and varied. As the field of quantum machine learning continues to grow, we can expect to see even more innovative uses of QSVMs in the future. This concludes our discussion on QSVMs. We hope this has been a helpful introduction to this exciting topic!

APPLICATIONS IN BIG DATA AND PATTERN RECOGNITION

Applications of Big Data

In today's world, there are a lot of data. Big companies utilize those data for their business growth. By analyzing this data, the useful decision can be made in various cases as discussed below:

- **Tracking Customer Spending Habit, Shopping Behavior:** In big retails store (like Amazon, Walmart, Big Bazar etc.) management team has to keep data of customer's spending habit (in which product customer spent, in which brand they wish to spent, how frequently they spent), shopping behavior, customer's most liked product (so that they can keep those products in the store). Which product is being searched/sold most, based on that data, production/collection rate of that product get fixed.
- Banking sector uses their customer's spending behavior-related data so that they can provide the offer to a particular customer to buy his particular liked product by using bank's credit or debit card with discount or cashback. By this way, they can send the right offer to the right person at the right time.
- **Recommendation:** By tracking customer spending habit, shopping behavior, Big retails store provide a recommendation to the customer. E-commerce site like Amazon, Walmart, Flipkart does product recommendation. They track what product a customer is searching, based on that data they recommend that type of product to that customer.
- As an example, suppose any customer searched bed cover on Amazon. So, Amazon got data that customer may be interested to buy bed cover. Next time when that customer will go to any google page, advertisement of various bed covers will be seen. Thus, advertisement of the right product to the right customer can be sent.

- YouTube also shows recommend video based on user's previous liked, watched video type. Based on the content of a video, the user is watching, relevant advertisement is shown during video running. As an example suppose someone watching a tutorial video of Big data, then advertisement of some other big data course will be shown during that video.
- **Smart Traffic System:** Data about the condition of the traffic of different road, collected through camera kept beside the road, at entry and exit point of the city, GPS device placed in the vehicle (Ola, Uber cab, etc.). All such data are analyzed and jam-free or less jam way, less time taking ways are recommended. Such a way smart traffic system can be built in the city by Big data analysis. One more profit is fuel consumption can be reduced.
- **Secure Air Traffic System:** At various places of flight (like propeller etc) sensors present. These sensors capture data like the speed of flight, moisture, temperature, other environmental condition. Based on such data analysis, an environmental parameter within flight are set up and varied.
- By analyzing flight's machine-generated data, it can be estimated how long the machine can operate flawlessly when it to be replaced/repaired.
- **Auto Driving Car:** Big data analysis helps drive a car without human interpretation. In the various spot of car camera, a sensor placed, that gather data like the size of the surrounding car, obstacle, distance from those, etc. These data are being analyzed, then various calculation like how many angles to rotate, what should be speed, when to stop, etc carried out. These calculations help to take action automatically.
- **Virtual Personal Assistant Tool:** Big data analysis helps virtual personal assistant tool (like Siri in Apple Device, Cortana in Windows, Google Assistant in Android) to provide the answer of the various question asked by users. This tool tracks the location of the user, their local time, season, other data related to question asked, etc. Analyzing all such data, it provides an answer.
- As an example, suppose one user asks "Do I need to take Umbrella?", the tool collects data like location of the user, season and weather condition at that location, then analyze these data to conclude if there is a chance of raining, then provide the answer.
- **IoT:**
  - Manufacturing company install IOT sensor into machines to collect operational data. Analyzing such data, it can be predicted how long machine will work without any problem when it requires repairing so that company can take action before the situation when machine facing

a lot of issues or gets totally down. Thus, the cost to replace the whole machine can be saved.

- In the Healthcare field, Big data is providing a significant contribution. Using big data tool, data regarding patient experience is collected and is used by doctors to give better treatment. IoT device can sense a symptom of probable coming disease in the human body and prevent it from giving advance treatment. IoT Sensor placed near-patient, new-born baby constantly keeps track of various health condition like heart bit rate, blood presser, etc. Whenever any parameter crosses the safe limit, an alarm sent to a doctor, so that they can take step remotely very soon.

- **Education Sector:** Online educational course conducting organization utilize big data to search candidate, interested in that course. If someone searches for YouTube tutorial video on a subject, then online or offline course provider organization on that subject send ad online to that person about their course.
- **Energy Sector:** Smart electric meter read consumed power every 15 minutes and sends this read data to the server, where data analyzed and it can be estimated what is the time in a day when the power load is less throughout the city. By this system manufacturing unit or housekeeper are suggested the time when they should drive their heavy machine in the night time when power load less to enjoy less electricity bill.
- **Media and Entertainment Sector:** Media and entertainment service providing company like Netflix, Amazon Prime, Spotify do analysis on data collected from their users. Data like what type of video, music users are watching, listening most, how long users are spending on site, etc are collected and analyzed to set the next business strategy.

Pattern Recognition and Machine Learning

Machine learning brings us cool innovations like self-driving cars, online shopping assistants/recommendations, and fraud detection. However, every amazing new tech needs a little help before it becomes fully realized. And that's why we're discussing pattern recognition.

This section discusses pattern recognition and machine learning. We will go over what it is, why it's important, its applications and techniques, and give some examples and pattern recognition and machine learning algorithms. We are also introducing a collection of mock answers for the pattern recognition test.

When you finish this article, you will gain a greater understanding and appreciation for pattern recognition and its role in machine learning. That's valuable knowledge to have in this world of ever-increasing smart machines.

Pattern is everything around in this digital world. A pattern can either be seen physically or it can be observed mathematically by applying algorithms.

Example: The colors on the clothes, speech pattern, etc. In computer science, a pattern is represented using vector feature values.

What is Pattern Recognition?

Pattern recognition is the process of recognizing patterns by using a machine learning algorithm. Pattern recognition can be defined as the classification of data based on knowledge already gained or on statistical information extracted from patterns and/or their representation. One of the important aspects of pattern recognition is its application potential.

Examples: Speech recognition, speaker identification, multimedia document recognition (MDR), automatic medical diagnosis.

In a typical pattern recognition application, the raw data is processed and converted into a form that is amenable for a machine to use. Pattern recognition involves the classification and cluster of patterns.

- In classification, an appropriate class label is assigned to a pattern based on an abstraction that is generated using a set of training patterns or domain knowledge. Classification is used in supervised learning.
- Clustering generated a partition of the data which helps decision making, the specific decision-making activity of interest to us. Clustering is used in unsupervised learning.

Features may be represented as continuous, discrete, or discrete binary variables. A feature is a function of one or more measurements, computed so that it quantifies some significant characteristics of the object.

Example: consider our face then eyes, ears, nose, etc are features of the face.

A set of features that are taken together, forms the **features vector.**

Example: In the above example of a face, if all the features (eyes, ears, nose, etc) are taken together then the sequence is a feature vector([eyes, ears, nose]). The feature vector is the sequence of a feature represented as a d-dimensional column vector. In the case of speech, MFCC (Mel-frequency Cepstral Coefficient) is the spectral feature of the speech. The sequence of the first 13 features forms a feature vector.

Pattern recognition possesses the following features:

- Pattern recognition system should recognize familiar patterns quickly and accurate
- Recognize and classify unfamiliar objects

- Accurately recognize shapes and objects from different angles
- Identify patterns and objects even when partly hidden
- Recognize patterns quickly with ease, and with automaticity.

Training and Learning in Pattern Recognition

Learning is a phenomenon through which a system gets trained and becomes adaptable to give results in an accurate manner. Learning is the most important phase as to how well the system performs on the data provided to the system depends on which algorithms are used on the data. The entire dataset is divided into two categories, one which is used in training the model i.e. Training set, and the other that is used in testing the model after training, i.e. Testing set.

- **Training set::** The training set is used to build a model. It consists of the set of images that are used to train the system. Training rules and algorithms are used to give relevant information on how to associate input data with output decisions. The system is trained by applying these algorithms to the dataset, all the relevant information is extracted from the data, and results are obtained. Generally, 80% of the data of the dataset is taken for training data.

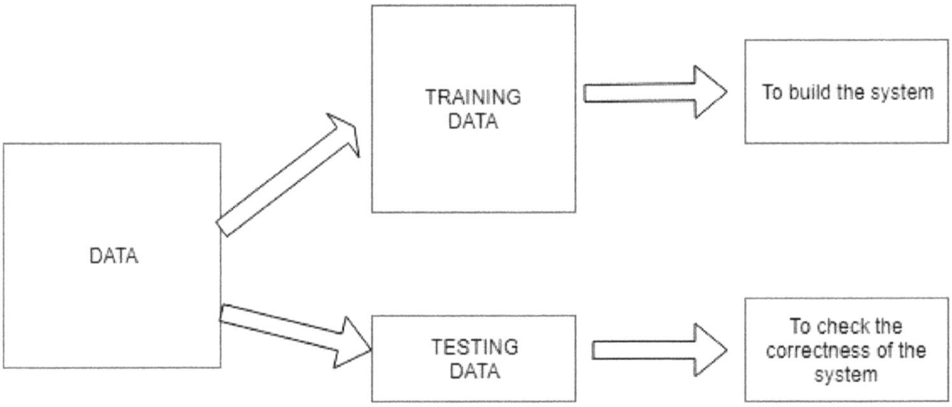

- **Testing set::** Testing data is used to test the system. It is the set of data that is used to verify whether the system is producing the correct output after being trained or not. Generally, 20% of the data of the dataset is used for testing. Testing data is used to measure the accuracy of the system. For example, a system that identifies which category a particular flower belongs to is able to identify seven categories of flowers correctly out of ten and the rest of others wrong, then the accuracy is 70 per cent.

Real-time Examples and Explanations:

A pattern is a physical object or an abstract notion. While talking about the classes of animals, a description of an animal would be a pattern. While talking about various types of balls, then a description of a ball is a pattern. In the case balls considered as pattern, the classes could be football, cricket ball, table tennis ball, etc. Given a new pattern, the class of the pattern is to be determined. The choice of attributes and representation of patterns is a very important step in pattern classification. A good representation is one that makes use of discriminating attributes and also reduces the computational burden in pattern classification.

An obvious representation of a pattern will be a **vector.** Each element of the vector can represent one attribute of the pattern. The first element of the vector will contain the value of the first attribute for the pattern being considered.

Example: While representing spherical objects, (25, 1) may be represented as a spherical object with 25 units of weight and 1 unit diameter. The class label can form a part of the vector. If spherical objects belong to class 1, the vector would be (25, 1, 1), where the first element represents the weight of the object, the second element, the diameter of the object and the third element represents the class of the object.

Advantages

- Pattern recognition solves classification problems
- Pattern recognition solves the problem of fake biometric detection.
- It is useful for cloth pattern recognition for visually impaired blind people.
- It helps in speaker diarization.
- We can recognize particular objects from different angles.

Disadvantages

- The syntactic pattern recognition approach is complex to implement and it is a very slow process.
- Sometimes to get better accuracy, a larger dataset is required.
- It cannot explain why a particular object is recognized.

Example: my face vs my friend's face.

Applications:

- **Image processing, segmentation, and analysis:** Pattern recognition is used to give human recognition intelligence to machines that are required in image processing.
- **Computer vision:** Pattern recognition is used to extract meaningful features from given image/video samples and is used in computer vision for various applications like biological and biomedical imaging.

- **Seismic analysis:** The pattern recognition approach is used for the discovery, imaging, and interpretation of temporal patterns in seismic array recordings. Statistical pattern recognition is implemented and used in different types of seismic analysis models.
- **Radar signal classification/analysis:** Pattern recognition and signal processing methods are used in various applications of radar signal classifications like AP mine detection and identification.
- **Speech recognition:** The greatest success in speech recognition has been obtained using pattern recognition paradigms. It is used in various algorithms of speech recognition which tries to avoid the problems of using a phoneme level of description and treats larger units such as words as pattern
- **Fingerprint identification:** Fingerprint recognition technology is a dominant technology in the biometric market. A number of recognition methods have been used to perform fingerprint matching out of which pattern recognition approaches are widely used.

Imagine we have a dataset containing information about apples and oranges. The features of each fruit are its color (red or yellow) and its shape (round or oval). We can represent each fruit using a list of strings, e.g. ['red', 'round'] for a red, round fruit.

Our goal is to write a function that can predict whether a given fruit is an apple or an orange. To do this, we will use a simple pattern recognition algorithm called k-nearest neighbors (k-NN).

CHAPTER-8

QUANTUM SUPREMACY AND MILESTONES

Quantum supremacy is a milestone in quantum computing that occurs when a quantum computer can solve a problem that no classical computer can solve in any feasible amount of time. Quantum advantage is the goal of combining quantum technology with CPUs, GPUs, and potentially NPUs to create a blended solution that can handle today's and tomorrow's jobs.

ABOUT QUANTUM SUPREMACY

- The phrase "quantum supremacy" was coined in 2011 by John Preskill, Professor of Theoretical Physics at the California Institute of Technology in a talk he delivered on the benefits of using quantum hardware over traditional computers.
- Quantum computing is the use of quantum-mechanical phenomena such as superposition and entanglement to perform computation.
  - A quantum computer is used to perform such computation, which can be implemented theoretically or physically.
  - Quantum supremacy refers to a quantum computer solving a problem that cannot be expected of a classical computer in a normal lifetime.
  - This relates to the speed at which a quantum computer preforms.
- Quantum supremacy is the point at which quantum computers can solve problems that are practically unsolvable for "classical" (nonquantum) computers to complete in any reasonable timeframe.
  - In principle, even the simplest universal computer can solve anything that is computable given infinite time to do so.
- It is generally believed that at least 49 qubits are required to cross the quantum supremacy line.
- Qubits behave very differently to bits in classical computers.

- Bits represent either a "1" or a "0," and computers read and perform operations on one bit at a time.

- In contrast, qubits can represent a combination state made up of both "1" and "0," due to the peculiar quantum effects in which properties like particle position, direction, and momentum are not well-defined.
- This allows for a system to be in multiple states at the same time, called quantum indeterminacy.

The algorithm used to demonstrate supremacy does not need to have wide application, just a clear-cut ability to run efficiently on a quantum processor compared with a classical computer where the algorithm is intractable. In this section, we discuss problems which researchers are considering to demonstrate quantum supremacy. Regardless of the particular problem used for the demonstration, quantum supremacy is a landmark achievement in the history of physics and computer science. While many proof-of-principle quantum computations have been performed on quantum processors, this will be the first to be executed at a large enough scale to reveal an experimentally verifiable computational separation.

This has implications for verifying quantum mechanics through largescale computation. Indeed, we can think of supremacy experiments as the computational analogue of Bell experiments. Just as Bell experiments refute local hidden variable models, supremacy experiments on an errorcorrected QC would refute the Extended Church-Turing Thesis (ECTT) which, asserts that any algorithmic process can be simulated efficiently using a probabilistic Turing machine PTM. The ability to carefully control quantum systems of this magnitude is also a crowning achievement of engineering and experimental physics.

Problems for Demonstrating Quantum Supremacy

While random circuit sampling is a very natural problem to consider for demonstrating quantum supremacy, it is not the only one. A recent survey paper provides a helpful discussion of additional major problems being considered to show quantum-classical separation.

The problem of boson sampling is another candidate for demonstrating quantum supremacy. Originally proposed, boson sampling involves sending n coincident photons into a randomly generated linear-optical network of m n modes (beam splitters); this generates a random unitary rotation. Detectors are then used to sample from the distribution of photons, a process which is believed to be classically hard. Boson sampling experiments have been performed with up to five photons and nine modes. Experimental systems are challenged by non-trivial photon loss in the optical network. Additionally, developing more efficient classical sampling techniques is a challenge for quantum supremacy via boson sampling.

Application of Quantum Computing

- **Artificial Intelligence (AI):** Quantum computers could empower machine learning by enabling AI programs to search through these gigantic datasets concerning medical research, consumer behavior, financial markets, etc—and make sense of them.
- **Computational Chemistry**: Today's digital computers can analyze only the simplest molecules. But quantum computers can do precision modelling of complex molecular interactions and also find the optimum configurations for chemical reactions.
  - Google has already made inroads in this field by simulating the energy of hydrogen molecules.
  - The implication of this is - more efficient products, from solar cells to pharmaceutical drugs, and particularly fertilizer production; since fertilizer accounts for 2 percent of global energy usage, the consequences for energy and the environment would be profound.
- **Financial services:** Quantum computers can be used for complex financial modelling and risk management in the financial industry by finding new ways to model financial data and isolating key global risk factors.
- **Cryptography:** Online security depends on the factoring large numbers into primes which can be done by digital computers themselves, however, it would consume an Immense amount of time that makes "cracking the code" expensive and impractical.
  - Quantum computers can perform such factoring more efficiently than digital computers = Quantum computing can soon replace those obsolete methods.
- **Weather Forecasting:** The ability to better predict the weather would have enormous benefits to many fields, not to mention more time to take cover from disasters.
  - Conventional computers would take longer than it takes for the actual weather to evolve. Equations governing the weather possess a hidden wave nature which can be analysed by quantum computers = better weather prediction.
- **Climate modelling:** Quantum computers could help build better climate models that could give us more insight into how humans are influencing the environment.

- **Particle Physics Simulation:** Models of particle physics are often extraordinarily complex which require vast amounts of computing time for numerical solution.
    - This makes them ideal for quantum computation, and researchers have already taken advantage of this.
- **Logistics and Scheduling:** Quantum computing can make significant strides in the logistics sector.
    - Although classical computing is used heavily to do these tasks, some of them may be too complicated for a classical computing solution whereas a quantum approach may be able to do it.

ACHIEVING QUANTUM SUPREMACY

Quantum supremacy is achieved by demonstrating that a quantum computer can perform a calculation that is infeasible for classical computers. The calculation should be well-defined, and the output should be verifiable using classical means.

Google, in partnership with NASA and Oak Ridge National Laboratory, has demonstrated the ability to compute in seconds what would take even the largest and most advanced supercomputers thousands of years, achieving a milestone known as quantum supremacy.

Quantum computing is still in its infancy, but this transformative achievement rockets us forward. "Our missions in the decades to come to the Moon, Mars and beyond are all fueled by innovations like this one."

Quantum computing is the study of how to harness the unique properties of quantum mechanics to solve certain types of problems far faster than on traditional computers. Potentially, NASA could one day use these techniques to support space missions, with quantum optimization making mission schedules more efficient and quantum simulation supporting the design of light and robust materials for modern spacecraft – just to name a few applications. This milestone is the first step toward that future.

"Achieving quantum supremacy means we've been able to do *one* thing faster, not everything faster," said Eleanor Rieffel, co-author on the paper on this result, published today in *Nature,* and the Quantum Artificial Intelligence Laboratory Lead at Ames. "And even though that one thing isn't terribly useful, that it has been done at all is groundbreaking."

The paper describes the experiments run by Google's Sycamore quantum processor to demonstrate quantum supremacy. Computations on a quantum computer are called "quantum circuits." These computer science abstractions work like programs, specifying a series of operations for the quantum processor to run.

The test itself involved running random quantum circuits on quantum processors as well as traditional supercomputers. Getting results from a random quantum circuit is difficult without a quantum processor, and theory suggests it may be impossible for tasks beyond a certain size, even on the largest imaginable supercomputer. You'd need more units of data than there are atoms in the universe. That's as close as you can get to an impossible task – making it the perfect test for quantum supremacy.

Both the quantum processor and supercomputer were given increasingly complex and random circuits to compute until the supercomputer wasn't able to process them. To find that limit, researchers at Ames advanced techniques for simulating these random quantum circuit computations using NASA's supercomputing facilities. At a certain point, even with all the tricks NASA's quantum computing and supercomputing experts threw at it, this simulated "computer within a computer" wasn't able to handle the random circuits given to it – and that became the bar set for Google's quantum computer to beat.

When a quantum computer outperforms a classical supercomputer on a well-defined computer science problem, this achievement is known as quantum supremacy.

- Superposition states allow qubits to carry more information.
- Because of quantum superposition, a quantum computer can mimic several classical computers working in parallel.
- This capacity of doing several computations in parallel gives quantum computers an advantage over classical computers, allowing them to perform a disproportionately greater number of operations.
- Google's quantum computer, named Sycamore, claimed 'supremacy' because it reportedly did the task in 200 seconds that would have apparently taken a supercomputer 10,000 years to complete.

Supercomputer

Supercomputer is a class of extremely powerful computers. The term is commonly applied to the fastest high-performance systems available at any given time.

- The performance of a supercomputer is commonly measured in floating-point operations per second (FLOPS) instead of million instructions per second (MIPS).
- Since 2017, there have existed supercomputers which can perform over 1017 FLOPS (a hundred quadrillion FLOPS, 100 petaFLOPS or 100 PFLOPS.

- These are very large classical computers, often with thousands of classical CPU and GPU cores capable of running very large calculations and advanced artificial intelligence.

Understanding the Basics of Quantum Computing

Quantum computing is a revolutionary approach to computation that utilizes quantum bits, or qubits, as the fundamental building blocks of information processing. While classical computers use binary digits, or bits, that can represent either a 0 or a 1, qubits can exist in a superposition, which allows them to represent multiple states simultaneously. This ability to exist in multiple states simultaneously is what gives quantum computers their potential for exponential computational power.

The Concept of Quantum Bits

A quantum bit, or qubit, is the basic unit of quantum information. It can be represented as a quantum system with two basis states, conventionally denoted as $|0\rangle$ and $|1\rangle$. However, unlike classical bits, qubits can also exist in a superposition of these two states, meaning they can simultaneously be $|0\rangle$ and $|1\rangle$. This opens up a whole new set of possibilities for computation.

Quantum bits are not limited to just two states, as classical bits are. They can exist in a continuum of states between $|0\rangle$ and $|1\rangle$. This means that a qubit can represent any number between 0 and 1, not just discrete values like 0 or 1. This continuous range of values allows for a much richer and more nuanced representation of information.

Furthermore, qubits can also exist in a state known as a superposition of multiple basis states. For example, a qubit can be in a state that is simultaneously |0é' and |1é' with a certain probability. This superposition of states enables quantum computers to perform calculations in parallel, exploring multiple possibilities simultaneously.

The Role of Superposition and Entanglement

Superposition and entanglement are two key concepts that make quantum computing unique. Superposition allows qubits to exist in multiple states at the same time, exponentially increasing the computational power of a quantum computer. This is because each additional qubit added to a quantum computer doubles the number of possible states it can represent.

Entanglement, on the other hand, refers to the phenomenon where the state of one qubit is linked to the state of another, regardless of the distance between them. When qubits are entangled, the state of one qubit cannot be described independently of the state of the other qubit. This entanglement allows for the creation of quantum gates that can operate on multiple qubits simultaneously, enabling complex calculations to be performed efficiently.

Entanglement also enables quantum computers to solve certain problems more efficiently than classical computers. For example, in certain optimization problems, the solutions can be represented as a superposition of states, and entanglement allows quantum computers to explore all possible solutions simultaneously, leading to potentially faster and more accurate results.

Now, let's explore the journey towards quantum supremacy and the milestones that have been achieved along the way.

In recent years, there has been significant progress in the field of quantum computing. Researchers have been able to create qubits using various physical systems, such as superconducting circuits, trapped ions, and topological states of matter. These qubits have been used to perform simple calculations and demonstrate the principles of quantum computation.

One of the key challenges in quantum computing is maintaining the delicate quantum states of qubits. Quantum systems are extremely sensitive to noise and interference from the environment, which can cause errors in calculations. Scientists are actively working on developing error-correction techniques and improving the stability of qubits to overcome these challenges.

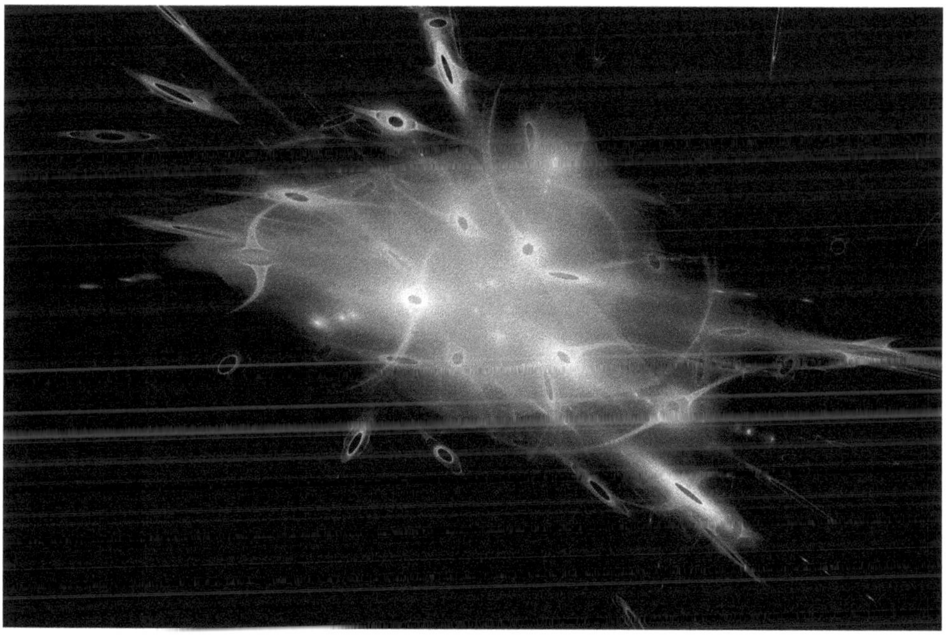

Fig. 1. Quantum bits, or qubits, are fundamental units of quantum information capable of existing in superposition states, enabling parallel computation.

Another important milestone in the development of quantum computing is the achievement of quantum supremacy. Quantum supremacy refers to the point at which a quantum computer can perform a calculation that is beyond the reach of any classical computer. While this milestone has not yet been reached, researchers are making significant strides towards it.

Quantum computing has the potential to revolutionize fields such as cryptography, optimization, drug discovery, and material science. It could enable us to solve complex problems that are currently intractable for classical computers, leading to breakthroughs in various scientific and technological domains.

The Journey Towards Quantum Supremacy

The development of quantum computing has been a gradual process, with notable breakthroughs and advancements over the years.

Quantum computing, a field that combines principles from quantum physics and computer science, has opened up new possibilities for solving complex problems that are beyond the reach of classical computers. It promises to revolutionize various industries, from cryptography and drug discovery to optimization and machine learning.

Historical Milestones in Quantum Computing

One of the earliest milestones in quantum computing was the invention of the quantum algorithm by physicist Paul Benioff in 1980. This ground-breaking work laid the foundation for the field, showing that quantum systems can perform computations that classical computers cannot.

Fig. 2. Entanglement is a key feature of quantum computing where qubits' states are linked, enabling simultaneous calculations and more efficient problem-solving than classical computers.

Building on Benioff's work, renowned physicist Richard Feynman introduced the concept of quantum simulators in 1982. He proposed that quantum computers could simulate physical systems, allowing scientists to study complex phenomena such as molecular interactions and quantum mechanics.

Another significant milestone was the creation of the first fully functional qubit in 1998 by a team of researchers at the IBM Thomas J. Watson Research Center. This breakthrough demonstrated the feasibility of building practical quantum computers. Qubits, the fundamental building blocks of quantum computers, harness the power of quantum mechanics to store and manipulate information.

Since then, researchers have made remarkable progress in scaling up the number of qubits and improving their coherence, the ability to maintain quantum states without interference. This progress has been driven by advancements in various technologies, including superconducting circuits, trapped ions, topological qubits, and photonics.

Key Players In Quantum Computing

Several organizations and research institutions are at the forefront of the quest for quantum supremacy. Companies like IBM, Google, Microsoft, and startups like Rigetti Computing and IonQ are investing heavily in quantum research and development, pushing the boundaries of what is possible.

IBM, for instance, has been actively working on developing quantum computers and making them accessible through cloud-based platforms. Their efforts have resulted in the creation of the IBM Quantum Experience, a platform that allows users to experiment with quantum circuits and algorithms.

Google, on the other hand, made headlines in 2019 when it claimed to have achieved quantum supremacy, a milestone where a quantum computer outperforms classical computers in a specific task. Their quantum processor, named Sycamore, reportedly solved a problem in just 200 seconds that would take the world's fastest supercomputer thousands of years to solve.

Microsoft is also making significant strides in quantum computing with its development of a topological qubit, a more robust and error-resistant qubit design. Their approach aims to overcome the challenges associated with qubit decoherence, a major hurdle in building large-scale quantum computers.

Rigetti Computing and IonQ, two prominent startups in the field, are exploring different technologies to build quantum computers. Rigetti focuses on superconducting qubits, while IonQ is developing trapped ion qubits. Both companies have made significant progress in improving qubit performance and are actively collaborating with researchers and industry partners. With a solid understanding of the journey so far, let's delve deeper into the definition of quantum supremacy and its theoretical underpinnings.

Defining Quantum Supremacy

Quantum supremacy is a term coined by John Preskill in 2012 to describe the point where quantum computers can outperform classical computers in solving certain problems. It is a threshold that marks a significant shift in computational power and has important implications in various fields.

Theoretical Underpinnings of Quantum Supremacy

Quantum supremacy is rooted in the unique properties of quantum systems. By harnessing the power of superposition and entanglement, quantum computers can perform certain computations exponentially faster than classical computers. Theoretical frameworks, such as quantum algorithms and quantum complexity theory, provide the foundations for understanding this phenomenon.

Practical Implications of Quantum Supremacy

The practical implications of achieving quantum supremacy are vast. Quantum computers could potentially revolutionize fields such as cryptography, optimization, drug discovery, and machine learning. They could enable us to solve complex problems more efficiently and unlock new possibilities that were previously unimaginable.

Now, let's compare the processing power of quantum computers to classical computers and evaluate their problem-solving capabilities.

Quantum Supremacy vs Classical Computing

When it comes to processing power and problem-solving capabilities, quantum computers have the potential to outperform classical computers in certain situations.

Fig. 3. Leading organizations like IBM, Google, Microsoft, and startups Rigetti Computing and IonQ are advancing quantum computing technology.

Comparing Processing Power

The processing power of a quantum computer can grow exponentially with the number of qubits, enabling it to solve problems that would take classical computers an impractical amount of time. However, it's worth noting that quantum computers are not superior in all scenarios, as there are still problems for which classical computers are better suited.

Evaluating Problem-Solving Capabilities

While quantum computers excel at certain types of problems, such as factoring large numbers and simulating quantum systems, they are not universally better than classical computers. Classical computers have been optimized over decades to efficiently handle a wide range of tasks, and for many problems, classical algorithms are still the most practical and efficient solution.

Finally, let's explore the impact of achieving quantum supremacy and consider the potential applications and ethical considerations.

The Impact of Achieving Quantum Supremacy

Achieving quantum supremacy would have far-reaching implications across various industries and scientific disciplines.

Fig. 4. Quantum supremacy is the point where quantum computers surpass classical computers in specific tasks, heralding a new era of computational power with significant real-world applications.

Potential Applications of Quantum Computing

Quantum computers could revolutionize cryptography by rendering many existing encryption algorithms obsolete. They could also accelerate drug discovery by simulating complex molecular interactions, leading to the development of more effective medications.

In addition, quantum computers could greatly enhance optimization and machine learning algorithms, enabling more efficient resource allocation and data analysis.

Ethical and Security Considerations

With great computational power comes great responsibility. Quantum computing raises ethical and security concerns, particularly in the realm of cryptography. As quantum computers become more powerful, they have the potential to break current encryption methods, jeopardizing the security of sensitive information.

As quantum supremacy looms on the horizon, researchers and policymakers are grappling with these challenges and working towards developing new encryption standards that can withstand quantum attacks.

NOTABLE QUANTUM COMPUTING MILESTONES

In the early days of quantum computing, a light-hearted anecdote began circulating among researchers: Two scientists were discussing a new quantum computer that could solve any problem instantly. One said, "Can I see it?" The other replied, "Sure, but only when you're not looking." This amusing tale sets the tone for the baffling nature of quantum mechanics and the challenges faced by pioneers in the field.

Diving into the world of quantum computing, we uncover a groundbreaking approach that taps into the mysterious principles of quantum mechanics for data processing and storage. Since its early 20th-century beginnings, this awe-inspiring field has captivated scientists and visionaries, with the potential to transform industries such as cryptography, drug discovery, and optimization. Join us on an enthralling journey, exploring the captivating history, intriguing theoretical foundations, and ongoing advancements that continue to shape the future of quantum computing.

We will divide the development of quantum computing into five distinct periods:

- The Theoretical Foundations of Quantum Computing (1900–1980)
- The Emergence of Quantum Computing (1980–1994)
- The Development of Quantum Algorithms (1994–2000)
- The Race to Build Quantum Computers (2000–2021)
- Ongoing Advancements (2021-present)

The Theoretical Foundations of Quantum Computing (1900–1980)

The origins of quantum computing can be traced back to the early 20th century when several groundbreaking discoveries in the field of quantum mechanics laid the foundation for this novel approach to computation. Key scientists, such as Max Planck, Albert Einstein, and Niels Bohr, contributed to the development of quantum mechanics, which would later provide the principles for quantum computing. In this section, we will explore the early theoretical foundations of quantum computing, focusing on the contributions of these pioneering scientists and the subsequent breakthroughs in the field.

- **Max Planck and the Quantum Hypothesis:** In 1900, Max Planck, a German theoretical physicist, introduced the concept of quantized energy levels to explain the phenomenon of black-body radiation. He proposed that energy is not emitted continuously but in discrete packets called quanta. Planck's quantum hypothesis marked the beginning of a new era in physics and set the stage for the development of quantum mechanics.
- **Albert Einstein and the Photoelectric Effect:** In 1905, Albert Einstein published a paper on the photoelectric effect, explaining that light consists of particles called photons, each carrying a discrete amount of energy proportional to its frequency. Einstein's work on the photoelectric effect further supported Planck's quantum hypothesis and contributed to the growing understanding of the particle-like behaviour of light.
- **Niels Bohr and the Bohr Model of the Atom:** In 1913, Danish physicist Niels Bohr developed the Bohr model of the atom, which proposed that electrons orbit the nucleus in quantized energy levels. Bohr's model provided a deeper understanding of the atomic structure and the quantized nature of energy. It also introduced the concept of quantum jumps, where electrons could move between energy levels by absorbing or emitting photons, further demonstrating the significance of quantization in atomic systems.
- **Werner Heisenberg and the Uncertainty Principle:** In 1927, Werner Heisenberg, a German physicist, formulated the uncertainty principle, a fundamental concept in quantum mechanics. The principle states that it is impossible to simultaneously know both the position and momentum of a particle with perfect accuracy. Heisenberg's uncertainty principle highlighted the inherent limitations in measuring quantum systems, which would later play a crucial role in the development of quantum computing.
- **Einstein-Podolsky-Rosen (EPR) Paradox and Bell Inequalities:** In 1935, Albert Einstein, Boris Podolsky, and Nathan Rosen published a paper introducing the EPR paradox, which questioned the completeness of

quantum mechanics due to the phenomenon of entanglement. Entanglement implies that the properties of two or more particles can be correlated in such a way that the state of one particle instantly affects the state of the other, regardless of the distance between them. In 1964, physicist John Bell formulated the Bell inequalities, which provided a way to test the validity of the EPR paradox experimentally. The violation of Bell inequalities in subsequent experiments confirmed the existence of entanglement, a key resource for quantum computing.

- **John von Neumann and the Mathematical Framework for Quantum Mechanics:** In the 1930s, John von Neumann, a Hungarian-American mathematician and physicist, developed the mathematical framework for quantum mechanics. His work, which included the development of the formalism of quantum states and operators, provided a rigorous foundation for understanding the behaviour of quantum systems. Von Neumann's contributions to the mathematical underpinnings of quantum mechanics were essential in paving the way for the development of quantum computing.
- **First Conference on Physics and Computation (PhysComp) in 1980:** The PhysComp conference in 1980 marked a significant milestone in the field of quantum computing. It brought together physicists, computer scientists, and mathematicians to discuss the potential applications of quantum mechanics in computation. This interdisciplinary gathering facilitated the exchange of ideas and the exploration of novel approaches to quantum computing, ultimately leading to the emergence of the field as we know it today. The PhysComp conference demonstrated the growing interest in and recognition of the potential impact of quantum mechanics on computation and information processing.
- Quantum mechanics is characterized by several unique features that distinguish it from classical mechanics, including superposition, entanglement, and wave-particle duality. These features enable quantum computing to perform tasks that are impossible or prohibitively slow on classical computers.
- As the understanding of quantum mechanics progressed, the mathematical framework developed by John von Neumann provided the necessary tools to explore the potential applications of quantum mechanics in computation. This development ultimately led to the emergence of quantum computing as a distinct field of study. The convergence of the foundational discoveries in quantum mechanics and the mathematical formalism laid the groundwork for the development of quantum computing, which seeks to harness

the unique properties of quantum systems to revolutionize the way we approach computation.

The Emergence of Quantum Computing

The concept of quantum computing started to gain momentum in the early 1980s as researchers began to explore the potential of leveraging quantum mechanics to enhance computational capabilities. Key figures such as Richard Feynman, Paul Benioff, and David Deutsch played pivotal roles in shaping the field during this period. In this section, we will delve deeper into the significant developments and breakthroughs that marked the emergence of quantum computing.

- **Richard Feynman's Vision of Quantum Computers:** In 1981, physicist Richard Feynman delivered a seminal lecture at the First Conference on the Physics of Computation, proposing that a computer operating on quantum principles could efficiently simulate quantum systems. Feynman's insight was crucial as it highlighted the limitations of classical computers in simulating quantum phenomena, and suggested that quantum computers could provide an efficient solution to this challenge.

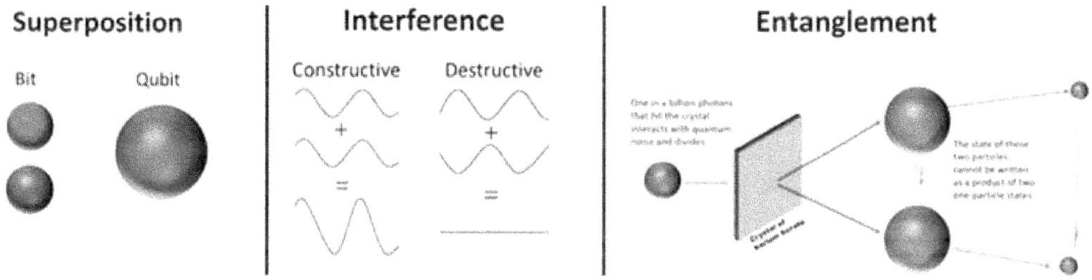

Fig. 5. Properties of Quantum Computers

- **Paul Benioff and Quantum Turing Machines:** In 1982, Paul Benioff, a theoretical physicist, published a paper describing a quantum mechanical model of a Turing machine. This model, now known as a Quantum Turing Machine (QTM), laid the groundwork for quantum computing models by demonstrating that quantum mechanical principles could be applied to the theoretical foundations of computation. Benioff's work showed that quantum systems could be used to perform computations in a manner analogous to classical Turing machines.

- **David Deutsch and the Universal Quantum Computer:** In 1985, David Deutsch, a British physicist, published a groundbreaking paper that introduced the concept of a universal quantum computer. Deutsch's work built upon the ideas of Feynman and Benioff, and provided a more concrete framework for understanding how quantum computers could operate. He demonstrated that a universal quantum computer could perform any computation that a classical computer could, but with the added advantages of quantum mechanics. Deutsch's work also laid the foundations for the development of quantum algorithms, which would later emerge as a crucial aspect of quantum computing research.

- **The Development of Quantum Logic Gates:** As the concept of quantum computing began to crystallize, researchers started to explore the development of quantum logic gates, which are the building blocks of quantum circuits. Quantum logic gates are analogous to classical logic gates but operate on qubits instead of bits, allowing them to harness the unique properties of quantum mechanics. During the late 1980s and early 1990s, researchers proposed various quantum logic gates, such as the CNOT gate and the Toffoli gate, which would later become essential components of quantum algorithms and circuits.

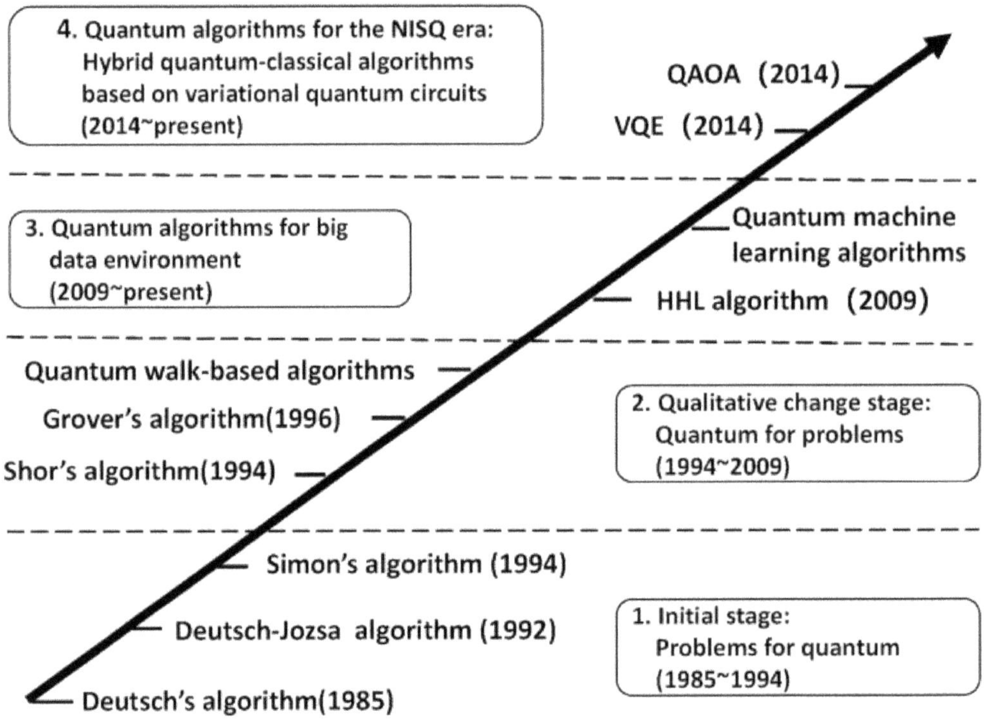

Fig. 6 Summary of quantum algorithms' development (Source: Springer)

The period between 1980 and 1994 marked the emergence of quantum computing as a distinct field of research. Visionary scientists like Richard Feynman, Paul Benioff, and David Deutsch played crucial roles in shaping the field, laying the groundwork for quantum computing models and demonstrating the potential advantages of harnessing quantum mechanics for computation. The development of quantum logic gates and the concept of a universal quantum computer provided a solid foundation for the future advancement of quantum computing research, paving the way for breakthroughs in quantum algorithms and hardware.

The Development of Quantum Algorithms (1994–2000)

The mid-1990s saw significant progress in the development of quantum algorithms, which are specialized computational methods designed to exploit the unique properties of quantum computers. The groundbreaking work of Peter Shor and Lov Grover in this period showcased the potential power of quantum computing, driving interest and investment in the field. In this section, we will delve deeper into the development of these early quantum algorithms and their impact on the field of quantum computing.

- **Shor's Algorithm**: In 1994, Peter Shor, an American mathematician and computer scientist, developed the first quantum algorithm, now known as Shor's algorithm. This algorithm leverages the principles of quantum mechanics to efficiently factorize large numbers — a task that would take exponentially longer on classical computers. The ability to factorize large numbers has significant implications for cryptography, as many encryption schemes, such as RSA, rely on the difficulty of this problem for their security. Shor's algorithm demonstrated the potential power of quantum computing, highlighting its ability to solve problems that were previously considered intractable for classical computers.
- **Grover's Algorithm**: In 1996, Lov Grover, an Indian-American computer scientist, developed another influential quantum algorithm, known as Grover's algorithm. This algorithm is designed to search unsorted databases more efficiently than classical algorithms. Grover's algorithm can search a database of N elements in roughly “N steps, offering a quadratic speedup compared to classical algorithms, which require approximately N steps. Although the speedup provided by Grover's algorithm is less dramatic than that of Shor's algorithm, it still demonstrates the potential of quantum computing to outperform classical computing in specific tasks.
- **Impact on Quantum Computing Research**: The development of Shor's and Grover's algorithms had a profound impact on the field of quantum computing. These early quantum algorithms provided concrete examples of the potential advantages of quantum computing, generating significant interest from both researchers and funding agencies. As a result, research in quantum computing accelerated, with scientists exploring the development of new quantum algorithms, error-correcting codes, and hardware implementations.
- **Theoretical Developments and New Quantum Algorithms**: Inspired by the success of Shor's and Grover's algorithms, researchers began to explore the development of additional quantum algorithms throughout the late 1990s. This period saw the proposal of various quantum algorithms

for problems such as the discrete logarithm problem, the hidden subgroup problem, and quantum simulation. These new algorithms further demonstrated the potential of quantum computing and expanded the range of problems for which quantum computers could offer significant advantages over classical computers.

The development of quantum algorithms, particularly Shor's and Grover's algorithms, played a crucial role in the advancement of quantum computing during the mid-to-late 1990s. These algorithms showcased the potential power of quantum computing and drove significant interest and investment in the field. The success of these early algorithms inspired researchers to explore new quantum algorithms and further develop the theoretical underpinnings of quantum computing, paving the way for ongoing advancements in the field.

The Race to Build Quantum Computers (2000–2021)

The early 21st century witnessed an intense race among researchers, tech giants, and startups to build practical quantum computers. This period saw significant progress in the development of various quantum computing technologies, as well as major milestones, such as Google's announcement of "quantum supremacy." In this section, we will discuss the key developments in the race to build quantum computers, focusing on different approaches, milestones, and ongoing challenges in the field.

- **Approaches to Quantum Computing**: Researchers explored various approaches to building quantum computers, with each approach having its unique advantages and challenges. Some of the prominent methods include (1) Tapped Ions, (2) Superconducting Qubits, (3) Topological Qubits and so on.
- **D-Wave Systems and Quantum Annealing**: In 2011, the Canadian company D-Wave Systems claimed to have built the first commercially available quantum computer, the D-Wave One. This system was based on quantum annealing, a specialized approach to quantum computing that focuses on solving optimization problems. However, the practical applicability and true quantum nature of D-Wave's systems were subjects of debate among researchers, with some arguing that the systems provided only limited speedup compared to classical computers.
- **Google's Quantum Supremacy**: In 2019, Google announced a major milestone in the development of quantum computing by achieving "quantum supremacy" with its 53-qubit Sycamore processor. Google's quantum computer solved a specific problem in 200 seconds that would take a classical supercomputer approximately 10,000 years to complete. This achievement marked the first time that a quantum computer outperformed

classical computers on a well-defined computational task, providing a proof-of-concept for the potential power of quantum computing.

- **Ongoing Challenges and Developments:** Despite the significant advancements in quantum computing during this period, several challenges remain. These include improving qubit coherence times, developing scalable and fault-tolerant architectures, and creating practical error correction techniques. Researchers continue to explore new materials, techniques, and algorithms to address these challenges and push the boundaries of quantum computing. Additionally, tech giants such as IBM, Microsoft, and Google, as well as numerous startups, continue to invest heavily in quantum computing research, fueling rapid progress in the field.

The race to build quantum computers in the early 21st century saw remarkable progre-ss and significant milestones, such as Google's demonstration of quantum supremacy. Researchers explored various approaches to quantum computing, with each method offering unique advantages and challenges. As the field continues to advance, overcoming the remaining hurdles will be crucial to realizing the full potential of quantum computing and enabling its practical application across a wide range of domains.

Ongoing Advancements (2021-present)

Quantum computing has continued to make rapid progress since 2021, with significant investment from governments, private companies, and academic institutions. The focus of research and development in the field has been on enhancing the capabilities of quantum computers, addressing existing challenges, and exploring new applications. In this section, we will discuss some of the ongoing advancements and areas of interest in quantum computing.

- **Scaling Up Quantum Computers:** One of the primary challenges in the field of quantum computing is to increase the number of qubits in a scalable and stable manner. Larger quantum computers with more qubits have the potential to solve increasingly complex problems and provide greater computational power. Researchers are actively working on techniques to scale up quantum systems while maintaining low error rates and long coherence times.

- **Error Correction and Fault Tolerance:** As quantum computers scale up, addressing issues related to error correction and fault tolerance becomes increasingly important. Quantum systems are highly susceptible to errors due to their fragile nature and sensitivity to environmental noise. Developing robust error-correction techniques and fault-tolerant architectures is crucial to ensure the practical usability of quantum computers for real-world applications.

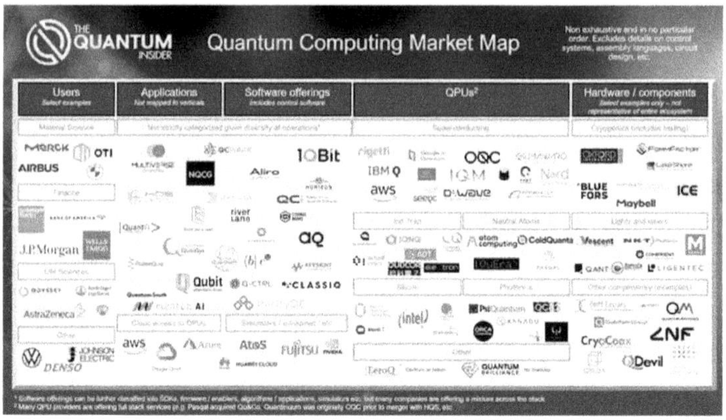

Fig. 7. Quantum Computing Market Map and Data 2022 (Source: The Quantum Insider)

- **New Quantum Algorithms:** Researchers continue to develop new quantum algorithms that take advantage of the unique properties of quantum computers. This ongoing research aims to discover efficient quantum algorithms for various problem domains, such as optimization, machine learning, and cryptography, further expanding the range of problems that quantum computers can tackle more efficiently than classical computers.
- **Quantum Cryptography and Post-Quantum Cryptography:** Quantum computing poses a significant threat to existing cryptographic schemes, such as RSA, which rely on the difficulty of factoring large numbers. Shor's algorithm, for instance, has the potential to break RSA encryption. This has prompted research into both quantum cryptography, which leverages the principles of quantum mechanics to secure communication, and post-quantum cryptography, which aims to develop new cryptographic schemes that can resist attacks from both classical and quantum computers.
- **Applications in Optimization, Artificial Intelligence, and Drug Discovery:** Quantum computing holds promise in various fields, including optimization problems, artificial intelligence, and drug discovery. Quantum computers can potentially solve certain optimization problems faster than classical computers, leading to improvements in areas such as logistics, finance, and supply chain management. In artificial intelligence, quantum computing can potentially enhance machine learning algorithms, enabling faster training and more accurate models. In drug discovery, quantum computers may be able to simulate complex molecular interactions, leading to the development of new pharmaceuticals and a deeper understanding of biological processes.

The ongoing advancements in quantum computing since 2021 highlight the rapid progress being made in the field. As researchers continue to address challenges related to scalability, error correction, and fault tolerance, and explore new algorithms and applications, the potential impact of quantum computing across various domains becomes increasingly apparent.

With sustained investment and research, quantum computing has the potential to revolutionize multiple industries and drive significant advancements in technology and science.

NOTABLE QUANTUM COMPUTING MILESTONES

Quantum computing, an emerging frontier in computing technology, holds the potential to revolutionize various industries and transform the way we approach complex problems. Over the past few decades, significant strides have been made in the field of quantum computing, leading to remarkable achievements and groundbreaking milestones. In this section, we will explore some of the most noteworthy achievements in quantum computing and discuss their implications for science, technology, and society.

Quantum Supremacy: A Milestone in Quantum Computing

One of the most significant achievements in quantum computing was achieved by Google's Quantum AI team in October 2019 when they claimed to achieve quantum supremacy. This milestone marked the moment when a quantum computer, Google's 53-qubit Sycamore processor, outperformed the world's most powerful classical supercomputers in solving a specific problem.

The problem chosen was a random sampling task, which would take thousands of years for even the fastest classical supercomputers to solve. However, Google's quantum computer completed the task in just over 3 minutes, demonstrating its superiority in handling complex computations.

Implications of Quantum Supremacy

The achievement of quantum supremacy has significant implications for both the field of quantum computing and the broader technological landscape:

- **Validation of Quantum Potential:** Quantum supremacy validated the potential of quantum computing to solve certain types of problems exponentially faster than classical computers. This milestone underscored the need for further research and investment in quantum computing technologies.
- **Cryptographic Implications:** Quantum computers have the potential to break many of the encryption methods currently used in cybersecurity. As quantum computing capabilities grow, there will be an increasing need for quantum-resistant cryptographic solutions to safeguard sensitive information.

- **Advancements in Scientific Research:** Quantum computing's ability to simulate complex quantum systems can significantly advance scientific research in areas such as materials science, drug discovery, and climate modeling.

Quantum Error Correction: Overcoming Quantum Noise

Quantum computing faces a significant challenge in maintaining qubits' delicate quantum states due to environmental noise and other factors. Quantum error correction (QEC) is a critical milestone that seeks to overcome this challenge by preserving the integrity of qubits' quantum information.

Researchers have made notable progress in developing quantum error correction codes that can detect and correct errors in quantum computations. These codes allow quantum computers to perform more reliably and scale up to larger numbers of qubits.

Implications of Quantum Error Correction

Quantum error correction has profound implications for the viability of practical quantum computing:

- **Enhanced Quantum Reliability:** Quantum error correction makes quantum computations more reliable, reducing the impact of quantum noise and increasing the accuracy of results.
- **Scalability of Quantum Computers:** Error correction techniques are vital for building large-scale quantum computers capable of handling complex real-world problems.
- **Fault-Tolerant Quantum Computing:** With robust error correction, quantum computers become more fault-tolerant, minimizing the impact of qubit errors and maintaining computational integrity.

Quantum Communication: Secure Data Transmission

Quantum communication, another significant milestone in quantum computing, aims to ensure secure data transmission by leveraging the principles of quantum mechanics. Quantum key distribution (QKD) is a central aspect of quantum communication, allowing parties to exchange cryptographic keys in a way that is inherently secure against eavesdropping.

Implications of Quantum Communication

The advent of quantum communication carries several implications for secure data transmission:

- **Unbreakable Encryption:** Quantum key distribution provides unbreakable encryption keys, making intercepted data practically impossible to decrypt without detection.

- **Quantum-Secured Networks:** Quantum communication can lead to the development of quantum-secured networks, safeguarding sensitive information in an era of increasingly sophisticated cyber threats.
- **Quantum Internet:** The concept of a quantum internet is envisioned, where quantum communication networks enable secure, instantaneous communication between quantum devices worldwide.

Quantum Computing and Drug Discovery

The field of quantum computing has shown great promise in the domain of drug discovery. Traditional drug discovery processes involve testing millions of compounds for potential drug candidates, which is time-consuming and costly. Quantum computing's ability to simulate molecular interactions and analyze quantum systems can accelerate this process significantly.

Implications for Drug Discovery

Quantum computing's application in drug discovery can have far-reaching implications:

- **Accelerated Drug Development:** Quantum simulations can predict the interactions between drugs and biological targets, enabling researchers to identify potential drug candidates faster and more accurately.
- **Precision Medicine:** Quantum computing can facilitate personalized medicine by tailoring treatments based on individual patients' genetic and molecular profiles.
- **Addressing Complex Diseases:** Quantum computing can tackle complex diseases like cancer by modeling molecular interactions and identifying potential therapeutic targets.

CHALLENGES AND PLANS TO OVERCOME THEM

Despite the remarkable advancements, quantum computing faces substantial challenges:

- **Decoherence and error mitigation:** Quantum states are delicate and easily disrupted by their environment, leading to errors. Error correction codes and quantum error correction techniques, such as surface codes and topological qubits, are being developed to mitigate the impact of errors and increase the reliability of quantum computations.
- **Interference:** Quantum systems exhibit interference phenomena, where qubits' superpositions interfere destructively or constructively, affecting computation outcomes. Techniques to control and mitigate interference are under exploration.

- **Cost:** Quantum computing's development and maintenance are costly, so research efforts are also focused on reducing hardware costs and optimising resource allocation.
- **Scalability:** Building large-scale, fault-tolerant quantum computers is a significant challenge. Quantum annealing and trapped ion technologies are being explored to create scalable quantum architectures.
- **Shortage of skilled workforce:** Quantum computing requires a specialised skill set. According to the World Economic Forum, more than half of quantum companies are hiring and struggling to find people with the right skills. Most current jobs are highly technical, and the only people trained in quantum technologies are highly academic. Educational programs and partnerships between academia and industry in countries like Ireland are helping to address the shortage of quantum experts.

Ireland's quantum computing leadership and global contributions

As the worldwide landscape of quantum computing evolves, several countries attempt to find solutions to these challenges. Ireland continues to enhance its position in quantum computing research and development. The country boasts several research institutions, including Trinity College Dublin, which hosts the Centre for Quantum Engineering and Science.

Additionally, multinational companies like IBM, Fidelity, and Microsoft have established quantum research initiatives in Ireland, fostering collaboration between academia and industry. In 2023, for instance, the Trinity Quantum Alliance (TQA) was launched. The TQA collaborates with Trinity, Microsoft, IBM, Horizon Quantum Computing, Algorithmiq and Moody's Analytics, bringing together experts from research and industry for innovative projects in quantum science and technology, simulation, education, and computation.

The TQA is the catalyst for investment in quantum technology in Ireland, with the ultimate goal being to construct a vibrant ecosystem to benefit various industry sectors, and it is already bringing results. In collaboration with IBM Dublin, Trinity's quantum physicists have successfully simulated super diffusion in a system of interacting quantum particles on a quantum computer, which is the first step in doing highly challenging quantum transport calculations on quantum hardware.

Moreover, Ireland's Walton Institute, a hub for quantum research and innovation, also plays a pivotal role in the country's quantum leadership, as it fosters quantum advancements. Fidelity Investments, a financial leader, is also actively engaged in quantum research. In Ireland, Fidelity's Center for Applied Technology (FCAT) collaborates on quantum projects, demonstrating the financial sector's keen interest in quantum's potential applications.

Ireland is partaking in the global race to quantum computing, as are several other countries also making substantial contributions to the quantum landscape. The United States is a quantum powerhouse, with major players like IBM and Google leading the charge. These companies are pushing the boundaries of both quantum hardware and algorithms. Institutions like the Perimeter Institute in Canada excel in quantum theory and quantum communication research.

China has made significant strides in quantum communication and quantum cryptography. Its launch of the world's first quantum satellite, Micius, and its experiments in quantum key distribution demonstrate a commitment to quantum communication's practical applications. The European Union's Quantum Flagship programme is a testament to its dedication to quantum research. This program fosters collaboration across member states, channelling resources and expertise into various quantum projects, from quantum computing to quantum communication.

Australia and Singapore have established quantum research hubs, contributing to quantum technology and applications innovation. All these countries recognise the potential of quantum computing and are actively investing in research and infrastructure to drive advancements.

QUANTUM ADVANTAGE IN SPECIFIC APPLICATIONS

Quantum computing is an advanced field of computer science, physics, and mathematics that harnesses the principles of quantum mechanics to process and manipulate information at an accelerated pace.

This remarkable field encompasses both hardware exploration and application development, pushing the boundaries of computational capabilities.

For instance, IBM Quantum is a pioneering company that has made quantum hardware a reality, making it accessible to hundreds of thousands of developers. This achievement represents a remarkable milestone, considering that the idea of real quantum processors seemed like a distant dream just thirty years ago.

Distinguished by their ability to leverage quantum mechanical phenomena like superposition and quantum interference, quantum computers excel in solving specific problem types more efficiently than their classical counterparts.

Quantum advantage refers to the scenario where quantum computers outperform classical computers in solving specific problems, offering a tangible benefit for certain applications. It doesn't imply absolute dominance across all tasks but rather highlights the quantum prowess in a particular computational domain. Quantum advantage is task-specific, showcasing the efficiency of quantum algorithms in areas like optimization, simulation, and machine learning.

Top Applications of Quantum Computing

Machine Learning has two roles within quantum computing. On the receiving side, quantum computers use classical machine learning to optimize hardware operations, control systems, and user interfaces. But, on the giving side, quantum computers perform machine learning tasks and solve traditional machine learning problems. Focusing on the latter, some of the most commonly cited quantum machine learning applications are:

- Enhance algorithms designed to solve optimization problems, which in turn have a broad range of potential applications across many industries
- Accelerate classification tasks for large datasets, particularly related to image and speech recognition, with quantum support vector machines (QSVM)
- Enable exploration of high-dimensional datasets, such as customer segmentation and anomaly detection, using algorithms such as K-means clustering
- Reduce dimensionality, using principal component analysis, to improve feature selection and thus improve the visualization and analysis of data
- Generate more realistic data for Variational Autoencoders (VAEs) and Generative Adversarial Networks (GANs) when the data either doesn't exist or needs to be augmented
- Discover complex patterns and correlations using Boltzmann machines for unsupervised learning, which has utility in recommendation systems and natural language processing
- Improve neural network training by leveraging interference, potentially saving time by reducing the number of iterations required to find the optimal parameters
- Solve near-term quantum chemistry problems, particularly applied to discovering new drugs and developing new materials, but also applied to a broad range of other problems
- Analyze data for features and anomalies, the latter of which has important implications for network traffic analysis and fraud detection for financial services
- Optimize policies for autonomous systems, including self-driving cars and unmanned aerial vehicles (UAV), using reinforcement learning

Although quantum computing is still in its infancy, cloud-based quantum machine learning solvers are already available. Some are proprietary and commercialized, but there are also open-source quantum machine learning services that are freely available.

What is Quantum Machine Learning?

Quantum Machine Learning (QML) is an interdisciplinary field that applies quantum computing to traditional machine learning tasks. But, classical machine learning already does that, so quantum machine learning algorithms must propose advantages over their classical counterparts:

- The basic unit of information, the qubit, is not a 0 or a 1, but a complex number; depending on several factors, a complex number is minimally several bytes, each of which is eight 0s and 1s.
- Entanglement exponentially increases the number of complex numbers required to describe a system, which means exponential compression of classical data
- Quantum computation is not sequential like classical computation; it is inherently parallel, which allows multiple solutions to effectively be discovered simultaneously
- Theoretical research supports the possibility of achieving significant computational speedups over known classical approaches
- Data can be mapped not only from classical sources but also from quantum sources such as the proposed Quantum Random Access Memory (QRAM)
- Interference can be leveraged to not only increase the probabilities of receiving correct solutions, but also to potentially provide speedups over classical algorithms

A paper by D.P. García, et al, titled "Systematic Literature Review: Quantum Machine Learning and its applications"identifying and describing 18 hybrid classical quantum machine learning algorithms as a result.

These algorithms include Boltzmann machines, parameterized circuits, autoencoders, reservoir computing, support vector machines (SVM), and an assortment of neural networks. This diversity of algorithms highlights the potential breadth of real world problems that might be solvable with quantum machine learning.

Quantum Advantage in Machine Learning

The term "quantum advantage" typically refers to speed, but the term is not strictly defined. When a claim is made that a computation can be performed in 200 seconds that would take a supercomputer thousands of years, that's a claim of quantum advantage. But, that suggests that there's only one classification of quantum advantage when, in fact, there are multiple potential advantages:

- **Speed.** The "holy grail" of quantum computing is to solve problems that consume considerable time and significant classical resources.

- **Precision.** Many hard problems can only be approximated classically, whereas quantum algorithms can offer precise solutions.
- **Complexity.** Quantum algorithms may solve problems in fewer timesteps than classical algorithms, indicating greater efficiency.
- Compression. Large datasets that require prohibitive amounts of classical memory may be mapped to a relatively small number of qubits.
- Dimensionality. As an extension of data compression, quantum computers are a natural fit for finding patterns and relationships in high-dimensional data.
- Sampling. Quantum computers can naturally sample probability distributions for a wide range of applications, including generative algorithms.
- Interference. Constructive and destructive interference can be leveraged to increase the probability of finding correct solutions and decrease the probability of incorrect solutions.

It's important to note that quantum algorithms are not guaranteed to be advantageous in any way. Nor can they be expected to realize all of the advantages above. However, the potential to realize these advantages exists, and some quantum machine learning solutions might prove to be exceptionally advantageous.

Quantum Machine Learning Applications

Quantum machine learning (QML) use cases overlap two other major classifications of quantum computing applications: quantum simulation and quantum optimization. Near-term solutions for both incorporate hybrid classical-quantum algorithms that utilize classical neural networks. And anywhere you find a classical neural network, is a potential application of quantum machine learning, as well:

- Molecular simulation, the original application of quantum computing, with use cases in drug discovery, material development, and climate modeling
- Optimization problems, with particular interest in financial applications, but with broad applicability across many industries, especially those with supply chains
- Natural language processing, including the quick and accurate interpretation, translation, and generation of spoken languages
- Imaging, including the classification and identification of objects in pictures and videos, and with applications ranging from health care to surveillance to autonomous vehicles

- Machine Learning model training, optimizing how artificial neural networks train on classical data to solve the problems above

Specific examples of some of these use cases, broken down by industry, include:

- Energy sector, including energy grid optimization, energy demand prediction, energy storage, energy storage distribution, and renewable energy integration
- Manufacturing, including production scheduling, shift scheduling, resource allocation, and defect detection, but also the optimization of individual processes
- Retail sales, including demand forecasting, inventory management, delivery route optimization, recommendation systems, loss prevention, and store layout optimization
- Government services, including traffic optimization, public transportation routing, policy modeling and simulation, and public health modeling
- Finance and insurance, including financial portfolio optimization, financial risk management, fraud detection, and trading strategy optimization
- Aerospace and space, including trajectory optimization and flight data analysis, both terrestrial and extraterrestrial, and communication optimization
- Environment and weather, including weather forecasting, disaster prediction, environmental modeling, and natural disaster response management
- Health care services, including medical image analysis, diagnosis assistance, treatment plan optimization, early detection screening, and clinical trial design
- Customer service and social media, including personal recommendations, sentiment analysis, support ticket routing, omnichannel experience optimization, and chatbots

The Impact of Quantum Computing on Artificial Intelligence

Quantum computing boosts the potential of AI by amplifying its velocity, efficacy, and precision. It transcends the limitations imposed on traditional computers by utilizing qubits and capitalizing on non-linear operations.

This remarkable advancement empowers quantum computing to find applications across diverse AI use cases. Sectors like maritime logistics, semiconductors, electric vehicles, luminescence, and power have already started reaping the rewards of quantum computing's exceptional problem-solving prowess.

Let's explore the impact of quantum computing on different industries and the transformative effects it brings to AI-driven processes.

Medical Care

Hospitals often form a medical board of specialists from diverse fields to address complex conditions in critically ill patients.

However, this traditional approach is time-consuming and hampers decision-making. Quantum computing offers a solution.

By inputting various possibilities and relevant historical data, **healthcare** professionals can leverage quantum computing to evaluate treatment effectiveness and receive optimal recommendations swiftly.

The quantum advantage allows providers to acquire valuable insights in a considerably reduced time frame.

Machine Learning (ML)

Machine learning (ML) relies on computers' ability to acquire knowledge from data and generate or recognize patterns, similar to how the human brain functions.

However, the effectiveness of machine learning can be hindered by subpar data quality and the sluggish availability of data. This is where quantum computing comes into play, offering the potential to rapidly process large volumes of data rapidly, thus granting machine learning the same advantage.

A notable example of this potential is a collaborative project, "Quantum Advantage in Learning from Experiments," involving scientists from renowned institutions like Caltech, Harvard, Berkeley, and Microsoft.

Published findings reveal the exceptional performance of their quantum computer, Sycamore, compared to classical learning agents, demonstrating exponential superiority across a diverse range of tasks, highlighting the remarkable capabilities of quantum learning agents.

Cryptography and Security

Quantum computing can make it harder for unauthorized parties to breach data using qubits to calculate all possible breach methods, allowing for stronger security measures.

However, critics argue that this very power of quantum computing could be leveraged by hackers to quickly devise strategies for infiltrating servers containing sensitive data, potentially compromising existing security measures.

That is why the development of quantum-resistant cryptography is a main focus of the National Institute of Standards and Technology (NIST). Through its Post-Quantum Cryptography Standardization Program, NIST aims to create a stronger cryptographic system that can withstand quantum attacks, surpassing the current widely adopted methods.

This pursuit of enhanced security measures is closely tied to the geopolitical landscape, as it fuels the competition between the United States and China in the race to advance quantum technology.

Financial Application

Quantum computing's integration promises to enhance market predictions and risk management.

Multiverse Computing, Pasqal, and Crédit Agricole recently completed a 1.5-year proof-of-concept study on quantum computing's potential in financial product valuation and credit risk assessment.

Notable advancements were achieved, reducing computing time and memory usage. Using a mere 50-qubit quantum processor, accurate results comparable to conventional methods were obtained, paving the way for real-world applications, specifically in derivatives valuation.

Anticipated advancements are on the horizon as a 300-qubit quantum processor is expected to become accessible in 2024. This breakthrough research marks the introduction of the inaugural quantum-enhanced machine learning algorithm designed specifically for forecasting credit rating downgrades.

Natural Language Processing (NLP)

Quantum computing can enhance natural language processing (NLP) and speech recognition, leading to more efficient and accurate communication. In that sense, quantum NLP (QNLP) aims to surpass the capabilities of traditional NLP by translating language into coded circuits processed by quantum computers.

Advancements in quantum computing enable QNLP to deliver enhanced effectiveness, faster processing, reduced power consumption, and a smaller environmental footprint. QNLP leverages quantum computing to accelerate the training process for data-intensive AI models, resulting in reduced training time.

For instance, Quantinuum (a company that integrates software and hardware solutions for quantum computing), with expertise in QNLP, recently collaborated with UCL and the BBC to explore the commercial potential in content discovery and archive retrieval.

Through the transformation of sentences into logical formats and the use of string diagrams, QNLP simplifies NLP design on quantum hardware. These encoded quantum circuits can be optimized for machine learning applications.

What are the Advantages of Quantum Computing in AI?

The exponential growth of complex data sets has surpassed the capabilities of traditional computers, putting a strain on our existing systems. However, quantum computing emerges as a promising solution to address these challenges in a matter of seconds.

The ability of quantum computing to process vast amounts of data at an astonishing speed is of utmost importance when it comes to tackling intricate problems.

Quantum simulations, in particular, hold significant promise in addressing complex issues like climate change and healthcare.

Apart from the incredible speed and the ability to handle complex data sets, quantum computing brings several other benefits to AI. Keep reading to find out what they are.

Optimizing Solutions

Quantum computing empowers us to make optimal decisions in portfolio analysis, delivery routes, and personalized treatment protocols.

As big data shapes our computer architecture, we require a different approach to effectively handle it. Quantum computers excel at solving sequential problems, offering better decision-making capabilities for businesses and consumers. This encourages investments in this emerging technology.

Spotting Patterns in Large Data Sets

Quantum computing can rapidly search for patterns or anomalies in vast, unsorted data sets. It has the ability to simultaneously access all items in a database, identifying similarities within seconds.

Current technologies rely on sequential examination, which is time-consuming and impractical for large data sets.

Facilitating Integration of Diverse Data Sets

Quantum computers will enable breakthroughs by integrating vastly different data sets. Initially, human intervention may be necessary to guide the integration process.

When we analyze raw data from diverse sources with distinct structures, it is crucial to understand how these structures are related to each other.

Advancements in natural language analysis, a significant challenge in artificial intelligence, are required for this task. Human input plays a vital role in training the system for future integration.

Challenges of Quantum Computing in AI

Qubit decoherence, the loss or degradation of quantum information in a qubit, stands as one of the most significant hurdles in the realm of quantum computing. These qubits are incredibly sensitive to their surroundings, meaning even minor disruptions can lead to the loss of their quantum properties.

Overcoming this challenge necessitates exploring novel quantum approaches, embracing new materials, and developing advanced computational techniques. It is crucial to recognize that the obstacles in quantum computing extend beyond hardware complexities.

Quantum algorithms are considerably more intricate than classical algorithms, demanding developers to adopt original strategies when approaching computational problems.

The field of quantum computing presents several additional challenges to scientists, engineers, and entrepreneurs. Let's examine eight of these remaining challenges:

Error Correction

Unquestionably, error correction stands as the foremost challenge faced by experts in the field. Quantum computers prove highly susceptible to noise and errors resulting from interactions with the environment.

Such errors can accumulate, compromising the accuracy of computations. Developing reliable techniques for error correction becomes imperative in constructing practical quantum computers.

Scalability

Although quantum computers have shown remarkable capabilities in specific areas, their current size and scale still fall short when compared to classical computers.

The primary hurdle is the need to expand quantum computers to support hundreds or even thousands of qubits while preserving coherence and minimizing errors.

The scalability of quantum computers poses a significant challenge, as it involves expanding their capacity to handle hundreds or even thousands of qubits while preserving coherence and minimizing errors.

Hardware Development

The development of high-quality quantum hardware, including qubits and control electronics, presents a significant obstacle. Various qubit technologies exist, each with its own advantages and disadvantages.

Therefore, extensive research focuses on creating a scalable and fault-tolerant qubit technology.

Software Development

Quantum algorithms and software development tools are currently in their early stages, necessitating the creation of new programming languages, compilers, and optimization tools. These innovations should effectively harness the power of quantum computers.

Classical Computers Interfaces

Quantum computers are not intended to replace classical computers; instead, they will serve as complementary technologies. Consequently, it is vital to develop efficient and reliable methods for transferring data between classical and quantum computers to enable practical applications.

Standards and Protocols

Establishing standards, protocols, and benchmarking in quantum computing is vital for compatibility, interoperability, and measuring performance. As the field matures, these aspects gain increasing importance across hardware, software, and communication interfaces.

Trained Talent

Finding qualified quantum workers is challenging. It's a catch-22 situation: more people won't join until practical quantum computers are widespread, yet the progress of quantum computers depends on more motivated individuals entering the field.

Overall Expense

Expense is a significant roadblock for quantum computing. Quantum talent, hardware, and complex supply chains are costly. Overcoming these expenses and seeking investments will be standard for scientists and entrepreneurs in the future.

CHAPTER-9

CHALLENGES AND CONSIDERATIONS IN QUANTUM COMPUTING

Quantum computing may seem like a technology that belongs in the distant future, but there are potential real-world applications today. Still, in order to take advantage of those, organizations need to address the challenges quantum computing poses.

Many organizations are looking into practical use cases of quantum computing and for good reason. Quantum computing has the potential to solve computational problems significantly faster than existing classical computing approaches. Businesses might want to use quantum computing for optimizing investments, improving cybersecurity or discovering new paths for value creation.

Whereas classical computing encodes data into logical bits using transistors that can process information only one decision at a time, quantum computers encode problems into basic units of information called *quantum bits* (qubits) that can store multiple states of information at the same time. This encoding makes them perfect for complex optimization problems and cracking existing encryption codes.

Despite some excitement that quantum computing is better at solving some obscure problems faster than classical computers, enterprises need to address the existing challenges of quantum computing before they can broadly adopt practical tools and systems.

"Quantum computing has the potential to be seismically disruptive, and the businesses that are experimenting now stand to amplify business value and innovation," said Carl Dukatz, tech innovation strategy executive at Accenture, an IT services and consulting firm headquartered in Dublin. "Quantum could change the world, but there are numerous factors to consider in getting this right."

Considerations in Quantum Computing

- **Increasing qubit count and coherence times in quantum devices:** The number of qubits (quantum bits) in a quantum computer is an important metric of its power. As the number of qubits increases, so does the computational power of the device. Coherence times refer to how long qubits can maintain their quantum state before decohering, and longer coherence times enable more complex computations.
- **Development of new quantum algorithms and optimization techniques:** As the capabilities of quantum computers are expanding, so is the development of new algorithms and techniques to take advantage of the unique properties of quantum computing. These include quantum machine learning, quantum error correction, and quantum optimization algorithms.
- **Emergence of quantum-inspired classical algorithms and hardware:** Researchers are studying the properties of quantum systems to develop new classical algorithms and hardware that mimic some of the advantages of quantum computing.
- **Growing interest and investment in quantum computing from industry and government:** As the potential applications of quantum computing become more apparent, there is growing interest and investment in the field from both industry and government.
- **Increased collaboration and sharing of resources among quantum research institutions and companies:** As quantum computing becomes more important, there is an increasing amount of collaboration and sharing of resources among quantum research institutions and companies.
- **The use of quantum machine learning and quantum artificial intelligence:** Researchers are exploring the use of quantum computing to develop new machine learning and artificial intelligence algorithms that can take advantage of the unique properties of quantum systems.
- **Rising of Quantum Cloud Services:** With the increasing qubit count and coherence times, many companies are now offering quantum cloud services to user, which allows them to access the power of quantum computing without the need of building their own quantum computer.
- **Advancement in Quantum Error Correction:** To make a quantum computer practically useful, it is necessary to have quantum error correction techniques to minimize the errors that occur during computation. Many new techniques are being developed to achieve this goal.

DECOHERENCE AND QUANTUM NOISE

The Theory of decoherence

Since experiments on quantum mechanical systems get more and more complex, it is no longer sufficient enough to describe this systems as closed. In practise any realistic system has an uncontrollable coupling to the environment which influences the time evolution of the system. Therefore the theory of open quantum systems describes their behaviour by considering different assumptions about the coupling or the environment since a complete description of the environmental degrees of freedom is not feasible. The dynamical evolution of the open system is then described with an effective equation of motion - the master equation.

Another motivation for the study of open quantum systems is of more fundamental origin. It is the question: How does the classical world emerge from the underlying quantum mechanical framework? This question is relatively young since the mainstream attitude in the 1970's and 1980's was that the boundary between the quantum and the classical world was a purely philosophical problem, out of physic's scope. A change of this opinion was initiated by theresearchers and by the understanding that there is no reason why one should deny quantum mechanics even for macroscopic objects.

From closed to open quantum systems

Closed systems

First of all we want to discuss how it is possible to describe the time evolution of closed quantum mechanical systems. If we consider a pure states $|\psi(t)\rho$, the time evolution of this state is given by the Schrodinger equation

$$i\,(d/dt)|\psi(t)i = H(t)|\psi(t)\rho, \quad (1)$$

where ħ is set to 1 and H(t) is the Hamiltonian of the system. Since we are describing closed systems, the evolution of the state can be expressed by an unitary time-evolution operator $U(t, t_0)$ which transforms the initial state $|\psi(t_0)\rho$ to the state $|\psi(t)\rho$,

$$|\psi(t)\rho = U(t, t0)|\psi(t_0)\rho \text{ with } U(t_0, t_0) = 1. \quad (2)$$

By substituting this state in Eq.(1) we get an operator equation for

$$U(t, t_0)\rho\,(\delta/\delta t)U(t, t_0) = H(t)U(t, t0). \quad (3)$$

In quantum information processing, the term decoherence is often used loosely to describe any kind of noise that can affect a quantum system. This can include sources of noise that seem, qualitatively, to be quite different from each other.

Quantum decoherence is the loss of quantum coherence, the process in which a system's behaviour changes from that which can be explained by quantum mechanics to that which can be explained by classical mechanics. Beginning out of attempts to extend the understanding of quantum mechanics, the theory has developed in several directions and experimental studies have confirmed some of the key issues. Quantum computing relies on quantum coherence and is the primary practical applications of the concept.

Quantum Noise

Noise refers to the multiple factors that can affect the accuracy of the calculations a quantum computer performs. Quantum computers are susceptible to noise from various sources, like disturbances in Earth's magnetic field, local radiation from Wi-Fi or mobile phones, cosmic rays, and even the influence that neighboring qubits –the building blocks of a quantum computer– exert on each other by mere proximity. These disruptions cause the information an idle qubit holds to fade away. Lastly, when performing a quantum logic operation, qubits can also suffer from errors that cause them to rotate by the wrong amount. In all cases, the final state of the quantum computer is not precisely the state one expects. Unless one can reverse the action of the noise, the information in the quantum system can become randomized or totally erased. This phenomenon is known as decoherence.

Since quantum information is highly prone to decoherence, the outlook for quantum computing appears bleak at first. Fortunately, a beautiful technique known as quantum error correction (QEC) provides a path forward: information is carefully and redundantly encoded into multiple qubits such that the effects of noise on the system can be, as the name suggests, corrected. QEC is a rich subject, but a key difficulty to reaching full fault-tolerant quantum computing (wherein the probability of logical errors can be made arbitrarily small) is that current schemes require a large overhead in the total number of qubits.

In addition to researching quantum error correction, AWS customers are also looking for ways to do more with less by studying applications of currently available noisy, intermediate-scale quantum (NISQ) devices. It is an open question whether or not we will be able to find quantum advantage using NISQ devices, but groups in academia and industry have been developing algorithms that nevertheless get the most performance out of current quantum computers, which are limited by their size and coherence. Researchers evaluate these algorithms in the presence of noise to understand how well near-term devices can perform in realistic scenarios. Noise simulation provides a systematic approach to evaluating noisy algorithms by making it possible to choose between different types of noise with tunable strength.

As quantum hardware efforts advance, researchers are keen to understand the way noise affects new devices by modeling errors and running noisy simulations with these error models. By comparing noisy simulations with hardware measurements, experimenters can characterize the noise in new hardware, informing future hardware advances, algorithm design, and quantum error correction research.

Quantum Noise refers to the unwanted disturbances that affect quantum systems, leading to errors in quantum computations. Unlike classical noise, which might simply add random errors to a signal, quantum noise can have more complex and detrimental effects. It's a major challenge in the development of quantum computers, as it can cause qubits to lose their delicate quantum state, known as decoherence.

Quantum noise can arise from various sources, including thermal fluctuations, electromagnetic interference, imperfections in quantum gates, and interactions with the environment. Different types of quantum noise affect qubits in distinct ways. For example, phase noise alters the relative phase between the basis states of a qubit, while amplitude noise affects the probabilities of measuring different states. Understanding and characterizing these noise sources is crucial for error mitigation.

Quantum noise poses a significant barrier to the development of large-scale, fault-tolerant quantum computers. Even small amounts of noise can lead to decoherence, causing qubits to lose their superposition and entanglement properties. This loss of quantum information can render computations meaningless and limit the size and complexity of feasible quantum algorithms. Quantum noise also complicates the implementation of error correction schemes, as correcting one type of error might inadvertently introduce others.

Efforts to mitigate quantum noise include improving the physical isolation of qubits, developing more precise control techniques, and implementing quantum error correction codes. Research into understanding the nature of quantum noise and developing methods to reduce or correct it is an active and vital area of quantum computing. Some algorithms, such as the Quantum Approximate Optimization Algorithm (QAOA), are designed to be more resilient to noise, making them suitable for near-term quantum devices.

Quantum noise is a multifaceted challenge that goes to the heart of the difficulties in building practical quantum computers. It represents an intersection of physics, engineering, and computer science, with ongoing research essential for advancing the field of quantum technology.

The Schrödinger equation describes the evolution of a quantum state over time, by way of unitary operators acting on the state. In a quantum computer, these unitary operators can be precisely controlled, giving rise to a set of logical gates for transforming the quantum state of the computer. Logic gates are the building blocks of quantum circuits, and they operate on one or several qubits. While these gates drive the evolution of so-called pure quantum states, they cannot describe noisy quantum evolution, decoherence, or open quantum systems. To model these things, a richer description of quantum states and quantum operations is needed, which we will describe in a later section.

In the code snippet that follows, the quantum computer is instructed to produce a Bell pair, in which a pair of qubits is maximally entangled. In the computational basis:

$$\frac{1}{\sqrt{2}}(|00\rangle + |11\rangle)$$

In a noiseless setting, measurements of this state would produce measurement outcomes of 00 and 11 with equal probability. However, in a noisy setting, the quantum computer can give erroneous results. Indeed, as observed in the measurement counts below, we find 01 and 10 bitstrings, along with the 00 and 11 results we expected. In fact, in this example, the states 01 and 10 represent 9.5% of the total results:

```
from braket.circuits import Circuit, Gate
from braket.aws import AwsDevice
from matplotlib import pyplot as plt
# set up device
rigetti = AwsDevice("arn:aws:braket:us-west-1::device/qpu/rigetti/Aspen-M-2")
# create a maximum entangled state.
bell = Circuit().h(0).cnot(0, 1)
# run circuit
rigetti_task = rigetti.run(bell, shots=1000)
# get measurement counts
rigetti_results = rigetti_task.result()
rigetti_counts = rigetti_results.measurement_counts
print('Measurement counts:', rigetti_counts)
# plot results: see effects of noise
%matplotlib inline
plt.bar(rigetti_counts.keys(), rigetti_counts.values())
plt.xlabel('bitstrings')
plt.ylabel('counts')
plt.tight_layout()
Python
Output:
Measurement counts: Counter({'00': 463, '11': 442, '10': 60, '01': 35})
```

How can this be? The answer is that noise corrupted the quantum information in the device, leading to the unexpected measurement results. The example above highlights the reality of all NISQ devices: they are prone to errors in the computation. In order to simulate the (noisy) evolution in NISQ hardware, we need a quantum simulator that can model general noise acting on the quantum circuit.

Density matrices

Since our goal is to model a wide variety of both pure and noisy quantum operations, we require a richer representation of quantum states than just state vectors and quantum circuits. What we really need are so-called *mixed quantum states*, which are required when we want to describe, for example, a physical system that is subject to noise and decoherence, or is entangled with other quantum systems in the environment outside of our control.

Mathematically, the more general description of quantum states we need makes use of "density matrices" to describe both pure and mixed quantum states. For pure quantum states, the state vector formalism and the density matrix formalism coincide: for each pure state |ψρ, there is a density matrix ρ=|ψρ⟨ψ| (the outer product of the state |ψρ and its conjugate transpose) that are equivalent representations of the same state. The density matrix formalism allows for more general quantum states than the pure states, and indeed mixed states can be represented by taking convex combinations of pure state density matrices: $\rho=''_i s_i |\psi_i\rho\langle\psi_i|$ with trρ=1.

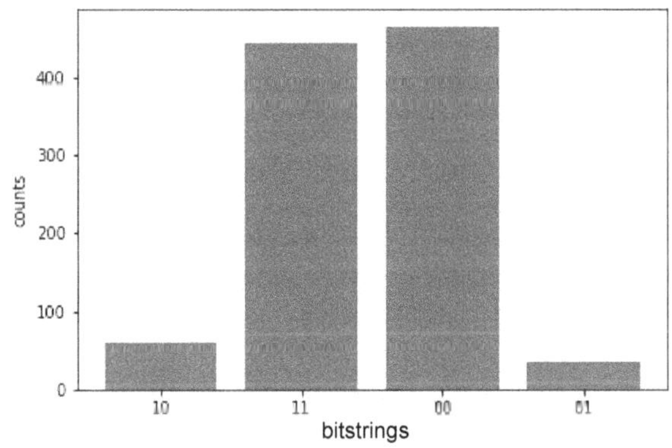

Fig. 1: Results of a Bell circuit run on noisy quantum hardware, highlighting the effects of the noise.

The beauty of the density matrix formalism is that it encompasses both pure and mixed states, which allows us to simulate more general processes in nature that involve noise and incomplete information. For example, a qubit in the |0ρ state that undergoes a bit flip error with probability s evolves from a (pure state) density matrix ρ=|0ρ⟨0| to a mixed state ρ'=(1-s)|0ρ⟨0|+s|1ρ⟨1|. This final density matrix is a mixed state representing a qubit that is either in |0ρ or |1ρ with a probability distribution {(1-s), s}. This density matrix represents an *incoherent mixture* of |0ρ and |1ρ, rather than a coherent superposition.

With density matrices in hand, we are now equipped to describe general types of operations that can be applied to a quantum system, known as quantum channels. We can accurately model noisy quantum dynamics and decoherence with quantum channels.

SCALABILITY AND QUANTUM ERROR CORRECTION CHALLENGES

Quantum error correction is a set of techniques used to protect the information stored in qubits from errors and decoherence caused by noise.

Quantum computers today have high error rates – around 1 error occurs in 100 operations before failure. For quantum computers to be useful, error rates need to be as low as 1 in a trillion. A huge improvement in performance is needed, however proven progress is already happening in the community.

We are focussed on breaking though this fundamental challenge, by building scalable control systems and fast decoders, and by understanding optimal quantum algorithms for error corrected quantum computers.

Quantum Error Correction Challenges

Quantum decoherence

Compared with standard computers, quantum computers are extremely susceptible to noise. The quantum state of qubits is extremely fragile and any disturbance, such as a slight vibration or a change in temperature, can uncontrollably affect the computer, causing information stored to be lost. It can be easily understood if we think of a flipped coin landing on its edge. Ideally, without wind or vibrations, the coin would stay upright.

Nevertheless, in the real world, any small disturbance can cause the coin to fall on one of its sides, like a qubit losing its quantum state and consequently causing errors in computations. This phenomenon is called quantum decoherence.

Decoherence poses a challenge in quantum computing since, in order to avoid errors, quantum computations must be completed before decoherence occurs, i.e., during the coherence time of a qubit, which is relatively short. Although increasing this timeframe is a significant area of research, a popular approach to tackle quantum decoherence is the development of error correction codes.

Quantum error correction techniques

The aim of quantum error correction techniques is to detect and correct errors caused by quantum decoherence before they can affect quantum computations. Although correcting errors using codes is not a new concept, it becomes more challenging in the quantum setting than in the classical one. While in classical computers errors are quite rare and often occur as bit flips (0 accidentally changes to 1 or vice versa), in quantum computers, the frequency of errors is much higher and they can manifest as phase flips, bit flips, or a combination of both. In addition, due to the no-cloning theorem in quantum mechanics, qubits cannot be simply replicated as it is done with classical bits. For all these reasons, quantum computing requires more complex error correction codes.

In Quantum Error Correction (QEC) the quantum information stored in one logical qubit is protected from errors by encoding it into several physical qubits. Logical qubits are used for programming and physical qubits are the physical materials we use to process information (ions, photons, superconductors). When we say that IBM built a 433-qubit quantum computer or Google announced a 72-qubits quantum processor, we are talking about physical qubits. The ratio between the number of logical and physical qubits varies depending on the hardware used, the algorithm run, or the specific application, but overall, the higher the error rate is, the more physical qubits you need.

There are many codes widely used for quantum error correction, each one representing a different way of encoding quantum information over physical qubits. Some examples are the Shor code (1 logical qubit is encoded into 9 physical qubits), Steane code (1 logical qubit is encoded into 7 physical qubits) or Surface code (family of quantum error correcting codes defined on a two-dimensional lattice of qubits). Also, both academia and industry are intensively researching this topic, although, as mentioned in a Quantum Insider post, "despite very impressive results, it is clear that we are still a long way from practical and usable QEC".

Scalability

Scalability refers to the ability to increase the number of qubits in a quantum system to allow for the resolution of more complex problems. As previously mentioned, qubits are notoriously fragile, and any small interference can cause errors in computations. This fact, together with the difficulty of connecting large numbers of qubits to create larger systems, makes scalability a challenging process. One possible solution is the use of error correction techniques which involve building redundancy into the system to allow for the detection and correction of errors. However, as previously mentioned, these techniques require the use of additional qubits and complex algorithms, which can further complicate the scaling process.

Currently the largest quantum computer has 1180 qubits, as is explained in a NewScientist article, and the number of physical qubits needed to factor an integer of 2048 bits in 8 hours is estimated at 20 million physical qubits. The authors of the latter assume that qubits are built using superconducting circuits, and the error correction code is done using the surface code.

So, how long until we have million-qubit machines? IBM predicts having a 1 million qubits quantum computer by 2030 and Google by 2029, both working on superconducting qubits. On the other hand, the start-up PsiQuantum is planning to make a one million photonic qubits quantum computer with error correction (about 1000 error corrected qubits) by 2025.

The Global Risk Institute publishes a report each year that "aims at providing an educated perspective of how far away the quantum threat is, by collecting and examining the perspectives of global experts from academia and industry, involved in diverse facets of quantum computing." In the 2023 report, 37 leading experts on quantum computing (Jay Gambetta from IBM, Dave Bacon from Google Quantum AI, Peter Shor from MIT, etc.) were interviewed. A significant number of experts agree that, considering the goal of implementing a quantum computer with roughly 100 logical qubits in the next 15 years, the leading candidates are superconducting systems and trapped-ions. To the question "Please indicate how likely you estimate it is that a quantum computer able to factorize a 2048-bit number in less than 24 hours will be built within the next 5 years, 10 years, 15 years, 20 years, and 30 years.", just over half of the experts answered that within 20 years the likelihood is greater than 70% and in 30, greater than 95%.

Quantum Hardware Limitations

Quantum hardware limitations are another significant challenge facing *quantum algorith*ms. Currently, most quantum devices are noisy and have a limited number of qubits. Moreover, the accuracy of the qubits is limited, and the coherence time is short. These limitations make it challenging to implement quantum algorithms efficiently and accurately. To address this challenge, researchers are developing new hardware architectures, improving the accuracy of qubits, and exploring the potential of hybrid quantum-classical computing.

While quantum algorithms hold tremendous promise for the advancement of QIP and faster computation, there are still numerous challenges and limitations that need to be addressed. Noise and error correction, scalability, limited applications, quantum supremacy, and quantum hardware limitations are some of the most significant challenges facing quantum algorithms. To address these challenges, researchers are exploring various approaches, such as developing novel error correction techniques, improving hardware architectures, and exploring the potential of hybrid quantum-classical computing.

Common Algorithms Used for Quantum Error Correction

Several quantum error correction algorithms have been developed, each with its own strengths and trade-offs. Here are some of the commonly used algorithms:

- **Shor's Code:** Proposed by Peter Shor in 1995, this code is one of the earliest and most fundamental quantum error-correcting codes. It can detect and correct a single qubit error in a logical qubit consisting of 9 physical qubits.
- **Steane Code:** Developed by Andrew Steane in 1996, this code can detect and correct a single qubit error in a logical qubit consisting of 7 physical qubits. It is more efficient than Shor's code in terms of the number of physical qubits required.
- **Bacon-Shor Code:** This code, introduced by Dave Bacon and Peter Shor in the late 1990s, is designed to protect against both bit-flip and phase-flip errors. It uses a larger number of physical qubits (13 or more) to encode a single logical qubit.
- **Surface Codes:** Surface codes, proposed by Alexei Kitaev in 1997, are a family of topological quantum error-correcting codes. They are particularly attractive due to their high fault-tolerance and the ability to correct errors without measuring individual qubits directly.
- **Color Codes:** Color codes are another class of topological quantum error-correcting codes that offer high fault-tolerance and efficient error correction. They are based on the principles of gauge theory and are particularly well-suited for hardware implementations.

These algorithms differ in their encoding schemes, error detection and correction methods, and the trade-offs between resource requirements (such as the number of physical qubits) and fault-tolerance capabilities.

Quantum Error Correction and Fault-Tolerant Quantum Computing

Quantum computing is an emerging technology that has the potential to solve problems that are beyond the capabilities of classical computers. However, quantum computers are prone to errors due to the inherent fragility of quantum states. These errors can propagate and lead to incorrect results, making it difficult to perform reliable computations. Therefore, developing techniques for quantum error correction (QEC) and fault-tolerant quantum computing (FTQC) is crucial for realizing the full potential of quantum computing.

Quantum Error Correction (QEC)

Quantum error correction is a technique for detecting and correcting errors in quantum states. QEC codes are designed to encode quantum information in a way that allows errors to be detected and corrected without destroying the information. The basic idea of QEC is to use redundant encoding to protect quantum information against errors. This is achieved by encoding the information in a larger quantum system that is more robust against errors.

FTQC

Fault-tolerant quantum computing is a technique for performing quantum computations reliably despite the presence of errors. FTQC involves the use of QEC codes to detect and correct errors in quantum states. However, FTQC goes beyond QEC by incorporating additional techniques such as quantum teleportation and quantum error correction thresholds to ensure that errors are corrected efficiently and reliably.

Types of QEC codes

There are several types of QEC codes that have been developed, including the Shor code, the Steane code, and the surface code. The Shor code is a block code that can correct any single-qubit error, while the Steane code is a block code that can correct any single-qubit error and any two-qubit error. The surface code is a two-dimensional lattice code that can correct any single-qubit error and any two-qubit error on a nearest-neighbor basis.

Threshold theorem

The threshold theorem is a fundamental result in FTQC that states that it is possible to perform arbitrarily long quantum computations reliably if the error rate is below a certain threshold. The threshold theorem provides a theoretical framework for designing fault-tolerant quantum computing schemes and is a key result in the development of practical quantum computers.

Challenges in implementing FTQC

Despite the progress made in the development of QEC and FTQC, there are still significant challenges in implementing fault-tolerant quantum computing. One of the main challenges is the need for high-quality qubits that can maintain their coherence for a sufficient amount of time. Another challenge is the need for efficient error correction algorithms that can correct errors quickly and reliably.

Quantum error correction and fault-tolerant quantum computing are crucial for realizing the full potential of quantum computing. QEC codes and FTQC techniques are designed to detect and correct errors in quantum states, allowing quantum computations to be performed reliably despite the presence of errors. While there are still significant challenges in implementing FTQC, the threshold theorem provides a theoretical framework for designing fault-tolerant quantum computing schemes.

Next Goals in Quantum Error Correction

While significant progress has been made in the field of quantum error correction, several challenges and goals remain:

- **Improving Fault-Tolerance:** Researchers are continuously working on developing more efficient and fault-tolerant quantum error correction codes that can handle higher error rates and require fewer physical qubits.
- **Hardware Integration:** Integrating quantum error correction techniques into actual quantum hardware is a crucial step towards practical quantum computing. This involves optimizing the algorithms for specific hardware architectures and addressing implementation challenges.
- **Real-Time Error Correction:** Developing techniques for real-time error correction, where errors are detected and corrected dynamically during quantum computations, is an important goal for achieving fault-tolerant quantum computing.
- **Scalability:** As quantum computers grow in size and complexity, scalable quantum error correction methods will be essential to maintain the reliability of large-scale quantum systems.
- **Noise Characterization:** Improving the understanding and characterization of different types of noise and errors in quantum systems can lead to more tailored and effective error correction strategies.

Quantum error correction is a vital component in the quest for practical and reliable quantum computing. By addressing the inherent fragility of quantum systems and mitigating the effects of errors, these techniques pave the way for harnessing the full potential of quantum algorithms and applications. As quantum hardware continues to advance, the development of robust and efficient quantum error correction methods will be crucial for realizing the transformative impact of quantum computing across various domains.

Major Players in the Quantum Computing Industry

The quantum computing industry is a rapidly growing field with several major players competing for a leading position. These companies are working towards developing quantum computers that can solve complex problems at a much faster rate than classical computers. The industry is attracting investment from governments, private companies, and venture capitalists due to its potential to revolutionize various sectors such as finance, healthcare, and energy.

- **IBM:** IBM is one of the leading players in the quantum computing industry. The company has been working on quantum computing for over 30 years and has made significant progress in the field. IBM's quantum computer, IBM Q, has been used by researchers and businesses to solve complex problems. The company has also developed a software platform, Qiskit, to help developers build quantum applications.

- **Google:** Google is another major player in the quantum computing industry. The company's quantum computer, Sycamore, was able to perform a task in just 200 seconds that would take a classical computer 10,000 years. This breakthrough demonstrated the potential of quantum computing and put Google at the forefront of the industry. Google has also developed a programming language, Cirq, to help developers write quantum algorithms.
- **Microsoft:** Microsoft has been investing in quantum computing for over a decade and has made significant progress in the field. The company's quantum computer, Azure Quantum, is a cloud-based service that allows developers to experiment with quantum computing. Microsoft has also developed a programming language, Q#, to help developers write quantum algorithms.
- **Rigetti Computing:** Rigetti Computing is a startup that has made significant progress in the quantum computing industry. The company's quantum computer, Aspen-8, is one of the most powerful quantum computers in the world. Rigetti Computing has also developed a software platform, Forest, to help developers build quantum applications.
- **Honeywell:** Honeywell is a diversified technology and manufacturing company that has recently entered the quantum computing industry. The company's quantum computer, H1, is one of the most powerful quantum computers in the world. Honeywell has also developed a software platform, System Model H1, to help developers build quantum applications.

Comparing the Options

All of these major players in the quantum computing industry have made significant progress and are working towards developing quantum computers that can solve complex problems. However, each company has its own strengths and weaknesses. IBM has a long history in the field and has developed a comprehensive software platform. Google has made a breakthrough in the field and has developed a programming language. Microsoft has a cloud-based service and has also developed a programming language. Rigetti Computing is a startup that has developed a powerful quantum computer and a software platform. Honeywell is a diversified technology company that has recently entered the quantum computing industry and has already developed a powerful quantum computer.

The quantum computing industry is a rapidly growing field with several major players competing for a leading position. Each company has made significant progress and is working towards developing quantum computers that can solve complex problems. Investors and businesses should consider the strengths and weaknesses of each company before investing in quantum computing.

ETHICAL AND SECURITY CONCERNS

Quantum computing is a rapidly developing field with the potential to revolutionise many aspects of our lives. However, it also raises a number of ethical concerns.

One of the most pressing ethical concerns is the potential for quantum computing to be used for malicious purposes. For example, quantum computers could be used to break current encryption methods, which could have a significant impact on the security of our online data. Quantum computers could also be used to develop new weapons, which could pose a threat to global security.

Another ethical concern is the potential for quantum computing to exacerbate existing inequalities. For example, quantum computers could be used to develop new medical treatments, but these treatments may only be available to those who can afford them. Quantum computers could also be used to develop new financial products, but these products may only be accessible to those who have a high level of wealth.

It is important to address these ethical concerns as quantum computing develops. We need to develop safeguards to prevent quantum computers from being used for malicious purposes, and we need to ensure that the benefits of quantum computing are shared equitably.

The Potential for Malicious Use

As mentioned above, quantum computers could be used to break current encryption methods. This could have a significant impact on the security of our online data. For example, quantum computers could be used to hack into government databases, steal financial information, or disrupt critical infrastructure.

In addition, quantum computers could be used to develop new weapons. For example, quantum computers could be used to simulate the behaviour of nuclear weapons, which could make it easier to develop new and more destructive weapons.

It is important to note that these are just a few of the potential malicious uses of quantum computing. As quantum computing technology develops, it is likely that new and more sophisticated malicious uses will be devised.

The Potential to Exacerbate Inequality

Quantum computing could also exacerbate existing inequalities. For example, quantum computers could be used to develop new medical treatments, but these treatments may only be available to those who can afford them. This is because the development and deployment of quantum computers is likely to be very expensive.

Quantum computers could also be used to develop new financial products, but these products may only be accessible to those who have a high level of wealth.

This is because the financial markets are already highly complex, and quantum computers could make them even more complex.

It is important to address these potential ethical concerns as quantum computing develops. We need to ensure that the benefits of quantum computing are shared equitably, and that quantum computing does not exacerbate existing inequalities.

Possible Solutions

There are a number of possible solutions to the ethical concerns raised by quantum computing. One solution is to develop international agreements that regulate the development and use of quantum computers. These agreements could prohibit the use of quantum computers for malicious purposes, and they could ensure that the benefits of quantum computing are shared equitably.

Another solution is to develop new encryption methods that are resistant to quantum computers. These new encryption methods would need to be based on different principles than current encryption methods, and they would need to be very secure.

It is also important to raise awareness of the ethical implications of quantum computing. This will help to ensure that the development and use of quantum computers is done in a responsible and ethical manner.

Ethical quantum concerns typically fall into several major categories:

- **Resource Allocation and Inequality**: Quantum computing is a resource-intensive technology, both in terms of the physical resources required to build quantum computers and the human resources needed to program and operate them. Such resources are available only to a few nations. Given this, and given the rise in "quantum nationalism" - the development of country-specific quantum programs - will the benefits of quantum computing primarily accrue to the wealthy, developed nations that can afford to invest in it? This could further deepen global socio-economic divides. Within the legal frameworks of the countries QuEra operates in, we seek to provide equitable access to potential users, whether via the cloud or by owning a quantum computer.
- **Misuse of power**: a sufficiently powerful quantum computer could one day break many current encryption schemes leading to unparalleled breaches of privacy and security. That's why many experts warn against bad actors that implement "Store Now Decrypt Later", capturing encrypted information today while hoping to decrypt it in a few years. This is especially relevant for information with a long shelf life such as medical records or certain financial transactions

- **Accountability and Transparency:** The complexity of quantum algorithms could lead to a lack of transparency and accountability. If a quantum algorithm, for instance, makes a mistake or causes harm, it may be difficult to understand why or how it happened. Ensuring such "explainability" is a key requirement of many algorithms such as those deciding the outcome of a loan application. At QuEra, we seek to understand the reasons certain algorithms work and share this knowledge with our customers.
- **Job Displacement:** The increased processing power and efficiency of quantum computers could automate many jobs currently performed by humans, leading to potential job displacement. We do our best to support education and re-training programs both to address the potential of job displacement as well as to train the next generation of scientists and technicians that will help build, program and maintain these advanced machines.

Some of these categories, such as job displacement, are not specific to quantum computing and present themselves when discussing other technologies such as AI or robotics. Others – breaking the encryption system - are specific to quantum, whereas AI presents its own unique challenges such as bias and discrimination, the ability to generate artificial consciousness.

Striving to address these concerns, several organisations have started constructing ethical frameworks for quantum computing. The World Economic Forum has developed a set of Quantum Computing Governance Principles that aim to guide the responsible development and use of quantum computing including inclusiveness and equity, security and safety, environmental sustainability, and transparency and accountability. The National Academies of Sciences, Engineering, and Medicine has published a report on The Ethics of Quantum Computing that identifies a number of ethical issues including the potential malicious use of quantum computing, the potential to disrupt existing industries, the negative environmental potential, and the need to ensure that quantum computing is developed and used in a way that is fair and equitable. Last, Deloitte has developed a Trustworthy & Ethical Tech Framework that can be used to guide the development and use of quantum computing.

Beyond ethical frameworks, one could imagine some solutions. Job displacement, for instance, is often associated with the introduction of transformative technologies. Factory workers that manually assembled cars might find themselves displaced by robots, but these robots need to be built and serviced by people. If quantum computers make certain jobs obsolete, they open other opportunities.

Other solutions might require multinational collaboration. For example, the World Health Organization serves an important function that ultimately helps both developed as well as developing nations. Promoting standards, monitoring global trends, and coordinating emergency responses have helped address inequality in healthcare, benefiting all. Similarly, a "World Quantum Organization" might provide shared quantum resources to benefit all, not just those that could develop an autonomous quantum ecosystem.

Concurrent with developing solutions and ethical frameworks, there is a need to educate and inform the public, policymakers, and stakeholders about the potential implications of quantum computing to foster informed discussions about its ethical, social, and economic impacts.

Quantum computing's potential to revolutionise industries is matched by the complexity of the ethical considerations it raises. At QuEra, we recognise these challenges and are committed to responsible innovation that prioritises inclusiveness, security, and sustainability. Collaborative efforts, such as the proposed 'World Quantum Organization,' resonate with our belief in shared quantum resources and global partnerships, and we invite interested parties to engage with us. As we navigate this exciting frontier, we must do so with both eyes open to the potential downsides, ready to tackle them head-on, and always guided by ethical principles.

Quantum Computing and the Cybersecurity Threats

Quantum computing will enable great innovations in the future, but it will be accompanied by diverse risks. The potential of quantum computers to break the current security of common activities in our daily lives could have severe consequences. The quantum cybersecurity threat forebodes data breaches of sensitive health and financial personal data, challenges to the integrity of digital assets, and breaking the fundamental cryptography underpinning cryptocurrencies.

The key cybersecurity threats

Threat 1: Harvest Now, Decrypt Later

According to a Deloitte poll, just over half of its surveyed professionals (50.2%) believe that their organizations are at risk for "harvest now, decrypt later" (or HNDL) cybersecurity attacks. This refers to an attack where threat actors collect encrypted data from target organizations today, fully anticipating that data can be decrypted later when quantum computing reaches a maturity level capable of rendering many publicly utilized cryptographic algorithms like RSA entirely obsolete. HNDL poses a risk to enterprises, banks, intelligence agencies, and even military capabilities – nothing will be safe from sophisticated threat actors equipped with advanced quantum computers.

Although the initial weight of resources required to conduct such an attack makes it unlikely to target your average enterprise, accelerating advancements in technology and volumes of data being regularly transmitted under encryption means we can anticipate them to become more likely in the future. In fact, it's entirely possible such attacks have already taken place, and the targeted organizations lack the sophisticated capabilities to detect them. Despite the risk, nearly 20% of enterprises appear to be taking a "wait and see" approach.

Whether or not organizations intend to turn to quantum computing, HBDL attacks are an inevitable threat to all enterprises in a post-quantum world.

Threat 2: Making Asymmetric Cryptography Obsolete

Implementation of a practical quantum computer will render most current asymmetric encryption methods unsafe, such as RSA, Diffie-Hellman (DH), and Elliptic Curve Cryptography (ECC).

Back in 1994, Peter Shor developed a theoretical quantum algorithm to find the prime factors of a large integer. While important research, it was not considered an immediate risk, given the lack of the technology to implement quantum computers.

Now, however, quantum computing is much closer to becoming mainstream. In 2021, IDC estimated that by 2027, the market for quantum computing may grow to $8.6 billion, a 50% compound annual growth rate since its value of $412 million in 2020. It poses a "Quantum Threat," a match for the complicated math problems previously unbeatable by classic computers. The world's data, currently protected by asymmetric cryptography algorithms such as RSA, DH and ECC, will soon become readable – and subsequently, easy for cybercriminals to infiltrate and bring down global digital security.

Put simply, a practical quantum computer could not only render traditional online activities insecure; it could break most of the security underpinning the internet.

Threat 3: The vulnerabilities of blockchain technology

Besides threatening current encryption schemes, quantum computing has the capacity to render blockchain technology extremely vulnerable. Because blockchain depends on the disseminated consensus of trust, achieved through the use of public-key cryptography, it is particularly susceptible to attacks that reveal a user's private key given, only the public key.

A recent study found that 25% of all bitcoins in circulation and 65% of ether — the tokens in the Ethereum network - reside in addresses with a public key that is published on the blockchain. This means they could be stolen by leveraging a quantum computer with sufficient resources. Hundreds of billions of dollars' worth of cryptocurrencies could be vulnerable to this attack vector.

Developing Post-Quantum Cryptography and Encryption Solutions

Although there is no consensus on a timeline for when practical quantum computers are expected to mature, it is clear that institutions with information that holds value beyond the next decade or so should prepare for quantum threats.

For organizations, it is important to build awareness of the threat quantum computing poses beyond the cybersecurity experts to the senior leaders and executive decision-makers. This will help organizations to develop a more cohesive response across different levels and stakeholders.

Governments and businesses have already begun preparing for a post-quantum world. For example, CISA and NSA recently released quantum-resistant algorithm recommendations and requirements for critical infrastructure and national security systems based on the post-quantum cryptography selections from NIST.

With time, it will become even more important to be agile. Organizations can focus their strategy on "crypto agility," by which they will be able to switch between crypto algorithms seamlessly in case one or more become vulnerable to attack. For enterprises hesitant to adopt new and untested algorithms, there is the option of integrating classical and quantum-based solutions for a hybrid approach.

Other technologies, like Post-Quantum Cryptography, or technologies based on the characteristics of quantum mechanics – think Quantum Key Distribution and Quantum Random Number Generation – is also a way to strengthen cryptography.

Cyber Threats to Quantum Computers

The current state of quantum computer systems is often referred to as the NISQ (noisy intermediate-scale quantum) era, characterized by quantum computers that offer moderate computing power and are still challenged by system fidelity. Current quantum computers are volatile and unstable, with error-correction for quantum calculations still being addressed. While researchers work to solve these challenges, it is apparent that in the near-term—and further into the near-future—quantum computers will most likely be used as co-processors in hybrid systems in which classical computers will hand off mathematical calculations to the quantum computer as part of a larger system workflow that still heavily depends on classical computers.

Understanding how quantum computers will be integrated with classical computers is essential to considering the cyber threats to quantum computers. The interface between classical and quantum computers in the hybrid computing environments typical of the NISQ-era is an area ripe for cybersecurity threats. This interface is literally the gateway between the classical and quantum environments, so it can serve as a conduit for known exploits of classical computers to traverse into quantum areas. In short, there are already many known cyber attack techniques for classical computers that can be leveraged to compromise a hybrid system.

Another attack vector stems from novel approaches for control and measurement of quantum devices that will be implemented in these interfaces. Application-specific integrated circuits (ASICs), field-programmable gate arrays (FPGAs), digital-to-analogue converters (DACs), and other elements of classical-quantum interfaces are being used in new ways. The current focus of research in designing these interfaces is on functionality and performance, yet security concerns also must be addressed. Given the many known techniques for compromising classical computers, it seems probable that attacks on quantum computers will originate in weaknesses in classical computers and then propagate to the quantum-classical interface.

Research sponsored by Microsoft Quantum Sydney outlines scalability issues related to current approaches for classical-quantum interfaces. The study highlighted challenges related to I/O management, heat and power dissipation, system footprint, noise and interference, and bandwidth. While these issues are presented in relation to scalability, the same issues provide avenues for attack. For instance, attackers can leverage the heat sensitivity to enable a denial-of-service attack or the proclivity for noise and interference to attack the integrity of operations. Our work in cybersecurity of classical computers has taught us that any system failure can provide an opening to exploit a system.

While securing the classical-quantum interface is a critical element in quantum cybersecurity, there are other areas to address. For instance, the output of quantum computing calculations will be much more valuable to protect (and valuable to steal) than most classical computer output, given the resources necessary to perform the calculations and derive the output. For instance, a commercial pharmaceutical company using a quantum computer to solve a complex chemistry problem will consider that output quite valuable because it may be hard to reproduce and the end-product will contain highly valuable intellectual property.

Moreover, the vast computing power in quantum computers necessitates protecting the quantum computational power itself. That is, not just protecting algorithms and their outputs but also detecting and protecting against hijacking of quantum computing capability, in the same way a botnet attack hijacks classical computing power. For example, if adversaries do not have quantum computing power of their own, but want to perform a resource-intensive calculation, then they may try to get unauthorized access to someone else's quantum capability. Likewise, an adversary may just want to disrupt quantum-based computations solely to adversely influence the results.

Lastly, a key difference between quantum computers and classical computers is their sensitivity to temperature and the physical world in general, which opens new vectors for denial-of-service-attacks. For instance, the refrigeration requirements for many quantum architectures opens an avenue to perform a denial-of-service attack: disrupt the cooling for these architectures and their entire operation can be halted. These are the most pressing of the many threats to quantum computers that the new discipline of quantum cybersecurity must address.

Areas of Future Research in Quantum Cybersecurity

Since the design and architecture of quantum computers is still an open area of research with many alternatives being explored, it is premature to focus on specific vulnerabilities in specific systems. Researchers in this field must first form an understanding of current and future threats to quantum computers to develop more effective protections. The preceding section highlighted various threats to the confiden-tiality, integrity, and availability of quantum computers. This section highlights areas of research needed to develop protections against these threats.

For example, one key area for future research is the development of capabilities for monitoring quantum computations. Quantum processing cannot be monitored in the same ways that system monitoring is done for classical computers, which makes it hard to both assess what algorithms quantum computers are running and determine whether malicious processing is occurring. This gap illustrates the need for developing a multi-layered instrumentation framework for quantum computers, which is one of the following six key areas for future quantum security research we identified in the Workshop on Cybersecurity of Quantum Computing:

- **Building secure large-scale control systems**. The scale of the classical computation involved in supporting a large-scale quantum computer can be extensive. This support includes control systems and error correction, but it can also include monitoring for intrusions. Research is needed on building secure classical control systems for quantum computers.
- **Enabling distributed high-performance quantum computing**. Classical high-performance computing systems are typically multi-tenant and distributed. Addressing the security of multi-tenant and distributed quantum computers now can lay the foundation for more secure quantum computers when they achieve scale.
- **Understanding attack vectors on different types of quantum computers**. Deeper research on potential attack vectors for various quantum system models, such as whether adversaries only access quantum devices through a user interface, is needed to more fully understand how to secure quantum computers.
- Creating formal methods for safe and secure quantum computing systems. In computing, formal methods refer to rigorous mathematical techniques for specifying, developing, and verifying computer software and hardware.

Research is needed on developing formal methods for quantum computing to achieve trustworthy quantum computing.

- Constructing a multi-layered instrumentation framework. Such a framework would allow security-relevant properties of quantum computers to be enforced or verified.
- Developing the necessary tools for service providers to verify quantum algorithms. These tools will enable the ability to verify and control which algorithms are running on a quantum computer, also helps ensure that a quantum computer will not perform undesirable behaviors.

While all these areas of research are critical for protecting quantum computers, the landscape of cyber threats will continually change as quantum computing technology evolves. All the above areas should be researched and, in tandem, additional areas for quantum cybersecurity research should be added as they become relevant. Techniques for protecting classical computers, such as threat modeling and considering ways to compromise the principles of the confidentiality, integrity, availability (CIA) triad, must be applied continually to quantum computers to discover emerging threats to research as this field of quantum cybersecurity advances.

INTERDISCIPLINARY COLLABORATION IN QUANTUM RESEARCH

Quantum computing represents a paradigm shift in our computational capabilities, offering the potential to solve complex problems that are currently beyond the reach of classical computers. This transformative technology, especially as explored through the lens of the McGinty Equation (MEQ), has broad implications across various domains, from enhancing research accessibility to influencing global geopolitical dynamics.

Quantum Computing Accessibility

The push towards making quantum computing more accessible to researchers and industries is akin to democratizing high level computational capabilities. Traditionally, the domain of quantum computing has been restricted to specialized research laboratories due to the sophisticated and expensive nature of quantum computers.

However, with advancements in technology and the introduction of quantum computing platforms through cloud services, there's a growing opportunity for a wider range of scientists, engineers, and businesses to access and leverage quantum computing for their research and development efforts.

Accessibility to quantum computing resources can accelerate innovation in drug discovery, materials science, and complex system simulation, among other areas. By providing computational resources that can process and analyze large datasets or simulate molecular interactions at an unprecedented scale and speed, quantum computing can significantly shorten the research and development cycles in these critical fields.

Interdisciplinary Research

The McGinty Equation (MEQ) exemplifies the potential of quantum computing to foster interdisciplinary research collaborations. By its nature, quantum computing sits at the confluence of physics, computer science, and engineering. However, the applications of MEQ extend beyond these fields, promising to bring together quantum physicists, biologists, chemists, and computer scientists in collaborative research efforts.

These interdisciplinary collaborations could lead to breakthroughs at the intersection of these fields, such as new treatments for diseases through advanced simulations of biological processes, or novel materials with unique properties for technological applications. The MEQ, with its capacity to analyze and interpret complex fractal patterns in quantum systems, serves as a bridge that unites diverse scientific disciplines towards common research goals.

Ethical and Security Considerations

With the power of quantum computing, including advancements driven by the MEQ, come significant ethical and security considerations. Quantum computing's potential to break current encryption standards poses a profound challenge to cybersecurity. The ability of quantum computers to solve complex cryptographic algorithms, which protect much of our digital communications, necessitates a rethinking of security protocols and encryption methods. This challenge also opens up ethical considerations regarding privacy and surveillance. As quantum computing becomes more accessible, the balance between national security interests and individual privacy rights will need careful navigation. The development of quantum-resistant encryption methods and the establishment of ethical guidelines for the use of quantum computing in surveillance and data analysis are critical steps in addressing these concerns.

Environmental Impact

The environmental impact of advancing quantum computing technology, including the energy consumption of quantum computers and the production of necessary materials, warrants attention. Quantum computers, particularly those based on superconducting qubits, require low temperatures, achieved through energy-intensive cooling systems. As the technology scales, so too could its carbon footprint. And, quantum computing offers the potential to address environmental challenges by optimizing energy usage in various industries, developing new materials for better energy storage, and modeling complex environmental systems to inform climate action strategies. Balancing the environmental costs of quantum computing with its potential benefits is essential for sustainable advancement in this field.

Economic Implications

The economic impact of quantum fractal analysis applications, as enabled by the MEQ, is profound. On one hand, quantum computing promises to create new industries and job opportunities, particularly in technology and research sectors. On the other hand, it poses potential displacement in traditional sectors reliant on classical computing solutions. Adapting to this shift requires a proactive approach to workforce development and education, ensuring that workers have the skills needed to thrive in an economy increasingly influenced by quantum technologies. Governments and industries must invest in training programs and educational initiatives to prepare for these changes, mitigating the risk of job displacement while capitalizing on the creation of new economic opportunities.

Legal and Regulatory Framework

The advancement of quantum technologies necessitates the development of a comprehensive legal and regulatory framework. This framework must address the use of quantum computing in sensitive applications, such as quantum cryptography and national security, while promoting innovation and protecting intellectual property rights. Regulations will need to balance the promotion of technological advancements with the prevention of misuse, ensuring that quantum computing technologies are developed and used in a manner that benefits society as a whole. This includes international cooperation to establish standards and norms for the use of quantum technologies, preventing an arms race and encouraging peaceful, collaborative progress.

Public Perception and Education

Public understanding and perception of quantum computing and its applications, including those driven by the MEQ, play a critical role in the technology's adoption and ethical use. Misconceptions about quantum computing's capabilities and implications can lead to unfounded fears or unrealistic expectations. Educational efforts aimed at demystifying quantum computing for the general public, alongside initiatives to integrate quantum computing concepts into STEM curricula, are essential. By increasing public awareness and understanding, we can foster informed discussions about the ethical use of quantum computing and ensure that its benefits are widely recognized and equitably distributed.

Quantum Supremacy and Competition

The race towards quantum supremacy, marked by milestones in quantum computing achievements, underscores the competitive nature of technological advancement in this field. Nations and corporations are investing heavily in quantum computing research and development, recognizing its strategic importance. This competition, while driving innovation, also raises questions about global collaboration and the equitable sharing of advancements. The pursuit of quantum supremacy must be balanced with efforts to ensure that the benefits of quantum computing, including those related to the MEQ, are accessible to all, promoting global scientific progress and addressing shared challenges. The implications of quantum computing, through the lens of the MEQ, extend far beyond specific technical applications. They touch on a wide range of societal, ethical, and environmental issues, necessitating a comprehensive and multifaceted approach to their development and deployment. By addressing these considerations thoughtfully, we can harness the transformative power of quantum computing to benefit humanity while mitigating its potential risks and challenges.

Interdisciplinary Research in Integrative Medicine

In the dynamic landscape of Integrative Medicine, collaboration and interdisciplinary research stand as pillars that bridge diverse fields of knowledge. By fostering cooperation between conventional medicine and complementary therapies, this approach creates a harmonious blend that is greater than the sum of its parts. The collaborative ethos within integrative medicine extends beyond professional boundaries, nurturing an environment where practitioners from various disciplines converge to shape the future of holistic healthcare.

Interdisciplinary Research Initiatives

Interdisciplinary research initiatives within integrative medicine bring together experts from diverse fields to explore complex healthcare challenges. For example, a team may include medical doctors, acupuncturists, nutritionists, and psychologists collaborating on a project aimed at understanding the holistic management of chronic pain. This cross-disciplinary approach fosters a holistic perspective that goes beyond individual specialties, addressing the multifaceted nature of health and well-being.

Holistic Patient Care Teams

In the practice of integrative medicine, patient care often involves a team-based approach. Holistic patient care teams may include professionals from various disciplines working collaboratively to develop and implement personalized treatment plans. This approach acknowledges that health is influenced by factors beyond biological aspects and integrates mental, emotional, and social well-being into the care continuum.

Education and Training Across Disciplines

Interdisciplinary collaboration in integrative medicine is not only evident in patient care but also in education and training programs. Institutions are increasingly offering courses that expose healthcare professionals to a spectrum of disciplines, fostering a shared understanding of integrative approaches. This educational model ensures that practitioners are equipped to collaborate effectively, appreciating the value of different perspectives in holistic patient care.

Research at the Intersection of Disciplines

In the pursuit of advancing integrative medicine, researchers are exploring the intersection of disciplines to uncover new insights and treatment modalities. For instance, studies may examine the combination of acupuncture and cognitive-behavioral therapy for mental health conditions or the integration of nutritional interventions in cancer care. These endeavors contribute to a growing body of evidence supporting the efficacy and safety of integrative approaches.

Patient-Centered Care through Collaboration

At the heart of collaborative and interdisciplinary research in integrative medicine is the commitment to patient-centered care. This approach recognizes that each individual is unique and may benefit from a combination of therapies tailored to their specific needs. Collaborative care plans empower patients to actively participate in their health journey, drawing on the expertise of professionals from different domains to achieve optimal outcomes.

Building Bridges between East and West

In the globalization of integrative medicine, collaboration extends beyond conventional and complementary practices to embrace cultural diversity. Collaborative research efforts are building bridges between Eastern and Western healing traditions, exploring the integration of practices such as acupuncture, herbal medicine, and mindfulness with conventional medical approaches. This cultural exchange enriches the field and enhances the options available to patients worldwide.

Overcoming Challenges through Dialogue

Collaboration and interdisciplinary research also involve navigating challenges arising from differing perspectives and methodologies. However, these challenges can be viewed as opportunities for growth and innovation. Open and ongoing dialogue between professionals from different disciplines fosters a shared understanding, leading to the development of common language and research protocols that benefit the entire field.

CHAPTER-10

QUANTUM COMPUTING IN INDUSTRY AND RESEARCH

Quantum computing is on the rise. Maybe not yet for the mainstream, but governments and industry giants have taken notice. Goldman Sachs is to introduce quantum algorithms in their pricing. Meanwhile, the US government added Chinese quantum computing firms to their export blacklist.

This level of attention is there for a good reason. Quantum computing is indomitable and could increase efficiency in various fields. Here's a quick lowdown on why it's such a big deal.

Manufacturing and Industrial Design

Manufacturing requires efficient processes and designs to produce high-quality products.

The design process can be incredibly tedious. Industrial designers need to consider multiple variables to craft a working product. This is especially important in machinery, transportation, and electronics.

For example, designers often need several drafts when manufacturing a high-speed jet. This process ensures that they have the most efficient wing design for high speeds. It also applies to other key parts of the machine.

Quantum computing can help designers fish through the different possibilities faster. This technology can help them save time and create better designs for a better product.

It can also help manufacturers troubleshoot better. They can give a quantum computer their data on machine failure, and it can help figure out the problem areas.

Logistics

Logistics is often a time and location-sensitive industry. Thus, it would benefit a lot from optimizing processes. There are a lot of factors to consider when transporting something from one place to another. You have supply chains, vehicle availability, traffic, and customer expectations, among others.

Quantum computing can help companies figure out the best routes for every shipment. This technology also considers real-life factors, such as weather and traffic.

Adopting quantum technology can change the game and fulfil customer standards for logistics. DHL and other logistics companies are already eyeing it as a trend with great potential.

Finance

Financial procedures often rely on a lot of complex mathematical processes. Analysts deal with many variables to predict possible outcomes of the market. Major events can require fast-paced responses that classic computers struggle to do.

Quantum computing can help make more accurate simulations and predictions of market activity. They are also a lot better at Monte Carlo simulations than traditional methods.

In finance, a Monte Carlo simulation allows analysts to look at many possible outcomes from an array of variables. These results help us understand the risks and possibilities, especially in financial forecasting. Quantum tech reduces the time and effort required for such operations.

Banking and financial giants recognize the possible applications of this emerging tech. JP Morgan Chase and Wells Fargo have already invested in quantum computing, powering the future of finance.

Chemical Engineering

Chemical engineering deals with the manipulation of atoms and molecules. The field itself involves the application of quantum principles.

It is also a widely-encompassing field. Chemical engineering has applications in manufacturing, healthcare, construction, food processing, electronics, etc.

With such a wide variety of chemical configurations available, it can take time to find the right one. Quantum computing can help speed up these processes.

This application is beneficial in pharmaceuticals and vaccine development. Our experience with the COVID-19 pandemic has emphasized the need for urgent solutions.

Artificial Intelligence

Artificial intelligence is another emergent technology already making waves in the mainstream. It involves "teaching" machines vast amounts of knowledge to perform various tasks.

AI already has many applications in various fields. These include healthcare, e-commerce, education, finance, security, and media, among others.

Quantum computing can be a significant help in AI efforts. AI development requires the processing of vast amounts of data for machine learning. This helps the AI recognize patterns and make decisions better.

Although classic computing is doing its job, AI would benefit a lot from quantum tech. Faster processing can lead to better AI performance. Eventually, this can result in more human-like responses from AI.

QUANTUM COMPUTING IN CHEMISTRY AND MATERIAL SCIENCE

Quantum chemistry is considered to be one of the first fields that could benefit from the development of quantum hardware and algorithms. The first applications of quantum computing to solve the electronic structure problem date back to 2005 and the field has since then received significant attention. A detailed overview of the state-of-the-art methods developed in this field can be found in the following two review papers (and references therein): Researchers focus on using digital quantum computers to solve the electronic structure problem *ab initio*, while researchers is aimed at the expert computational chemist and highlights the advantages quantum computing brings to the field.

At this early technological stage, several strategies to employ quantum effects in computing are being explored. The two most well-developed at present are quantum gate-based and quantum annealing. The former can be thought of as the quantum equivalent of classical computers, where the classical bits are replaced by quantum bits (qubits) and classical gates are replaced by quantum gates, which operate in discrete time. The latter relies on the quantum adiabatic theorem and requires the problem of interest to be mapped to a physical set of qubits, whose states are allowed to evolve by slowly changing the Hamiltonian parameters of the quantum annealer, at all times remaining in the instantaneous ground state. However, current quantum annealers experience coupling to their thermal environment beyond the ~10–100 ns timescale. Quantum annealers, therefore, behave in a way that is intermediate between the idealized quantum adiabatic theorem and inevitable experimental limitations.

From a chemical point of view, quantum gate-based algorithms have been employed mainly to solve the Fermion Hamiltonian that describes the motion of electrons in molecules and materials, i.e., the Shrödinger equation. Typically, the terms that account for electron correlation make this equation intractable to solve classically for all but the simplest systems. Thus, post-Hartree-Fock (post-HF) approaches have been developed such as configurational interaction (CI) and ideally applied in the full-CI limit. Several algorithms have proved to be promising in this field. However, results are still limited due to the size and stability of available quantum hardwares.

Quantum annealing in its current hardware implementation solves problems that can be formulated as an Ising model. Unfortunately, the electronic Hamiltonian cannot be mapped to the Ising form without an exponential growth of the number of variables required to solve the problem, as discussed from a classical point of view in researchers. This introduces an intrinsic limitation in using quantum annealers for solving this type of problem. Nevertheless, several algorithms to solve the electronic structure problem through quantum annealing have been explored for small systems.

Quantum annealing is suited to solving optimization and global minimum search problems. Therefore, it finds applications in chemistry, where several configurations of the same structure are energetically viable. For example, in the analysis of the conformation of transition states, configurations of dense polymers mixtures, protein design, screening of chemicals to discover new materials and materials design such as configurational analysis of doped materials.

Here, we will focus on this last application using vacancies in graphene as a test model to explore how to map a chemical system to an Ising Hamiltonian and to the quadratic unconstrained binary optimisation (QUBO) model. These models are the respective natural language for QA and chemistry and they both belong to the binary quadratic model (*BQM*) class of problems.

Despite the simplicity of the problem, it can be seen as the test model for the combinatorial optimization class of problems, which are often found in chemistry and materials science. The configuration space to explore is proportional to the binomial coefficient

$$\binom{N_{sites}}{N_{vac}}$$

where N_{sites} is the number of sites in the unit cell and N_{vac} is the number of vacancies. For small values of N_{sites} or N_{vac}, the problem can be treated exactly by completing an exhaustive search, i.e., by calculating the energy of each possible outcome. However, as the size of the cell increases, the problem becomes quickly intractable (for example, for N_{sites}=50 and N_{sites}=10‘, there are more than one billion possible configurations). Various heuristic classical algorithms are available to tackle this type of problem, for example, Monte-Carlo methods, random walks, tree search optimization, tabu algorithm, and simulated annealing (SA). However, these approaches suffer from limitations, such as getting stuck in local minima, sampling the same location more than once, and completely missing the best configurations because of the randomness of the sampling. A method to overcome these limitations is, therefore, required to analyze large configurational spaces encountered in materials science.

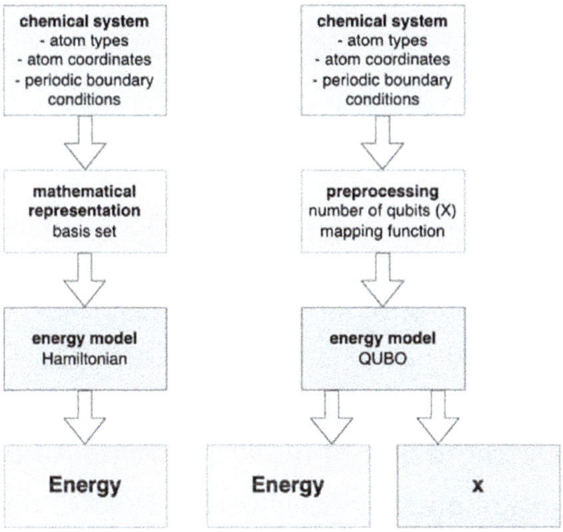

Fig. 1. Left: computational materials chemistry workflow for classical computers. Right: computational materials chemistry workflow for quantum computers. The vector x represents the lowest energy configuration of the system.

Simulated annealing borrows ideas from the thermal annealing of metals. A fictional temperature, which decreases as the annealing evolves, is introduced as a tunable parameter. By reducing the temperature, the size of the accessible configurational space decreases during annealing. The process typically stops when either a minimum threshold on the energy or the maximum number of iterations, defined by the user, has been reached. The progress of the SA can be determined by using sophisticated methods such as holding points and checking to see if the holding point is within a local basin.

Quantum annealing (QA) is based on the same principles as SA but uses an auxiliary quantum mechanical system to find the minimum energy of the system. Unlike the SA algorithm that uses classical search techniques, QA exploits two quantum mechanical phenomena: superposition and tunneling. The former means that at the beginning of the anneal, the qubits represent all possible final states, corresponding to all combinations of 1 and 0 simultaneously. The latter means that the system can move from one configuration to another by tunneling through the energy barrier. Therefore, it is possible for QA to escape deep local minima that trap other optimization techniques.

Simulating and predicting the behavior of complex, quantum-mechanical systems is critical for new design, such as new types of batteries or pharmaceutical drugs. McKinsey & Company predicts that quantum chemistry will be an early disruptive application of quantum computing. Modeling polymers, solids, molecules at high precision without experimentally synthesizing materials in the lab enables identification of effective molecular structures that satisfy desirable properties such as high energy density or stiffness. Classic examples include drug discovery or the Haber-Bosch process: Industrial production of chemicals such as the catalytic nitrogen fixation of ammonia in the Haber-Bosch process uses up 1% of the world's energy production and is responsible for 1.4% of the carbon-dioxide emission. On a large scale, even relatively small improvements would cause a relevant absolute impact.

The global relevance of quantum computing in Material Science is also reflected in our working group. There are various QUTAC material science examples, including prediction of chemical reactivity in the chemical industry (BASF), molecular dynamics for drug discovery (Boehringer Ingelheim, Merck), and battery research (VW).

Quantum chemistry in the age of quantum computing

A fundamental goal of quantum chemistry is to solve the time-independent, non-relativistic Schrodinger equation for molecular systems,

$$\hat{H}_{mol}(\vec{r})\psi(\vec{r}, t) = E\psi(\vec{r}, t) \qquad (1)$$

where $\hat{H}_{mol}$ is the molecular Hamiltonian, $\psi(\vec{r}, t)$ is the multi-particle wave function of the system, and E is the energy eigenvalue. In atomic units, the molecular Hamiltonian is given by

$$\hat{H}_{mol} = -\sum_{i} \frac{\nabla^2_{\vec{R}_i}}{2M} - \sum_{i} \frac{\nabla^2_{\vec{r}_i}}{2} - \sum_{ij} \frac{Z_i}{|\vec{R}_i - \vec{r}_j|} + \sum_{ij>i} \frac{Z_i Z_j}{|\vec{R}_i - \vec{r}_j|} + \sum_{ij>i} \frac{Z_i Z_j}{|\vec{r}_i - \vec{r}_j|} \qquad (2)$$

where $\vec{R}_i$, M_i and Z_i indicate the spatial coordinates, masses and charges of the nuclei in the molecule and $\vec{r}_i$ are the electronic coordinates. However, an exact solution quickly becomes intractable due to the exponential growth of the size of the wave function with the particle number. This has inspired formulations of various physically-motivated wave function approximations as well as quantum chemistry algorithms on classical computers. This section starts from challenges as such and discusses how classical computers may fall short in addressing some of the challenges while quantum computers are able to circumvent the limitations.

For some time, the underlying trend in the observed improvement of hardware capabilities was remarkable and became known as the Moore's Law. However, the initially observed pattern of roughly doubling the density of transistors in a chip every 18–24 months is showing signs of slowing down, calling for new computing paradigms to meet the growing computational demands in several scientific and technological fields. Among the candidates expected to provide the next quantum leap in computational technology, quantum computing emerges as the most promising. Yet, because quantum computing is still in its infancy, it is a long way toward capabilities exceeding what has been achieved through classical compute machinery. Tying back to the main topic of this manuscript, this means that once more a great effort spanning many different disciplines is expected to be necessary in order to elevate quantum computers to be the main workhorse behind the quantum chemistry inquiry.

The initial case for quantum computing came from Richard Feynman, who is often credited for conceiving the idea that a computing device working under the laws of quantum mechanics could be exponentially faster than a classical machine for certain classes of problems, an idea which was independently reached (somewhat earlier) by researcher. One of the most immediate and natural applications of a quantum computer envisioned by Feynman was the simulation of other quantum systems. On one hand, this opens the door to the solution of many problems that would otherwise be "practically impossible."

On the other hand, as it will become clear later, it often demands a complete rethinking of these problems, and quantum chemistry is no exception, which practically means revisiting the three foundational pillars that helped elevate quantum chemistry in the first place. The phrase "practically impossible" appears in quotes for a reason. For our purposes, it means that problems whose resource demands do not scale polynomially with the size/time of the simulation. In other words, if upon varying the dimension of the Hilbert space or the propagated time one observes an exponential response in the computational resources necessary to carry out the underlying computation, this signals that this type of simulation is very limited in scope.

The question of which problems are practically possible in this sense is addressed in a rich field of theoretical computer science known as computational complexity theory. However, such considerations are beyond the practical concerns of most chemists and will not be addressed here.

To start putting things in perspective, one can look at quantum chemistry from the standpoint of electronic structure theory, which has long benefited from the second quantization formalism, representing states in an occupation basis, that is, Fock space. The exact eigenspectrum for a non-relativistic Hamiltonian in a given basis can be found by diagonalization of the full Hamiltonian, amounting to solving the full configuration interaction (FCI) problem. Yet, it is easy to verify that the dimension of the Hilbert space in question grows as 2^N, with N being the number of basis functions, that is, exhibits exponential growth. In practical terms, the number of matrix elements that need to be evaluated scales as 4^N, alleviated to $2^N(2^N + 1)^{-2}$ in the case of an observable, such as the molecular Hamiltonian, due to the Hermiticity constraint.

Turning to the dynamics problem, the textbook example of a separable wave function in terms of time and spatial domain points to an exponential dependence with the time variable, which holds in the adiabatic approximation (the Hamiltonian is constant or varies only slowly in time). Thus, in simple terms, such methods are amenable only for implementation within a compute paradigm where information can be stored and processed exponentially with the number of resources available. The great potential from quantum computing is due to the superposition and entanglement found among qubits, which enables a quantum computer to naturally achieve such an exponential increase in performance.

In light of Feynman's proposal and keeping in mind that chemistry is also governed by the laws of quantum mechanics, quantum chemistry has been seen by many as one of the first fields to showcase a tangible advantage from the employment of quantum computers. Yet, for a long time the majority of the quantum algorithms were not directly related to chemistry, such as the Bernstein–Vazirani algorithm to determine an unknown string of bits (bit string) and its more general Deutsch–Jozsa algorithm, Grover's search algorithm, Shor's prime number factoring, and so forth. The quantum phase estimation (QPE) algorithm is pervasive in many other quantum computing algorithms, and even though it is not specific to quantum chemistry, it allows one to compute an eigenvalue for a given eigenstate of an observable with tunable precision.

This made the QPE algorithm a prominent candidate in quantum chemical simulations, since many quantum chemistry methods aim at just that, particularly at recovering the ground state energy via the diagonalization of the Hamiltonian in a basis of trial wave functions that are variationally optimized. However, its application to even relatively small molecules/basis sets is accompanied by quantum circuits with prohibitive implementation at present.

Given the early stage of quantum computing at the moment, understanding the availability and demand of quantum resources is of paramount importance. In evaluating the suitability of a quantum algorithm, a crucial metric is the so-called *circuit depth*. In short, the entire algorithm is comprised of a time-ordered series of relatively simple operations (gates) and each takes some amount of time to be executed. As we add more and more of these *gates* (these will be better explained later), the more time it requires to complete the circuit that executes an algorithm.

However, qubits can survive in a defined state for a limited time before external effects push them out of that state, negatively impacting the reliability of the information they can provide. The length of time in which assertions about the state can be made reliably is known as *coherence time*. Because present qubits have shown significant resistance to endure for prolonged coherence times, it is one of the main limiting factors preventing quantum computers to reach their expected performance. Another factor in curtailing a more widespread adoption of quantum computers is the small-to-moderate number of qubits in the current quantum chips, which are collectively known as noisy intermediate-scale quantum (NISQ) devices.

While these current technological challenges severely curtail the performance and operation of quantum computers, they have spurred the development of a new compute paradigm with the goal of circumventing the inherent shortcomings of the present technology.

It recognizes that the quantum computer is better suited to specific tasks, such as the preparation of highly entangled states and the associated measurements, from which some cost function can be computed given a set of parameters that can tune the quantum circuit. The output of the cost function (a scalar) is provided to a classical optimization routine that in turn searches the parameter space in order to meet user-defined optimal criteria. It is this interplay between classical and quantum technologies that has led to the rise of hybrid quantum-classical computing. From a computer science/software engineering standpoint, this idea can be seen as a natural extension of heterogeneous compute approaches, highlighted by the concerted usage of central and graphical processing units (CPUs and GPUs, respectively), and has proven a pivotal move in the development of quantum computing at large as it constitutes an avenue for showcasing the strengths of quantum computers even before it reaches full maturity, a future milestone that is commonly referred to as the fault-tolerance regime.

The main goal of this review is to gently introduce quantum chemistry practitioners to the most important aspects of quantum computing that are of relevance in quantum chemistry. It is important to bear in mind that quantum computing is actually an umbrella term that encompasses several distinct computational models and architectures. The most widely used, and the one receiving most attention in this review, is the one inspired by the circuit logic model underlying many of the conventional computers. A more modest emphasis is given to adiabatic quantum computing (AQC), as it has not experience nearly as much success in the chemistry domain.

Other paradigms exist, such as measurement-based/one-way quantum computing, which have not served quantum chemistry at present. In order to better follow this review, basic understanding of quantum mechanics and its linear algebra formulation, tied back to Dirac's postulates, is assumed as well as familiarity with quantum chemistry, primarily electronic structure theory and its second quantization formulation, as exposed in researchers. The most prominent topics will be illustrated largely in light of quantum computing applications in the domain of electronic structure theory. The extension to problems of relevance in dynamics is believed to only be accessible in the fault-tolerant stage of quantum computing.

Furthermore, this review is not intended to give a comprehensive overview of every single development in quantum computing that touches on quantum chemistry or vice-versa. For this purpose, the foundation given by this manuscript can be augmented by lengthier, more encompassing reviews. Valuable resources for the beginner researcher looking into a more practical take on quantum computing is the Qiskit textbook [25] and the tutorial in researchers. Finally, the quintessential textbook in the field of quantum computing is the one authored by Nielsen and Chuang.

Information and bits

In analogy with classical computing, where the bit is the basic building block of information, we have the quantum bit, yet with key differences from its classical counterpart. A classical bit, simply bit hereafter, is only ever found in two different "states," $|0\rangle$ and $|1\rangle$, often associated with whether or not a transistor is charged, and consequently can be ascribed a binary value: 0 or 1. In principle, the state of the transistor and the value of the associated bit is always known (or knowable) except when faults occur, which are relatively rare in current classical computers, but are still the focus of ongoing research.

The Bloch sphere

While the classical bit can only be found in the two poles of the sphere along the z-axis, the surface of the sphere is comprised of all superpositions of the two states. The ability of superimposing quantum states is partly responsible for the speedup that can be harnessed from quantum computers. In contrast to classical bits, which can always be ascribed individual states, two or more qubits can be found in *entanglement*. Entanglement can be identified with qubits in a superposition of states that results in a uniquely quantum kind of correlation that prevents any qubit to be able to be addressed independently from the other qubits it is entangled with. And it is the entanglement property in conjunction with superposition, which are exclusive to quantum entities, the responsible factors for the attractive prospect speedup of quantum computing.

Drug Discovery and Materials Science

The pharmaceutical and materials science industries face the formidable task of searching vast chemical spaces to discover new drugs and materials with desired properties. Quantum computing offers the potential to simulate molecular interactions and properties at the quantum level accurately. Quantum algorithms, like the Variational Quantum Eigensolver (VQE) and Quantum Chemistry Variational Eigensolver (QCVQE), enable researchers to perform quantum simulations of molecules and materials. This capability accelerates the discovery of new drugs, predicts material properties, and optimizes chemical reactions with unprecedented precision.

Quantum Computing Applications in Materials Science

Cases of material science use are being investigated as some of the first applications of quantum computing to show practical quantum advantages. This is because many materials science problems are quantum. A computational advancement in the field will have consequences in many areas, from scientific exploration to industrial upgrades and sustainability. Quantum computers present an attractive alternative, as many quantum algorithms avoid the exponential memory overheads of classical quantum matter computations.

Critical algorithms for materials science applications are identified, considering practical applications and potential for quantum advantage. The requirements for quantum-centric supercomputing architectures are discussed, including evaluating the computational and operational demands, scalability, and integration hurdles of deploying these algorithms in combined quantum-classical high-performance computing environments.

Specific use cases in materials science where quantum and high-performance computing algorithms can be most effectively utilized are highlighted. The use case must be classically hard in some limit, amenable to execution on a noisy or fault-tolerant quantum computer, and represent an interesting problem in materials science.

Quantum algorithms that can be used for materials science applications are summarized. These include algorithms that simulate quantum systems and quantum computing approaches to simulate partial differential equations (PDEs). The simulation of quantum systems is the most natural application of quantum computers in the materials science space.

Classical Information Processing in Quantum-Classical Workflows

To simulate a physical quantum system, the governing physical Hamiltonian must be appropriately mapped to a qubit Hamiltonian such that the quantum computer faithfully simulates the physical system of interest. This involves deciding how to encode a nonnegative integer representing the occupation of the mode into qubits.

Scientific Discoveries and Innovations

Quantum computing is poised to accelerate scientific discoveries and innovations in fields such as materials science, drug discovery, and climate modeling. It could provide solutions to some of humanity's most pressing challenges and revolutionize industries like pharmaceuticals, energy, and transportation.

Looking Ahead: Quantum Computing's Role in the Future of Technology

Quantum computing holds the potential to reshape the future of technology in profound ways. As the field advances, we can expect several key developments and impacts:

- **Quantum Advantage and Practical Applications:** Achieving quantum advantage, where quantum computers can outperform classical computers in practical applications, will unlock new possibilities for solving complex problems. Quantum computing's impact on drug discovery, materials science, optimization, and artificial intelligence will accelerate scientific discoveries and drive innovation in various industries.
- **Quantum Supremacy and Beyond:** As quantum computers continue to scale and improve in performance, the achievement of quantum supremacy will mark a significant milestone in the field. Beyond quantum supremacy, researchers will explore new frontiers of quantum computing, aiming for even greater computational power and efficiency.
- **Quantum Internet and Communication:** Quantum networking and quantum communication protocols will pave the way for quantum internet applications. Secure quantum communication using quantum key distribution will revolutionize cryptography and cybersecurity, ensuring future-proof communication channels.
- **Quantum Machine Learning and Artificial Intelligence:** Quantum machine learning will enhance data processing, pattern recognition, and optimization tasks, offering new opportunities for artificial intelligence and data-driven technologies.
- **Quantum Simulation and Scientific Discovery:** Quantum simulation will enable scientists to explore complex quantum systems and condensed matter phenomena, driving advances in physics, chemistry, and materials science.
- **Societal Impact and Ethical Considerations:** Quantum computing will raise important societal and ethical considerations, particularly in the areas of privacy, cryptography, and the potential impacts on industries and employment. Responsible development and governance of quantum technologies will be crucial.

Embracing the Quantum Era

As we conclude our exploration of quantum computing, we stand at the threshold of a new era in computing and information processing. Quantum computing holds the promise to unlock unparalleled computational power, enabling us to tackle some of the world's most challenging problems and revolutionize the way we approach scientific research and technological innovation.

Embracing the quantum era requires collaboration, investment, and the collective efforts of researchers, industries, and governments worldwide. As we venture into the quantum realm, let us be guided by a spirit of curiosity, responsibility, and ethical consideration.

SIMULATION CHALLENGES IN MOLECULAR AND MATERIALS SCIENCE

We now turn to survey a representative, but certainly non-exhaustive, set of scientific problems that could be interesting for quantum simulation. We group these roughly into a few areas: *quantum chemistry*, the problem of determining the low-lying states of electrons in molecules; *quantum molecular spectroscopy*, concerned with stationary states of the nuclei vibrating and rotating in molecules; *chemical quantum dynamics*, that studies the non-equilibrium electronic and nuclear motion of molecules associated with reactions and external fields; *correlated electronic structure in materials*, a close cousin of quantum chemistry in the materials domain, but with several important differences in practice and in emphasis; and *dynamical quantum effects in materials*, concerned with driven and out-of-equilibrium material systems.

Quantum chemistry

Quantum chemistry is concerned with determining the low-lying eigenstates of the electronic Hamiltonian of a molecule. The eigenstates are determined for fixed sets of nuclear positions, i.e. within the Born-Oppenheimer approximation. Determining the main features of the resulting potential energy surface, i.e. the electronic energy as a function of nuclear positions, its minima and saddle points, is key to understanding chemical reactivity, product distributions, and reaction rates.

There exists a wide range of quantum chemical methods with different accuracy and speed tradeoffs, ranging from density functional methods that routinely treat a few thousand atoms or more on modern cluster resources Jones, to high-level many-electron wavefunction methods, such as coupled cluster theory, that can attain chemical accuracy of 1 kcal/mol and better, on systems of tens of atoms. However, most methods in quantum chemistry are most accurate for problems where there is a dominant electronic configuration, a subset of the quantum chemistry problem known as the single-reference problem. Single-reference quantum chemistry is found in the ground-states of many simple molecules (e.g. hydrocarbons), but in many molecular excited states, at stretched bond geometries, and in transition metal chemistry, multiple electronic configurations can come into play, which is referred to as multi-reference quantum chemistry. The distinction between single- and multi-reference problems in quantum chemistry is sketched in Figure 2. Despite much work (and progress) in extending quantum chemistry to multi-reference situations, the attainable accuracy in molecules with more than a few atoms is significantly lower than in the single-reference case.

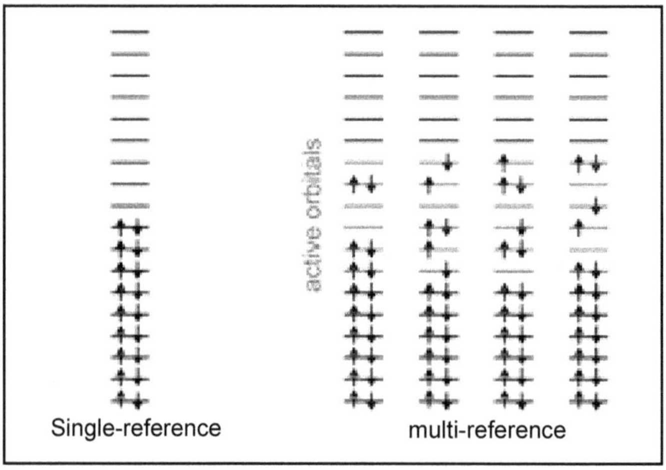

Fig. 2: Single-reference (left) and multi-reference (right) wavefunctions. The former is qualitatively described by a single Slater determinant, the latter by a linear combination of a potentially large number of Slater determinants. Often such determinants correspond to different configurations of electrons in an "active space" of orbitals.

The chemistry of enzyme active sites. Such active sites can involve multiple coupled transition metals, famous examples being the 4 manganese ions in the oxygen evolving complex, or the 8 transition metals in the iron-sulfur clusters of nitrogenase; researchers shown in Figure 3. They present some of the most complicated multi-reference quantum chemistry problems in the biological world. Combined theoretical and experimental studies, primarily at the level of density functional theory, have proven successful in unravelling many structural and electronic features of such enzyme active sites. However, a detailed understanding of the interplay between spin-coupling and delocalization between metals, which requires true multi-reference quantum chemistry and is needed to interpret aspects of experimental spectroscopy, remains in its infancy.

Transition metal nanocatalysts and surface catalysts. Similarly to enzyme active sites, simulating the mechanism of action of synthetic heterogeneous catalysts remains a major challenge. While density functional theory has been widely employed, predictions of even basic quantities such as the adsorption energy of small molecules are unreliable. While not all such problems are expected to be multi-reference in character, even the single-reference modeling of such chemistry, at a level significantly beyond density functional theory, is currently challenging or impossible. In addition, multi-reference effects are expected to play a role in certain catalysts, such as transition metal oxides, or at intermediate geometries in reaction pathways.

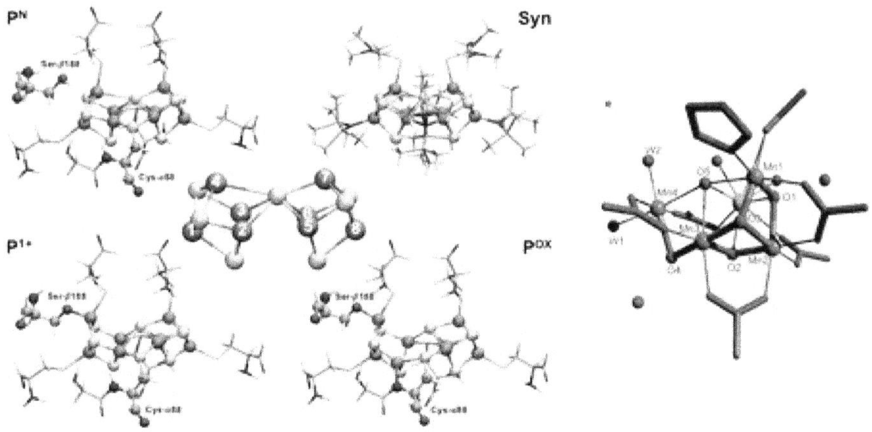

Fig. 3: Left: Iron-sulfur clusters associated with different oxidation states (P^N, syn (a synthetic model of P^N), P^{1+} and $P^{\alpha x}$) of the P cluster of the nitrogenase enzyme

Light harvesting and the vision process. The photochemistry of conjugated organic molecules is the means by which nature interacts with light. Some prominent examples of such natural conjugated systems include the carotenoid and chlorophyll pigments in the light-harvesting complex of plants, as well as the rhodopsin system associated with vision. While describing the interaction with light is not purely a question of electronic structure, as it involves the quantum dynamical evolution of quantum states, the quantum chemical questions revolve around the potential energy surfaces of the ground- and excited-states, and the influence of the environment on the spectrum. These questions are currently challenging due to the size of the systems involved as well as the varying degree of single- and multi-reference character in many of the conjugated excited states.

The basic quantum simulation problem is the ground-state (or low-energy eigenstate) problem for the electronic Hamiltonians, and the basic metric is whether ground-state or low-energy eigenstate quantum algorithms yield more accurate energies (for comparable computational resources) than the best classical algorithms, for the problem sizes of interest. Proof-of-principle demonstrations could be carried out in simplified models of the above problems (e.g. in small active spaces of orbitals).

However, to make real progress, one should also consider more quantitative models, which requires treating a large number of electrons in a large number of orbitals; at minimum, tens of electrons in hundreds of orbitals. This poses new challenges for ground-state algorithms, and raises questions of how best to represent and encode the resulting Hamiltonians and states. In addition, there are many aspects of the chemical problems beyond the modeling of the electronic wavefunctions, for example, to treat environmental, solvent, and dynamical effects. It is natural to handle these by interfacing the quantum simulation with other classical simulation methods, for example, in molecular dynamics, where Newton's equation could be integrated using forces determined from the quantum simulation, in QM/MM (quantum mechanics/molecular mechanics) models, where part of the environment would be modeled by classical charges and force-fields, and in simulations using implicit continuum models of solvation.

Finally, although the above examples have focused on multireference and strongly correlated quantum chemistry, weakly correlated chemistry itself becomes hard to model classically when the number of degrees of freedom is very large. These may also be interesting to target with quantum algorithms when sufficiently large quantum machines are available.

Quantum molecular spectroscopy

High-resolution gas-phase rovibrational spectroscopy provides an extremely precise experimental probe of molecular structure. Such spectroscopy is important not only for the fundamental understanding of small molecules and the quantum control of atomic and molecular states, but also to provide insight into the basic chemical processes and species involved, for example, in atmospheric chemistry and in astrochemistry. In larger molecules, with more than a few atoms, even the low-energy rovibrational spectrum contains many peaks which cannot be interpreted without theoretical simulation. The theoretical goal is to compute the eigenstates of the nuclear Schrödinger equation.

However, unlike the electronic structure problem, there are several challenges even in setting up the best form of the nuclear Schrödinger equation to solve. The first is that the nuclear Hamiltonian (in particular, the nuclear-nuclear interactions) are not known a priori because the interactions are mediated by the electrons. This nuclear potential energy term must instead be determined from quantum chemical calculations at fixed nuclear geometries and then fitted to an appropriate functional form; this requires a large number of high accuracy quantum chemistry calculations. The second is that nuclear ro-vibrational motion is often far from harmonic and not well approximated by simple mean-field theories, unlike many electronic structure problems. Thus there is a need for a proper choice of curvilinear nuclear coordinates that decreases coupling in the nuclear potential energy (e.g. in a harmonic system, normal modes are such a choice of coordinates) while retaining a simple form for the kinetic energy operator, and which also exposes the symmetry of the molecular system.

Once the nuclear Schrödinger equation has been properly formulated, one then faces the problem of representing the eigenstates. While methods such as diffusion Monte Carlo have made progress on vibrational ground-states, spectroscopy involves transitions to excited states. In this setting, tensor factorization researchers approaches Christiansen have been explored to approximate the rovibrational wavefunctions. However, the high dimensionality and spectral congestion, requiring resolution between peaks on the scale of 1 wavenumber, proves extremely challenging. Some famous examples include:

- *Spectra of floppy molecules.* Floppy molecules are by their nature very anharmonic and thus far from a simple vibrational description. CH+5 is a prototypical floppy molecule (see Fig. 4): the five hydrogen atoms move around the central carbon and the molecule has almost no structure in the traditional sense.
- *Hydrogen bonded clusters.* Another vibrational problem with large anharmonicity is found in hydrogen bonded clusters, such as in the spectroscopy of water molecules and protonated water clusters. The hydrogen bond network is fluid and even small clusters can transition between many different minima on the potential energy surface. Resolving the peaks and tunnelling splittings is important for interpreting water spectra in the atmosphere, as well as in understanding reaction mechanisms in water. Further, the spectroscopy of molecules with intermolecular hydrogen bonds, such as the malonaldehyde molecule, has also posed long-standing challenges for the field.

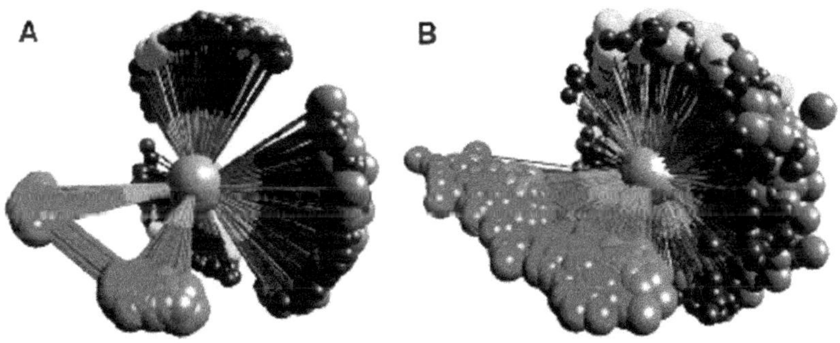

Fig. 4: Dominant families of configurations of fluxional CH_{+}^{5}.

From a quantum algorithms perspective, although there are similarities with the quantum chemistry problem (in particular one is interested in low-energy eigenstates), there are significant differences. One important difference is that the Hamiltonian is no longer of simple two-particle form due to the effective nuclear-nuclear interaction and typically includes important three- and four-mode terms. Also, one is often interested in an order of magnitude more states (e.g. hundreds of excited states) than in the electronic structure problem. All these features are sufficiently distinct from the usual quantum chemical scenarios that quantum algorithms are likely to require additional innovation to be useful in the nuclear problem. Some steps in this direction have recently appeared. One simplification is that many nuclei are distinguishable avoiding the need to consider indistinguishable particles. The lack of a good mean-field starting point together with the various technical complications means that one can find relatively small systems (in terms of the Hilbert space size) where classical methods already have trouble; for example, a minimal quantum model of the CH_+^5 molecule can be formulated as a 12 dimensional problem with 10 basis functions per mode.

Chemical quantum dynamics

Chemical quantum dynamics is another important target for quantum simulation. This field is concerned with modeling time-dependent electronic and nuclear quantum effects in molecules (as distinct from computing the time-independent electronic or nuclear eigenstates in quantum chemistry and quantum molecular spectroscopy). Quantum molecular dynamics is primarily concerned with the nuclear motion and describes the rates of chemical processes as well as the dynamical interaction of molecules with light, as involved in spectroscopy and quantum control. However, with the development of short X-ray pulses direct experimental access to electron dynamics in molecules is now also available.

Currently these dynamical simulations are challenging. For example, nuclear motion is poorly described by mean-field theory and the classical limit is often a better starting point, but offers no zeroth order description of quantum effects. Thus classical simulations of quantum dynamics either invoke methods based on the classical limit that scale to large systems but which are difficult to systematically improve (such as approximate path integral methods), or methods which model the wave-function dynamics or the path integral accurately for a small number of degrees of freedom, but which are not scalable due to dimensionality or the dynamical sign problem.

A subfield of quantum molecular dynamics, but one of important chemical interest, is the description of non-adiabatic quantum effect. At nuclear configurations where different electronic surfaces approach each other, the Born-Oppenheimer approximation can break down and the quantum behavior of the nuclei, coupled indirectly via the electrons, is enhanced.

The associated quantum non-adiabatic effects govern non-radiative energy relaxation via the crossing of electronic surfaces (so-called conical intersections) and are thus central in describing energy transfer. The faithful description of non-adiabatic quantum effects requires the simultaneous treatment of quantum electrons and quantum nuclei. The complexity of this problem together with the often large system sizes where non-adiabatic effects are of interest means that current classical methods rely on simple heuristic approximations, such as surface hopping, for which a rigorous quantum formulation is lacking. Examples of relevant chemical problems in the area of chemical quantum dynamics include:

- *Proton coupled electron transfer* (PCET). PCET is known to be an important mechanism in catalysis and energy storage: electrons are transferred at lower overpotentials when thermodynamically coupled to proton transfer. Examples range from homogeneous catalysts and heterogeneous electrocatalysts to enzymes that perform PCET, such as soybean lipoxygenase (that catalyzes the oxidation of unsaturated fatty acids), photosystem II (in the tyrosine oxidation step); and the redox-leveling mechanism of catalytic water oxidation. While semiclassical predictions are often good enough for describing electron transfer, the quantum nature of molecular dynamics is paramount with PCET because of the quantum nature of the proton as evidenced in kinetic isotope effects (referring to the ratio of the proton to deuteron reaction rates) which can be very large. Thus, classical mechanics is not sufficient, and quantum simulations of PCET would be extremely helpful for making predictions in large (especially biological) systems.
- *Vibrational dynamics in complex environments*. For many systems of interest, vibrational spectroscopy is the key tool available for characterization. The questions here focus on larger scale systems and condensed phase problems, where the line-shapes as well as frequencies are important, and the system size limits the use of fully quantum formalisms. Indeed, from the librations of water to the high frequency motion of C-H bonds, much of physical chemistry uses nuclear vibrational frequencies to characterize complex systems.
- Nevertheless, because of computational limitations, the standard approach today for modeling vibrational dynamics in large complex environments is to invoke a very old flavor of theory. In this case, one focuses on energy gaps and uses a semiclassical expansion of the line-shape. However, even for the energy gaps one relies on diagonalization of the quantum subsystem and this limits the problems that are accessible; systems with many interacting quantum states – for instance, very large H/J molecular aggregates Riehl and Richardson (1986) – are difficult or out of reach.
- *Plasmonic chemistry*. A recent development is the possibility of using metal particles (with large cross sections) as a tool to absorb light and, with the resulting plasmonic excitations, initiate "plasmonic chemistry". Already, there are a few well-studied examples in the literature of hot plasmonic chemistry, such as the plasmon induced dissociation of hydrogen molecules on nanoparticles. To better understand this arena, however, one of the key questions is: how do we characterize plasmonic excitations? While classical descriptions of plasmons are easy to obtain, quantum descriptions are necessary to model quantum processes, e.g. electron transfer. Covering the disparate length scales of plasmonic excitations and the chemical process remains extremely difficult.

While quantum dynamics is in principle an ideal simulation problem for a quantum computer, the quantum simulation of quantum molecular dynamics entails several practical challenges. Some of this may be viewed as an issue of representation. As in the problem of quantum molecular spectroscopy, the nuclear quantum Hamiltonian contains complicated interactions which must be tabulated or calculated on the fly. In addition to this, the dynamical quantum state involves near continuum degrees of freedom, posing a challenge for the standard discretizations of Hilbert space considered in quantum algorithms.

Finally, typical spectroscopic observables may be accessible to relatively simple treatments, not requiring the full fidelity of the quantum wave-function evolution. These technical issues mean that implementing quantum molecular dynamics with a quantum advantage is likely to remain challenging in practice, despite the favorable theoretical complexity on a quantum device.

Dynamical quantum effects in materials

Many experiments on condensed-matter systems do not probe the equilibrium properties of the system, but rather dynamical properties. For example, the main workhorse of mesoscopic quantum physics is electron transport, i.e. the response of the system when it is coupled to electron reservoirs and a voltage is applied. Likewise, material properties are often probed through scattering experiments, such as neutron scattering or angle-resolved photoemission spectroscopy (ARPES), which probe dynamical properties such as the structure factor or spectral function.

Going beyond spectral properties, the non-equilibrium real-time dynamics of quantum systems has increasingly come into focus, both because of experiments that can probe quantum dynamics at atomic scales, and because of fundamental interest in studying the equilibration of quantum systems, which serves as a bridge between the theories of quantum mechanics and statistical mechanics, as discussed below. Experimental setups that can probe ultra-fast dynamics in materials include, for example, free-electron lasers as well as other pulsed laser systems. These allow the application of experimental techniques, such as pump-probe spectroscopy, illustrated in Fig. 5, to provide novel insights into the behavior of correlated quantum systems.

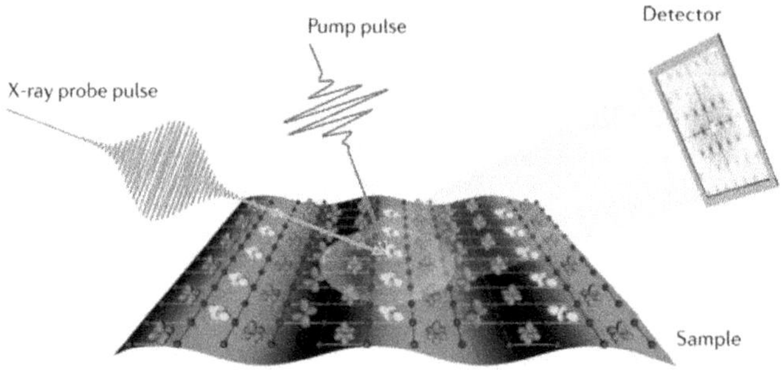

Fig. 5: Illustration of pump-probe spectroscopy using X-ray probes.

On the other hand, *cold atomic gases* provide a highly controllable environment that allows systematic exploration of quantum dynamics even in the strongly interacting regime, see Fig. 6. A key advantage is that one can engineer the evolution of the system to closely follow a target model; this approach is also referred to as analog quantum simulation. However, classical simulation still plays a crucial role in establishing the accuracy of cold atom setups.

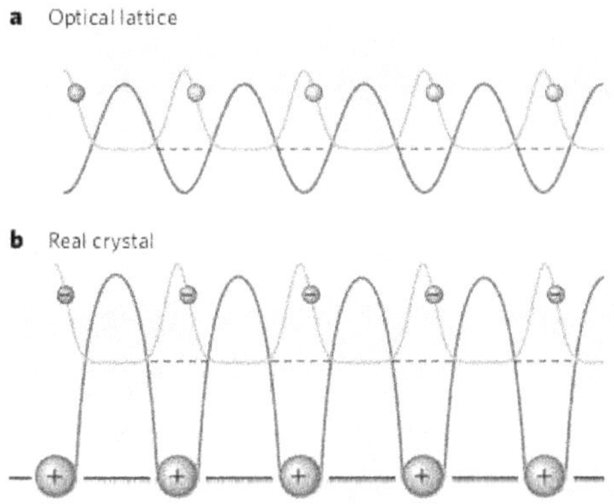

Figure 6: Cold atomic gases are controllable quantum systems that can be arranged in a lattice (a). They can be tuned to provide analog simulators of real crystal potentials (b).

From a conceptual point of view, a central question has become the connection between statistical mechanics and the dynamics of closed quantum systems. The general goal is to put quantum statistical mechanics on a solid conceptual foundation as well as understanding the cases where it does not apply, such as many-body localized systems.

Numerically simulating all these systems has been a severe challenge. While many approaches to quantum dynamics exist, none are universally applicable. At short times, tensor-network methods can accurately describe the dynamics. However, in general the computational cost grows exponentially with the desired simulation time, thus severely limiting the timescales that can be resolved.

Conversely, at long times, the system is often effectively described by classical dynamics controlled by conservation laws. However, the interesting strongly correlated behavior is generally exhibited at intermediate times, inaccessible to the established classical methods. For example, quantum Monte Carlo methods can scale exponentially in time even for unfrustrated systems. Non-equilibrium dynamical mean field theory researchers has emerged as a powerful method especially for systems in high dimensions, but requires uncontrolled approximations (both in the setup of the method and its numerical solution). Finally, in the regime of weak interactions, time-dependent density functional theory can be used, but likewise implies uncontrolled approximations.

Challenges for quantum algorithms in quantum simulation

Overview of algorithms

We described three quantum problems that lie at the heart of chemistry and materials physics: the problem of quantum dynamics, representative of computational tasks that can be efficiently tackled by a quantum computer, aside from the initial state preparation; quantum ground- and low-energy state determination, central to quantum chemistry, condensed phase electronic structure, and quantum molecular spectroscopy; and thermal averages or *quantum statistical mechanics*, to describe finite-temperature chemistry and physics. In next sections, we survey the current status and theoretical and practical challenges to implement quantum algorithms for these problems, and some future directions.

Regardless of the problem we are studying, the first step in a quantum simulation is to choose a representation for the Hamiltonian and the states.

Quantum ground-state algorithms fall into several classes. Quantum phase estimation is a direct route to (near exact) eigenstate determination, but has been challenging to implement so far.

A complementary technique is to prepare the exact ground-state via a prescribed "exact" evolution path, either in real time (adiabatic state preparation), or in imaginary time (quantum imaginary time evolution).

On the other hand, variational quantum algorithms provide the possibility to introduce approximations with adjustable circuit depth, which are determined via a non-linear optimization, usually implemented in a hybrid-quantum classical loop. While polynomial time algorithms for *quantum time evolution* have been known for some time, algorithms with optimal asymptotic complexity (linear in time) as well as favorable scaling with error and low prefactors, remain an area of active research. Also, much work remains to be done to optimize Hamiltonian simulation algorithms for the Hamiltonians of interest in chemistry and materials science. Quantum time evolution is a fundamental building block in many quantum algorithms, such as phase estimation.

Hardware-efficient ansatz

The unitary coupled cluster ansatz involves non-local gate operations and is expensive to implement on near-term devices with limited qubit connectivity. An alternative variational approach, pursued and termed "hardware-efficient" there, is to tailor the ansatz specifically to the underlying hardware characteristics. The circuits considered in and sketched in Fig. 7, consist of alternating layers of arbitrary single-qubit gates and an entangling gate that relies on the intrinsic drift Hamiltonian of the system. While this drift Hamiltonian and thus the entangling gate is not known precisely, for the variational approach it is sufficient to know that the gate is reproducible. The variational parameters are only the rotations in the layer of single-qubit gates. While it is not guaranteed that such an ansatz contains a good approximation to the state of interest, it is an example of an adaption of a method to NISQ devices. An application to BeH_2 is seen in Fig. 7.

FINANCE AND OPTIMIZATION WITH QUANTUM COMPUTING

Financial services has a history of successfully applying physics to help solve its thorniest problems. The Black-Scholes-Merton model, for example, uses the concept of Brownian motion to price financial instruments - like European call options - over time.

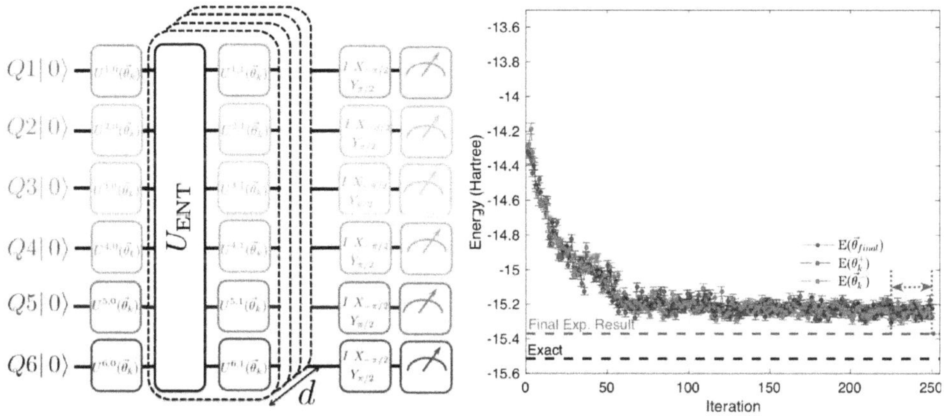

Fig. 7: Left: Hardware-efficient quantum circuit for trial state preparation and energy estimation, shown here for 6 qubits. The circuit is composed of a sequence of interleaved single-qubit rotations, and entangling unitary operations UENT that entangle all the qubits in the circuit. A final set of post-rotations prior to qubit readout are used to measure the expectation values of the terms in the qubit Hamiltonian, and estimate the energy of the trial state. Right: energy minimization for the six-qubit Hamiltonian describing BeH2.

Applying emerging quantum technology to financial problems - particularly those dealing with uncertainty and constrained optimization - should also prove hugely advantageous for first movers. Imagine being able to make calculations that reveal dynamic arbitrage possibilities that competitors are unable to see. Beyond that, greater compliance, employing behavioral data to enhance customer engagement, and faster reaction to market volatility are some of the specific benefits we expect quantum computing to deliver.

What gives quantum computing this enormous advantage? The solution space of a quantum computer is orders of magnitude larger than traditional computers—even immensely powerful ones. That's because doubling the power of a classical computer requires about double the number of transistors working on a problem. The power of a quantum computer can be approximately doubled each time only one qubit is added.

While broad commercial applications may remain several years away, quantum computing is expected to produce breakthrough products and services likely to successfully solve very specific business problems within three-to-five years.

Quantum computing can also enable financial services organizations to re-engineer operational processes, such as:

- Front-office and back-office decisions on client management for "know your customer," credit origination, and onboarding,
- Treasury management, trading and asset management,
- Business optimization, including risk management and compliance.

Quantum computing's specific use cases for financial services can be classified into three main categories: targeting and prediction, trading optimization, and risk profiling.

We explore potential use cases in each of these categories, providing examples that apply to three main industries in financial services: banking, financial markets, and insurance.

Powerful quantum use cases

Quantum computing's specific use cases for financial services can be classified into three main categories: targeting and prediction, trading optimization, and risk profiling.

We explore potential use cases in each of these categories, providing examples that apply to three main industries in financial services: banking, financial markets, and insurance.

Fig. 8 Expected quantum computing use cases in financial services

Targeting and prediction

Today's financial services customers demand personalized products and services that rapidly anticipate their evolving needs and behaviors. Twenty-five percent of small- and medium-sized financial institutions lose customers due to offerings that don't prioritize customer experience. It's difficult to create analytical models that sift through mounds of behavioral data quickly and accurately enough to target which products are needed by specific customers in near real-time. This constrains financial institutions from providing preemptive product recommendations with optimal feature selection in an agile manner, missing opportunities to expand current customer share of wallet or reaching the 1.7 billion adults worldwide who are unbanked.

A similar problem exists in fraud detection. It is estimated that financial institutions are losing between USD 10 billion and 40 billion in revenue a year due to fraud and poor data management practices. Fraud detection systems remain highly inaccurate, returning 80 percent false positives, causing financial institutions to be overly risk averse. To help ensure proper credit scoring, the customer onboarding process can take as long as 12 weeks. In today's digital age, where 70 percent of banking takes place digitally, consumers are just not willing to wait that long. Financial institutions too slow in engaging effectively with new customers are losing them to more nimble competitors.

For customer targeting and prediction modeling, quantum computing could be a game changer. The data modeling capabilities of quantum computers are expected to prove superior in finding patterns, performing classifications, and making predictions that are not possible today because of the challenges of complex data structures.

Trading optimization

Complexity in financial markets trading activity is skyrocketing. For example, the valuation adjustments model for derivatives, the XVA umbrella, has greatly increased in complexity, now including credit (CVA), debit (DVA), funding (FVA), capital (KVA) and margin (MVA). Due to greater transparency requirements from regulations, stricter validation processes are applied to trading, impacting risk-management calculations that need to align counterparty credit exposures with creditlimit utilization of derivatives portfolios.

Furthermore, significant investment frameworks and vehicles have changed. For example, bond exchange traded funds (ETFs) are projected to reach USD 2 trillion by 2024, and environmental, social, and government (ESG) investments are gaining traction, with USD 35 trillion invested in this asset taxonomy in 2019.

In this complicated trading landscape, investment managers struggle to incorporate real-life constraints, such as market volatility and customer life-event changes, into portfolio optimization. Ideally, money managers would like to simulate large numbers of potential scenarios and investment options to validate sensitivities when estimating expected returns. Currently, rebalancing investment portfolios that keep up with market movements is significantly constrained by computational limitations and transaction costs.

Quantum technology could help cut through the complexity of today's trading environments. Quantum computing's combinatorial optimization capabilities may enable investment managers to improve portfolio diversification, rebalance portfolio investments to more precisely respond to market conditions and investor goals, and more cost-effectively streamline trading settlement processes.

Risk profiling

Financial services institutions are under increasing pressure to balance risk, hedge positions more effectively, and perform a wider range of stress tests to comply with regulatory requirements. Liquidity management, derivatives pricing, and risk measurement can be complex and calculations difficult to perform, making it hard to properly manage the costs of risk on trades. Today, Monte Carlo simulations—the preferred technique to analyze the impact of risk and uncertainty in financial models—are limited by the scaling of the estimation error.

Looking forward, we expect continual waves of overlapping amendments to regulations, directives, and standards, such as Basel III and its revisions. They will require a much larger array of risk-management stress scenarios. As a result, compliance costs are expected to more than double in the coming years, including regulatory penalties and remediation in cases of non-compliance.

In the face of more sophisticated risk-profiling demands and rising regulatory hurdles, the data-processing capabilities of quantum computers may speed up risk scenario simulations with higher precision, while testing more outcomes.

Benefits of the Quantum Era

Quantum computing's business value for financial services institutions result from four main scenarios:

- Enhancing investment gains
- Reducing capital requirements
- Opening new investment opportunities
- Improving the identification and management of risk and compliance

A Quantum Leap in Portfolio Optimization

Applications in Finance Portfolio Optimization

As we turn our focus toward the impact of quantum computing on finance, it's particularly interesting to examine its potential role in portfolio optimization. Before delving into how quantum computing can revolutionize this field, let's take a moment to understand what portfolio optimization entails.

$$\min_{x \in \{0,1\}^n} \text{risk aversion coef} * X'\Sigma X - \mu' X$$

s.t. : 1'X = budget

Portfolio optimization is a mathematical framework used in finance to identify the best possible portfolio out of a set of potential investments. The aim is to allocate investments among different financial instruments in a manner that maximizes return and minimizes risk. This involves careful analysis of various parameters such as expected returns, variances, and covariances of asset returns. In essence, portfolio optimization aids investors in making data-driven, strategic investment decisions, thereby maximizing their financial gain while managing potential risks.

Despite its significant role in finance, traditional methods of portfolio optimization face a few major challenges. A prominent hurdle is computational complexity. Classical computers solve optimization problems one step at a time, and as the number of assets in a portfolio grows, the possible combinations and the complexities of the computations increase exponentially. This can result in intractable problems that require prohibitive amounts of computational time and resources.

The second significant challenge is scalability. Classical portfolio optimization methods struggle to scale effectively with increasing portfolio size. As the number of assets increases, classical methods often experience a decline in performance due to the enormous computational resources required to process large datasets. This scalability issue limits the applicability of classical portfolio optimization, particularly for large, complex portfolios.

While traditional methods of portfolio optimization have served us well to date, they are not without their limitations. Computational complexity and limited scalability pose significant challenges, particularly as we handle increasingly large and diverse portfolios. These are precisely the challenges that quantum computing, with its superior speed and ability to handle complexity, promises to overcome. As we will see, the advent of quantum computing in finance may well herald a new era of portfolio optimization.

Benefits of quantum portfolio optimization

With a grasp of the challenges faced by classical methods in portfolio optimization, we can now better appreciate the **significant benefits** brought about by the incorporation of quantum computing into this field.

The key strength of quantum computing lies in its intrinsic properties of **parallelism and interference**. Quantum parallelism, derived from the superposition of qubits, allows quantum computers to explore a multitude of potential solutions simultaneously. This is particularly beneficial for portfolio optimization, which often requires a search through a vast space of potential asset combinations. In addition, quantum interference, another fundamental quantum mechanical property, can be harnessed to guide the computational resources toward the most promising solutions, thereby improving the efficiency of the search. Moreover, a new class of quantum-inspired algorithms, often based on principles like **quantum Hamiltonian mechanics**, provides fresh approaches to handle complex optimization tasks. These algorithms leverage the principles of quantum mechanics to enhance computational speed and efficiency, even on classical computers. In the domain of quantum portfolio optimization, several algorithms have already emerged. For instance, the Variational Quantum Eigensolver (VQE) and Quantum Approximate Optimization Algorithm (QAOA) are two notable examples of quantum algorithms applied to financial portfolio optimization. These algorithms exploit the computational power of quantum computers to tackle optimization problems that are intractable for classical computers.

The benefits of quantum portfolio optimization are manifold. The most immediate advantage is speed. Quantum computers, with their ability to process vast amounts of data simultaneously, can dramatically reduce the time taken to optimize portfolios. This, in turn, can lead to more timely investment decisions and strategies.

Furthermore, quantum portfolio optimization offers the potential for greater accuracy. By managing the computational complexities associated with large, diverse portfolios, quantum algorithms can yield solutions that better reflect the true optimal portfolio.

Lastly, the application of quantum computing in portfolio optimization offers unprecedented flexibility. As financial markets become increasingly complex, the ability to adapt and scale with evolving market conditions becomes crucial. Quantum computing, with its exceptional processing power, provides this much-needed flexibility.

Quantum portfolio optimization, empowered by the unparalleled processing capabilities of quantum computing, offers the potential for faster, more accurate, and highly adaptable solutions. This innovative approach holds promise to transform the way we navigate and optimize investment portfolios, ushering in a new era of quantum finance.

What does this look like in MATLAB?

The following example provides a preview of a simulation of the Variational Quantum Eigensolver routine using the Conditional Value at Risk aggregation function. The goal is to show how the problem can be setup and simulated using MATLAB.

Problem Definition

Given a set of assets corresponding to expected returns and covariances, along with a risk factor and budget, we seek a subset of assets such that the resulting weighted mean-variance is maximized.

```
% Covariance between assets
params.sigma = [ 0.0064 0.00408 0.00192 0;
    0.00408 0.0289 0.0204 0.0119;
    0.00192 0.0204 0.0576 0.0336;
    0 0.0119 0.0336 0.1225 ];

% Expected returns for assets
params.mu = [0.05; 0.1; 0.12; 0.18];

% Risk appetite
params.q = 0.5;

% Budget
params.B = 3;

% Penality for budget
params.lambda = 10;

% Number of qubits
params.N = length(params.mu);
```

VQE-CVaR Parameters:

To reduce compilation overhead, an ansatz is used that respects the native gate set and connectivity of the Aspen-M-3 device

```
% Number of repeated entangling blocks
params.ansatzDepth = 2;

% Number of learnable angles for the ansatz circuit
numAngles = params.N*(params.ansatzDepth+1);

% Number of simulated runs
params.numSimShots = 1000;

% Plot the ansatz with arbitrary angles to view its structure
randAnsatz = buildAnsatz(rand(numAngles, 1), params.N);
plot(randAnsatz)
```

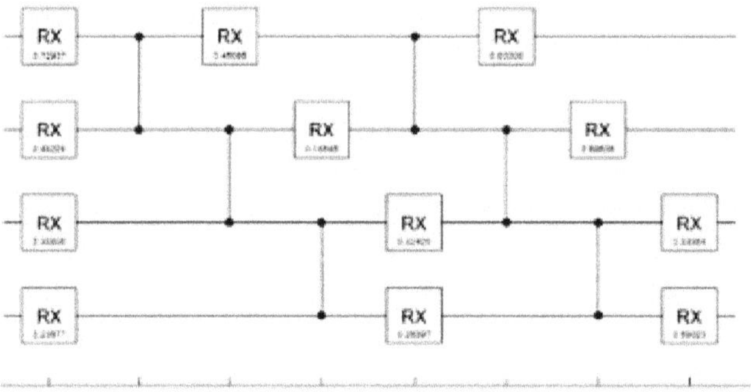

Simulate the Variational Quantum Eigensolver on a local machine

The objective function for the optimizer takes the angles and simulates an iteration of the VQE-CVaR routine.

```
objFcn = @(theta) simVQECVAR(theta, params);

options = optimoptions("surrogateopt", "MaxFunctionEvaluations",10);

lb = repmat(-pi, numAngles, 1);
ub = repmat(pi, numAngles, 1);
[optAngles, ~] = surrogateopt(objFcn,lb,ub,[],[],[],[],[],options);
```

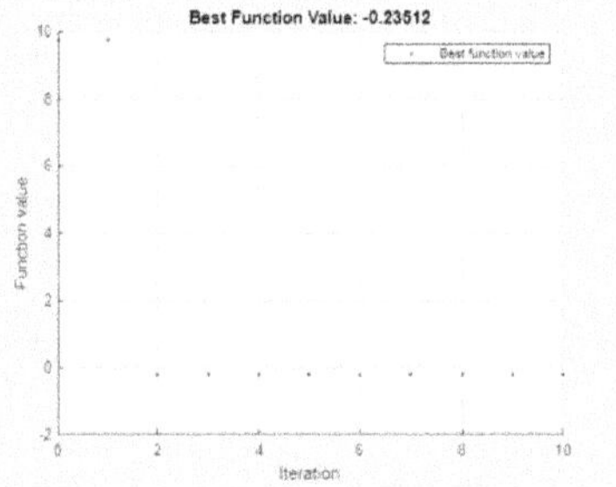


```
optAnsatz = buildAnsatz(optAngles, params.N);
sv = simulate(optAnsatz);
figure
histogram(sv)
```

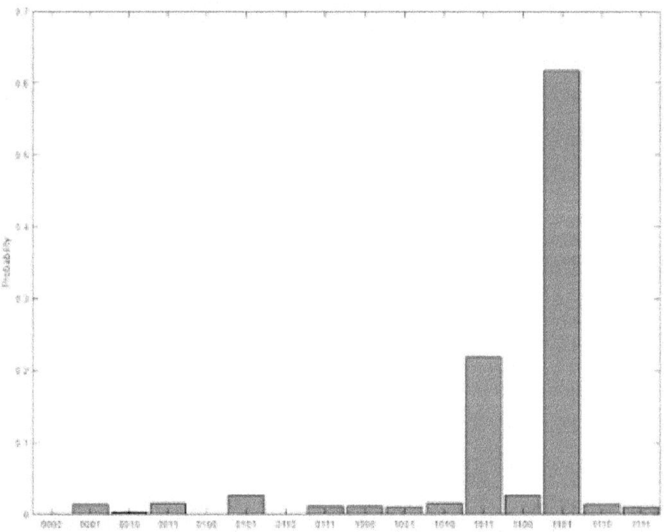

Run the Final Circuit on Quantum Hardware

Run the optimized ansatz circuit on the Aspen-M-3 device provided through Amazon Braket.

```
device = quantum.backend.QuantumDeviceAWS("Aspen-M-3");
task = run(optAnsatz, device, NumShots=100);
result = fetchOutput(task);
histogram(result)
```

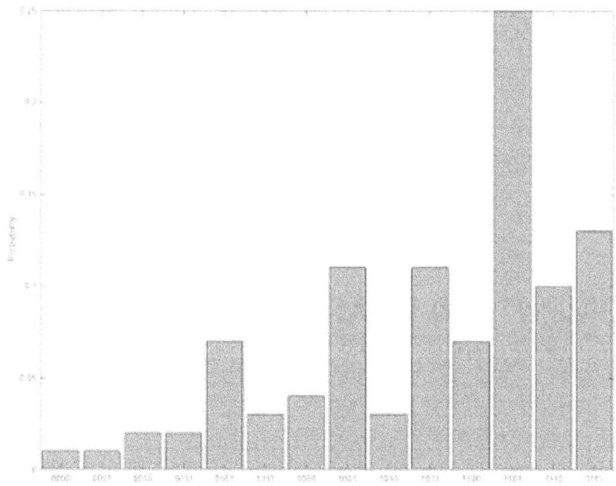

The last 2 plots show, that out of the 14 different portfolio options available, portfolio "1101" returned the highest probability that it was optimal solution.

Deep Dive: Expanding Your Quantum Knowledge

As we delve into the exciting world of quantum computing and its potential applications in finance, it's always helpful to expand our knowledge base and explore further. Here are some excellent resources that can enhance your understanding of quantum computing.

A fantastic starting point is the article titled "Quantum Computing: Definition, How It's Used, and Example"on Investopedia. This piece offers a comprehensive overview of quantum computing, its various applications across sectors, and concrete examples to help you grasp the core concepts. This user-friendly guide is a must-read for anyone eager to explore the world of quantum computing.

For those interested in delving into the practical aspects of quantum computing, Mathworks.com provides an extensive resource through the "Quantum Computing with MATLAB" page. This resource offers insightful tutorials and guides that allow you to experiment with quantum algorithms using MATLAB. The Quantum Computing **Documentation** on MathWorks is another excellent reference, providing an in-depth understanding of how quantum computing works, complete with illustrative examples and useful links.

For readers who want to explore some hands-on applications of quantum computing, we would like to share some examples from my own work and other insightful projects. You can visit this GitHub repository, where we have shared my "PortOpt" project that applies quantum computing principles to portfolio optimization. This will give you a practical example of how quantum algorithms can be implemented to solve real-world problems.

Lastly, the Quantum Support Package is a treasure trove of examples showcasing various quantum computing applications. It's a brilliant resource if you're looking to understand the wide-ranging uses of quantum computing across different industries.

In conclusion, while our exploration of quantum computing and portfolio optimization has only scratched the surface, these resources provide an excellent starting point for deeper learning. Quantum computing is a rapidly evolving field, and staying informed and updated is the key to harnessing its potential.

QUANTUM COMPUTING IN ARTIFICIAL INTELLIGENCE

Quantum artificial intelligence (QAI) is an emerging field of computer science that applies the transformative power of quantum computing to the research and development of improved artificial intelligence products, such as machine learning algorithms, neural networks and large language models (LLM).

If AI could be powered by a new generation of computing power - -quantum processing - then it would leave today's innovation in the dust.

Quantum computing, an entirely new way of processing information, when combined with AI, has the potential, without exaggeration, to bring about a new computing revolution. Transformation may be an understatement.

Instead of processing information in terms of 1s and 0s - called bits - and doing it serially, which is how classical computing works, quantum computers use qubits which can represent a 1 and a 0 simultaneously. Like a guitar, bits are similar to playing one note at a time, whereas, qubits play several notes together. With enough qubits, quantum computers could theoretically be millions of times faster than the fastest microchip computers today.

But quantum computing isn't confined anymore to research labs, although technological hurdles must still be overcome. Big tech firms such as IBM, Microsoft, and Google, and many compelling market entrants such as IonQ and D-Wave Systems, provide capabilities that can be used today. That said, usage is still fairly specialized and often experimental in nature. Practical uses today can be found in pharmaceutical development, cybersecurity, financial services, and weather forecasting.

There's a lot of optimism that the pace of quantum computing innovation will continue to accelerate, and we could see mainstream adoption by the end of the decade. That's just around the corner.

Independent of artificial intelligence, quantum computing is going to be a big deal. However, coupled with AI, it will be a gamechanger.

Revolutionary innovation is not an exaggeration.

In the interim, work to integrate artificial intelligence with quantum computing will continue. Research is nascent and non-trivial technological hurdles exist.

Quantum Artificial Intelligence (QAI) - and in particular, its subset research area Quantum Machine Learning (QML) - will use new quantum-designed algorithms with superpowers that result in much more powerful AI models. As QAI gradually emerges, we can expect significant improvements in the speed, efficiency, and accuracy of AI. We should also anticipate the emergence of completely new and surprising business capabilities.

At first, the benefits will be reaped by certain industries and needs, particularly those with optimization requirements. But later, as QAI becomes more mainstream, almost every enterprise will need to have a strategy.

An example of work-in-progress today is a partnership between IonQ and Hyundai who are researching the use of QAI to process images such as road signs.

For learning and experimenting, Google currently offers a platform, TensorFlow Quantum (TFQ), for prototyping hybrid quantum-classical AI models.

Rather than playing catch-up when QAI arrives, organizations should have the technology on their radar and follow developments closely. Those lucky enough to have an innovation lab or equivalent, should consider some experimental and research work, if only for the purposes of acquiring skills and knowledge.

The high level of interest from industry and the pace of scientific research clearly suggests that QAI is coming, and the question will be whether you are ready. It's probably closer than you think and it's likely going to be a very big deal.

The true strength of quantum computing lies in its ability to navigate vast quantities of possibilities, sifting through them to extract potential solutions to intricate challenges.

At the core of this technology are qubits, which encode information in a quantum state that transcends the binary limitations of 0 and 1, encompassing a multidimensional spectrum.

What are qubits made of in quantum systems? The composition of qubits varies depending on the architecture, with specific requirements for optimal functionality. Cold temperatures are often necessary. Qubits can consist of trapped ions, photons, artificial or natural atoms, or even quasiparticles.

Operating on the principles of quantum mechanics, these computers introduce a new lexicon of terms requiring comprehension.

Superposition

Just as classical physics allows adding waves, quantum states can be combined, resulting in new valid ones. Moreover, any quantum state can be expressed as a sum of multiple distinct states.

This remarkable feature, known as superposition, grants quantum computers inherent parallelism. Harnessing this parallelism enables these machines to execute millions of operations simultaneously.

Entanglement

Quantum entanglement occurs when two systems become intricately connected, regardless of their physical distance. Entanglement is remarkable because acquiring information about one particle instantly reveals details about the other, regardless of their spatial separation.

This unique relationship forms the basis for quantum algorithms designed to tackle complex problems. Moreover, the addition of qubits results in an exponential surge in computational capabilities.

Decoherence

Decoherence arises when qubits lose their quantum behavior due to external factors like vibrations or temperature fluctuations. Such disturbances can cause qubits to lose their superposition state and introduce errors in computations.

To mitigate this issue, protective measures are necessary, such as utilizing insulation, supercooled refrigerators, and vacuum chambers to shield qubits from external interference.

Quantum Computing vs. Classical Computing: What is the Difference?

Classical and quantum computing differ in their building blocks. Traditional computers use binary digits (0s and 1s), while quantum computers use qubits. This makes quantum computers highly efficient for complex AI applications, as they are less prone to errors than classical computers.

Quantum computing enhances classical computing by improving specialized functions and offering greater accuracy and efficiency. They process data faster, enabling faster learning and improvement for AI systems. Quantum entanglement optimizes correlations between variables.

Quantum computers excel at solving complex optimization problems, leading to more powerful and intelligent AI systems beyond classical physics laws. They benefit various AI applications like planning and scheduling.

They accelerate AI architecture development, performing calculations and creating new algorithms that classical computers can't. They provide solutions to unsolvable problems using classical methods.

Quantum computers enable faster learning and robust simulations for real-world scenarios without catastrophic forgetting, ensuring lifelong learning without losing previous knowledge.

Quantum computers also provide data security and can counter cybercrime through parallel processing. Their ability to exist in multiple states simultaneously aids in discovering superior algorithms.

The Case for Existing AI Tools

AI tools have proven their worth across various sectors, from healthcare and finance to transportation and entertainment. Machine learning algorithms can process vast amounts of data, learning and improving over time. Deep learning, a subset of machine learning, has enabled the development of neural networks that can recognize patterns and make decisions with a high degree of accuracy. These tools have been successful in solving complex problems and are continually improving.

Moreover, these AI tools are accessible and practical. They operate on classical computers, which are widely available and relatively affordable. They can be deployed in real-world applications today, providing immediate benefits to businesses and society. Since AI models are so good, perhaps help from quantum computers is not required.

The Quantum Leap: Potential and Challenges

Quantum computing, on the other hand, is often touted as the next big thing in AI. Quantum computers can process a vast number of possibilities simultaneously. This could potentially speed up AI algorithms and process larger datasets more efficiently, leading to more powerful AI models.

A recent Boston Consulting Group study identified a market potential of $50B to $100B of quantum opportunities in generative, foundation, and horizontal AI, impacting practically all industries. According to BCG, additional multi-billion-dollar opportunities exist in preventing fraud and money laundering, as well as automotive AI algorithms.

However, quantum computing is still in its infancy. Today's quantum computers have a limited number of qubits, and maintaining their quantum state, known as coherence, is a significant challenge. limiting the complexity of the computations that can be performed.

Moreover, quantum computers are not just an upgrade to classical computers; they require entirely new algorithms. For instance, classical machine learning models, such as neural networks, are trained by adjusting parameters (weights and biases) based on the input data, aiming to minimize the difference between the model's predictions and the actual output. Sophisticated models have millions or billions of parameters and are tuned by a process called gradient descent – determining the direction in which changing the parameters results in minimizing that difference.

However, measuring or estimating the gradients in a quantum computer is exceptionally difficult. Thus, trying to use a classical algorithm on a quantum computer is a recipe for failure, and new algorithms are required. Developing these algorithms is a complex task that, while promising, is still in the early stages. For instance, a new type of machine learning algorithm called "reservoir computing" appears to leverage unique quantum properties to achieve good results in both classification and prediction applications.

Quantum Computing and Generative Models

One area where quantum computers excel today is generating randomness. In classical computers, random numbers are generated using algorithms or from some external source of randomness (like atmospheric noise), but these numbers are not truly random: if you know the algorithm and its initial conditions (the seed), you can predict all the numbers that the algorithm will generate. In contrast, thanks to core principles of quantum mechanics - superposition - quantum computers can generate truly random numbers. Superposition shows that a quantum bit can exist in multiple states at once, and when measured, the outcome is inherently random.

Generative modeling, an unsupervised machine learning scheme, can benefit from this randomness. Quantum computers can create statistical correlations that are otherwise very difficult to replicate, making them ideal for this application. Such generative models can be used in numerous problems, such as portfolio optimization, where the generative model attempts to replicate high-performing portfolios discovered by the algorithm, leading to portfolios with much lower risk than those discovered by classical algorithms. Similar uses have been suggested for molecular generation for drug discovery and even for factory floor scheduling.

The Future of Quantum Computing and AI

Despite these early challenges, the potential of quantum computing for AI is immense. Quantum machine learning could classify larger datasets in less time, and quantum neural networks could process information in ways that classical neural networks cannot. While existing AI tools are powerful and practical for many applications today, quantum computing represents a new frontier with the potential to significantly advance the field. However, the road to practical quantum computing is long and filled with challenges. It will likely be some time before quantum computers are more powerful and ready for widespread use in AI. Until then, the focus could be on maximizing the capabilities of our existing AI tools while continuing to explore the exciting possibilities that quantum computing offers.

The Impact of Quantum Computing on Artificial Intelligence

Quantum computing boosts the potential of AI by amplifying its velocity, efficacy, and precision. It transcends the limitations imposed on traditional computers by utilizing qubits and capitalizing on non-linear operations.

This remarkable advancement empowers quantum computing to find applications across diverse AI use cases. Sectors like maritime logistics, semiconductors, electric vehicles, luminescence, and power have already started reaping the rewards of quantum computing's exceptional problem-solving prowess.

Now explore the impact of quantum computing on different industries and the transformative effects it brings to AI-driven processes.

Medical Care

Hospitals often form a medical board of specialists from diverse fields to address complex conditions in critically ill patients.

However, this traditional approach is time-consuming and hampers decision-making. Quantum computing offers a solution.

By inputting various possibilities and relevant historical data, healthcare professionals can leverage quantum computing to evaluate treatment effectiveness and receive optimal recommendations swiftly. The quantum advantage allows providers to acquire valuable insights in a considerably reduced time frame.

Machine Learning (ML)

Machine learning (ML) relies on computers' ability to acquire knowledge from data and generate or recognize patterns, similar to how the human brain functions.

However, the effectiveness of machine learning can be hindered by subpar data quality and the sluggish availability of data. This is where quantum computing comes into play, offering the potential to rapidly process large volumes of data rapidly, thus granting machine learning the same advantage.

A notable example of this potential is a collaborative project, "Quantum Advantage in Learning from Experiments," involving scientists from renowned institutions like Caltech, Harvard, Berkeley, and Microsoft.

Published findings reveal the exceptional performance of their quantum computer, Sycamore, compared to classical learning agents, demonstrating exponential superiority across a diverse range of tasks, highlighting the remarkable capabilities of quantum learning agents.

Cryptography and Security

Quantum computing can make it harder for unauthorized parties to breach data using qubits to calculate all possible breach methods, allowing for stronger security measures.

However, critics argue that this very power of quantum computing could be leveraged by hackers to quickly devise strategies for infiltrating servers containing sensitive data, potentially compromising existing security measures.

That is why the development of quantum-resistant cryptography is a main focus of the National Institute of Standards and Technology (NIST). Through its Post-Quantum Cryptography Standardization Program, NIST aims to create a stronger cryptographic system that can withstand quantum attacks, surpassing the current widely adopted methods.

This pursuit of enhanced security measures is closely tied to the geopolitical landscape, as it fuels the competition between the United States and China in the race to advance quantum technology.

Financial Application

Quantum computing's integration promises to enhance market predictions and risk management.

Multiverse Computing, Pasqal, and Crédit Agricole recently completed a 1.5-year proof-of-concept study on quantum computing's potential in financial product valuation and credit risk assessment.

Notable advancements were achieved, reducing computing time and memory usage. Using a mere 50-qubit quantum processor, accurate results comparable to conventional methods were obtained, paving the way for real-world applications, specifically in derivatives valuation.

Anticipated advancements are on the horizon as a 300-qubit quantum processor is expected to become accessible in 2024. This breakthrough research marks the introduction of the inaugural quantum-enhanced machine learning algorithm designed specifically for forecasting credit rating downgrades.

Natural Language Processing (NLP)

Quantum computing can enhance natural language processing (NLP) and speech recognition, leading to more efficient and accurate communication. In that sense, quantum NLP (QNLP) aims to surpass the capabilities of traditional NLP by translating language into coded circuits processed by quantum computers.

Advancements in quantum computing enable QNLP to deliver enhanced effectiveness, faster processing, reduced power consumption, and a smaller environmental footprint. QNLP leverages quantum computing to accelerate the training process for data-intensive AI models, resulting in reduced training time.

For instance, Quantinuum (a company that integrates software and hardware solutions for quantum computing), with expertise in QNLP, recently collaborated with UCL and the BBC to explore the commercial potential in content discovery and archive retrieval.

Through the transformation of sentences into logical formats and the use of string diagrams, QNLP simplifies NLP design on quantum hardware. These encoded quantum circuits can be optimized for machine learning applications.

Advantages of Quantum Computing in AI?

The exponential growth of complex data sets has surpassed the capabilities of traditional computers, putting a strain on our existing systems. However, quantum computing emerges as a promising solution to address these challenges in a matter of seconds. The ability of quantum computing to process vast amounts of data at an astonishing speed is of utmost importance when it comes to tackling intricate problems.

Quantum simulations, in particular, hold significant promise in addressing complex issues like climate change and healthcare.

Apart from the incredible speed and the ability to handle complex data sets, quantum computing brings several other benefits to AI. Keep reading to find out what they are.

Optimizing Solutions

Quantum computing empowers us to make optimal decisions in portfolio analysis, delivery routes, and personalized treatment protocols.

As big data shapes our computer architecture, we require a different approach to effectively handle it. Quantum computers excel at solving sequential problems, offering better decision-making capabilities for businesses and consumers. This encourages investments in this emerging technology.

Spotting Patterns in Large Data Sets

Quantum computing can rapidly search for patterns or anomalies in vast, unsorted data sets. It has the ability to simultaneously access all items in a database, identifying similarities within seconds.

Current technologies rely on sequential examination, which is time-consuming and impractical for large data sets.

Facilitating Integration of Diverse Data Sets

Quantum computers will enable breakthroughs by integrating vastly different data sets. Initially, human intervention may be necessary to guide the integration process.

When we analyze raw data from diverse sources with distinct structures, it is crucial to understand how these structures are related to each other.

Advancements in natural language analysis, a significant challenge in artificial intelligence, are required for this task. Human input plays a vital role in training the system for future integration.

Challenges of Quantum Computing in AI?

Qubit decoherence, the loss or degradation of quantum information in a qubit, stands as one of the most significant hurdles in the realm of quantum computing. These qubits are incredibly sensitive to their surroundings, meaning even minor disruptions can lead to the loss of their quantum properties.

Overcoming this challenge necessitates exploring novel quantum approaches, embracing new materials, and developing advanced computational techniques. It is crucial to recognize that the obstacles in quantum computing extend beyond hardware complexities.

Quantum algorithms are considerably more intricate than classical algorithms, demanding developers to adopt original strategies when approaching computational problems. The field of quantum computing presents several additional challenges to scientists, engineers, and entrepreneurs. Let's examine eight of these remaining challenges:

Error Correction

Unquestionably, error correction stands as the foremost challenge faced by experts in the field. Quantum computers prove highly susceptible to noise and errors resulting from interactions with the environment.

Such errors can accumulate, compromising the accuracy of computations. Developing reliable techniques for error correction becomes imperative in constructing practical quantum computers.

Scalability

Although quantum computers have shown remarkable capabilities in specific areas, their current size and scale still fall short when compared to classical computers.

The primary hurdle is the need to expand quantum computers to support hundreds or even thousands of qubits while preserving coherence and minimizing errors.

The scalability of quantum computers poses a significant challenge, as it involves expanding their capacity to handle hundreds or even thousands of qubits while preserving coherence and minimizing errors.

Hardware Development

The development of high-quality quantum hardware, including qubits and control electronics, presents a significant obstacle. Various qubit technologies exist, each with its own advantages and disadvantages.

Therefore, extensive research focuses on creating a scalable and fault-tolerant qubit technology.

Software Development

Quantum algorithms and software development tools are currently in their early stages, necessitating the creation of new programming languages, compilers, and optimization tools. These innovations should effectively harness the power of quantum computers.

Classical Computers Interfaces

Quantum computers are not intended to replace classical computers; instead, they will serve as complementary technologies. Consequently, it is vital to develop efficient and reliable methods for transferring data between classical and quantum computers to enable practical applications.

Standards and Protocols

Establishing standards, protocols, and benchmarking in quantum computing is vital for compatibility, interoperability, and measuring performance. As the field matures, these aspects gain increasing importance across hardware, software, and communication interfaces.

Trained Talent

Finding qualified quantum workers is challenging. It's a catch-22 situation: more people won't join until practical quantum computers are widespread, yet the progress of quantum computers depends on more motivated individuals entering the field.

Overall Expense

Expense is a significant roadblock for quantum computing. Quantum talent, hardware, and complex supply chains are costly. Overcoming these expenses and seeking investments will be standard for scientists and entrepreneurs in the future.

When Will Commercial Quantum Computing Emerge?

Industry experts suggest that the competition to deliver quantum computing on a commercial scale is not expected to reach a conclusion prior to 2027.

The continuous advancement of quantum computing technology is expected to gradually decrease the cost of hardware, making it more accessible to businesses and organizations.

Factors like advancements in the field, market demand, and competition among quantum computing companies will play a crucial role in determining the cost of quantum computers.

Leading companies such as IBM, Amazon and Google have already developed highly sophisticated quantum computers with hundreds of qubits. However, to have a significant impact on commercial applications, it may be necessary to scale up the number of qubits to thousands or even millions.

Despite these advancements, there are challenges that impede progress. For instance, superconducting quantum computing requires complex cooling systems to maintain the optimal functioning of qubits at low temperatures, along with reliable error correction systems.

These challenges contribute to the uncertainty surrounding the exact timeframe for the availability of commercial quantum computers.

Nonetheless, influential figures in various industries remain optimistic that practical applications of this transformative technology will emerge within the next ten to twenty years.

How Close Are We To Quantum Artificial Intelligence?

Quantum artificial intelligence (QAI) holds great potential across various fields, including ML, chemistry and materials science, climate modeling, optimization, finance, cryptography, and artificial general intelligence (AGI).

However, despite its wide-ranging applications, we are still in the early stages of QAI's development, and further progress is needed.

To maximize the effectiveness of QAI, it is vital to focus on the development of advanced quantum algorithms, drawing upon expertise in quantum mechanics, computer science, and mathematical optimization.

This process involves a series of steps:

- Identifying the problem at hand,
- Carefully selecting the most suitable quantum algorithm,
- Optimizing the quantum circuit to maximize efficiency,
- Implementing error correction techniques,

- Iteratively refining and analyzing the results,
- Collaborating with domain experts to further enhance the algorithm's performance.

Still, research and excitement in this field are thriving, as QAI is considered a promising avenue for future AI breakthroughs. Although some experiments have used quantum computing to enhance machine learning algorithms, they are currently in the initial trial stages and not yet ready for real-world applications.

Nonetheless, the partnership between IonQ and Hyundai Motor in 2022, leveraging quantum machine learning for road sign image classification and simulation, serves as a tangible example of QAI's real-world application.

Quantum Computing and AI: Key Takeaways

The impact of quantum computing on artificial intelligence (AI) is substantial and holds great promise for various industries and applications. Quantum computing amplifies the speed, efficacy, and precision of AI systems, surpassing the limitations of traditional computers.

As a result, areas such as medical care, machine learning, cryptography and security, financial applications, and natural language processing benefit from the transformative effects of quantum computing.

Quantum computing brings several advantages to AI, including the ability to:

- Optimize solutions,
- Spot patterns in large data sets,
- Facilitate the integration of diverse data sets.

These benefits enable optimal decision-making, efficient analysis of unsorted data, and breakthroughs through the integration of disparate data sources.

As quantum technology continues to advance, its impact on AI will undoubtedly grow, unlocking new possibilities and driving innovation across industries.

It is an exciting time where the convergence of quantum computing and AI holds tremendous potential for transformative quantum leaps and advancements in various fields.

FUTURE POTENTIAL AND EMERGING APPLICATIONS

Quantum computing applications to know

- Artificial intelligence
- Better batteries
- Cleaner fertilization
- Cybersecurity

- Drug development
- Electronic materials discovery
- Financial modeling
- Solar capture
- Traffic optimization
- Weather forecasting and climate change

But quantum computers are inching closer to reality, thanks to Microsoft focusing on another key issue. Microsoft and Quantinuum have figured out a way to check qubit errors without altering a quantum computer's environment, signaling a new era in quantum computing.

Quantum computers have a reputation for being unreliable since even the most minute changes can create 'noise' that makes it difficult to get accurate results, if any. The discovery by Microsoft and Quantinuum addresses this problem and reignites the heated race between top tech companies like Microsoft, Google and IBM to conquer quantum computing.

But even once quantum computing reigns supreme, its potential impact remains largely theoretical. Still, quantum's hypothetical nature hasn't stopped a steady stream of investment in the hope quantum computing could be a game-changer for various industries. From cybersecurity to pharmaceutical research to finance, here are some ways quantum computing facilitates major advancements.

Future of Quantum Computing

Quantum computing is a rapidly developing field, and its future is full of exciting possibilities. Several potential directions for quantum computing in the future are listed below:

Improved Hardware

Developing hardware that can reliably perform quantum computations is one of the main challenges in quantum computing. In order to mitigate the effects of noise and decoherence, researchers are developing better quantum processors and improving error correction techniques.

Applications in chemistry & materials science

By simulating complex chemical reactions and interactions that are difficult or impossible to model with classical computers, quantum computing may be able to greatly accelerate the discovery of new materials and drugs.

Advancements in cryptography

Quantum computing could potentially break many of the encryption algorithms used to secure sensitive information today. However, researchers are also working on developing new quantum-safe encryption methods that would be resistant to attacks by quantum computers.

Optimization and machine learning

Quantum computing could be used to solve optimization problems that are intractable for classical computers, such as those encountered in logistics and supply chain management. Quantum machine learning could also offer significant improvements in data analysis and pattern recognition.

Hybrid classical-quantum computing

Many applications may require a combination of classical and quantum computing to achieve the best results. Researchers are developing methods for integrating classical and quantum algorithms to take advantage of the strengths of each approach.

Overall, the future of quantum computing is bright, with the potential to revolutionize fields ranging from medicine to finance to cybersecurity. Even so, quantum computing may not be widely accessible and practical for real-world applications for several years.

Quantum Computing Companies of The Future

We will now take a look at some of those newer startups and companies in the space, founded within the last year or two, that are innovative in their approaches and have a good chance to unlock some of the possibilities of quantum technology.

Abelian

Abelian applies post-quantum cryptographic algorithms to ensure the long-term security and privacy of customers' digital gold, ABEL. Abelian ensures that wallet addresses are hidden and untraceable, while also securing the amount in transactions hidden by using lattice-based linkable ring signature schemes. Side chains, smart contracts, and interoperability will be developed for supporting various DeFi, Metaverse, and Web3 applications and initiatives.

Abelian is based in Irvine, California, and is led by cryptographers, mathematicians, engineers, developers, and cybersecurity experts.

Planqc

A neutral atom quantum computing startup emerged from the Munich Quantum Valley in 2022 (and is the first to do so), planqc's founding team of Alexander Glätzle, Sebastian Blatt, Johannes Zeiher, Lukas Reichsöllner, Ann-Kristin Achleitner, and

Markus Wagner combines decades of international research on neutral-atom quantum technologies.

Planqc's quantum computers are built on the precision of atomic clocks, quantum gas microscopes and high-speed Rydberg gates and store information in individual atoms — nature's best qubits.

Bohr Quantum Technology

Bohr Quantum Technology is a Pasadena, California-based startup that has developed a commercial-ready quantum networking system that it intends to commercialize from IP published in December 2020 (licensed technology from CalTech and Fermilab). They are moving the complexity of light-based networking into a rack allowing for the networking of quantum data. This enables scaling of quantum computers (i.e. being able to connect QPUs that are restricted by a cryo chamber) and their overall usefulness (e.g. entangle and disentangle chips across a building or even across towns).

The business is also interested in distance networking and enabling long-distance networking of quantum memories. Its technology offers precision timing, networking computers, and provably secure communication.

Diraq

Diraq is a full-stack quantum company building a quantum computer based on silicon CMOS spin qubits. The startup, based in Sydney, Australia and founded in 2022, invented this revolutionary technology in 2014 and filed patents for it.

Focused on building fault-tolerant quantum computers, Diraq's patented CMOS qubits are the same size as today's transistors and use the same manufacturing. Diraq maintains 28 patents and patent applications across major jurisdictions. Diraq's founder is CEO Andrew Dzurak, whose intention over the next ten years is for the business to progress its chips from prototypes to silicon quantum processor chips at nanometer scales.

SCALINQ

Based on research derived from years of research and development at the Chalmers University of Technology and founded in 2021, SCALINQ has the goal to make the scaling of quantum computers easier. Experts in the field of superconducting quantum computing and committed to helping firms and customers efficiently realize larger quantum processors, SCALINQ is based in Gothenburg, Sweden.

Its interdisciplinary team of leading researchers with competencies ranging from quantum engineering, microwave engineering, and hardware design, combined with business developers who have backgrounds in engineering.

SandboxAQ

SandboxAQ is harnessing the exponential power of AI + Quantum Technology - AQ. Sandbox AQ and some of its team originated at Alphabet Inc., which became an independent entity in 2022. The mission of the company is to develop computationally intensive products for the financial services, healthcare, telecommunications, and public sectors.

Blue Qubit

Based in the Bay area of California, Blue Qubit builds first-in-class quantum software for current and upcoming quantum computers and was founded in 2022 by Hrant Gharibyan and Hayk Tepanyan.

The Future of Quantum Computing

As quantum computing advances, a world that is currently science fiction will become a reality. With it, we will be able to process enormous amounts of data extremely fast, enabling simulations that are unimaginable at the moment. As a result, a whole new level of AI will be possible that will accelerate advances in genomics, disease management and renewable energy technologies, just to name a few. In a world in which the cost of energy is rapidly falling toward zero, we will live longer, healthier lives.

Let us hope, however, that when the technology becomes more powerful and more mainstream, we use it for only good intentions.

Potential Applications of Quantum Computing

The potential applications of quantum computing span across diverse fields, where its unparalleled computational power can bring about transformative changes:

Cryptography and Security

One of the most intriguing aspects of quantum computing is its potential impact on cryptography. Shor's algorithm, a quantum algorithm, can factor large numbers quickly, breaking widely-used cryptographic schemes like RSA and ECC. To counter this, research into post-quantum cryptography is underway, developing quantum-safe cryptographic algorithms to protect sensitive data from quantum attacks.

Drug Discovery and Material Science

Quantum simulations can analyze molecular interactions and simulate complex chemical processes, facilitating drug discovery and material design. Quantum computers can significantly speed up the process of finding new drugs and materials with specific properties.

Optimization in Finance and Logistics

Quantum computing's optimization capabilities can revolutionize financial modeling and portfolio optimization. It can efficiently analyze vast amounts of financial data and optimize investment strategies to achieve better returns with reduced risks.

Artificial Intelligence and Machine Learning

Combining quantum computing with machine learning could lead to new breakthroughs in artificial intelligence. Quantum algorithms for pattern recognition, data analysis, and optimization could significantly improve AI models' capabilities.

The Current State of Quantum Computing

The current state of quantum computing is characterized by significant progress and advancements, but it is still in its early stages. Here are some key aspects that reflect the current state of quantum computing:

- **Quantum Hardware Development**: Several companies and research institutions have made significant strides in developing quantum hardware. Quantum processors, based on various technologies such as superconducting qubits, trapped ions, and topological qubits, have been created with increasing qubit counts and coherence times. Companies like IBM, Google, Rigetti Computing, IonQ, and others have demonstrated quantum processors with tens to hundreds of qubits.
- **Quantum Volume and NISQ Era**: Quantum Volume is a metric used to assess the overall capabilities of quantum processors, taking into account factors like qubit count, gate fidelity, and connectivity. Quantum computers in the current state belong to the Noisy Intermediate-Scale Quantum (NISQ) era, where the machines have limited qubits and are susceptible to noise and errors. They are useful for certain specialized tasks, but full-scale fault-tolerant quantum computing remains a long-term goal.
- **Quantum Algorithms and Applications**: Research on quantum algorithms has led to groundbreaking achievements like Shor's algorithm for factoring large numbers exponentially faster than classical algorithms and Grover's algorithm for unstructured search. Quantum algorithms have

shown promise in fields like cryptography, optimization, and machine learning. Researchers are actively exploring more quantum algorithms and their potential applications in various domains.

- **Cloud-Based Quantum Computing Services**: Some companies, including IBM and Google, have launched cloud-based quantum computing services. These services allow researchers and developers to access and experiment with quantum processors remotely, democratizing access to quantum computing resources.
- **Quantum Error Correction**: Quantum error correction is a crucial area of research to address the inherent errors and decoherence in quantum processors. Developing fault-tolerant quantum error correction codes is vital for scalable and reliable quantum computing.
- **Quantum Software and Tools**: The quantum software ecosystem is evolving rapidly, providing tools and frameworks for quantum programming, simulation, and optimization. Open-source quantum software platforms like Qiskit (IBM) and Cirq (Google) have gained popularity and fostered the quantum software community.
- **Public and Private Quantum Research Initiatives**: Governments and private sector companies have invested heavily in quantum research and development. Various countries have established national quantum initiatives to support quantum research and propel advancements in quantum technologies.
- **Quantum Network and Communication:** Quantum communication, specifically quantum key distribution (QKD), has advanced, demonstrating secure and unbreakable communication using quantum principles. Quantum networks are being developed to establish secure quantum connections between different locations.

CHAPTER-11

THE FUTURE OF QUANTUM COMPUTING

INTRODUCTION

Quantum computing is a revolutionary field that combines principles from quantum mechanics and computer science to create a new paradigm of computing. Unlike traditional computers that use bits to represent information as either a 0 or a 1, quantum computers use qubits, which can exist in multiple states simultaneously. This allows quantum computers to perform complex calculations at an exponentially faster rate than classical computers. The concept of quantum computing dates back to the early 1980s when physicist Richard Feynman first proposed the idea of using quantum systems to simulate physical processes. However, it wasn't until the late 1990s that researchers were able to build the first working quantum computers. Since then, there has been significant progress in the field, with companies like IBM, Google, and Microsoft investing heavily in quantum computing research. Quantum computing has the potential to revolutionize various industries, including cryptography, drug discovery, machine learning, artificial intelligence, big data analytics, and cybersecurity. Its ability to solve complex problems at an unprecedented speed opens up new possibilities for scientific research and technological advancements.

Quantum computing is poised to revolutionize data processing, and Cloud 7 IT Services Inc is at the forefront of embracing this technological advancement. As we delve into the future of IT, the power of quantum computing, with its qubits, is becoming increasingly evident.

Traditional computers rely on bits, which can represent either 0 or 1. Quantum computers, on the other hand, utilize qubits, which can represent 0, 1, or both simultaneously due to the principles of superposition. This allows them to perform complex calculations exponentially faster than classical computers.

Applications of quantum computing are vast, from optimizing supply chains to simulating complex quantum systems. This technology promises breakthroughs in fields like cryptography, drug discovery, and artificial intelligence.

At Cloud 7 IT Services Inc, we are actively exploring how quantum computing can benefit businesses. Our experts are harnessing the power of quantum algorithms to solve complex problems efficiently. We invite you to join us on this exciting journey into the future of IT.

The digital devices that we rely on so heavily in our day-to-day and professional lives today—smartphones, tablets, laptops, fitness trackers, etc.—use traditional computational technology. Traditional computers rely on a series of mathematical equations that use electrical impulses to encode information in a binary system of 1s and 0s. This information is transmitted through quantitative measurements called "bits."

Unlike traditional computing, quantum computing relies on the principles of quantum theory, which address principles of matter and energy on an atomic and subatomic scale. With quantum computing, equations are no longer limited to 1s and 0s, but instead can transmit information in which particles exist in both states, the 1 and the 0, at the same time.

Quantum computing measures electrons or photons. These subatomic particles are known as quantum bits, or "qubits." The more qubits are used in a computational exercise, the more exponentially powerful the scope of the computation can be. Quantum computing has the potential to solve equations in a matter of minutes that would take traditional computers tens of thousands of years to work out.

Cutting-edge Uses of Quantum Computing Technology

With its remarkable ability to process vast quantities of information in moments and transmit multidimensional information, quantum computing provides huge potential for evolving technology. Quantum computing will have an impact on the trajectory of manufacturing, artificial intelligence, and cybersecurity, to name just a few evolving applications.

For financial institutions, the power of quantum computing can be harnessed to craft sophisticated trade simulations using high-speed financial modeling to make marketplace predictions. Financial institutions can use quantum computing to increase security, boost fraud detection capabilities, and perform in-depth risk analyses.

Soon we will begin to see financial institutions using quantum computers to develop highly advanced, streamlined investment portfolios for their clients. Recent studies have shown that 80% of financial institutions recognize the possibilities presented by AI. Many of us in the industry believe that, coupled with quantum computing, we will see a burst of fintech developments and technological evolutions of traditional brick-and-mortar financial institutions.

The pharmaceutical industry is also adopting quantum computers, as researchers can use quantum computing to simulate molecular interactions, which will allow for the quick development of new medications. Using quantum computing for intensive DNA studies may lead to healthcare providers' ability to offer gene-specific cures.

In the fields of engineering, aerospace, and military development, researchers and designers can use quantum computers to create sleeker, more efficient aircraft models. Air traffic controls and traffic coordination systems can likely be made safer using quantum computing. And military intelligence can also benefit from the vast power of quantum computing.

In addition, quantum computing can be used to enhance cybersecurity and intelligence gathering, providing stronger data encryption services and high-level intrusion-detection systems. Quantum computing will contribute to big data search processes, as well as the rapid development of AI and machine learning.

Quantum computing may even revolutionize our domestic power sources, providing electrical energy based on nuclear fusion processes.

QUANTUM COMPUTING ROADMAP

Quantum computers use the concepts of quantum coherence, superposition, and entanglement to process information in such a way that classical computing cannot do. The ability of quantum states to be in superposition can lead to a substantial speedup of a computation in terms of complexity since operations can be executed on many states at the same time.

A quantum algorithm is the stepwise procedure performed on a quantum computer to solve a problem, for example- searching a database, factorization of large numbers, and optimization with the latter effectively used in a speed-up of machine learning algorithms. In quantum machine learning, quantum algorithms are developed to solve typical sort of problems of machine learning using the concepts and efficiency of quantum computing. This is usually done by adapting classical algorithms or their expensive subroutines to run on a quantum computer.

So, basically, we can grab two concepts here, ML techniques can be used to output the quantum processes. Also, quantum computational concepts can be used to design and enhance ML algorithms.

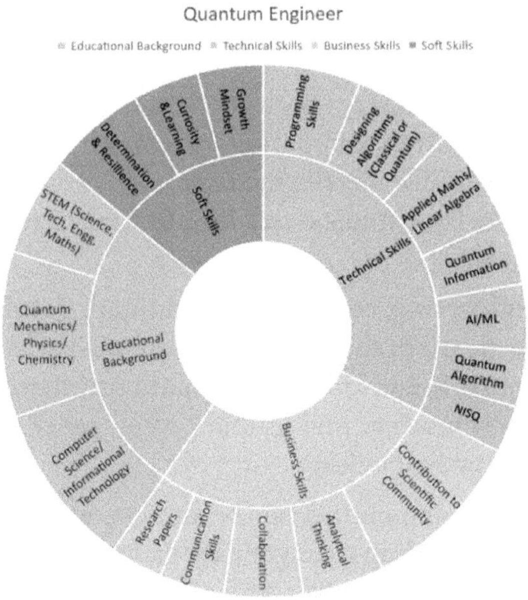

Quantum engineers may or may not require a background in quantum science depending upon the area of engineering we focus on. But for software engineers, bringing the quantum engineering mindset to project execution and development of enterprise programs is important. "As the layers of abstraction increases, and we are agreed upon the standards in community, it's going to make less and less necessary for engineers to know what quantum Hamiltonian, unitary transformations, superposition, and entanglement concepts is, because the functionalities are quite tough to understand and it's going to be packaged and you know software modules and application layer that are easier to plug and play into existing application."

The important aspect for a person who is new to quantum physics or a mathematics background is to develop intuition for key quantum computing concepts and how that intuition can be leveraged with engineering skills.

The wheel graphic below illustrates the primary skills that are required in the areas of educational background, technical background, business, and soft skills:

The role of Quantum Engineer is a complex one, involving deep education, technical, business, and soft skills. The following describes each area in more detail.

Educational Background

STEM – Any discipline within Science, Technology, Engineering, Mathematics, Computer Science, and Information technology. Masters and PhD. in Science is preferred, however Bachelor's in Engineering with Computer Science or Electronics is a requirement.

Quantum Mechanics/Physics/ Chemistry – Quantum mechanics is a desired skillset. Quantum mechanics is the fundamental theory of physics that provides the description of nature at atomic and subatomic level. Quantum computing leverages the underlying complex laws of quantum mechanics like entanglement, superposition, teleportation etc.

Technical Skills

Programming skillset:

- Quantum Engineers do not require PhD, however a strong grasp of programming languages like Python, R and Quantum SDKs like Qiskit (IBM), Pennylane (Xanadu), Cirq (Google), and/or TensorFlow (Google) is important.
- Primarily Classical Computing Languages such as Python, C, C++ is required and is supported by SDKs like Qiskit and Cirq for programming.
- However, Quantum Programming Languages are broadly classified into:
  - Imperative Quantum Programming Language
  - Functional Quantum Programming Language
  - Multi-Paradigm Languages

Refer to image below for detailed visualization:]

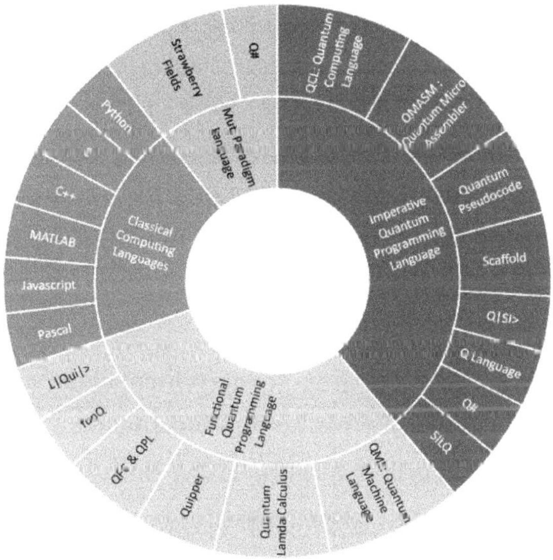

Quantum Programming Language

Quantum Software Development Kits are required to run Quantum Circuits on Simulators or prototype Quantum Devices.

The below figure illustrates Quantum Software Development Kits from different organizations:

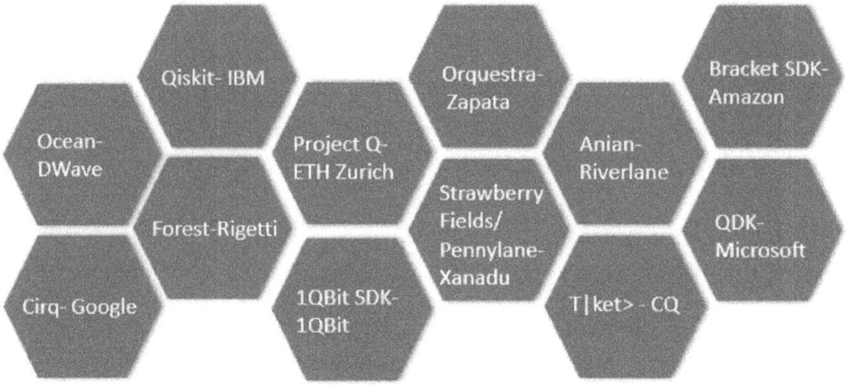

Mathematical Concepts Linear Algebra, Complex Numbers and Probability Theory is a desired skillset.

Quantum Information and Computation including Quantum Algorithms, Quantum Communication, Quantum Cryptography, and Information Processing is applicable in all the areas of quantum technology like Ion Traps, Cavity QED, NMR, photonics quantum computers and solid-state systems. QIC covers all the concepts from Quantum Mechanics to Physical realizations and Quantum Information Theory.

Noisy Intermediate-Scale Quantum (NISQ) marks the 'NISQ' era of Quantum Computing with 50- 100 qubits able to perform complex operations and surpass the capabilities of classical computing. Quantum engineers and quantum hardware manufacturers strive for the implementation of more accurate and less-noisy fault- tolerant quantum systems.

Artificial Intelligence and Machine learning plays a significant role in building hybrid environments of classical and quantum computing algorithms. The evolving quantum technology requires more AI Engineers transforming themselves into Quantum Engineers to build and implement Enterprise AI-Quantum Strategy.

Business Skills

Quantum Engineers must be able to convince others of the benefits and alignment with organizational goals of their solutions.

- **Communication:** Strong communication skills both written and verbal
- **Collaboration:** Ability to work with diverse team of Engineers, scientists, and Business stakeholders.
- **Analytical and Logical Thinking**
- **Research Papers:** Contribution to research papers and experience working in R&D environment

- **Contribution to Scientific Community:** Transforming from a Software Engineer to Quantum Engineer requires active communication, collaboration, contribution to communities (such as GitHub, Qiskit Community etc.), and publishing and reviewing research papers.

Soft Skills

Soft skills are an abstract skillset that is critical for an individual and an organization to evolve and grow. The ability and motivation to learn, to be curious to discover, to be determined, to have growth mindset, to be able to work in a team, to be able to express and communicate, are major factors for transitioning to successful Quantum Engineering.

Networking is a key factor; you need to know people who can point you to the right people.

Quantum Engineering is intense form of science, and there is no substitute for learning. There are tremendous number of resources available on the internet today in comparison to what it was 5 years back and its increasing.

A very important lesson that we understood is focusing and learning, as it has no substitute, and having connection with maybe a small group of brilliant people who can help in getting what is a real fit to your quantum journey.

The power of nature has always been there, but only a pioneer mindset can unfold those mysteries.

Education Requirements

- **Masters/PhD. in Quantum Computing, Science (Physics/Chemistry) or Engineering-** Masters/ PhD. in quantum computing, machine learning, artificial intelligence, physics, mathematics, chemistry, or related fields are an ideal fit. However, organizations like United Health Group, JP Morgan, Standard Chartered, Accenture, HSBC, etc. are working on designing training programs with the focus on software engineers, technologists, and C Suites. The industry has started realizing the impact of quantum with a primary focus on transportation, space, life sciences, insurance and healthcare sectors. Since the field of quantum machine learning is still in its budding phase and, therefore, PhD roles are an ideal fit for the organization to pursue research. However, we will see a lot of dynamics in terms of Industry roles coming in the span of 5 10 years.
- **Machine Learning Engineer/AI Engineer** – Machine Learning /AI is one of the important skills for quantum machine learning. However, for an AI/ML Engineer, exposure to and understanding of quantum theory and computation is very much required.

- **Research Associate/Scientist**– A research associate or scientist already working in quantum computation, optimization and AI/ML is a plus. Such experience can bring great expertise in this domain.
- **Internships and Certifications**– There are a lot of internships and certification programs available. However, one should know, not all internships and certification courses provide in-depth knowledge of quantum computing or machine learning. You need to self-invest a lot to acquire depth in both subjects.
- **Industry Experience** – Experience and knowledge gained from the commercial industry is a great addition. Understanding of the business and consumer helps in determining and deriving several use cases of a particular Industry front.

Technical Skills

Talking to academic and industry experts on what technical skills could define a quantum machine learning engineer, Adrian Perez Salinas, Research Engineer and pursuing PhD at Barcelona Supercomputing Center, casts some light on the technical requirements for QML Engineer and Quantum Computing in general. As per some of the pointers that I grabbed from our discussion and my research:

- **AI/ Machine Learning** – Quantum AI/ML needs to achieve several milestones to become mature in the field of quantum engineering. Widespread adoption of open-source modelling and training frameworks is one critical point. Before starting with quantum machine learning, one should know the AI and ML algorithms in depth.
- **Applied Mathematics/ Linear Algebra**– Linear algebra, complex numbers, probability theory are required skillsets.
- **Quantum Computation and Quantum Information** – Harnessing quantum physics for the purpose of computation holds significant promise for the development of data science and machine learning. Also, in turn, data science and especially machine learning can play a major role in the development of quantum computation and quantum information.
- **Quantum Machine Learning Algorithms** – Understanding of quantum machine learning algorithms and how they can work with classical machine learning algorithms. Some examples include:
    - Quantum Machine Learning Algorithms for supervised and Unsupervised Learning
    - Quantum Principal Component Analysis
    - Quantum Support Vector Machines and Kernel Methods
    - Optimization Techniques

- **Quantum Optimization and Simulation** – Quantum computers have a natural tendency to simulate the dynamics of quantum systems. Also, algorithms such as classical discrete optimization problem becomes an eigen problem on a large matrix, that can be visualized with quantum systems. Understanding of both quantum optimization and simulation is a plus.
- **NISQ** – We are still amid what we call as "Noisy Intermediate Scale System". The noisy intermediate scale quantum devices (NISQ) are being constructed out of cold atoms, superconducting quantum circuits, trapped ions, and other quantum systems for which we have achieved an exquisite degree of control. Some of the tasks for these NISQ devices will be as simulators (or emulators) of other highly entangled quantum many-body systems. The goal is to supplant our current conventional computer simulation technology, such as exact diagonalization, quantum Monte Carlo, or tensor network methods.
- **Tensor Networks** – "Tensor Networks are extremely powerful because they represent huge amount of data, so it is a way to represent large amounts of data in a very efficient way. We think that it would be like the linear algebra of 21st century and maybe you want to know that because there are some extremely useful methodologies that can be used for processing images, processing sound." says Adrian Perez Salinas, Research Engineer and pursuing PhD at Barcelona Supercomputing Center.

Business Skills

The science of quantum machine learning is complicated. For success in this field, along with strong educational and technical background, there are a few other parameters that are required as well:

- **Right Mentorship**: Finding the right mentorship is very important. Few initiatives, such as the Quantum Open-Source Foundation (QOSF) programs, are entirely designed in the framework of Mentee-Mentors that helps in connecting with the quantum enthusiasts and right mentors.
- **Contribution to Scientific community**– Contributing to the scientific community by participating in hackathons, slack channels, and networking helps in finding the right people and a great value add to the knowledge content. In order to enhance your networking skills, there is this interesting website to check: http://quantumapalooza.com/, which aggregates a list of all the free quantum computing meetup events going on globally.
- **Contribution to research papers**– Writing research papers, original content, or maintaining a GitHub account with your coding projects shows the level of depth. It is not, however, a mandate for certain roles. But it is

always an added advantage, especially if a person is seeking for scientific and research domains.

- **Understanding the Business and Industry requirements-** In the commercial world, it doesn't matter how cool your tech is if it's not getting to the customer. Things like timescales, hard deadlines, user experience, economic cycles, quantum cycles (Spring, winter, managing hype etc.), message to market, product creation etc. are all critical skills that the workforce as a whole needs to know. Business development and Quantum Research Architects are some of the challenging roles in the quantum machine learning area.
- **Understanding the Consumer**– Understanding the consumers requires more outlook into what type of market or industry you are selling your products to. Experience Manager roles aare some of the challenging roles as they have daily interactions with the customers to understand their requirements and also how they want to see the software packages.

Soft Skills

Soft skills play a major role in enhancing the path to development. Continuous development, strong determination, perseverance, curiosity are very important to evolve and grow. In the case of quantum machine learning, shaping the right mindset and setting the right expectation plays a major role.

A word of caution, there is a lot of potential in Quantum AI/ML, but it is still in the process of realization. We might get immediate results, or we may have to wait for this field to mature. But the important aspect is to set the right expectations and not to get impatient if we do not get results immediately, like in classical machine learning. All we need to do is to work and contribute for breakthroughs that are much expected to happen, especially in the quantum machine learning area.

Quantum machine learning is an intense science. The intersection of multi-disciplinary areas makes it more complex both in theoretical and practical terms. There is optimism towards the advancement of quantum machine learning field, all we need to work towards is realizing the potential it could bring to AI and ML domain.

QUANTUM COMPUTING AND THE CLASSICAL WORLD

Basically in essence quantum computers differ significantly from classical computers, which are the computers we currently use. Here are some key differences between the two:

- **Data Representation:** Classical computers use bits to represent and process information. A bit can be in one of two states: 0 or 1. Quantum computers, on the other hand, use quantum bits or qubits, which can represent 0, 1, or a superposition of both states simultaneously. This superposition allows quantum computers to process multiple states and perform complex computations in parallel.

- **Computation Method:** Classical computers perform computations using algorithms based on binary logic gates, such as AND, OR, and NOT gates. Quantum computers utilize quantum gates, which are analogous to classical gates but operate on qubits and can manipulate their quantum states. Quantum algorithms, such as Shor's algorithm and Grover's algorithm, take advantage of quantum properties to solve certain problems more efficiently than classical algorithms.
- **Parallelism:** Quantum computers leverage a phenomenon called quantum parallelism. Due to the superposition property of qubits, quantum computers can perform computations on many possible solutions simultaneously. This enables them to explore a vast number of combinations and find solutions much faster for specific problems compared to classical computers.
- **Quantum Entanglement:** Quantum entanglement is a unique property of quantum systems where two or more qubits become correlated in such a way that the state of one qubit is dependent on the state of the other(s), regardless of the distance between them. This property allows quantum computers to perform operations on multiple qubits collectively, increasing computational power and enabling secure communication through quantum cryptography.
- **Error Correction:** Quantum computers are susceptible to errors due to environmental interference, called quantum noise or decoherence. Quantum error correction techniques are employed to mitigate these errors and preserve the integrity of computations. Classical computers also deal with errors, but they rely on error correction codes specifically designed for classical bits.
- **Application Potential:** Quantum computers have the potential to solve complex problems in various domains more efficiently than classical computers. They hold promise for applications in cryptography, optimization, drug discovery, materials science, artificial intelligence, and simulating quantum systems. However, quantum computers are still in the early stages of development, and practical, large-scale quantum computers are yet to be realized.

It's important to note that while quantum computers offer advantages in certain computations, they are not intended to replace classical computers entirely. Classical computers excel in tasks involving simple logic operations, everyday computing needs, and most software applications. Quantum computers are expected to complement classical computers and be utilized for specific problems that can benefit from their unique capabilities.

So What Are The Risks?

While quantum computers hold great promise for advancing scientific research and solving complex problems, they also present some risks and challenges. Here are a few potential risks associated with quantum computers:

- **Cryptographic Breakthroughs:** Quantum computers have the potential to break certain encryption algorithms that are widely used today. For example, Shor's algorithm, when implemented on a large-scale quantum computer, could render many commonly used public-key encryption algorithms, such as RSA and ECC, vulnerable. This poses a significant risk to secure communication, data protection, and financial transactions that rely on these encryption methods.
- **Data Security:** Quantum computers could potentially undermine the security of sensitive data that was encrypted using current cryptographic protocols. As quantum computers advance, previously encrypted data could be decrypted using powerful quantum algorithms, compromising confidentiality and privacy.
- **Defence and National Security:** Quantum computers could disrupt current defence and national security systems. Encryption plays a vital role in protecting sensitive information in areas like military communications, intelligence gathering, and critical infrastructure. If quantum computers can break existing encryption methods, it could have implications for national security and defence strategies.
- **Impact on Blockchain Technology:** Blockchain technology, which is used in cryptocurrencies and decentralised systems, relies on cryptographic algorithms to ensure security and trust. If quantum computers can break the cryptographic foundations of blockchain systems, it could impact the integrity and immutability of transactions and compromise the security of decentralised networks.
- **Misuse of Quantum Computing Power:** As quantum computers become more powerful, there is a risk that they could be used for malicious purposes. For example, quantum computing could potentially be used to break into secure systems, decrypt sensitive information, or create new forms of cyber threats that are currently unseen.
- **Ethical Considerations:** The advancement of quantum computing raises ethical questions and concerns. It is crucial to ensure that the power of quantum computers is used responsibly and ethically. Ethical considerations

include issues of privacy, data protection, fairness, and the potential impact on society as a whole.

It's worth noting that many of these risks are still hypothetical and dependent on the development of large-scale, error-corrected quantum computers. Researchers and organisations are actively working on post-quantum cryptography methods to develop new encryption algorithms that can withstand quantum attacks. Additionally, efforts are being made to enhance data security and develop quantum-resistant technologies to address these risks.

So what are the Benefits?

Quantum computers offer several potential benefits across various fields. While practical, large-scale quantum computers are still in development, here are some potential advantages they may bring:

- **Faster Computations:** Quantum computers have the potential to solve certain problems much faster than classical computers. Quantum algorithms can leverage quantum parallelism and superposition to perform computations on multiple possibilities simultaneously. This speedup could significantly impact areas such as optimisation, cryptography, and complex simulations.
- **Improved Optimisation:** Quantum computers excel at solving optimisation problems, which involve finding the best solution among a vast number of possibilities. This has implications for various fields, including logistics, supply chain management, scheduling, and financial portfolio optimisation. Quantum algorithms can potentially find optimal solutions more efficiently, leading to improved resource allocation and cost reduction.
- **Enhanced Simulation Capabilities:** Quantum computers have the ability to simulate complex quantum systems, which is difficult for classical computers. This can accelerate advancements in materials science, drug discovery, chemical reactions, and understanding physical phenomena at the quantum level. Simulating quantum systems accurately can help researchers design better materials, understand quantum processes, and drive innovation in various scientific domains.
- **Advanced Machine Learning and AI:** Quantum computers have the potential to enhance machine learning and artificial intelligence (AI) algorithms. Quantum machine learning algorithms can efficiently process and analyse large datasets, leading to improved pattern recognition, optimisation of neural networks, and more accurate predictions. Quantum computers could also contribute to the development of novel AI algorithms and models.

- **Quantum Cryptography**: Quantum computers can offer enhanced security through the use of quantum cryptography protocols. Quantum key distribution (QKD) enables the secure exchange of cryptographic keys, leveraging the principles of quantum mechanics to detect eavesdropping attempts. Quantum cryptography can provide unbreakable encryption methods and ensure secure communication channels.
- **Advancements in Scientific Research**: Quantum computers have the potential to revolutionise scientific research across disciplines. They can enable more accurate modeling and simulation of complex phenomena, leading to breakthroughs in chemistry, physics, biology, and materials science. Quantum computers can help scientists explore uncharted territories and gain a deeper understanding of the natural world.

It's important to note that while quantum computers offer significant potential benefits, they are not intended to replace classical computers. Quantum computers are expected to complement classical computers and be utilised for specific problems that can benefit from their unique capabilities.

IMPACT ON SOCIETY AND SCIENTIFIC DISCOVERY

Quantum computing offers new possibilities for drug discovery and pharmaceutical research, as it can simulate the behavior of complex molecules more accurately than classical computers. This capability can lead to the development of new drugs and therapies through a faster and more efficient drug discovery process.

Quantum computing will be used for a variety of innovations and calculations across all industries that were not possible with previous computers. Quantum computers have potential to benefit society in various ways, including making smarter investment decisions, developing drugs and vaccines faster and revolutionizing transportation. However, one disadvantage of quantum computing is that it could break current cryptography. Here is what the experts are saying about how quantum computing may impact society in each industry.

Healthcare

The benefits of quantum computing for healthcare include increased speed to develop vaccines and pharmaceuticals, helping to diagnose patients earlier and personalizing treatment. Developing new drugs is a slow process, and as we saw with the coronavirus vaccine, it can only be sped up so much with current processes. Part of the reason it takes so long is that scientists must develop molecules to test their interactions with other molecules; however, with quantum computers, scientists will be able to simulate molecules for testing. Quantum computers will give scientists and extremely precise simulation of even single molecules.

Finance

According to some studies, the finance sector stands to benefit the most from quantum computers in the short term. The first benefit of quantum computing for finance is the ability to calculate outcomes in the stock market that were previously too random and numerous to calculate. Investors increasingly want more accurate risk assessments under various potential scenarios, which quantum computers will be able to handle. Additionally, when calculating loans and portfolios, quantum computers will offer more precise calculations of credit, which will enable better lending decisions.

Climate forecasting

Quantum computers could also potentially predict the weather. According to a PBS interview with an MIT professor, "Currently, a classical computer might take more time than it actually takes the weather to evolve to predict the weather." This improved climate forecasting could impact many other industries that are weather-dependent, including transportation, food production and more. In the United States, weather affects nearly 30% of GDP, either directly or indirectly. Plus, weather prediction would also allow for more time to prepare for disasters.

Travel and transportation

Quantum computing, combined with AI, will benefit travel and transportation through traffic signal optimization, developing autonomous vehicles, air traffic control and more. Although it may take a few years to reap the fruits of quantum computers in transportation, they have the potential to revolutionize the industry. Quantum computers will be able to calculate optimal traffic routes quickly, reducing congestion and ensuring faster delivery for cargo. For companies like Amazon and FedEx, this increased efficiency could mean a profit increase of up to 600%.

Additionally, quantum computers may help quicken the development of autonomous vehicles, which must be trained through AI. Currently, it can take weeks or months with the world's fastest computers to train AI algorithms, but with quantum computers that development could be exponentially faster.

Quantum computers will impact society in other industries as well, including media and entertainment, consumer goods and insurance. However, quantum computers will also disrupt privacy and cybersecurity with potentially serious negative consequences if organizations are not prepared.

Privacy/security

Perhaps the most imminent impact of quantum computers on society will be in regard to digital security and privacy. Quantum computers will be able to break current cryptographic algorithms because they can perform exponentially more factors than current computers. This means that classical encryption methods will be vulnerable to quantum computers and there is already a quantum algorithm developed that could do just that: Shor's algorithm.

In a DigiCert study, 71% of IT professionals reported knowing the threat quantum computing poses to encryption, yet how well organizations understand this threat varies, and there are equally wide variations in the levels of preparation. To close that gap, DigiCert is currently working to innovate tools and products to better equip our customers for the impact of post-quantum cryptography.

Impact on the Economy

Quantum computing is a rapidly growing field and has attracted significant investment from venture capital and private equity firms. The compound annual growth rate (CAGR) of quantum venture capital and private equity investments is difficult to quantify; however, the latest report published estimates the global quantum computing market size to be valued at around USD 457.9 million in 2021 and is predicted to reach around USD 5274.9 million by 2030 while growing at a compound annual growth rate (CAGR) of roughly 31.21% between 2022 and 2030. The impact of quantum will be notable with all the recent investments in the technology.

Quantum computing has the potential to revolutionize various industries and be a powerful catalyst for the digital economy. Quantum computing can provide significant advantages in areas such as cryptography, which is critical for secure digital transactions and communications in numerous industries.

Impact on Society

While quantum technology is poised to have a significant positive impact on various industries, the economy, and society, it is important to address the associated digital trust challenges and be proactive in developing legal, regulatory, ethical, and cybersecurity programs.

Ethics

The development and deployment of quantum technology raise specific ethical issues, such as justice, fairness, equity, inclusion, respect for persons, ESG, human rights, etc.

Cyber

Quantum computing can have a dual role as a cyber attack or cyber defense mechanism. Quantum computing could be used to break encryption or build optimal zero-trust cyber defense systems. Zero-trust is a cybersecurity approach that assumes that all devices, networks, and users are untrusted until proven otherwise.

Governance

Quantum computing could also be used to perform complex simulations and modeling for voting, crisis and resource management, and public policy.

Citizenship

Quantum computing combined with advanced biometric techniques and decentralized ledger technologies such as blockchain can be foundational for the development of robust digital identities for global citizens.

BIBLIOGRAPHY

Akshay, V., D. Rabinovich, E. Campos, and J. Biamonte, "Parameter concentrations in quantum approximate optimization", *Physical Review* A 104 1, L010401 (2021).

Akshay, V., H. Philathong, E. Campos, D. Rabinovich, I. Zacharov, Xiao-Ming Zhang, and J. D. Biamonte, "Circuit depth scaling for quantum approximate optimization", *Physical Review* A 106 4, 042438 (2022).

Albrecht, Martin R., Miloš Prokop, Yixin Shen, and Petros Wallden, "Variational quantum solutions to the Shortest Vector Problem", *Quantum* 7, 933 (2023).

Anschuetz, Eric R. and Bobak T. Kiani, "Quantum variational algorithms are swamped with traps", *Nature Communications* 13 1, 7760 (2022).

Arute, F., Arya, K., Babbush, R., Bacon, D., Bardin, J. C., Barends, R., ... & Castelnovo, M. (2019). Quantum supremacy using a programmable superconducting processor. Nature, 574(7779), 505–510.

Bae, J. -H., Paul M. Alsing, Doyeol Ahn, and Warner A. Miller, "Quantum circuit optimization using quantum Karnaugh map", *Scientific Reports* 10, 15651 (2020).

Basso, Joao, David Gamarnik, Song Mei, and Leo Zhou, "Performance and limitations of the QAOA at constant levels on large sparse hypergraphs and spin glass models", arXiv:2204.10306, (2022).

Basso, Joao, Edward Farhi, Kunal Marwaha, Benjamin Villalonga, and Leo Zhou, "The Quantum Approximate Optimization Algorithm at High Depth for MaxCut on Large-Girth Regular Graphs and the Sherrington-Kirkpatrick Model", arXiv:2110.14206, (2021).

Bonde, Bhushan, Pratik Patil, and Bhaskar Choubey, Methods in Molecular Biology 2716, 153 (2024) ISBN:978-1-0716-3448-6.

Bouwmeester, D., A. Ekert, A. Zeilinger (eds.) *The Physics of Quantum Information*, Springer, Berlin (2001).

Brown, J., *The Quest for the Quantum Computer*, Simon and Schuster, New York (2000).

Campos, E., D. Rabinovich, V. Akshay, and J. Biamonte, "Training Saturation in Layerwise Quantum Approximate Optimisation", arXiv:2106.13814, (2021).

Cao, Chenfeng, Zheng An, Shi-Yao Hou, D. L. Zhou, and Bei Zeng, "Quantum imaginary time evolution steered by reinforcement learning", *Communications Physics* 5 1, 57 (2022).

Chandarana, P., N. N. Hegade, K. Paul, F. Albarrán-Arriagada, E. Solano, A. del Campo, and Xi Chen, "Digitized-counterdiabatic quantum approximate optimization algorithm", *Physical Review* Research 4 1, 013141 (2022).

Chen, Ye-Hong, Adam Miranowicz, Xi Chen, Yan Xia, and Franco Nori, "Enhanced-Fidelity Ultrafast Geometric Quantum Computation Using Strong Classical Drives", *Physical Review Applied* 18 6, 064059 (2022).

Chi-Ning Chou, Peter J. Love, Juspreet Singh Sandhu, and Jonathan Shi, "Limitations of Local Quantum Algorithms on Random Max-k-XOR and Beyond", arXiv:2108.06049, (2021).

Choy, Boy and David J. Wales, "Molecular Energy Landscapes of Hardware-Efficient Ansätze in Quantum Computing", *Journal of Chemical Theory and Computation* 19 4, 1197 (2023).

Cirac, J. I., & Zoller, P. (2000). A scalable quantum computer with ions in an array of microtraps. *Nature*, 404(6778), 579–581.

Claes, Jahan and Wim van Dam, "Instance Independence of Single Layer Quantum Approximate Optimization Algorithm on Mixed-Spin Models at Infinite Size", *Quantum* 5, 542 (2021).

Cohen-Tannoudji, C, B. Dui, F. Laloe¨, *Quantum Mechanics*, VolI, Wiley, New York, (1977).

Díez-Valle, Pablo, Jorge Luis-Hita, Senaida Hernández-Santana, Fernando Martínez-García, Álvaro Díaz-Fernández, Eva Andrés, Juan José García-Ripoll, Escolástico Sánchez-Martínez, and Diego Porras, "Multiobjective variational quantum optimization for constrained problems: an application to cash handling", *Quantum Science and Technology* 8 4, 045009 (2023).

Dlaska, Clemens, Kilian Ender, Glen Bigan Mbeng, Andreas Kruckenhauser, Wolfgang Lechner, and Rick van Bijnen, "Quantum Optimization via Four-Body Rydberg Gates", *Physical Review Letters* 128 12, 120503 (2022).

Faílde, Daniel, José Daniel Viqueira, Mariamo Mussa Juane, and Andrés Gómez, "Using Differential Evolution to avoid local minima in Variational Quantum Algorithms", *Scientific Reports* 13 1, 16230 (2023).

Farhi, Edward, David Gamarnik, and Sam Gutmann, "The Quantum Approximate Optimization Algorithm Needs to See the Whole Graph: A Typical Case", arXiv:2004.09002, (2020).

Giacomo De Palma, Milad Marvian, Cambyse Rouzé, and Daniel Stilck França, "Limitations of Variational Quantum Algorithms: A Quantum Optimal Transport Approach", *PRX Quantum* 4 1, 010309 (2023).

Gidi, J., B. Candia, A. D. Muñoz-Moller, A. Rojas, L. Pereira, M. Muñoz, L. Zambrano, and A. Delgado, "Stochastic optimization algorithms for quantum applications", *Physical Review* A 108 3, 032409 (2023).

Gregory Quiroz, Paraj Titum, Phillip Lotshaw, Pavel Lougovski, Kevin Schultz, Eugene Dumitrescu, and Itay Hen, "Quantifying the Impact of Precision Errors on Quantum Approximate Optimization Algorithms", arXiv:2109.04482, (2021).

Guillermo González-García, Rahul Trivedi, and J. Ignacio Cirac, "Error Propagation in NISQ Devices for Solving Classical Optimization Problems", *PRX Quantum* 3 4, 040326 (2022).

Hajo Leschke, Chokri Manai, Rainer Ruder, and Simone Warzel, "Existence of Replica-Symmetry Breaking in Quantum Glasses", *Physical Review Letters* 127 20, 207204 (2021).

Han Zheng, Zimu Li, Junyu Liu, Sergii Strelchuk, and Risi Kondor, "Speeding Up Learning Quantum States Through Group Equivariant Convolutional Quantum Ansätze", *PRX Quantum* 4 2, 020327 (2023).

Hari Krovi, "Average-case hardness of estimating probabilities of random quantum circuits with a linear scaling in the error exponent", arXiv:2206.05642, (2022).

Harrigan, Matthew P., Kevin J. Sung, Matthew Neeley, Kevin J. Satzinger, Frank Arute, Kunal Arya, Juan Atalaya, Joseph C. Bardin, Rami Barends, Sergio Boixo, Michael Broughton, Bob B. Buckley, David A. Buell, Brian Burkett, Nicholas Bushnell, Yu Chen,Francisco Chicano, Zakaria Dahi, and Gabriel Luque, Proceedings of the Companion Conference on Genetic and Evolutionary Computation 2187 (2023) ISBN:9798400701207.

Hashim, Akel, Rich Rines, Victory Omole, Ravi K. Naik, John Mark Kreikebaum, David I. Santiago, Frederic T. Chong, Irfan Siddiqi, and Pranav Gokhale, "Optimized SWAP networks with equivalent circuit averaging for QAOA", *Physical Review* Research 4 3, 033028 (2022).

Headley, David and Frank K. Wilhelm, "Problem-size-independent angles for a Grover-driven quantum approximate optimization algorithm", *Physical Review* A 107 1, 012412 (2023).

Hita-Pérez, M., Jaumà, G., Pino, M., & García-Ripoll, J.J. (2021). Three-Josephson junctions flux qubit couplings. *Applied Physics Letters* **119**, 222601.

Hita-Pérez, M., Jaumà, G., Pino, M., & García-Ripoll, J.J. (2022). *Ultrastrong capacitive coupling of flux qubits. Physical Review Applied* **17**, 014028.

Hita-Pérez, M., Orellana, P., García-Ripoll, J.J., Pino M. (2022). Bound states in the continuum in a heavy fluxonium qutrit. *Phys. Rev.* A **106**, 062602.http://beige.ovpit.indiana.edu/M743/

http://en.wikipedia.org/w/index.php?title=POVM&oldid=88260272. Accessed December 29, 2006.http://en.wikipedia.org/w/index.php?title=Quantum_entanglement&oldid=93333870. Accessed December 31, 2006.

http://www.cs.uwaterloo.ca/~watrous/lecture-notes.html

http://www.cs.washington.edu/education/courses/cse599d/06wi/

Hua, Fei, Yuwei Jin, Yanhao Chen, Suhas Vittal, Kevin Krsulich, Lev S. Bishop, John Lapeyre, Ali Javadi-Abhari, and Eddy Z. Zhang, Proceedings of the 28th ACM International Conference on Architectural Support for Programming Languages and Operating Systems, Volume 3 59 (2023) ISBN:9781450399180.

IBM Quantum. (2020). IBM Quantum Roadmap. Retrieved from https://www.ibm.com/quantum-computing/technology/roadmap/

Jain, Nishant, Brian Coyle, Elham Kashefi, and Niraj Kumar, "Graph neural network initialisation of quantum approximate optimisation", Quantum 6, 861 (2022).

Johnson, M. W., Amin, M. H. S., Gildert, S., Lanting, T., Hamze, F., Dickson, N., ... & Berkley, A. J. (2011). Quantum annealing with manufactured spins. Nature, 473(7346), 194–198.

Joseph, David, Antonio J. Martinez, Cong Ling, and Florian Mintert, "Quantum mean-value approximator for hard integer-value problems", *Physical Review* A 105 5, 052419 (2022).

Kaitlin N. Smith, Michael A. Perlin, Pranav Gokhale, Paige Frederick, David Owusu-Antwi, Richard Rines, Victory Omole, and Frederic Chong, Proceedings of the 50th Annual International Symposium on Computer Architecture 1 (2023) ISBN:9798400700958.

Kishor Bharti, Alba Cervera-Lierta, Thi Ha Kyaw, Tobias Haug, Sumner Alperin-Lea, Abhinav Anand, Matthias Degroote, Hermanni Heimonen, Jakob S. Kottmann, Tim Menke, Wai-Keong Mok, Sukin Sim, Leong-Chuan Kwek, and Alán Aspuru-Guzik, "Noisy intermediate-scale quantum algorithms", Reviews of Modern Physics 94 1, 015004 (2022).

Kolotouros, Ioannis and Petros Wallden, "Evolving objective function for improved variational quantum optimization", *Physical Review* Research 4 2, 023225 (2022).

Lacroix, Nathan, Christoph Hellings, Christian Kraglund Andersen, Agustin Di Paolo, Ants Remm, Stefania Lazar, Sebastian Krinner, Graham J. Norris, Mihai Gabureac, Johannes Heinsoo, Alexandre Blais, Christopher Eichler, and

Andreas Wallraff, “Improving the Performance of Deep Quantum Optimization Algorithms with Continuous Gate Sets”, *PRX Quantum* 1 2, 020304 (2020).

Larkin, Jason, Matías Jonsson, Daniel Justice, and Gian Giacomo Guerreschi, “Evaluation of QAOA based on the approximation ratio of individual samples”, Quantum Science and Technology 7 4, 045014 (2022).

Leonidas, Ioannis D., Alexander Dukakis, Benjamin Tan, and Dimitris G. Angelakis, “Qubit efficient quantum algorithms for the vehicle routing problem on NISQ processors”, arXiv:2306.08507, (2023).

Lumia, Luca, Pietro Torta, Glen B. Mbeng, Giuseppe E. Santoro, Elisa Ercolessi, Michele Burrello, and Matteo M. Wauters, “Two-Dimensional Z₂ Lattice Gauge Theory on a Near-Term Quantum Simulator: Variational Quantum Optimization, Confinement, and Topological Order”, *PRX Quantum* 3 2, 020320 (2022).

Maciejewski, Filip B., Flavio Baccari, Zoltán Zimborás, and Micha^{3} Oszmaniec, “Modeling and mitigation of cross-talk effects in readout noise with applications to the Quantum Approximate Optimization Algorithm”, Quantum 5, 464 (2021).

McClean, Jarrod R., Matthew P. Harrigan, Masoud Mohseni, Nicholas C. Rubin, Zhang Jiang, Sergio Boixo, Vadim N. Smelyanskiy, Ryan Babbush, and Hartmut Neven, “Low-Depth Mechanisms for Quantum Optimization”, *PRX Quantum* 2 3, 030312 (2021).

McMahon, D., *Quantum Mechanics Demystified*, McGraw Hill, New York (2005).

Meglicki, Z., *Introduction to Quantum Computing*

Mele, Antonio A., Glen B. Mbeng, Giuseppe E. Santoro, Mario Collura, and Pietro Torta, “Avoiding barren plateaus via transferability of smooth solutions in a Hamiltonian variational ansatz”, *Physical Review* A 106 6, L060401 (2022).

Misra-Spieldenner, Aditi, Tim Bode, Peter K. Schuhmacher, Tobias Stollenwerk, Dmitry Bagrets, and Frank K. Wilhelm, “Mean-Field Approximate Optimization Algorithm”, *PRX Quantum* 4 3, 030335 (2023).

Nielsen, M., and I. L. Chuang, *Quantum Computation and Quantum Information*, Cambridge University Press, Cambridge (2000)

Niu, Yun-Fei, Shuo Zhang, Chen Ding, Wan-Su Bao, and He-Liang Huang, “Parameter-parallel distributed variational quantum algorithm”, SciPost Physics 14 5, 132 (2023).

Ozaeta, Asier, Wim van Dam, and Peter L. McMahon, “Expectation values from the single-layer quantum approximate optimization algorithm on Ising problems”, Quantum Science and Technology 7 4, 045036 (2022).

Pederiva, G., A. Bazavov, B. Henke, L. Hostetler, D. Lee, H. W. Lin, and A. Shindler, "Quantum State Preparation for the Schwinger Model", The 38th International Symposium on Lattice Field Theory 47 (2022).

Pelofske, Elijah, Andreas Bärtschi, Lukasz Cincio, John Golden, and Stephan Eidenbenz, "Scaling Whole-Chip QAOA for Higher-Order Ising Spin Glass Models on Heavy-Hex Graphs", arXiv:2312.00997, (2023).

Peñas, G.F., Puebla, R., Ramos, T., Rabl, P., García-Ripoll, J.J. (2022). *Universal Deterministic Quantum Operations in Microwave Quantum Links. Physical Review Applied* **17**, 054038.

Pengzhan Zhao, Xiongfei Wu, Junjie Luo, Zhuo Li, and Jianjun Zhao, 2023 IEEE International Conference on Quantum Software (QSW) 68 (2023) ISBN:979-8-3503-0479-4.

Peropadre, B., Forn-Díaz, P., Solano, E., & García-Ripoll, J. J. (2010). *Switchable Ultrastrong Coupling in Circuit QED. Physical Review Letters* **105**, 023601.

Phillip C. Lotshaw, George Siopsis, James Ostrowski, Rebekah Herrman, Rizwanul Alam, Sarah Powers, and Travis S. Humble, "Approximate Boltzmann distributions in quantum approximate optimization", *Physical Review* A 108 4, 042411 (2023).

Phillip C. Lotshaw, Kevin D. Battles, Bryan Gard, Gilles Buchs, Travis S. Humble, and Creston D. Herold, "Modeling noise in global Mølmer-Sørensen interactions applied to quantum approximate optimization", *Physical Review* A 107 6, 062406 (2023).

Pietro Torta, Glen B. Mbeng, Carlo Baldassi, Riccardo Zecchina, and Giuseppe E. Santoro, "Quantum approximate optimization algorithm applied to the binary perceptron", *Physical Review* B 107 9, 094202 (2023).

Pontus Vikstål, Mattias Grönkvist, Marika Svensson, Martin Andersson, Göran Johansson, and Giulia Ferrini, "Applying the Quantum Approximate Optimization Algorithm to the Tail-Assignment Problem", *Physical Review Applied* 14 3, 034009 (2020).

Pradeep Niroula, Ruslan Shaydulin, Romina Yalovetzky, Pierre Minssen, Dylan Herman, Shaohan Hu, and Marco Pistoia, "Constrained quantum optimization for extractive summarization on a trapped-ion quantum computer", *Scientific Reports* 12, (2022).

Prasanna Date, Davis Arthur, and Lauren Pusey-Nazzaro, "QUBO formulations for training machine learning models", Scientific Reports 11, 10029 (2021).

Rabinovich, Daniil, Ernesto Campos, Soumik Adhikary, Ekaterina Pankovets, Dmitry Vinichenko, and Jacob Biamonte, "On the gate-error robustness of variational quantum algorithms", arXiv:2301.00048, (2022).

Rabinovich, Daniil, Richik Sengupta, Ernesto Campos, Vishwanathan Akshay, and Jacob Biamonte, "Progress towards Analytically Optimal Angles in Quantum Approximate Optimisation", Mathematics 10 15, 2601 (2022).

Rabinovich, Daniil, Soumik Adhikary, Ernesto Campos, Vishwanathan Akshay, Evgeny Anikin, Richik Sengupta, Olga Lakhmanskaya, Kirill Lakhmanskiy, and Jacob Biamonte, "Ion-native variational ansatz for quantum approximate optimization", *Physical Review* A 106 3, 032418 (2022).

Rehman, Junaid ur, Hayder Al-Hraishawi, and Symeon Chatzinotas, ICC 2023 - IEEE International Conference on Communications 2674 (2023) ISBN:978-1-5386-7462-8.

Romero-Alvarez, Javier, Jaime Alvarado-Valiente, Enrique Moguel, Jose Garcia-Alonso, and Juan M. Murillo, 2023 IEEE International Conference on Software Services Engineering (SSE) 1 (2023) ISBN:979-8-3503-4075-4.

Ruslan Shaydulin, Phillip C. Lotshaw, Jeffrey Larson, James Ostrowski, and Travis S. Humble, "Parameter Transfer for Quantum Approximate Optimization of Weighted MaxCut", arXiv:2201.11785, (2022).

Sami Boulebnane and Ashley Montanaro, "Predicting parameters for the Quantum Approximate Optimization Algorithm for MAX-CUT from the infinite-size limit", arXiv:2110.10685, (2021).

Sanders, Yuval R., Dominic W. Berry, Pedro C. S. Costa, Louis W. Tessler, Nathan Wiebe, Craig Gidney, Hartmut Neven, and Ryan Babbush, "Compilation of Fault-Tolerant Quantum Heuristics for Combinatorial Optimization", arXiv:2007.07391, (2020).

Sandhu, J. S. and J. Shi, "A Sum-of-Squares Hierarchy in the Absence of Pointwise Proofs I: Energy Certificates", arXiv:2401.14383, (2024).

Schindler, Paul M., Tommaso Guaita, Tao Shi, Eugene Demler, and J. Ignacio Cirac, "VariationalAnsatzfor the Ground State of the Quantum Sherrington-Kirkpatrick Model", *Physical Review Letters* 129 22, 220401 (2022).

Steeb, W. H. and Y. Hardy, *Problems and solutions in Quantum Computing and Quantum Information*, World Scientific, New Jersey (2004).

Stuart Hadfield, Tad Hogg, and Eleanor G Rieffel, "Analytical framework for quantum alternating operator ansätze", *Quantum Science and Technology* 8 1, 015017 (2023).

Tan, Benjamin, Marc-Antoine Lemonde, Supanut Thanasilp, Jirawat Tangpanitanon, and Dimitris G. Angelakis, "Qubit-efficient encoding schemes for binary optimisation problems", *Quantum* 5, 454 (2021).

Teague Tomesh, Pranav Gokhale, Victory Omole, Gokul Subramanian Ravi, Kaitlin N. Smith, Joshua Viszlai, Xin-Chuan Wu, Nikos Hardavellas, Margaret R. Martonosi, and Frederic T. Chong, "SupermarQ: A Scalable Quantum Benchmark Suite", arXiv:2202.11045, (2022).

Teppei Suzuki and Michio Katouda, "Predicting toxicity by quantum machine learning", Journal of Physics Communications 4 12, 125012 (2020).

Thais L. Silva, Márcio M. Taddei, Stefano Carrazza, and Leandro Aolita, "Fragmented imaginary-time evolution for early-stage quantum signal processors", *Scientific Reports* 13 1, 18258 (2023).

Thomas Grurl, Jürgen Fuß, and Robert Wille, 2023 IEEE 53rd International Symposium on Multiple-Valued Logic (ISMVL) 141 (2023) ISBN:978-1-6654-6416-1.

Tobias Fankhauser, Marc E. Solèr, Rudolf Marcel Füchslin, and Kurt Stockinger, "Multiple Query Optimization Using a Gate-Based Quantum Computer", *IEEE Access* 11, 114031 (2023).

Usatyuk, Vasiliy, Sergey Egorov, and Denis Sapozhnikov, "Spherical and Hyperbolic Toric Topology-Based Codes On Graph Embedding for Ising MRF Models: Classical and Quantum Topology Machine Learning", arXiv:2307.15778, (2023).

Wang, Lu, Zhao-Yun Chen, Feng-Yu Le, Zhi-Qian Yu, Cheng Xue, Xi-Ning Zhuang, Qing Yan, Yang Yang, Wu, Yu-Chun, and Guo-Ping Guo, "A quantum feature selection framework via ground state preparation", *Physica Scripta* 98 11, 115121 (2023).

Wauters, Matteo M., Emanuele Panizon, Glen B. Mbeng, and Giuseppe E. Santoro, "Reinforcement Learning assisted Quantum Optimization", arXiv:2004.12323, (2020).

Weggemans, Jordi R., Alexander Urech, Alexander Rausch, Robert Spreeuw, Richard Boucherie, Florian Schreck, Kareljan Schoutens, Jiøí Mináø, and Florian Speelman, "Solving correlation clustering with QAOA and a Rydberg qudit system: a full-stack approach", *Quantum* 6, 687 (2022).

Wei-Feng Zhuang, Ya-Nan Pu, Hong-Ze Xu, Xudan Chai, Yanwu Gu, Yunheng Ma, Shahid Qamar, Chen Qian, Peng Qian, Xiao Xiao, Meng-Jun Hu, and Dong E. Liu, "Efficient Classical Computation of Quantum Mean Values for Shallow QAOA Circuits", (2021).

Wendin, G., "Quantum information processing with superconducting circuits: a perspective" (2023).

Wendin, G., Encyclopedia of Condensed Matter Physics 246 (2024) ISBN:9780323914086.

Willsch, Dennis, Madita Willsch, Fengping Jin, Kristel Michielsen, and Hans De Raedt, "GPU-accelerated simulations of quantum annealing and the quantum approximate optimization algorithm", Computer Physics Communications 278, 108411 (2022).

Xuchen You and Xiaodi Wu, "Exponentially Many Local Minima in Quantum Neural Networks", arXiv:2110.02479, (2021).

Yanbin Chen and Yannick Stade, Lecture Notes in Computer Science 14284, 164 (2023).

Zettili, N, *Quantum Mechanics: Concepts and Applications*, Wiley New York, (2001).

GLOSSARY OF QUANTUM COMPUTING TERMS

Abstraction: A different model (a representation or way of thinking) about a computer system design that allows the user to focus on the critical aspects of the system components to be designed.

Adiabatic quantum computer: An idealized analog universal quantum computer that operates at 0 K (absolute zero). It is known to have the same computational power as a gate-based quantum computer.

Algorithm: A specific approach, often described in mathematical terms, used by a computer to solve a certain problem or carry out a certain task.

Analog computer: A computer whose operation is based on analog signals and that does not use Boolean logic operations and does not reject noise.

Analog quantum computer: A quantum computer that carries out a computation without breaking the operations down to a small set of primitive operations (gates) on qubits, there is currently no model of full fault tolerance for such machines.

Analog signal: A signal whose value varies smoothly within a range of real or complex numbers.

Asymmetric cryptography (also public key cryptography): A category of cryptography where the system uses public keys that are widely known and private keys that are secret to the owner; such systems are commonly used for key exchange protocols in the encryption of most of today's electronic communications.

Basis: Any set of linearly independent vectors that span their vector space. The wave function of a qubit or system of qubits is commonly written as a linear combination of basis functions or states. For a single qubit, the most common basis is {| 0é', | 1é'}, corresponding to the states of a classical bit.

Binary representation: A series of binary digits where each digit has only two possible values, 0 or 1, used to encode data and upon which machine-level computations are performed.

Certificate authority: An entity that issues a digital certificate to certify the ownership of a public key used in online transactions.

Cipher: An approach to concealing the meaning of information by encoding it.

Ciphertext: The encrypted form of a message, which appears scrambled or nonsensical.

Classical attack: An attempt by a classical computer to break or subvert encryption.

Classical computer: A computer: for example, one of the many deployed commercially today: whose processing of information is not based upon quantum information theory.

Coding theory: The science of designing encoding schemes for specific applications: for example, to enable two parties to communicate over a noisy channel.

Coherence: The quality of a quantum system that enables quantum phenomena such as interference, superposition, and entanglement. Mathematically speaking, a quantum system is coherent when the complex coefficients of the contributing quantum states are clearly defined in relation to each other, and the system can be expressed in terms of a single wave function.

Collapse: The phenomenon that occurs upon measurement of a quantum system where the system reverts to a single observable state, resulting in the loss of contributions from all other states to the system's wave function.

Collision: In hashing, the circumstance where two different inputs are mapped to the same output, or hash value.

Complexity class: A category that is used to define and group computational tasks according to their complexity.

Computational complexity: The difficulty of carrying out a specific computational task, typically expressed as a mathematical expression that reflects how the number of steps required to complete the task varies with the size of the input to the problem.

Compute depth: The number of sequential operations required to carry out a given task.

Concatenation: The ordered combination of two sequences in order. In the context of quantum error correction (QEC), this refers to carrying out two or more QEC protocols sequentially.

Control and measurement plane: An abstraction used to describe components of a quantum computer, which refers to the elements required to carry out operations on qubits and to measure their states.

Control processor plane: An abstraction used to describe components of a quantum computer, which includes the classical processor responsible for determining what signals and measurements are required to implement a quantum program.

Cryostat: A device that regulates the temperature of a physical system at very low temperatures, generally in an experimental laboratory.

Cryptanalysis: The use of a computer to defeat encryption.

Cryptography: The study and practice of encoding information in order to obfuscate its content that relies upon the difficulty of solving certain mathematical problems.

Cryptosystem: A method of deploying a specific cryptographic algorithm to protect data and communications from being read by an unintended recipient.

Decoherence: A process where a quantum system will ultimately exchange some energy and information with the broader environment over time, which cannot be recovered once lost. This process is one source of error in qubit systems. Mathematically speaking, decoherence occurs when the relationship between the coefficients of a quantum system's contributing states become ill-defined.

Decryption algorithm: A set of instructions for returning an encrypted message to its unencrypted form. Such an algorithm takes as input a cipher text and its encryption key, and returns a cleartext, or readable, version of the message.

Digital gate: A transistor circuit that performs a binary operation using a number of binary single bit inputs to create a single-bit binary output.

Digital quantum computer: A quantum system where the computation is done by using a small set of primitive operations, or gates, on qubits.

Digital signature: An important cryptographic mechanism used to verify data integrity.

Dilution refrigerator: A specialized cooling device capable of maintaining an apparatus at temperatures near absolute zero.

Discrete-log problem on elliptic curves: A specific algebraic problem used as the basis of a specific cryptographic protocol where, given the output, it is computationally hard to compute the inputs.

Distance: In an error-correcting code, the number of bit errors that would be required to convert one valid state of a computer to another. When the number of errors is less than (D–1)/2, one can still extract the error-free state.

Encryption: The application of cryptography to protect information, currently widely used in computer systems and Internet communications.

Encryption algorithm: A set of instructions for converting understandable data to an incomprehensible cipher, or ciphertext. In practice, the algorithm takes as input the message to be encrypted along with an encryption key and scrambles the message according to a mathematical procedure.

Entanglement: The property where two or more quantum objects in a system are correlated, or intrinsically linked, such that measurement of one changes the possible measurement outcomes for another, regardless of how far apart the two objects are.

Error-corrected quantum computer: An instance of a quantum computer that emulates an ideal, fault-tolerant quantum computer by running a quantum error correction algorithm.

Fault tolerant: Resilient against errors.

Fidelity: The quality of a hardware operation, sometimes quantified in terms of the probability that a particular operation will be carried out correctly.

Fundamental noise: Noise resulting from energy fluctuations arising spontaneously within any object that is above absolute zero in temperature.

Gate: A computational operation that takes in and puts out one or more bits (in the case of a classical computer) or qubits (in the case of a quantum computer).

Gate synthesis: Construction of a gate out of a series of simpler gates.

Hamiltonian: A mathematical representation of the energy environment of a physical system. In the mathematics of quantum mechanics, a Hamiltonian takes the form of a linear algebraic operator. Sometimes, the term is used to denote the physical environment itself, rather than its mathematical representation.

Host processor: An abstraction used to describe the components of a quantum computing system, referring to the classical computer components driving the part of the system that is user controlled.

Key exchange: A step in cryptographic algorithms and protocols where keys are shared among intended recipients to enable their use in encrypting and decrypting information.

Logical qubit: An abstraction that describes a collection of physical qubits implementing quantum error correction in order to carry out a fault-tolerant qubit operation.

Logic gate: In classical computing, a collection of transistors that input and output digital signals, and that can be represented and modeled using Boolean logic (rules that combine signals that can be either false, 0, or true, 1).

Lossless: No energy is dissipated.

Measurement: Observation of a quantum system, which yields only a single classical output and collapses the system's wave function onto the corresponding state.

Microprocessor: An integrated circuit that contains the elements of a central processing unit on a single chip.

Noise: Unwanted variations in a physical system that can lead to error and unwanted results.

Noise immunity: The ability to remove noise (unwanted variations) in a signal to minimize error.

Noisy intermediate-scale quantum (NISQ) computer: A quantum computer that is not error-corrected, but is stable enough to effectively carry out a computation before the system loses coherence. A NISQ can be digital or analog.

Nondeterministic polynomial time (NP): A specific computational complexity class.

One-way functions: Functions that are easy to compute in one direction while being for all intents and purposes impossible to compute in the other direction.

Overhead: The amount of work (for example, number of operations) or quantity of resources (for example, number of qubits or bits) required to carry out a computational task; "cost" is sometimes used synonymously.

Post-quantum cryptography: The set of methods for cryptography that are expected to be resistant to cryptanalysis by a quantum computer.

Primitive: A fundamental computational operation.

Program: An abstraction that refers to the sequence of instructions and rules that a computer must perform in order to complete one or more tasks (or solve one or more tasks) using a specific approach, or algorithm.

Quantum annealer: An analog quantum computer that operates through coherent manipulation of qubits by changing the analog values of the system's Hamiltonian, rather than by using quantum gates. In particular, aquantum annealer performs computations by preparing a set of qubits in some initial state and changing their energy environment until it defines the parameters of a given problem, such that the final state of the qubits corresponds, with a high probability, to the answer of the problem. In general, a quantum annealer is not necessarily universal: there are some problems that it cannot solve.

Quantum communication: The transport or exchange of information as encoded into a quantum system.

Quantum computation: The use of quantum mechanical phenomena such as interference, superposition, and entanglement to perform computations that are roughly analogous to (although operate quite differently from) those performed on a classical computer.

Quantum computer: The general term for a device (whether theoretical or practically realized) that carries out quantum computation. A quantum computer may be analog or gate-based, universal or not, and noisy or fault tolerant.

Quantum cryptography: A subfield of quantum communication where quantum properties are used to design communication systems that may not be eavesdropped upon by an observer.

Quantum information science: The study of how information is or can be encoded in a quantum system, including the associated statistics, limitations, and unique affordances of quantum mechanics.

Quantum interference: When states contributing to coherent superpositions combine constructively or destructively, like waves, with coefficients adding or subtracting.

Quantum sensing and metrology: The study and development of quantum systems whose extreme sensitivity to environmental disturbances can be exploited in order to measure important physical properties with more precision than is possible with classical technologies.

Quantum system: A collection of (typically very small) physical objects whose behavior cannot be adequately approximated by equations of classical physics.

Qubit: A quantum bit, the fundamental hardware component of a quantum computer, embodied by a quantum object. Analogous to a classical bit (or binary digit), a qubit can represent a state corresponding to either zero or one; unlike a classical bit, a qubit can also exist in a superposition of both states at once, with any possible relative contribution of each. In a quantum computer, qubits are generally entangled, meaning that any qubit's state is inextricably linked to the state of the other qubits, and thus cannot be defined independently.

Run time: The amount of time required to carry out a computational task. In practice, the actual time required for a task depends heavily on the design of a device and of its particular physical embodiment, so run time may be described in terms of the number of computational steps.

Scalable, fault-tolerant, universal gate-based quantum computer: A system that operates through gate-based operations on qubits, analogous to circuit-based classical computers, and uses quantum error correction to correct any system noise (including errors introduced by imperfect control signals, or unintended coupling of qubits to each other or to the environment) that occurs during the time frame of the calculation.

SHA256: A specific hash function that outputs a 256-bit hash value regardless of the input size.

Shor's algorithm: A quantum algorithm developed by Peter Shor in the 1990s that, if implemented on a real quantum computer of sufficient scale, would be capable of breaking the encryption used to protect Internet communications and data.

Signal: An electromagnetic field used to convey information in an electronic circuit.

Software tool: A computer program that helps a user design and compose a new computer program.

Standard cell library: A set of predesigned and tested logic gates.

Superposition: A quantum phenomenon where a system is in more than one state at a time. Mathematically speaking, the wave function of a quantum system in a superposition state is expressed as the sum of the contributing states, each weighted by a complex coefficient.

Surface code: A quantum error correction code (QECC) that is less sensitive to noise than other established QECCs, but has higher overheads.

Symmetric encryption: A type of encryption where a secret key, shared by both the sender and the receiver, is used to encrypt and decrypt communications.

Systematic noise: Noise resulting from signal interactions that is always present under certain conditions and could in principle be modeled and corrected.

Transport Layer Security (TLS) handshake: The most common key exchange protocol, used to protect Internet traffic.

Unitary operation: An algebraic operation on a vector that preserves the vector length.

Universal computer: A computer that can perform any computation that could be performed by a Turing machine.

Wave function: A mathematical description of the state of a quantum system, so named to reflect their wave-like characteristics.

Wave-particle duality: The phenomenon where a quantum object is sometimes best described in terms of wave-like properties and sometimes in terms of particle-like properties.

QUANTUM COMPUTING RESEARCH ORGANIZATIONS AND INSTITUTES

ARC Centre of Excellence for Engineered Quantum Systems (EQUS), Australia

Canadian Institute for Advanced Research (CIFAR) – Quantum Information Science Program, Canada

Center for Quantum Devices (CQD) – University of Copenhagen, Denmark

Centre for Quantum Computation & Communication Technology (CQC2T) – Australia

Centre for Quantum Information and Control (CQuIC) – USA

Centre for Quantum Technologies (CQT) – Singapore

Hefei National Laboratory for Physical Sciences at the Microscale (HFNL), China (USTC) in Hefei, Anhui Province

Institut de Recherche en Informatique Fondamentale (IRIF) – University of Paris

Institut Néel – CNRS

Institute for Quantum Computing (IQC) – University of Waterloo, Canada

Institute for Quantum Computing (IQOQI) Vienna

Joint Quantum Institute (JQI) – University of Maryland and NIST, United States

Korea Advanced Institute of Science and Technology (KAIST) – South Korea

Korea Institute for Advanced Study (KIAS) – South Korea

Max Planck Institute of Quantum Optics (MPQ) – Garching, Germany

National Institute of Informatics (NII) – Japan

National Institute of Standards and Technology (NIST) – United States

Paul Scherrer Institute (PSI) – Switzerland

Perimeter Institute for Theoretical Physics – Waterloo, Canada

Quantum Artificial Intelligence Lab (QuAIL) – NASA Ames Research Center, USA

Quantum Engineering and Space-Time Research (QUEST) – Leibniz University Hannover, Germany

Quantum Information and Computing Group at the National Institute for Theoretical Physics (NITheP), South Africa

Quantum Information Science and Technology (QIST) – South Korea

Quantum Information Science and Technology (QuTech) – Delft University of Technology, Netherlands

Quantum Materials and Devices (QMD) Lab at the University of British Columbia

Quantum Research Group at the University of KwaZulu-Natal, South Africa

Quantum Science and Technologies Hub (QST) – United Kingdom

Shanghai Branch of the Chinese Academy of Sciences

Trinity College Dublin – Trinity Centre for Quantum Information Science and Quantum Computing

University College London – UCL Quantum Science and Technology Institute (UCLQ), University College London

University of Cambridge – Centre for Quantum Information and Foundations

University of Oxford – Oxford Quantum

Yale Quantum Institute (YQI) – Yale University, USA.

INDIA'S TOP QUANTUM COMPUTING RESEARCH INSTITUTES

Indian Institute of Science – Initiative on Quantum Technologies (IQT@IISc)

Indian Institute of Technology Jodhpur

Indian Institute of Technology Madras

Tata Institute of Fundamental Research (TIFR) - Quantum Measurement and Control Laboratory

Indian Institute of Science Education and Research (IISER) Pune

Quantum Information and Computing (QuIC) lab at the Raman Research Institute, Bangalore

Harish-Chandra Research Institute (HRI) – Quantum Information and Computation Group

INDEX

O

P

Q

R

S

T

V

W

X

Y

www.ingramcontent.com/pod-product-compliance
Ingram Content Group UK Ltd.
Pitfield, Milton Keynes, MK11 3LW, UK
UKHW050948290926
15470UKWH00005B/1703

9 781787 153059